T0321995

Business Models and Strategies for Open Source Projects

Francisco José Monaco
Universidade de São Paulo, Brazil

A volume in the Advances in
Systems Analysis, Software
Engineering, and High Performance
Computing (ASASEHPC) Book Series

Published in the United States of America by
IGI Global
Business Science Reference (an imprint of IGI Global)
701 E. Chocolate Avenue
Hershey PA, USA 17033
Tel: 717-533-8845
Fax: 717-533-8661
E-mail: cust@igi-global.com
Web site: http://www.igi-global.com

Library of Congress Cataloging-in-Publication Data

Names: Monaco, Francisco José, 1971- editor.
Title: Business models and strategies for open source projects / editor,
    Francisco José Monaco.
Description: Hershey, PA : Business Science Reference, [2023] | Includes
    bibliographical references and index. | Summary: "Business Models and
    Strategies for Open Source Projects investigates the rationales and the
    strategy underlying companies' decisions to produce and release open
    source products, as well as which business models have succeeded.
    Covering topics such as embedded systems, open source ecosystems, and
    software companies, this premier reference source is a valuable resource
    for entrepreneurs, business leaders and managers, students and educators
    of higher education, librarians, software developers, researchers, and
    academicians"-- Provided by publisher.
Identifiers: LCCN 2022053586 (print) | LCCN 2022053587 (ebook) | ISBN
    9781668447857 (hardcover) | ISBN 9781668447864 (paperback) | ISBN
    9781668447871 (ebook)
Subjects: LCSH: Business planning. | Strategic planning. | Embedded
    computer systems. | Open source software.
Classification: LCC HD30.28 .B84377 2023 (print) | LCC HD30.28 (ebook) |
    DDC 658.4/012--dc23/eng/20221104
LC record available at https://lccn.loc.gov/2022053586
LC ebook record available at https://lccn.loc.gov/2022053587

This book is published in the IGI Global book series Advances in Systems Analysis, Software Engineering, and High Performance Computing (ASASEHPC) (ISSN: 2327-3453; eISSN: 2327-3461)

British Cataloguing in Publication Data
A Cataloguing in Publication record for this book is available from the British Library.

All work contributed to this book is new, previously-unpublished material.
The views expressed in this book are those of the authors, but not necessarily of the publisher.

For electronic access to this publication, please contact: eresources@igi-global.com.

Advances in Systems Analysis, Software Engineering, and High Performance Computing (ASASEHPC) Book Series

ISSN:2327-3453
EISSN:2327-3461

Editor-in-Chief: Vijayan Sugumaran, Oakland University, USA

MISSION

The theory and practice of computing applications and distributed systems has emerged as one of the key areas of research driving innovations in business, engineering, and science. The fields of software engineering, systems analysis, and high performance computing offer a wide range of applications and solutions in solving computational problems for any modern organization.

The **Advances in Systems Analysis, Software Engineering, and High Performance Computing (ASASEHPC) Book Series** brings together research in the areas of distributed computing, systems and software engineering, high performance computing, and service science. This collection of publications is useful for academics, researchers, and practitioners seeking the latest practices and knowledge in this field.

COVERAGE

- Computer Networking
- Metadata and Semantic Web
- Human-Computer Interaction
- Engineering Environments
- Network Management
- Distributed Cloud Computing
- Software Engineering
- Computer Graphics
- Enterprise Information Systems
- Parallel Architectures

IGI Global is currently accepting manuscripts for publication within this series. To submit a proposal for a volume in this series, please contact our Acquisition Editors at Acquisitions@igi-global.com or visit: http://www.igi-global.com/publish/.

Titles in this Series

For a list of additional titles in this series, please visit:
http://www.igi-global.com/book-series/advances-systems-analysis-software-engineering/73689

Advanced Applications of Python Data Structures and Algorithms
Mohammad Gouse Galety (Department of Computer Science, Samarkand International University of Technology, Uzbekistan) Arul Kumar Natarajan (CHRIST University (Deemed), India) and A. V. Sriharsha (MB University, India)
Engineering Science Reference • copyright 2023 • 298pp • H/C (ISBN: 9781668471005) • US $270.00 (our price)

Handbook of Research on Machine Learning-Enabled IoT for Smart Applications Across Industries
Neha Goel (Raj Kumar Goel Institute of Technology, India) and Ravindra Kumar Yadav (Raj Kumar Goel Institute of Technology, India)
Engineering Science Reference • copyright 2023 • 542pp • H/C (ISBN: 9781668487853) • US $345.00 (our price)

Quantum Computing and Cryptography in Future Computers
Shyam R. Sihare (Dr. APJ Abdul Kalam Govt. College, India)
Engineering Science Reference • copyright 2023 • 300pp • H/C (ISBN: 9781799895220) • US $270.00 (our price)

Handbook of Research on Integrating Machine Learning Into HPC-Based Simulations and Analytics
Belgacem Ben Youssef (King Saud University, Saudi Arabia) and Mohamed Maher Ben Ismail (King Saud University, Saudi Arabia)
Engineering Science Reference • copyright 2023 • 400pp • H/C (ISBN: 9781668437957) • US $325.00 (our price)

Perspectives and Considerations on the Evolution of Smart Systems
Maki K. Habib (American University in Cairo, Egypt)
Engineering Science Reference • copyright 2023 • 320pp • H/C (ISBN: 9781668476840) • US $270.00 (our price)

For an entire list of titles in this series, please visit:
http://www.igi-global.com/book-series/advances-systems-analysis-software-engineering/73689

701 East Chocolate Avenue, Hershey, PA 17033, USA
Tel: 717-533-8845 x100 • Fax: 717-533-8661
E-Mail: cust@igi-global.com • www.igi-global.com

Table of Contents

Detailed Table of Contents

Chapter 1
Karl-Michael Popp, SAP SE, Germany

Open-source software companies represent growing businesses with specific business models. Here, the authors look at different business models for companies that base their business model completely or in part on open-source software or open-source licenses. They analyze different building blocks of such business models and reuse an existing business model framework to categorize these building blocks. This view reveals different hybrid business models for open-source software and ways for commercial open-source companies to create differentiation and competitive advantage.

Chapter 2
Marco Berlinguer, IGOP, Spain

Despite being a commons, free and open source software has come to dominate software production. FOSS surprising trajectory passed so far through two distinct stages. It originated within self-organized communities of developers and was later sustained by market adoption and innovative forms of economic competition. Its economic model was initially interpreted as a gift economy. Today it is better understood as based on hybrids that modulate markets and commons. By analyzing the trajectory of FOSS through two approaches with roots in evolutionary economics— the multi-level perspective and the techno-economic paradigms—FOSS takes on the characteristics of a development and innovation system that has grown with the digital paradigm and is destined to occupy an important function in its further development. The evolution of FOSS has not ended. On the contrary, a third phase of FOSS development is looming, which will be characterized by greater government involvement and further innovations in FOSS governance systems and economic models.

Chapter 3
Laetitia Marie Thomas, Université Grenoble Alpes, France
Karine Evrard-Samuel, Université Grenoble Alpes, France
Peter Troxler, Hogeschool Rotterdam, The Netherlands

Open source hardware (OSH) initiatives are collectively managed projects enabled by the internet and digital fabrication tools. They allow people to create products in a cheaper, faster, and more efficient manner. To date, there is no strategic and actionable framework using the commons theory for analyzing how these hardware initiatives develop economically effective and sustainable business models. Based on an analysis of the business models of 27 community-based and community-oriented OSH initiatives studied over a 3-year period, this chapter presents such a framework. The five-stages spiral framework offers to guide companies and startups involved in OSH to interact with their surrounding innovation ecosystems progressively, enrich their value propositions and grow in impact.

Chapter 4
Renê de Souza Pinto, Zededa GmbH, Germany

Several open source operating systems are being used in commercial embedded applications, such as smartphones, set-top boxes, routers, video game consoles, and many other consumer electronics. One of the best examples is the Linux kernel, which is present in millions of different embedded devices. That said, the Linux kernel is licensed under GNU General Public License version 2 (GPLv2), which enforces any derivative work to be licensed under the same terms as the original license. Embedded device manufacturers must be aware of such clauses and understand how to handle the distribution of their systems, including free software and open source operating systems, such as Linux kernel. This chapter covers relevant aspects of different open source licenses regarding operating systems and some common issues faced by developers of commercial applications. The foundation knowledge is presented to guide readers to choose an open source operating system according to its license for embedded commercial applications.

Chapter 5
Francisco Jose Monaco, Universidade de Sao Paulo, Brazil

The open-source paradigm has evolved from the early enthusiasts' circles to enter the agenda of the mainstream industry, while related initiatives have been extending the idea of open, collaborative development to other kinds of intellectual artifacts. Against this background, it is pertinent to ask how an innovation-based business that deliberately renounces the exclusive prerogatives endowed by intellectual property can foster continuous innovation. In order to shed light on those questions, this article addresses the open-source model as a new paradigm of innovation fostering that does not rely on the IP-enforcement model. The investigation brings up a comprehensive conceptual framework to understand different kinds of open-source business models in a unified and systematic way. By introducing a broader definition of open-source innovation, the study formulates the notion of coherent synergy: a property that determines the roles of the intellectual creation and the different stakeholders in innovation ecosystems.

Chapter 6
    Marcelo Schmitt, Universidade de Sao Paulo, Brazil
    Paulo Meirelles, Universidade de Sao Paulo, Brazil

Device drivers are an elementary part of the Linux kernel and comprise roughly 2/3 of the project's lines of code. Even though the fraction of device driver code in a conventional operating system (OS) can vary, some of these components are essential for system functioning. In addition, the Linux kernel is used in a wide range of applications, from cloud service providers to embedded systems and supercomputers. If GNU/Linux systems should be trustworthy to justify running them in those environments, then testing the kernel is fundamental. However, since device drivers are designed to interface with hardware, conventional test approaches may not suit the occasions when devices are unavailable at test time. This raises the question: How are device drivers tested?

Chapter 7
    Hillary Nyakundi, freeCodeCamp, Kenya
    Cesar Henrique De Souza, Universidade de Sao Paulo, Brazil

In this chapter, the authors explore the importance of creating a welcoming and supportive community for new contributors trying to venture into the field of open-source. They cover the best practices for creating a positive and inclusive environment, such as clear documentation, accessible communication channels, and active mentorship programs. Additionally, they delve into some of the key challenges that new contributors often face and also offer strategies for overcoming these obstacles. By promoting a supportive and welcoming community, open-source projects can encourage more people to participate, thereby increasing their overall impact and diversity in society.

The world has been recovering from the COVID-19 pandemic and is coming towards its post-pandemic era. Although many IT companies have experienced big growth during the pandemic caused by the increasing demand of several kinds of services, finding highly skilled IT professionals is essential to the expansion of the business and was never an easy task, even before the pandemic. The leveraging of remote work during the last years collaborated substantially with companies in order to expand their teams across the globe and find talented people that would never have been found within the pre-pandemic environment. However, apart from the new working models and environments in the IT sector, the FOSS model always posed as an outstanding framework not only to leverage projects but also to help in finding talented people throughout the world. This short chapter presents a brief overview about how FOSS can be used to help companies leverage their businesses and expand teams by reaching professionals with a good matching profile.

Open source implies shared knowledge, one of the central virtues of the FOSS model. It is therefore natural that open-source technology constitutes a key resource for building accessible educational tools. Cost-effectiveness is not the only benefit brought about by the FOSS paradigm. Along with the flexibility permitted by unrestricted access to the source code, FOSS also implies public sovereignty, as community-driven development allows the society to regain control over the technology it uses and upon which it relies. Educational tools are especially critical in this context, as it directly impacts our autonomy to implement education programs free from technical, economic, or ideological biases dictated by corporate big tech. This chapter delves into this matter, exploring an illustrative case study based on the OSLAP experience. As in other application fields calling for new sustainable FOSS business models, open-source educational technology emerges as an area where fresh ideas are demanded, along with strategies for how to finance collaborative projects in the long term.

Red Hat, Inc. is a leading software company known worldwide for pioneering the FOSS industry. Its history offers a concrete example of a successful open-source business model. Red Hat Enterprise Linux (RHEL), taken as a study case, is one of the most successful commercial Linux distributions, thanks to its components' stability and company support. This chapter brings a brief historical perspective of the several Red Hat distributions and their communities, highlighting how decisions have impacted the enterprise product. The chapter also introduces the open-source model behind Red Hat's Linux development flow. For this purpose, the Linux kernel provides an excellent example of collaboration that goes through all distributions, maturing to their final destination. The discussion presents some aspects of quality, security, and testing that make RHEL one of the most reliable and secure distributions.

Preface

Since it emerged in the mid-80s through the protagonism of pioneer organized movements, the notion of freely shareable, collaboratively developed technology has steadily established itself in the following decades to enter the 21st century as a leading industrial paradigm.

Today, nearly 40 years after the concept of *free and open source* (FOSS) was introduced, and despite the initial skepticism that has gradually been dissipated by positive empiric evidence, some questions still baffle newcomers and even experienced practitioners.

How have many large community-run open-source ventures evolved from experimental undertakings into long-standing, economically sustainable projects?

Why are major commercial enterprises increasingly engaging in developing open-source systems, and how do such decisions meet their business goals?

How to design an economically-effective business model and a sustainable development strategy for an open-source product or service in a given industry segment?

By shedding light on those issues, this book aims at offering a starting point both for individual entrepreneurs venturing into innovative undertakings and for already established organizations willing to consider the open, collaborative paradigm for a new product or service.

More than *"why use open-source,"* the book is about *"why create open-source."* It is inspired by the observation that while, on the one hand, it is not difficult to enumerate advantages of FOSS from the users' standpoint — whether related to cost, socio-technological inclusion, flexibility, dependability, or transparency — on the other hand, understanding the driving interests of individuals and organizations that invest massively in FOSS development is not so straightforward. Why would anyone commit resources — money, labor, time — in producing intellectual creations, only to deliberately relinquish the exclusive profiting prerogatives endowed by intellectual-propriety enforcement? True, it is plausible to look for clues in initiatives conceived on ethical grounds, like GNU, and intellectual enjoyment, like Linux — as well as portfolio building, like the ever-growing collection of personal projects hosted in source-code management platforms. However, while such hints may point to valid origins of many community-driven projects, they do not address how those endeavors matured into lasting, sustainable enterprises. Moreover, arguably, neither hobby nor philanthropy is to be accounted for as the only goal of the large corporations that have decided to embrace the open-source development model.

Against this background, while successful experiences of FOSS have been around for over three decades, more often than not, when considering the option of delivering a given innovation product under an open-source license, a preeminent question that arises for both new entrepreneurs and industry veterans is how to figure out a suitable business strategy that is economically sustainable in the long-term.

The present book dwells on those questions. In exploring study cases, the investigation aims at understanding the rationales and strategies underlying some companies' decisions to produce and release open-source products. By addressing the topic from varying perspectives, the book's chapters examine which business models have succeeded, and which ones might apply to leverage the open-source industry in areas where world-class FOSS solutions have not flourished yet.

From a contemporary perspective, the book embraces the realization that the principles of collaborative construction of publicly accessible knowledge grounding the open-source paradigm have been extended beyond the software industry's original ambit, coming to encompass any intellectual artifact made available under non-exclusive rights of utilization, adaptation, and distribution. From this standpoint, the study assumes a comprehensive view of *free and open-source* systems that applies to all technological, educational, artistic, or other creations, including computer programs, hardware design, artwork, scientific data, and other intellectual artifacts.

The contents of this volume cover relevant topics such as the foundations of the free and open-source paradigm, scientific and technological innovation, business models, industry cases, community fostering, decision-making, licensing, project governance, community ethics, challenges to the FOSS industry, and the dynamics of collaborative ecosystems.

By calling forth the knowledge of experienced authors, the material is expected to offer a state-or-art reference for researchers and practitioners involved in developing or managing open-source projects, and for decision-makers considering the appropriate strategy to design open-source business models for their products and services.

To give a glimpse of what is in the book, we can briefly refer to some of the original ideas discussed by the authors.

For instance, it is fair to say that the FOSS debut was less of a timid rookie attempt than of a rebel call to action, and its success was not initially received without a good deal of surprise. In the chapter "Open Source and Economic Models in an Evolutionary Approach," Dr. Marco Berlinguer lays a comprehensive review of the trajectory of FOSS along its history, and the different interpretations that have been tried to explain its seemingly paradoxical success in the context of the traditional innovation industry. In his analysis, the author criticizes the premature bid to co-opt FOSS into the conventional logic of the capitalist market, as well as the naive trivialization of FOSS as yet another more-of-the-same hype — as those narratives fail to account for the transformations FOSS has been yielding in the mainstream digital production standards. Berlinguer discusses the varying phases through which FOSS has evolved, from the self-organizing volunteer communities to widespread market adoption, and highlights the new phase we are entering now, when public policies and significant geopolitical unfoldings are expected to call forth a more organic involvement of the government sphere in the trajectory of FOSS. By assuming an evolutionary-economic perspective, the chapter frames FOSS as a digital commons and dissertates on how the success of FOSS may be evidence of a broader role of this concept in the emerging digital economy. Anyone venturing into the FOSS-based enterprise domain would benefit from glancing at what is to come.

That is especially true for individuals and organizations considering an open-source strategy for a new enterprise, as devising an appropriate business is crucial for the project's economic viability. Many different approaches have been developed for commercial open-source products over the years. The chapter "A Business Model Framework for Open Source Software Companies," by Dr. Karl-Michael Popp, analyzes varying such models through a unified framework. The author distinguishes between community and commercial open-source projects, and looks at various alternatives based either entirely or partially on open-source licenses. Pop breaks down the several examples into basic building blocks, and explores the possible combinations of main business models to reveal different hybrid instances capable of delivering differentiated value. The chapter overviews how commercial open-source companies foster contributor communities for their enterprises, and look further into the future of on-demand and software-as-a-service deployments.

Opportunely, while certainly the canonical example, the software case is not the only representative of the open-source concept under the industry's attention, as the influential success of that segment has also impacted other fields where the concept of free open collaboration has been felt. Among those new extents lies the emergence of the open-source hardware (OSH) technology. Elaborating on that new compelling topic, the chapter "Building Open Source Hardware Business Models" by Dr. Laetitia Marie Thomas, Prof. Karine Evrard-Samuel, and Prof. Peter Troxler reviews the state-of-the-art of OHS communities. The authors build on the Commons theory to shed length on how OSH initiatives have developed economically effective and sustainable business models. Thomas, Evrard-Samuel, and Troxler develop the ideas grounded on empirical evidence collected through nearly 30 study cases which they followed over an extended period. Their findings propose a framework for helping OHS practitioners design viable business models, enumerating actionable, strategic steps for this purpose, and raising the potential of the open-source approach to meet the sought-after equilibrium between our social demands and the environmental capacity of the planet.

At this point, it is worth remembering that when examining the digital economy, the scope of the discussion is no longer confined to how people use laptops and smartphones. Modern electronic equipment is increasingly being designed as a collection of peripherals around embedded computer hardware: smart TVs, internet routers, smartwatches, vehicular control units, and a myriad of wearable internet-enabled gadgets are, essentially, computers. Today FOSS runs in those computers to such an extent that open-source technology has become pervasive in our daily lives, even when we are not typing on a keyboard or swapping a touch screen. In the chapter "Open Source and Free Software Licenses for Embedded Systems," Dr. Renê de Souza Pinto discusses the effect of FOSS in the embedded system industry and analyzes how open-source licensing impacts the consumer electronics market. The author evokes one of the best examples, the Linux kernel, which is present in millions of embedded devices. Renê discusses Linux's copyleft license, which enforces any derivative work to be released under the same terms as the original license. Embedded device manufacturers should be aware of such clauses and understand how to handle the distribution of their open-source systems. The chapter covers relevant aspects of different open-source licenses and common issues of interest for the business model design.

Still concerning Linux, the chapter "Trusting Critical Open Source Components: The Linux Case Study" by Marcelo Schmitt and Dr. Paulo Meirelles raises the question of dependability in FOSS systems. Exploring Linux device drivers as a study case, the authors invite us to ask how much we can trust the FOSS infrastructure that sustains so much of the software and online systems we rely upon for our business and lives. Schmit and Meirelles conduct an extensive analysis of the software testing methodologies employed by the Linux project to evaluate the quality of device drivers. From their discussion, it is interesting to ponder on the transparency allowed by the FOSS model, as it is not equally feasible to inspect the inner workings of many of the proprietary products that power mission-critical systems. Linux is a long-lasting project whose outcome grounds much of today's modern computational infrastructure — and it is fortunate that the community has been able to devise successful strategies to justify the system's positive reputation. That has been possible thanks to innovative business models that connect individuals and organizations with varying perspectives, allowing them to take advantage of the shared resources, while being encouraged to give back to the community through investment and technological contributions.

In the same vein as free and open-source hardware extended the original idea of free and open-source software, related concepts have gradually emerged in the context of other kinds of intellectual creations, including open-source educational content, scientific communication, commercial artwork, and research data, to name only a few examples. In the chapter "Coherent Synergy: Fostering Innovation in Open Source Ecosystems," Dr. Francisco José Monaco abstracts the fundamental principles shared by those varying instances into the unified notion of open-source innovation, referring to any kind of intellectual creation, irrespective of its nature, whether technological, artistic, scientific or other. The author addressed the question of how an innovation-based business that deliberately renounces the exclusive prerogatives endowed by intellectual property can foster continuous innovation. Against this background, Monaco approaches the open-source model as a new paradigm of innovation fostering that does not rely on the IP-enforcement model, bringing up a comprehensive conceptual framework to understand different kinds of open-source business models in a unified and systematic way. The study formulates the notion of coherent synergy: a property that determines the roles of intellectual creation and the essence of value delivery in open-source innovation ecosystems. The chapter examines some fundamental criteria when designing open-source business models concerning their adequacy to sustain a consistent, continuous innovation process.

The concept of FOSS ecosystem, in turn, can not be separated from that of Community, as it is through the latter that the cooperative feedback flows. The long-term sustainability of an open-source project, either a commercial enterprise or a community-driven effort, inherently depends on an engaged and enthusiastic community. Fostering a FOSS community around a project is a key concern for the long-term sustainability of the project. This aspect comprises the theme of the chapter "Fostering FOSS Communities: A Guide for Newcomers" by Hillary Nyakundi and Cesar Henrique De Souza. The authors conduct an extensive literature review addressing the technical and social barriers that cause newcomers to cease their contribution to a FOSS project, and complement the discussion with best practices to build a productive and long-lasting community.

Still on FOSS communities, the chapter "Building Teams and Developing a Career in the FOSS Industry" by Dr. Renê de Souza Pinto discusses aspects of FOSS as a professional path, highlighting the possibilities open for both individuals and organizations. The chapter approaches the potential frictions that may emerge from conflicts between the company's exclusive commercial goals and the community's collective interests, pointing to ways such dynamics can be addressed. The author elaborates on why companies should invest in building FOSS teams, and the opportunities open for entrepreneurs and young professionals.

The concept of open source embodies the idea of shared knowledge, which lies at the core of the FOSS model. Therefore, it is only natural that open-source technology plays a crucial role in the development of inclusive educational tools. This is the topic approached in the chapter "The Open Source Perspective in the Education Technology: A Digital Kon-Tiki Journey" by Martin Dow and Dr. David Preston. The authors highlight how the benefits of the FOSS paradigm extend beyond cost-effectiveness. In addition to the flexibility enabled by unrestricted access to source code, the chapter discuss how FOSS also promotes public sovereignty by empowering communities to regain control over the technology they rely on. In the context of education, this becomes particularly significant as it directly influences our ability to implement educational programs without being constrained by technical, economic, or ideological biases imposed by corporate giants in the tech industry. This chapter delves into this subject, exploring a compelling case study based on the OSLAP (Open-Source Learning Academy Protocol) initiative. Similar to other domains that require sustainable FOSS business models, open-source educational technology emerges as a realm where innovative ideas and strategies for long-term project financing are in high demand.

Finally, the chapter "The Red Hat Enterprise Linux Business Model" by Cesar Henrique De Souza addresses one of the most iconic practical illustrations of open-source-based enterprise, the case of Red Hat Inc. The author introduces the business model behind Red Hat's Linux development, highlighting its contribution to the Linux kernel. Faracco describes the main aspects of Red Hat Enterprise Linux, undoubtedly one of the most successful commercial Linux distributions, and the company's experience in using other open-source distributions such as Fedora and CentOS. The chapter brings a brief historical overview of each distribution and their communities, and comments on how their histories impacted the enterprise's products.

Through an in-depth discussion of these and related topics, the authors gather valuable information and critical analysis to help the interested audience understand the open-source development's rationales. The studies explore novel referential frameworks upon which individuals and organizations can devise strategies and design appropriate business models for a particular product or service.

We hope this book serves as a valuable resource to researchers, students, and practitioners investigating the foundations of the open-source model and its economic, social, technological, and ethical implications.

A Word About the Authors

This volume was brought about by many hands. It gathers the thoughts shared by academics and practitioners in response to the open call for contributions distributed through professional mailing lists, special interest groups, scientific forums, and other public channels.

   We are enormously glad that we could count on the contribution of the acknowledged authors who helped write this book.

Francisco José Monaco
Universidade de São Paulo, Brazil

Acknowledgment

This work was developed under the scope of the *Free and Open Source Research and Education Center,* a permanent project of the *Open-Source Competence Center (CCOS)* of ICMC, at the University of São Paulo, Brazil. Special thanks are due to the graduate and undergraduate collaborators of the U*SP's Free and Open-Source Extension Group.* The editor also acknowledges the research fellows who kindly contributed with valuable suggestions and advice, as well as to all the FOSS community, including individual enthusiasts and the organizations that bravely and generously have gifted us with the exciting present and promising future of the Free and Open Source technology. Thanks are also due to the authors who contributed their thoughts and ideas to this book and, not least, to my wife Michele and my kids Pedro and Eva for making everything worthwhile.

Editorial Advisory Board

Chapter 1
A Business Model Framework for Open Source Software Companies

Karl-Michael Popp
SAP SE, Germany

ABSTRACT

Open-source software companies represent growing businesses with specific business models. Here, the authors look at different business models for companies that base their business model completely or in part on open-source software or open-source licenses. They analyze different building blocks of such business models and reuse an existing business model framework to categorize these building blocks. This view reveals different hybrid business models for open-source software and ways for commercial open-source companies to create differentiation and competitive advantage.

1. A BUSINESS MODEL FRAMEWORK FOR OPEN-SOURCE SOFTWARE COMPANIES

Open-source software companies represent growing businesses with specific business models (Deshpande & Riehle, 2006, Popp, 2019). Here, we look at different business models for companies, that base their business model completely or in part on open-source software or open-source licenses. We analyze different building blocks of such business models and reuse an existing business model framework to categorize these building blocks.

DOI: 10.4018/978-1-6684-4785-7.ch001

1.1 Open-Source Licenses as a Key Factor for the Variety of Business Models

An open-source license comes with rights and obligations and the search for the optimal license continues (Lerner & Tirole, 2005, Jaeger et al., 2005). A license creates limitations as well as opportunities in creating business models around open-source software.

For example, for a company using open-source software as part of its products, the limitations can be described as follows.

Example

A software vendor may make use of the rights, like usage or redistribution of the open-source software, but it also has to fulfill the obligations, like e.g. delivering the copy of the license text with the software or revealing the source code of a software product.

Another restriction is that some licenses do not allow modifications of the open-source software. This would exclude the ability of a commercial open-source company to provide maintenance and to fix security vulnerabilities, because the open-source code must not be changed.

But the limitations of open-source licenses can also be an advantage for software vendors providing open-source software, which will be shown later in this chapter, when we talk about dual licensing models.

The key point for a commercial company is if it is willing and able to comply with the license terms of a specific open-source component. The rights and obligations in conjunction with the open-source software have to be analyzed diligently to make sure there is no violation of the license terms and the license terms are not in conflict with the commercial company´s business model (Onetti & Verma, 2009, Krishnamurthy, 2005). If this is ensured, the company can leverage this piece of open-source software.

1.2 Suppliers of Open-Source Software for Commercial Use

Often, open-source software is being supplied by a community or by a commercial company (Popp & Meyer, 2010). We speak of community open-source and commercial open-source respectively.

Community involvement with open-source products means that a community of people provides creation, maintenance and support for an open-source software (Stürmer & Myrach, 2006). Sometimes the community even provides presales and

Figure 1. Business model variations

Open Source Business Model variations

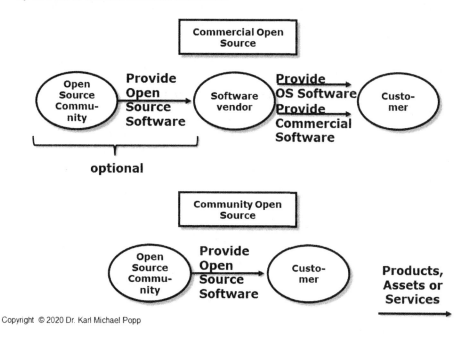

sales activities for companies offering an open-source version and a commercial version of their software. In most of the cases the community provides these services free of charge.

By providing an open-source licensed version of a product, a software vendor has the opportunity to outsource certain activities, like development, maintenance and support to the community (Dahlander & Magnusson, 2006).

There are, of course, differences between a company and the open-source community in providing open-source software. These differences are important to understand, because they influence a customer's software license selection and they also create niches for companies to establish a business. The differences are listed in Figure 2.

Looking at licenses, community open-source usually comes with a single type of license and standard terms. If a commercial company would like to use the open-source software and to have changes of the license, it is usually not possible to change the license terms with a community. Commercial open-source has the advantage that a commercial company issues the license. A software vendor willing

Figure 2. Commercial open-source vs. community open-source models

Community vs. Commercial Open Source

	Community Open Source	Commercial open source
License	Open source license, standard terms only	Commercial license, customized terms possible
Consulting	Some help by community, free of charge	Paid consulting services to customer needs
Maintenance	Community provides new versions	Paid maintenance to customer needs
Support	Community supports without guaranteed service level agreements	Paid support to customer needs with guaranteed service level agreements

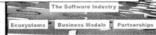

to change terms can get in contact and start negotiations of the license terms with that commercial company.

Consulting services for community open-source might come from the community itself or from companies who have specialized on providing commercial consulting services for community open-source software.

Maintenance service for community open-source is provided by the community only. While this is free of charge, there is no way to enforce changes and updates of the software.

Nevertheless, active communities have shown to perform timely updates for security vulnerabilities. A software vendor using the community open-source can escape this issue by donating a source code change to the open-source community. This should be a well considered decision, because the software vendor might be giving up intellectual property rights for that change.

Looking at support services, a community provides support services without guaranteed service level agreements, which is a big issue for commercial companies using that open-source software. In commercial open-source, there usually is a support services offering by the software vendor granting the commercial open-source license.

In addition, there is often the option to choose a commercial license for the open-source software, too, which might also come with a commercial support offering.

1.3 Open-Source Business Models in Detail

Now let us have a more detailed look at the different open-source business models.

Classification of Open-Source Business Models

Based on a general classification of business models (Malone et al., 2006) we will have a look at open-source business models. The following section arguments along the lines of (Popp & Meyer, 2010).

Figure 3 shows a business model framework containing a classification of generic business models. The business models relevant for commercial open-source business are marked in bold. In this general classification of business models, software classifies as an intangible product, see the corresponding column "Intangible" in Figure 3.

Software can be created or written ("Inventor"), distributed ("IP Distributor") or licensed or rented to customers ("IP Lessor"). In addition, the customer needs services to run and maintain the software, like implementation, support and maintenance services. These classify as "Contractor" business (Popp & Meyer, 2010). We assume here that all open-source businesses make use of at least a subset of these four business models. No matter if it is a community or a commercial software vendor, one or many of these business models are applied. By choosing a specific subset of business models, a so-called hybrid business model is created (Popp, 2011, Popp, 2012). Creating a hybrid business model means combining different business models with their specific goals, requirements and cost structures.

Since these business models are models on a type level, there might be different implementations of how a certain business model is run. An open-source community might run the Inventor business for creating software in a different way (leveraging the community) than a commercial software vendor (leveraging a proprietary development team), from a process as well as from a resource perspective. But on a type level, both run the same type of business called Inventor.

It is important to note that business model type level and business implementation level are design dimensions for describing existing and designing new open-source business models (Lindman & Rajala, 2012). So, creating a new open-source business might start with selecting one or more type level business models and then select from existing or new implementations for each of the business models to create a business.

Figure 3. Components of the commercial open-source business model

Commercial Open Source Business Model				
	Type of Products/Services offered			
	Financial	Physical	Intangible	Human
Creator	Entrepreneur	Manufacturer	**Inventor**	n/a
Distributor	Financial trader	Wholesaler, Retailer	**IP distributor**	n/a
Lessor	Financial lessor	Physical lessor	**IP lessor**	**Contractor**
Broker	Financial broker	Physical broker	IP broker	HR broker

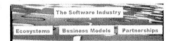

It is important to note that selecting certain business models, combining them and implementing them give a company the opportunity to differentiate themselves from competitors (Popp, 2011).

Going forward, we will analyze existing commercial and community open-source business models as a selection of a subset of the business models identified here: Inventor, IP Lessor, IP distributor and Contractor.

Community Open-Source Business Model

The community open-source business model usually makes use of the following business models: Inventor, IP Lessor and Contractor.

For the community, the inventor business is what the community is most involved in. It is about creating open-source software and engaging with the community members to coordinate the work and collect the contributions of the community members.

The IP lessor business is also important for the community. The IP lessor business defines the terms and conditions of the open-source license and makes the software available to customers. The license is defined by the community and all customers using the software have to comply with it. In some cases, there are multiple different licenses for an open-source software that a customer can choose from.

The contractor business contains all human services to customers. The community typically provides these via email and they contain services like maintenance, support, translation for country specific versions and the like. They are all carried out by community members. In almost every case, the customer does not pay for these services, but the customer has no rights to enforce any of these services and he does not have service level agreements, like a definition of minimum reaction time for support incidents.

The community can serve two types of customers: software vendors and (end) customers. For software vendors, the open-source community works as a supplier of software, for the customer, the open-source community works as a software vendor licensing software to the customer.

These two relationships differ in the way that customers and software vendors might make use of the software. Customers usually license the software for internal use only. Software vendors license software for internal use and/or for distribution to customers or for providing cloud solutions to customers. Often open-source software is included in commercial software and provided to customers by the software vendor. In this case, the software vendor has to make sure he complies with all licenses of all open-source software he is including in his software product.

Commercial Open-Source Business Models

In the last section we described the community business model, now we turn to the commercial open-source business model. As mentioned before, a commercial software vendor does not have to implement all of these business models, but can rather build a unique business model by selecting a subset of available business models. One basic difference to community open-source is that the IP Distributor business model is an option for commercial companies.

The history of commercial open-source companies shows that in the beginning the companies focused on services around open-source software, which matches the Contractor business. The next step was to build distributions for open-source software, like, e.g., for Linux. This matches to the IP Distributor business model.

Today, we find all kinds of hybrid business models around open-source. Companies are building software and donate it, completely or partially to the open-source community (Inventor business model) (Henkel, 2004). Commercial software vendors often package or change or extend existing community open-source software, so the community acts as a supplier of open-source software to the software vendor. In some cases the software vendor does not use existing open-source software from

Figure 4. Commercial open-source business model

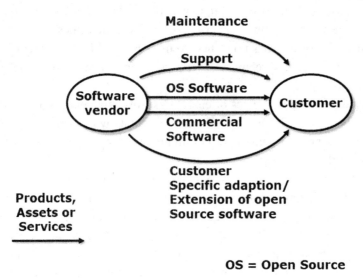

a community, but chooses to offer its proprietary software under a dual licensing strategy, e.g. under a commercial as well as an open-source license.

Please note that there are at least two delivery models for open-source software: either the software is distributed to the customer and run at the customer´s site or the software is provided in a hosted, cloud or on demand or cloud delivery model.

Commercial Services for Open-Source Software

Since open-source licenses are usually free of charge, many commercial companies are focused on providing services around open-source software (Lindman & Rajala, 2012). The expectation was simply that customers would still need services and since the license was free, that customers would have more money to spend on services. So, open-source software increased the share of wallet for commercial services.

Commercial open-source companies mainly provide the following services for open-source software: Hosting, Maintenance, Support, Consulting and Extension or Adaptation of open-source software to a customer´s needs.

Hosting services mean providing hardware and access to that hardware on which open-source software runs. Maintenance services consist of the following activities: building versions, provide bug fixes and upgrades and providing them to the customers. Support services contain of accepting, maintaining, and resolving incidents that the customer experiences while using the software. Consulting services mean planning and executing the installation and go-live of customers´ system landscapes containing the software.

Extension or adaptation of open-source software based on customer´s requests is designing, programming, testing and delivering open-source software that has been modified or expanded. Examples for extensions and modifications are:

- Functional Extensions for open-source applications with country-specific functionality or customer specific functionality;
- Extending the usage scenarios for open-source to additional countries by adding additional translations of user interfaces;
- Adapting open-source software, e.g. to make modifications of open-source software to run on a currently unsupported hardware platforms.

Commercial Licensing Business for Open-Source Companies

In the industry, we see three ways how commercial open-source companies offer software to customers executing the IP Lessor business model:

- Offer or redistribute open-source software only, no commercial software offered. In this case, the software vendor needs a hybrid business model containing one or more revenue streams to fund the open-source business.
- Offer identical products under two licenses (dual license model) (Valimaki, 2002).
- Offer different versions of the same product under two licenses to customers (dual product model).

For a commercial open-source company, there are two choices for dual licensing, dual license strategy for identical products or dual product strategy with dual licenses.

Dual License for Identical Products

Following the dual license strategy for identical products (Valimaki, 2002) a commercial open-source company would offer the same product under an open-source license and a commercial license. There are good reasons for the company and customers alike to have the choice between the two licenses As mentioned earlier,

Figure 5. Multiproduct and multilicensing strategy for open-source

Multiproduct and multilicense strategies for open source

	Single product	Dual products
Single License	„classic case" of Open source license only or of commercial license only	Dual product strategy (market segmentation by product and license)
Dual License (commercial & open source)	Dual license strategy for identical product (customer segmentation by license)	Dual product strategy (market segmentation by product and license)
Dual License (two open source licenses)	Dual license strategy for license compatibility (usage segmentation by license, more usages are possible)	Dual product strategy

Ecosystems Business Models Partnerships

customers could choose the commercial license for several reasons, like to ensure they get support service level agreements, warranty or liability from the software vendor. The commercial open-source software vendor could use a license that does not allow commercial use of the open-source software to force commercial users to buy a commercial license. Another variant of this is used by SugarCRM, which licenses parts of the offering under open-source license and premium features under commercial license (Waltl, 2013).

Dual Product With Dual Licensing

In the strategy dual product with dual licensing, the software vendor usually applies versioning. This could mean that a product with limited functionality can be licensed under an open-source license and the full product is available under a commercial license.

There are basically two examples for this strategy, freemium (Bekkelund, 2011, Pujol, 2010) and customer specific version of open-source under commercial license. Freemium in the context of open-source means that a free version of a product under an open-source license exists with restrictions compared to a commercial version of the product, like e. g. a reduced set of functionalities. The customer has to pay a premium, a commercial license fee, to get the full version of the product.

1.4 Revenue Models of Open-Source Companies

The key question for each open-source company is: how do they make money? Since there is usually no license revenue or very limited license revenue, there have to be other revenue streams that keep the company alive. This means that a hybrid commercial open-source business model combines free-of-charge services and products with services and products that are being charged for.

Relating to Figure 6, there might be a revenue stream for each of the products and services provided for customers.

In addition to the revenue streams shown, some open-source companies use other services to create revenues, like certification and compliance testing, hardware sales and advertising.

Figure 6. Commercial open-source revenue model

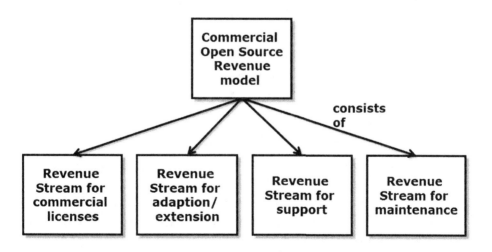

Commercial Open Source Revenue Model

In creating the operations plan for the company you have to make sure that the sum of the planned revenue of all revenue streams is big enough to sustain as a profitable company in the long term.

1.5 Customer View: Value of Commercial Licenses for Open-Source Software

Commercial open-source vendors offer open-source licensed software to their customers. There are different ways software vendors can add value to the open-source software like:

- By packaging (Wasserman, 2009): the software vendor creates a distribution by shrinkwrapping open-source software and distributes that to the customers (IP distributor business model). The customer can rely on the professional configuration of the package and does not have to have expert knowledge on open-source.
- By providing a commercial license (Ascher, 2004) with significant differences to the open-source license, like warranty and liability, no copyleft effect, clearly stated usage scenarios of the software and others. So the customer gets some license (or contract) terms that he could not get with the open-source license.
- By creating customer specific adaptation or integration of open-source software as commercial software. When a customer needs Perl on an exotic hardware platform with 64 bit support, he will contact a company that is specialized in this business and order that specific adaptation of the open-source software under a commercial license.
- By omitting advertising in the commercial version of the software while the open-source software is containing advertising.
- By providing better service level agreements, more storage space or other features for a higher service fee. This case applies for open-source software in a hosted, cloud or on demand delivery model.
    But even without the extra value a customer might decide against an open-source license and in favor of commercial open-source. This is the case, if e.g. a customer needs customized license terms, runs open-source in a mission-critical environment and thus needs service level agreements for support or if he needs maintenance provided in a different way than via the open-source community. In many business contexts it makes also sense to have liability and warranty provisions from a supplier when using open-source. In most of the existing open-source licenses there is exclusion of any warranty or liability (Jaeger et al., 2005). This is

another reason why companies might choose commercial open-source over community open-source.

1.6 Leveraging the Open-Source Community for Commercial Purposes

Besides providing open-source software to customers, software companies can leverage open-source software and the corresponding open-source community for their business in the following ways (Popp & Meyer, 2010):

- Leverage the open-source community as supplier, as development resource, marketing, presales, sales, maintenance or support resource.
- Leveraging the open-source community as product owner, maintainer and supporter and
- Leveraging the open-source community as sales channel.

To create a commercial open-source business model, software companies choose one or several of these levers. This is why there is no single open-source business model out there. Let us look closer at the different advantages of a commercial open-source model.

Leveraging the Open-Source Community as a Supplier

Software vendors often use the open-source community as a supplier of software. Almost any commercial software on the market contains components that are under an open-source license or the solutions use open-source software as a runtime environment.

The main reasons to use open-source "as supplied material" are quality, security and cost advantages. Quality advantages have been shown by several studies in the following way: open-source software with a community of significant size has a higher quality than similar commercial software.

Regarding cost advantages: If the community is inventing the software, it carries the cost of development. There is no sunk cost for a company to develop the software. As shown in chapter 4, this cost advantage can be disruptive to industries.

So, for the software vendor, the value of open-source software is that it comes for free, and it provides a significant cost advantage compared to programming a similar, proprietary functionality from scratch. The software vendor might also include and ship the open-source software with its solutions. As mentioned before, there is no license fee paid from the software vendor to the open-source community.

Figure 7. Flow of open-source products in a commercial setting

Flow of Open Source Products

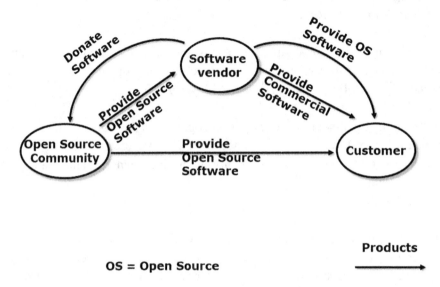

OS = Open Source

Products

As every open-source software comes with license terms, the software vendor has to comply with the license terms of the open-source software used (Cusumano, 2004).

If the software vendor ships the open-source software, the software vendor is responsible for support and maintenance of the software shipped, which includes the open-source software. So the software vendor has to make sure he is able to maintain and support the open-source software.

Since compliance with the license terms of open-source software is important, help for doing that is available. There are companies specialized on analyzing open-source usage and on analyzing the attached license terms. They offer tools that automatically analyze the source code and determine the list of open-source software components used. With this list you can determine if you can comply with the license terms and if you want to continue to use the open-source software.

Leveraging the Open-Source Community as Product Owner, Maintainer, and Supporter

The software vendor might decide to donate the source code to the community and let the community drive the product innovation as well as maintenance activities. By doing that, the software vendor further lowers its cost to develop and maintain software.

Commercial software vendors might have different reasons for donating software to the open-source community, e.g.:

- To create visibility of a software company's expertise. This is especially interesting for small companies to gain visibility and reputation within a larger community of subject matter experts.
- To get rid of the cost for product development, maintenance and support if a product is in the late stages of the product lifecycle or if the product is commoditized or did not create enough revenue.

But how do you make the community owner of a product? You donate proprietary software to the community and make it open-source. The following picture shows the flow of products. From this point in time, you lose some control over the product and trade this for the cost saved and the innovation speed of the product.

At the same time, if the community is big enough and active, the quality of the software increases. There is also a good chance that the community, due to its heterogeneity, is a better breeding ground for evolutionary innovation of the product.

1.7 Leveraging the Community as a Sales Channel

Software vendors might leverage the community to endorse products via viral marketing. It works like this: community members like the software and endorse its use (at companies). The companies can choose between the open-source and the commercial license of the software. If it chooses the commercial license, it will be provided by the software vendor.

Depending on the open-source license chosen, the software vendor can force customers into a commercial license for commercial use. This is the case for open-source licenses, which do not allow commercial use of the software under the open-source license. Another case is the customer wanting to do proprietary changes on the software and keep the ownership of the software, which conflicts with copyleft licenses. Copyleft licenses enforce that all versions, including modified and extended versions, are available for free to the community.

1.8 Summary and Outlook

Here, it was shown that a framework exists that can be used to describe business models and that these business models can be combined to create different hybrid business models of commercial open-source companies. In addition, an overview was given, how commercial open-source companies leverage open-source communities for their purposes.

The evolution of open-source business and commercial open-source business is still underway. We will see, which new hybrid business models will be created in the future, just like the ones we recently saw in open-source on demand applications or open-source software in cloud environments.

REFERENCES

Ascher, D. (2004). Is Open Source Right for You? *ACM Queue; Tomorrow's Computing Today*, 2(3), 32–38. doi:10.1145/1005062.1005065

Bekkelund, K. J. (2011). *Succeeding with freemium*. Norwegian University of Science and Technology.

Cusumano, M. (2004). The business of software. Free Press.

Deshpande, A., & Riehle, D. (2006). The Total Growth of Open-source. *Open-source Development Communities and Quality*, 275, 197–209. doi:10.1007/978-0-387-09684-1_16

Henkel, J. (2004). Open-source software from commercial firms–tools, complements, and collective invention. *Journal of Business Economics*, 4(4), 1–23.

Jaeger, T., Koglin, O., Kreutzer, T., Metzger, A., & Schulz, C. (2005). Die GPL kommentiert und erklärt. O'Reilly.

Krishnamurthy, S. (2005). An Analysis of Open-source Business Models. *Source*, 54, 267–278.

Lerner, J., & Tirole, J. (2005). Economic Perspectives on Open-source. *Perspectives on Free and Open-Source Software, 15*, 47-78.

Lindman, J., & Rajala, R. (2012). How Open Source Has Changed the Software Industry: Perspectives from Open Source Entrepreneurs. *Technology Innovation Management Review*, 2(1), 5–11. doi:10.22215/timreview/510

Malone, T., Weill, P., Lai, R., D'Urso, V., Herman, G., Apel, T., & Woerner, S. (2006). Do Some Business Models Perform Better than Others? SSRN *Electronic Journal*. doi:10.2139/ssrn.920667

Onetti, A., & Verma, S. (2009). Open-source Licensing and Business Models, ICFAI. *Journal of Knowledge Management, VII*(1), 68–95.

Popp, K. (2011). Hybrid revenue models of software companies and their relationship to hybrid business models. In B. Regnell & I. Weerd (Eds.), *Software business* (pp. 77–88). Springer.

Popp, K. (2012). Leveraging open source licenses and open source communities in hybrid commercial open source business models. *CEUR Workshop Proceedings, 879*, 33–40.

Popp, K. (2019). *Best practices for commercial use of open source software*. Books on Demand.

Popp, K., & Meyer, R. (2010). *Profit from Software Ecosystems: Business Models, Ecosystems and Partnerships in the Software Industry*. Books on Demand.

Pujol, N. (2010). Freemium: Attributes of an Emerging Business Model. SSRN *Electronic Journal*. doi:10.2139/ssrn.1718663

Stürmer, M., & Myrach, T. (2006). Open-source community building. In Business Models and Community Relationships of Open-source Software Firms. Elsevier.

Valimaki, M. (2002). Dual Licensing in Open Source Software Industry. SSRN *Electronic Journal*. doi:10.2139/ssrn.1261644

Waltl, J. (2013). *IP modularity in software products and software platform ecosystems*. Books on Demand.

Wasserman, T. (2009). *Building a Business on Open Source Software*. Academic Press.

Chapter 2

Open Source and Economic Models in an Evolutionary Approach

Marco Berlinguer
IGOP, Spain

ABSTRACT

Despite being a commons, free and open source software has come to dominate software production. FOSS surprising trajectory passed so far through two distinct stages. It originated within self-organized communities of developers and was later sustained by market adoption and innovative forms of economic competition. Its economic model was initially interpreted as a gift economy. Today it is better understood as based on hybrids that modulate markets and commons. By analyzing the trajectory of FOSS through two approaches with roots in evolutionary economics— the multi-level perspective and the techno-economic paradigms—FOSS takes on the characteristics of a development and innovation system that has grown with the digital paradigm and is destined to occupy an important function in its further development. The evolution of FOSS has not ended. On the contrary, a third phase of FOSS development is looming, which will be characterized by greater government involvement and further innovations in FOSS governance systems and economic models.

INTRODUCTION

Free and open source software (FOSS) has come to largely dominate software production, i.e., the leading technology and industry of the digital revolution (Berlinguer, 2021).

DOI: 10.4018/978-1-6684-4785-7.ch002

Open source plays a central role on all the main frontiers of digital innovation, from Cloud computing, to IoT, AI, 5G, DLT, and even Quantum computing; and open source solutions have become a central terrain for capitalist competition as well as an arena for convergence, standardization and industry-wide forms of collaboration.

FOSS had a spectacular evolution. Its unconventional way of organizing the production of software in fact has taken its first steps at the margins of industry, within informal communities of autonomous developers. This evolution is even more surprising since this has happened despite FOSS challenging characteristics. In fact, FOSS is a digital commons (Benkler, 2013). The most distinctive feature of FOSS is that it is governed by licenses that allow anyone to access, use, copy, modify, develop and redistribute it. It radically overturns the principle of exclusivity enforced by the Intellectual Property Rights (IPR). And this basic institutional arrangement has crucial implications for models of governance and ways of appropriating the value of the resource (Benkler, 2013; Berlinguer, 2018).

For this and other characteristics - such as the voluntary character of the contributions, the absence of hierarchical ties and market exchanges - initial characterizations of FOSS have often been of a utopian hue. FOSS was described as a "gift economy" (Raymonds, 1999;), a "third model of production" – "commons-based peer production" (Benkler, 2001; 2006;) – and sometimes as an illustration of an emerging post-capitalistic mode of production (Bauwens 2005; Vercellone et al. 2015; Mason 2016; Rifkin, 2014).

At the beginning of its trajectory, these unconventional features created quite a few challenges and many obstacles to the spread and adoption of FOSS. Microsoft, which has long been the quintessential adversary of FOSS, used it to foment the FUD (fear, uncertainty, doubt) syndrome, which was widespread among the managerial class and long surrounded FOSS discouraging its adoption by companies, organizations and governments.

Today the picture is radically different. So much so that Microsoft itself likes to present itself as the company that contributes most to the open source world. In this new situation, the widespread temptation might be to consider the unconventional features of FOSS gone. This "normalization" could be argued either by pointing to the selective capture and co-optation of its alternative instances by the market and capitalism (O'Neil et al., 2021), or by hollowing out, domesticating, and trivializing its original novelties: as if to say that, in fact, there was nothing really new under the sun.

There is some truth in both of these narratives, which capture aspects of the evolution of FOSS. However, on the whole, they fail to account for the trajectory of FOSS and the many innovations that have accompanied its growth and expansion. Above all, they draw premature conclusions about the evolution of this new approach to technological development and digital production, which is instead about to enter a new phase of development.

What is needed instead is an interpretation of the trajectory of FOSS that can better understand some of the challenging and changing characteristics of the FOSS ecosystem and at the same time shed light on its possible future evolution. This also applies to the economic models that have underpinned the development of FOSS to date, which have changed at different stages of FOSS development and will evolve further in the future.

To develop the building blocks of such an interpretation, in this chapter FOSS will first be framed as a digital commons, as this characteristic is fundamental to understanding the economic models that have emerged around FOSS. Indeed, its ownership regime undermines the possibility of exclusive private appropriation of its value. Moreover, this characterization is important because not only has FOSS emerged in the area of software, that is, in the central technology of the digital revolution, where it is about to become the standard model of production. But its innovative ways have also inspired similar developments in many other areas. This means that the success of FOSS may be evidence of a broader role for these new types of commons in the emerging networked digital economy and society.

Along with this characterization as a digital commons, the evolution of the economic models of FOSS - from its first appearance to its current stage - will be organized in two different phases. The first focused on self-organized communities of developers and voluntary contributions. The second characterized by market adoption and new forms of capitalist competition (Perens, 2005; Berlinguer, 2018). Although communities and enterprises have coexisted throughout the history of FOSS, the prevailing characteristics, driving forces, and dynamics of each period allow for such a distinction, which also highlights the distinctive areas of innovations that occurred in each phase in FOSS economic models.

Overall, the presence of a commons and this periodization will allow some lessons to be learned about some challenging features of the economic models that have emerged so far around FOSS. The most important is that FOSS economic models are based on a plurality of systems of ownership, governance, and value generation and appropriation (Jessop, 2001; Lepak et al., 2007; Berlinguer, 2018). It is this hybridity between commons and markets that characterizes the economic models that support FOSS at its current stage of development. These hybrids can take different configurations, and a synthetic framework organized on the basis of three concepts - semicommons, shared infrastructure, and ecosystem creation - can help distinguish the different rationales, actors, and strategies operating behind these hybrid models.

However, the trajectory of FOSS is far from concluded. Therefore, after analyzing the first two stages of the FOSS evolution, the trajectory of FOSS will be further placed in the broader context of transformation occurring in production systems. This will be done by applying to the trajectory of FOSS two approaches - with roots in evolutionary economics - that have been developed to analyze radical technological transitions: the "multilevel perspective" (Geels, 2010) and the theory of "techno-economic paradigms" (Perez, 2003; 2010). Both approaches will provide insights to better understand why FOSS economic models have gone through different phases; and both will shed light on what to expect in the future of FOSS (Berlinguer, 2019b).

Overall, the characterization of FOSS that will emerge is that of a development model and innovation system that has grown along with the digital paradigm and is set to occupy a central function in its further development. Following this characterization, the last section will outline the most salient contours of a third phase of FOSS development, which is just beginning to take shape.

In conclusion, the most important new development expected in the FOSS ecosystem will be identified in a more organic participation and involvement of governments. This shift will represent a third phase in the evolution of FOSS and will inevitably bring new challenges and opportunities and generate further innovations in the governance systems and economic models of FOSS.

THE FIRST PHASE: COMMUNITIES OF DEVELOPERS REINVENT THE COMMONS

The origins of the free software movement date back to the early 1980s. The root cause was the expansion of intellectual property rights (IPRs) to software, which clashed with the habits and values of some software developers and researchers, who perceived IPRs as an obstacle to their freedom and a burden on their productivity. Richard Stallman laid the foundation for the free software movement, organizing it around what he called the "four fundamental freedoms of the user" in relation to software: the freedom to run, study, modify, and redistribute copies of a program. The most important legacy of this first step was the invention of a new type of license - the General Public License (GPL) - aimed at protecting these freedoms. However, it was not until the 1990s, thanks to the growth of the World Wide Web, that the free software movement was able to really take off. This happened when dispersed developers, driven by different motivations - initially not primarily economic - began to band together, forming new types of communities, based on collaboration, voluntary contributions and original forms of governance.

Yet these new licenses also served to provide a surprising new anchor that functioned—under certain conditions—as a new institutional arrangement that fostered collaboration and trust, and an innovative organizational lever to coordinate independent and dispersed contributors (Weber, 2004). It was in this way that, pragmatically, the autonomous communities that emerged around FOSS turned out to be a critical experience in the rediscovery or reinvention of the commons at the new frontier of the digital revolution (Berlinguer, 2017).[1]

With varying blends of ideological and pragmatic values, these loose-knit communities discovered and experimented with mechanisms that anchored and fostered collaboration among dispersed and highly diverse individuals and motivations, in the absence of institutional ties, direct economic transactions or formal hierarchies.

The main innovation, however, hinged on the innovative system of property rights. The GPL license created by Stallman, like all licenses that have flourished in the FOSS world, actually involves the radical overturning of the principle of exclusivity enforced by, and central to, intellectual property rights (Rose, 1986: 2003; Coriat, 2015). The original rationale for this institutional innovation was to ensure that no one could withdraw and appropriate a collaboratively produced resource, thus undermining the fundamental freedoms. However, these new licenses also served to provide a surprising new anchor that functioned, under certain conditions, as a new institutional arrangement that fostered collaboration and trust, and an innovative organizational lever to coordinate independent and dispersed collaborators (Weber 2004). In this way, pragmatically, the autonomous communities that emerged around FOSS turned out to be a critical experience in rediscovering or reinventing the commons at the new frontier of the digital revolution (Berlinguer, 2017).

This radical reversal of the principle of exclusivity introduced by FOSS licenses has many important implications, both in the modes of governance and in the forms of value generation and appropriation. The most relevant in economic terms is that this regime denies the "right to exclude" or the exclusive rights of the owner (Coriat, 2015). By this, it excludes the possibility of selling ownership or the right to access and use the resource, and in this way to appropriate its value, at least privately and exclusively.

THE FIRST ECONOMIC MODEL: HIGH TECH GIFT ECONOMY

As Yochai Benkler recently recalled, "When free and open source software emerged into the public consciousness in the late 1990s, it was an 'impossible' phenomenon. There were thousands of volunteers collaborating to develop some of the most complex software infrastructure on the model of a common good: anyone could contribute, no one had exclusive rights to use, adapt or distribute the software, and most of the people contributing were not paid to do so. The fact that this mission-critical infrastructure was being built on a largely voluntary and completely non-proprietary model, in direct competition with the world's largest software companies, was a complete mystery to the prevailing economic wisdom of the time." (Benkler, 2019).

The voluntary nature of the contributions and the success of these initiatives stimulated a first wave of studies on FOSS, which mainly investigated the motivations of developers in the absence of direct monetary incentives (Kollock, 1999; Hippel & Krogh 2003; Lakhani & Wolf, 2005; David & Shapiro, 2008; O'Neil 2009), and the models of organizing production in situations where there was no possibility of exercising direct hierarchical command.

The common perception was that FOSS expansion could undermine and disrupt the software markets. What, at the beginning, was seen as either exciting or frightening. On one side, it was relatively easy for Microsoft – for long the fiercest enemy of FOSS to leverage instinctive fears in the business and managerial world and to launch smear campaigns depicting the free software as an "hippie" and "anti-American" enterprise for its presumed anti-commercial aim. Conversely, on the other side, initially, FOSS was celebrated by many with characterizations often of a utopian and anarchic hue.

At this early stage, the prevailing characterization of FOSS was that of a "high-tech gift economy" (Barbrook, 1998; Raymond, 1998; 2001; Weber, 2000; Zeitlyn, 2003). The notion of a gift economy was recovered from historical economic anthropology (Mauss, 2002; Polanyi, 1957) and the growth of this new gift culture and economy was seen as a possibility created by the new technical, economic and cultural conditions in a "new economy" (Kelly, 1999) in which non-rival digital information was going to be the central resource.

Benkler, expanding his analysis beyond FOSS to include other experiences such as for example Wikipedia, theorized the emergence of a third model of production, distinct from both the market and the institutional public sphere, which he called "commons-based peer production" (Benkler 2006). The emphasis in general was on the voluntary, not paid contributions, and on a "pragmatic anarchy" in relation to the organization of labor (Benkler, 2004).

This characterization of FOSS as an organic alternative economy has never entirely disappeared. Even today, there are still quite a few who look at FOSS as an expression of an emerging post-capitalist mode of production (Rifkin, 2014; Kostakis & Bauwens 2014; Rigi, 2014; Vercellone et al., 2015; Mason 2016).

However, as FOSS evolved and begun to diffuse and be increasingly adopted by companies and in the market both these initial opposite characterizations of FOSS – the utopian and the liquidationist – has progressively lost meaning. Rather it became clear that the idea of an opposition between FOSS and markets required thorough revision (Berlinguer, 2020). Indeed this re-interpretation of FOSS was also the deliberate aim pursued by the Open source movement, a brunch of the Free software movement which split the movement in the late 1990s, with the intention of crafting a narrative around FOSS more business-friendly.

SHARED VALUE: AN ENDURING UNRESOLVED MISMATCH

In 2000s the linkages between FOSS and the world of business began to grow steadily. Nevertheless, the communities, the way they function and their forms of governance have not disappeared; and most importantly the ownership regime of the resources has remained unchanged.

In this sense, there are many legacies of the "economic models" and organizational innovations which sustained this first "heroic" phase of FOSS development which have continued to influence the economic models which have emerged around FOSS in its second stage development. Indeed they exerted an important influence on the evolution of the digital economy more broadly.

In economic terms, one of the most important directly depends on the presence of a commons at the core of FOSS development. One of the consequences of this regime of ownership is that FOSS as such cannot be directly sold and monetized. This also means that FOSS economy is difficult to measure in monetary values. One complementary consequence is that FOSS economy is also poor monetarily, at least in comparison with its "real" value. The result is that FOSS economy is structurally underestimated, for example by public policy.

Linux is a good example. The Linux Foundation presents it on its website as "the most valuable shared technological investment in history". With good reasons. Linux is the product of the contributions of thousands of developers and hundreds of companies. Its value however can only be calculated by the hypothetical cost of labor necessary to build all its lines of code. Linux foundations estimated it at 16 billions dollars. This value can be compared with the Linux Foundation's budget. In 2021 it was 184 millions dollars. A large and rapidly growing budget. However devoid of any relation to the value of the resource for which the Linux Foundation is the main Trust.

The broader point is that FOSS value manifests a structural misalignment and mismatch with the conventional and institutionalized systems of economic account, such as GDP, balance sheets, consumption indexes, which have regulated for long the economy, at micro and macro level (Rullani, 2000; Morell et al. 2016; Berlinguer 2016; 2018).

This mismatch is a wider phenomenon (Martinez-Alier et al., 1998; Moore, 2014; Berlinguer, 2016). In this sense FOSS belongs to a large family of intangibles, which have been growing in the last decades. But FOSS is one of the more interesting and puzzling of these intangibles. For this reason. Because FOSS highlights a form of wealth generation that originates from the sharing of common resources and which often multiplies through that sharing. A feature, the latter, for which a neologism has been created to name it: "antirivality" (Weber, 2004). Furthermore this is a mechanic which FOSS shares with other phenomena that have come markedly to the fore in networked digital economies, in parallel with FOSS, like for example standards (Blind, 2004; Blind, & Jungmittag, 2008; Swann, 2010; Sidak, 2016) and network effects (Katz & Shapiro, 1994; Parker & Van Alstyne, 2005; Farrell & Klemperer, 2007; Tucker, 2018).

Overall, this mismatch – and the relative invisibility of FOSS value in GDP, balance sheets, consumption metrics - remains a blind spot that has been scarcely addressed in studies on FOSS.

Yet it may result in micro and macro injustices, inefficiencies and fragility within FOSS economy and in its relationship with the wider economy. To say it with feminist philosopher Nancy Frazer, it can be a source of "mis-representation", "mis-recognition", "maldistribution" (Fraser, 2017).

A recent study sponsored by the EU Commission has attempted to render visible and quantify the value of FOSS economy at the EU level, focusing on its spill over effects (Blind et al., 2021). However, there is yet a lack of consolidated methodologies for addressing this issue.

THE SECOND DRIVER: MARKET INCORPORATES OPEN SOURCE

Projects and ecosystems that maintain community-centered forms of collaboration continue to exist or new ones emerge in the FOSS ecosystem. Indeed, in some cases it is from these kinds of informal communities that the most disruptive innovations emerge, as has been the case with blockchain technologies, for example. These largely informal coalitions continue to influence and contribute significantly to widespread and accelerated innovation in the digital world. The explosion of digital entrepreneurship itself has been based largely on FOSS. The availability of freely reusable and recombinable FOSS commons has dramatically reduced the barriers to experimentation and prototyping and given a huge boost to entrepreneurship and innovation in the startup ecosystem (Egbal, 2016).

Sometimes it is from these communities that the resources that support the infrastructure of the digital economy globally come, often with little awareness on the part of the organizations and institutions that rely on them. And sometimes these communities continue to rely in part on volunteer labor and face precariousness and lack of resources. These fragilities can translate into unexpected systemic vulnerability, as was widely experienced during the Heartbleed case[2]. This condition underscores the distortions and opportunistic exploits that characterize, in many cases, the FOSS economy and the exploitation of "open access" resources. In terms of their internal functioning, FOSS communities are still anchored in principles such as voluntary involvement and alignment, social and symbolic capital of leaders and projects, meritocracy, "do-ocracy." This is also true for the work systems of the powerful nonprofit foundations that have sprung up and grown in the FOSS ecosystem.

However, the relationships of most of these foundations and the broader FOSS ecosystem with market forces and companies have changed radically.

Indeed, the spectacular growth of FOSS would not have been possible without its progressive adoption in the market and the increasing involvement of companies in its development. The growth of this symbiosis has followed a path that was sometimes difficult to imagine. Linux, for example, has not succeeded as an operating system for personal computers (where Microsoft has maintained its dominance), as was in its initial ambitions. Instead, it quickly found its way as a dominant platform in other areas such as servers, which was the use that began to be made of Linux, starting in the mid-1990s, by large organizations with supercomputing needs, such as NASA or Google, who leveraged it to build huge data centers and large processing capacities relatively inexpensively.

In general, FOSS found an easier way into new areas of development at the frontiers of innovation - such as Web servers, mobile telephony, data centers, the Internet of Things, and cloud computing - that were not already occupied by dominant proprietary standards or platforms. In these areas, FOSS has been able to exploit its advantages as a low-cost, distributed approach to experimentation and development, with a critical mass of developers and companies coalescing around it. Other areas where FOSS solutions prevailed more easily were those where end users were primarily developers, such as development tools, programming languages, databases, servers, and low-level libraries. For developers, in fact, the lack of easy or attractive interfaces or the fact that a program is a work in progress (which is often the case in FOSS compared to commercial products) are secondary issues, while the freedom to study, reuse, transform, and redistribute software makes a huge difference to them. Finally, another unexpected boost that has helped tip the balance between proprietary software and FOSS, came from the new Web companies - Google, Facebook, Twitter, and Amazon - when they began to use it to build their infrastructures and because they have gradually learned the importance of opening up some layers of their platforms to nurture communities of developers and third-party applications.

In any case, slowly but surely, FOSS has step by step managed to penetrate and gradually transform the entire software industry. By the end of the first decade of the 2000s, FOSS began to be commonly recognized as a pillar of information technology. In the early 2010s, the "open source won" meme began to spread. The following "conversion" of a company like Microsoft proved that it was becoming suicidal - even for the largest software company - not to integrate into the open source ecosystem.

Popular platforms for software development began to incorporate the logic of "forking" (the ability to clone software and divide its development). Initially, thought of as a tool of last resort in the hands of communities to hold project leadership accountable or as a way to resolve internal conflicts over project development, forks have become the ordinary, default mechanism for facilitating parallel development of workflows on the same program.

Today it is virtually impossible to find a company that does not use FOSS programs. And it is extremely rare to find a major technology company that does not participate in the development of some FOSS project. Instead, it is common for top technology companies to launch FOSS projects to compete in the most critical and innovative areas of development.

The connections between markets and FOSS ecosystem have become capillary, increasing the speed and ease with which the most "promising" innovations are picked up, adopted and integrated by venture capital, tech giants, or by industry more broadly (as is happening with blockchain technologies in banking, logistics or communication, for example). At the same time, the promise of rapid valorization that these connections sometimes provide to successful startups has become the pole star in the minds of many FOSS developers.

Ultimately, in this way, market forces, companies and new forms of capitalist competition have gradually become, after communities, the second main driver of FOSS development. And this symbiosis with open source has become a laboratory for new kinds of economic models and organizations.

MARKETS-COMMONS HYBRIDS: THREE TEMPLATES

FOSS is thriving in the central industry of the digital revolution, despite being a common good and not fitting into the dominant regime of economic production and exploitation centered on monetary exchange value.

How can this surprising success be explained?

A key explanation is that the FOSS ecosystem and its economy are governed by a new type of hybrid or mixed economy. Indeed, to analyze the FOSS economy it is necessary to recognize that there are several overlapping and interdependent layers, organized according to differentiated systems of ownership, regimes of value generation and appropriation, and forms of governance. (Jessop 2001; Berlinguer, 2017)

The second related explanation is that, despite their idiosyncratic structures, markets and open-access commons not only can coexist but can expand in parallel or synergistically. For a long time they were considered antithetical. What is true. Each regime threatens the other. Commons and commodities remain irreconcilable. Yet, on the other hand, they are not only in conflict with each other, but can also develop symbiotically and can both expand in parallel through mutual collaboration. Markets can be eliminated in some areas by introducing a commons, to be expanded or created tout court in others, where they can be facilitated or fostered by those same commons: for example, by reducing the costs of products or services or accelerating the digital transformation of processes and resources.

A scheme organized around three concepts - semicommons, shared infrastructure, ecosystem building - can help analyze the hybrids that have emerged in FOSS ecosystems and the different configurations these hybrids between commons and markets can take (Berlinguer, 2017).

Each concept represents a rationale. In practice, these rationales often overlap. However, keeping them conceptually separate provides a means to distinguish the different logics, types of actors, outcomes, and dilemmas that can arise from these hybrid arrangements. (Berlinguer, 2017, 2020a)

The first concept is that of semicommons. The concept was proposed by Smith (2000), who extrapolated it from an analysis of the medieval open field system and applied it to modern communication networks. Medieval commons have historically accommodated two types of activity - agriculture and grazing - and two different property regimes - commons and private property - at different times of the year. The concept is useful insofar as it highlights a two-tiered structure based on the coexistence of a dual regime of ownership and economic exploitation within the same resource system (Fennell, 2011). The "open business models" that have gradually emerged around FOSS can be collected under this heading (Chesbrough, 2006). It clarifies how, on the one hand, the primary value of software remains a common good that cannot be exclusively appropriated. On the other hand, various forms of commercialization can be generated on it: the sale of services, support, certifications, packaged distributions, the use of "freemium" models, the integration of additional features of proprietary software, and the integration of software inside hardware and complementary products (Herraiz et al., 2009). There are important differences among these models, which have gradually taken shape around FOSS. However, they all share the same two-level structure, organized according to two logics: a common good as a shared base and the different markets that are generated on it. This two-tiered structure also explains the cross-subsidization basis that finances the production of the "public good " in a market context.

The second concept is that of shared infrastructure. It is one of the most commonly used motivations to explain the adoption of FOSS by companies (Perens 2005; Eghbal 2016; Fogel 2017). This concept also proposes a two-tiered structure. The difference here is that companies are conceived primarily as users and buyers of software, rather than as producers and sellers. Most companies, in most cases, belong to this category. They are not interested in software commercialization and most of the software they use does not constitute a specific "differentiating component" for their business model (Perens, 2005). This well explains the crucial role that companies that are primarily users and consumers of software have played in expanding the adoption of FOSS solutions in the market. For these companies, FOSS provides a way to share and economize costs and risks in the access and provision (development, maintenance, adaptation, and upgrading) of necessary components of production.

The third way of framing the hybridism between FOSS and new forms of capitalism describes the strategic use of FOSS that has sometimes been made by the largest and most successful companies of the Internet era (Berlinguer, 2018). In this case, FOSS is used to build an ecosystem. Initially it was typically a single company that introduced a specific FOSS product, often retaining control over its development. It is actually more common for these initiatives to be promoted by a coalition of companies. In both cases, the strategy typically aims to attract users, developers, and commercial ecosystems around a new standard or platform, and is designed to leverage the growth or creation of complementary markets adjacent to and related to the FOSS commons. "Surveillance capitalism" (Zuboff 2015), based on hoarding and exploiting user data, has been fertile ground for these strategies. Google's Android represents the first and most successful example of this strategy. At the same time, Google's recent condemnation by the European Commission for abusing the dominant position it achieved with Android demonstrates how this economic model of cross-subsidization can be used as a kind of innovative dumping strategy to wipe out competitors, unleash various network effects, and prepare the ground for new forms of monopolization. What is certain, however, is that these modes of competition have increasingly expanded in the marketplace. Even beyond software. Facebook's Open Compute Project, aimed at sharing and accelerating knowledge and design of data center hardware products, is one example. In the automotive industry, Tesla has used it to break resistance toward electric cars and to mobilize the global investment needed for an extremely expensive transition, while leveraging its leading position. In the microchip industry, Risc-V is an open-standard instruction set architecture (ISA) developed under open source licenses and supported by a global coalition of companies and organizations, with particular interest from those in China. To date, it is becoming almost standard for large technology companies or coalitions of companies to adopt this strategy. Especially if they are struggling and need to catch up with their competitors. Some current examples include the struggle among the most powerful technology companies over artificial intelligence frameworks; the Open 5G promoted by the U.S. telecommunications industry; Huawei's new Harmony mobile operating system.

NEW ECONOMIC ARCHITECTURES: BEYOND MARKET AND HIERARCHIES

Indeed, as with other innovative arrangements that have emerged in the FOSS economy, this multilayered articulation of technology stacks and legal and economic regimes that have emerged in FOSS hybrids seems to have broader significance for the study of contemporary forms of value production and appropriation.

In fact, FOSS as a digital commons has grown in parallel with the rise of new types of economic organization (Rullani, 2009; Muegge, 2013; Berlinguer, 2018), such as networks (Powell, 1989; Castells, 2004; Benkler, 2006; McIntyre & Srinivasan, 2017), ecosystems (Jacobides et al. 2018; Baldwin, 2018); Cennamo et al., 2018), and platforms (Baldwin & Woodard 2009; Gawer, 2014; Gawer & Cusumano, 2014; Srnicek, 2017; Constantinides et al., 2018). All somehow belong to a new family of economic architectures or "meta-organizations" (Gawer, 2014) that have gradually supplanted the organizational forms that characterized the Fordist era (Coase, 1937; Chandler, 1993). And they share some common characteristics.

A common feature, for example, of these organizations is that they are all characterized by porous and elusive boundaries (Parker et al., 2016; Berlinguer, 2018). It is difficult to define the relevant economic unit within them. Who owns Linux? Who works for Google? These are questions that would be difficult to answer.

Another common feature is that there is more in these economic meta-organizations than just markets. Markets are only part of the whole. Much of what is produced, circulates and is appropriated in these new architectures of the digital economy is not mediated by monetary market transactions (Berlinguer, 2018). And, just as there are not just markets, there is not just competition either. In these economic organizations much value is produced by other mechanisms, for example, aggregation on common platforms, alignment on standards, integration through protocols and interfaces, and data generated by technology design.

Rather, one can see how leading companies in the platform economy have learned to use the hybrid economy that underlies FOSS and strategically modulate the creation and destruction of markets (Parker et al., 2016; Berlinguer, 2018).

Indeed, the strategic modulation of differentiated technological, legal and economic layers appears to be a critical locus for investigating not only the emergence of a new typology of economic organizations and their modes of governance, but also for investigating the mechanisms by which the value generated by the complex flows that characterize contemporary digital ecosystems is disproportionately captured (Baldwin, 2015; Mazzucato et al., 2020; Blanke & Pybus, 2020).

This also means that FOSS should be integrated into the ongoing revision of traditional antitrust doctrine.

FOSS has proven to function effectively as a system to generate 'collective value', govern technological interdependencies or foster collaboration in conditions where, as Powell (1989) put it, 'neither markets nor hierarchies' can guarantee it. FOSS has democratised and accelerated innovation in a multitude of areas, supporting developer autonomy, and small businesses and start-ups. By its very nature, FOSS as such cannot be monopolised. Nevertheless, as the case of Android has made clear, FOSS is not exempt from the risk of new forms of monopolisation arising from the intricate systems within which FOSS layers can be embedded. What is happening in Cloud computing is another example. Important technology stacks in Cloud computing are standardised by FOSS solutions (e.g. Linux, OpenStack, Kubernetes). However, this is accompanied by an extreme market concentration, where a few companies (Amazon, Microsoft, Google, Alibaba) dominate unchallenged.

Indeed, this unequal distribution of the benefits of FOSS in monetised markets is a structural feature that has been rather overlooked. After all, the spread of FOSS with its open access regime has grown symbiotically with the formation of a hypercentralised digital economy.

Moreover, the FOSS ecosystem itself is not exempt from the risks of undue influence or capture. In this sense, the recent mega-acquisitions of GitHub by Microsoft (for $7.5 billion, almost four times the last valuation received by the start-up) and of Red Hat by IBM for $34 billion, about 40 per cent more than its stock market value) should sound as a warning.

So far, FOSS foundations are the main institutions or "meta-organizations" that have emerged in the FOSS ecosystem to provide answer to the multiple issues which progressively emerged in FOSS governance along its development.

Their main function remains that of a trust that ensures - along with the ownership system - equitable governance of the collective development effort and the common resource.

However FOSS foundations have evolved together with the governance problems of the FOSS ecosystem (O'Mahony, 2007; Riehle, 2010; Hunter & Walli, 2013; Izquierdo & Cabo, 2018; 2020).

In the beginning, foundations provided communities with a legal entity to manage scarce financial resources and residual intellectual property rights (e.g., trademark). As they developed know-how on the governance of FOSS collaborative undertakings, they began to provide services and mentoring to new projects. Later, in the second phase of FOSS development, they grew out of their proven ability to ensure neutrality in managing the development of common resources and, in this way, keep cooperation between companies, sometimes competing in the same markets, alive. The current membership of the Linux Foundation - which includes all of the world's major technology companies - is in itself a striking proof of the trust that the global industry has progressively placed in some FOSS foundations, as well as a testament to how radically the FOSS world has changed.

More recently, there has been an incipient consolidation among foundations in the FOSS ecosystem, with some - for example, Linux Foundation (LF) and Apache Foundation - beginning to assume more "macro" and "systemic" functions of representation and governance of the entire FOSS ecosystem.

This evolution is happening hand in hand with the expansion of FOSS's role as a provider of critical components in the intricate global digital infrastructure system. This structural dependence of global information systems on FOSS has raised concerns among industry and governments about the possible existence of unknown fragilities and risks. Initiatives such as the Core Infrastructure Initiative, FOSSA, the Open Source Security Foundation, reflect the growing demand for more structured governance to prevent unexpected vulnerabilities and security problems.

The second critical area in which foundations are expanding their role is as innovative *de facto* standards provider organizations (Blind & Böhm, 2019; Lundell et al., 2021; Berlinguer, 2021). FOSS is increasingly supplanting traditional standards development organizations (SDOs), following a model that is more informal, agile, and suitable for digital systems, as it is based on continuous and direct implementation (rather than going from specifications to follow a cumbersome path, as is customary for SDOs), and at the same time more equitable, accessible, and transparent, as FOSS standards ensure a drastic reduction in barriers to adoption, development, testing, thanks to the absence of royalties and the freedoms guaranteed by FOSS licenses.

However, this growth in scale and complexity in the governance of FOSS ecosystems is only embryonic. It only hints at the necessity to elaborate more sophisticated, transparent and trustworthy mechanisms (Prattico, 2012; Izquierdo & Cabot, 2020) at a higher scale. Its future development is going to be part of and will make a contribution to the broader search for new governance models for the many unresolved challenges related to the governance of critical digital infrastructures, the platform economy and the digital society at large (Katz & Sallet, 2018; O'Reilly, 2019; Gorwa, 2019; Mazzucato et al., 2020; O'Neil et al., 2021; Berlinguer, 2021; De Streel & Ledger, 2021; Mazzucato et al., 2021).

AN EVOLUTIONARY APPROACH TO FOSS

Profound changes have drastically transformed the FOSS ecosystem, especially over the last decade. FOSS has been increasingly integrated into the market. It has become a core ingredient in the competitive strategies on the frontier of digital innovation. In other cases FOSS has become a terrain of convergence and *de facto* standardization for thousands of companies. FOSS ecosystem has also undergone a process of consolidation and incipient "institutionalization".

Overall, these developments clearly require a revision of FOSS early characterizations, which Benkler aptly defined as a common-based peer-to-peer model of production (Benkler, 2006).

But how should this development be interpreted?

FOSS has often been interpreted as a social movement, with cultural roots in the libertarian culture of the 1960s and 1970s movements and the ethics and practice of open science. Early on, it emerged as a disruptive innovation driven primarily by noneconomic motivations, within communities of developers and researchers, for whom (Castells, 2004; Sodeberg, 2015; Vercellone, 2015) it embodied aspirations for freedom, autonomy, self-management and meritocracy, as well as the collaborative requirements needed for better productivity in networked knowledge production (Lazzarato, 1996; Weber, 2004; Vercellone et al., 2015). Its trajectory could thus be interpreted as a classical case of capitalist recuperation, appropriation or co-optation of instances introduced by critical social movements (Boltanski & Chiapello, 2005).

A second interpretation can be called "normalization." From the beginning, economists and the pro-business branch of the FOSS movement have tended to domesticate the "anomalies" of FOSS. (Lerner & Tirole, 2002; Perens, 2005). This has been argued in different ways. For example, some have applied the traits of homo economicus to volunteers contributing to FOSS, emphasizing motivations such as human capital development, reputation, social capital or employability as economic motivations.

But FOSS could also be seen as an extension of the alliances in R&D that have characterized the most innovative technology sectors since at least the 1980s and 1990s (Powell, 1990); or rather, as a radicalization of outsourcing practices, extended to R&D and prototyping (Berlinguer, 2019). Otherwise, some historical precedents could be cited. Common pools of patents between companies have played a crucial role in some earlier technological transitions: for example, in the automotive or aeronautics industries.

Each of these interpretations captures some aspects of the evolution of FOSS. However, overall, their main limitation is that they tend to treat as solved the challenges brought by FOSS as a new model of innovation, production, and governance that emerged on the frontier of the digital revolution. In this way, they draw premature conclusions about FOSS and its ecosystem. Instead, the FOSS ecosystem is still evolving. Rather, there are quite clear signs that FOSS is moving into a new phase of development, that will produce, as in previous phases, significant reorganizations and further innovations in its governance systems and economic models.

Two approaches, recently developed to analyze radical technological transitions, can help to build an understanding of the trajectory of FOSS that can simultaneously account for its past evolution and shed light on its future developments.

They are the multi-level perspective (Geels, 2010) and the theory of techno-economic paradigms (Perez, 2002). Both are rooted in evolutionary economics (Winter & Nelson, 1982; Geels, 2002; Kattel et al., 2009) and the notion of "technological paradigm" (Dosi, 1982). MLP's approach is meso (Dopfer et al., 2004). TEP's approach is instead macro-historical.

FOSS AS A NEW 'REGIME' IN THE MAKING IN SOFTWARE PRODUCTION

The main objective of the multi-level perspective (MLP) is to understand the complexity and resistance to change in transitions to ecological sustainability (Köhler et al., 2019). MLP's unit of analysis is changes in functions "socio-technical regimes" (e.g., urban mobility) and focuses on the socio-economic dynamics of radical technological transition. The study of previous transformations in socio-technical systems led MLP to develop an analytical tool organized on three levels - niche, regime, landscape - that stylizes a sequence of stages in radical technological transitions (Geels & Schot 2007).

According to the MLP, radical innovations typically begin in niches, because in this way they are protected from "mainstream market selection." It is this characteristic that allows radical innovations to emerge. Because radical innovations in the beginning are highly experimental, characterized by great uncertainty and non-competitive in their performance. For the same reason, initially the motivations and selection mechanisms are primarily "social," i.e., not economic. Niche innovations usually grow within small networks of highly committed actors. If they later manage to break out of their niche, this happens - according to the MLP - through two main mechanisms: internal consolidation that stabilizes the patterns of new solutions and a linkage with some incumbent actors, who begin to support the innovation. In this way, a feedback loop begins to generate synergies and network effects within the ecosystem that grows around the innovation, which in turn accelerates its expansion. Further consolidation - which begins to "close," standardize, the innovation path - contributes to improve efficiency and further reduce risks, uncertainties, and cognitive barriers. In this way, the new system becomes accessible to a wider mass of users. Finally, when fully successful, these innovations come to overtake and replace the old dominant players and their regime, establishing their own routines, selective mechanisms and path dependence which consolidate the new regime.

It is not difficult to recognize in this stylized sequence many features of the evolution of FOSS. FOSS began as a niche, highly experimental innovation. It was nurtured in small, committed networks driven primarily by noneconomic motivations. It then began to grow through internal consolidation and external linkages. It has gradually moved from the margins to the center of the software industry, spreading its new set of cognitive and normative "routines" (which in the MLP framework form the backbone of a "regime"). And it is now in the process of becoming the new "standard" or regime in software production. As happens in the stylized MLP sequence, along with this evolution, the FOSS ecosystem and its major players have changed function. FOSS has shifted from being an environment suitable primarily for experimentation and exploration within small and poorly coordinated networks, to becoming an actor with a growing role as a builder and maintainer of large systems and critical infrastructure, coordinating its activities with a large and growing ecosystem of organizations. As a result, the prevailing internal ideologies have also changed from the anarchic-libertarian celebration of individual freedom in the early days to the current emphasis on security and efficiency, with selection mechanisms that have become increasingly economic (Berlinguer, 2020b).

The MLP scheme thus works quite well to describe the trajectory of FOSS so far. It also anticipates the next phase of FOSS development. FOSS is on the verge of becoming the new regime or standard in software production.

Instead, the main limitation of the MLP framework seems to be that FOSS cannot be fully encompassed within the notion of a "socio-technical system" that fulfills a social function, which is MLP's unit of analysis. For two reasons: because FOSS is a new model of production and innovation; and because it has emerged in a "general purpose" technology (David & Wright, 1999) such as software, which is penetrating and transforming the entire society.

FOSS AS EXEMPLAR IN THE EMERGING TECHNO-ECONOMIC PARADIGM

This expansion in scale and scope of the potential significance of FOSS can be better framed through Perez's theory of technological revolutions and techno-economic paradigms (TEP) (Perez, 2002).

TEP also has roots in evolutionary economics, particularly in neo-Schumperian studies of technological revolutions (Kattel et al., 2009) and the notion of a "technological paradigm" (Dosi, 1982), which it expands to a "macro-historical" scale. Perez's theory also schematizes a periodization. In this case, it is based on a recurring sequence of stages that characterized the social and economic assimilation of previous technological revolutions. The theory's central innovation is based on the notion of a historical succession of distinct techno-economic paradigms.

In TEP, a technological revolution is defined as "a set of interrelated radical breakthroughs, forming a major constellation of interdependent technologies" (Perez, 2010). The emphasis is on the strong interconnection and interdependence of the systems that make it up, both in their technological and in their economic aspects; it also emphasizes the power of these breakthroughs to profoundly and simultaneously transform the entire economy and society as a whole.

In TEP, a technological revolution is defined as "a set of interrelated radical breakthroughs, forming a major constellation of interdependent technologies" (Perez, 2010). The emphasis is on the strong interconnectedness and interdependence of its component systems, both in their technological and economic aspects; and the power of these breakthroughs to profoundly and simultaneously transform the entire economy and society as a whole is also emphasized.

The notion of "techno-economic paradigm" captures, instead, the set of highly interconnected technical, economic and organizational innovations that define a new "common sense" in each revolution regarding the best model of efficient production that will guide the dissemination process across all sectors and provide the patterns for framing both problems and solutions. A paradigm can be thought of as a new shared common sense regarding techno-economic organizational principles. A new paradigm spreads when the new forms of exploitation of the set of interconnected technical and organizational innovations that are the basis of the technological revolution prove to be the most efficient, and consolidate into new models and organizational principles, thus displacing old ideas and practices among managers, entrepreneurs, engineers, and inventors.

TEP frames techno-economic transitions in two distinct phases: the installation period and the deployment period. Technological revolutions historically begin when a previous paradigm has exhausted its potential for productivity growth. Perez links this first phase with the beginning of an era of financialization. For, the first phase of these technological revolutions is typically driven by finance capital, speculative bubbles and a *laissez-faire* ideology. The aim is twofold: to override the power of the dominant actors and production structures of the old paradigm and to finance new entrepreneurs to allow a period of extensive experimentation through trial and error. This phase typically ends with excesses of speculation, a growing divorce between the financial and real economies, and a financial collapse.

It is precisely in emerging from the subsequent depression that periods of great prosperity were unleashed, exploiting the enormous potential for transformation that emerged only embryonically in the first period (Perez, 2013). However, according to Perez, these transitions have historically required " bold" government intervention to "tilt the playing field" and push the potential innovation in specific directions, ending the domination of *laissez-faire* policies and shifting the balance of power from finance to real production (Perez, 2012). Moreover, previous historical experience shows that these readjustments occurred only under radical political pressure to reverse the dislocations and inequalities produced by the previous period of rampant market dominance. Only this pressure, in fact, allowed the necessary revision of the institutional order to be undertaken. Indeed, according to Perez, each paradigm required institutional and cultural discontinuities so profound that one can speak of a succession of "different modes of growth in the history of capitalism" (Perez, 2002; Valenduc, 2018).

This pattern organized through two phases, separated by a collapse of the old system and a radical reorganization of the growth regime, is best exemplified by the crisis of the 1930s, which - following this pattern - exploded at the end of the period of installation of the Fordist paradigm and required fundamental changes in economic thought, policy and institutional structures, such as those that subsequently shaped and channeled the Keynesian-Fordist regime after World War II (Jessop, 2013).

According to this theory, the world is currently at an "impasse," at the critical stage that typically marks the transition from the "installation period" to the "deployment period" of the new paradigm.

Now, how might the FOSS trajectory fit within the TEP? And what might it add to TEP, to better understand the current unresolved impasse?

FOSS hints at a new model of organizing digital production, and the importance of FOSS in the new techno-economic paradigm can be argued in numerous ways. Indeed, it has many characteristics of an "exemplar" (Kuhn, 1974) of the new techno-economic paradigm: that is, it offers an innovative model for framing and solving the problems of digital production systems.

FOSS emerged in the core technology and industry of the new paradigm. It took form as an anomaly, or as a puzzle for the "conventional wisdom". It did not depend on financial capital in its beginning, but it certainly was born on the margins of the dominant model of production. It has challenged the inherited "common sense". Despite being neglected by the existing legal and economic regime, it grew steadily and strongly throughout the installation phase of the new TEP. It has gained a central role in all the new areas that have emerged along with the new paradigm (Web services, mobile telephony, data centers, cloud computing, artificial intelligence, Internet of Things); and it is on its way to becoming a central ingredient or standard of the information systems and infrastructure that will permeate the new TEP. On the other hand, as it has been the case with previous historical "techno-economic paradigms", along with this spectacular growth, FOSS has also been a laboratory for the diffusion of new organizational forms, systems of governance, business organizations, forms of capitalist competition, and logics of value generation. In other words, it has established or inspired innovative ways of framing and solving production systems problems.

The importance of FOSS in the new techno-economic paradigm seems clear. Its spectacular success, despite its challenging characteristics, testifies to the fit of FOSS with the socio-economic and technical characteristics of the digital paradigm.

But what role might FOSS play in the next troubled phase toward which the world economic system is heading? And how might the evolution of FOSS be affected by this period of radical transformation?

The Upcoming Third Phase of FOSS Development

The trajectory of FOSS has been surprising so far. It has not been linear and has no single explanation. The most influential forces behind its development have changed. In the beginning, the first steps were taken in self-organizing communities of developers. In its second phase, the most powerful engine has been market adoption and new forms of economic competition.

To a large extent, FOSS is winning its challenge with proprietary software and is reaching its own "momentum" in this battle (Hughes, 1987). FOSS is on the verge of becoming the dominant regime in software production. Not only because it is spreading along all frontiers of digital innovation, but because more generally it is beginning to overturn the lock-in mechanisms and broader "path dependence" (David 2001) that have long operated in favor of proprietary software in many dimensions (Berliguer, 2021).

The trajectory of FOSS as an ecosystem and as a new model of digital production, however, has not ended. This is partly due to the internal dynamics of FOSS. The FOSS governance system, especially on a macro scale, is still embryonic and has unresolved challenges, weaknesses, and is exposed to risks of inequities, imbalances, and structural fragilities. However, the future evolution of FOSS will be even more influenced by the broader context, in which, as Perez puts it, the new techno-economic paradigm is reaching its tipping point (Perez, 2010; Knell, 2021). FOSS will be an integral part of the forthcoming radical transformations and the broader search for new systems of governance.

So far, FOSS has already made its contributions to this search for new models of governance in a different paradigm of growth. It has succeeded in "installing" a new institution - a "contractually reconstructed commons" (Reichman & Uhlir, 2003) - that potentially has implications for the entire information paradigm. This rediscovery of the commons at the frontier of the digital revolution is an innovation that is yet to be adequately metabolized by political, economic, and legal theory, but which cannot be trivialized. It displaces the market-state dichotomy, which has long been the dominant template for "framing problems and solutions." It enriches the repertoire of organisational or institutional policies and solutions (Benkler, 2013). Moreover, the increasing presence of FOSS in contemporary economic and technological systems paves the way for a rethinking about the actual functioning of markets in the digital economy and their possible governance. The same potentially applies to the public sector as well. In very broad terms, FOSS alludes to a new type of mixed economy whose understanding and capacity for governance has not yet developed. And at the same time to a new kind of 'tripartite system of governance', composed of governments, markets and communities, which should learn to compensate for the relative shortcomings and failures of each of these systems (Berlinguer, 2021).

A second important contribution of FOSS is emerging in the architecture of future digital techno-infrastructures. A closer look at the latest generation of digital technologies (e.g., cloud computing, Internet of Things) shows that FOSS, in combination with standardization and modularity, is driving an innovative matrix that increasingly informs the design, architecture, and governance of this latest generation of techno-infrastructures (Blind et al., 2019; Kostakis, 2019; Council of the European Union, 2020; Berlinguer, 2021). This matrix reflects the structural conditions that characterise the development of these technological systems, such as the need to simplify the management of their complexity, scale, scope and dynamism, and to meet contradictory requirements such as providing flexibility and stability, resilience and ease of mass adoption. It accommodates hybrid regimes of ownership, governance and value generation and appropriation. And it may have wider significance for the governance of future techno-economic systems in a context of green digital growth.

Nevertheless, FOSS as a new model of digital development is probably still in its early stages. And it would be difficult to imagine how it will develop, perhaps as much as it would have been to imagine at the outset its subsequent trajectory.

What however can be glimpsed is that, in the near future, the most complicated change with the greatest consequences within the FOSS ecosystem is likely to come from greater government involvement (Berlinguer, 2020a; 2021). FOSS will have to contend with the current resurgence of government intervention, industrial policy (Cherif & Hasanov, 2019; Mazzucato et al. 2021) and the related explosion of geopolitical conflicts centered on control of the next generation of technologies. As a consequence, a more organic involvement of governments, public policy and public sector looms as the third driver that is likely to deeply mark the future trajectory of FOSS.

It will not be an easy road. So far, public policies on FOSS have been largely ineffective. Experimentation and innovation in the relationship between FOSS, public policy and the public sector will therefore be necessary (Berlinguer, 2020a). Furthermore, increased government and public policy involvement will bring tensions and challenges, not only opportunities for FOSS.

At first glance, one might even observe that FOSS - which is because of its legal nature, a global commons - has traits idiosyncratic with national sovereignty and geopolitical divisions. However, if the past trajectory of FOSS teaches us anything, it is that, as happened with private property, the arrangements that will emerge will be more nuanced, blended and "layered." That is, a new generation of hybrids is likely to begin to emerge, as a further evolution of the FOSS foundations or rather as a new type of organizations experimenting with innovative "tripartite system of governance" (Berlinguer, 2021), as has begun to happen, for example, with Gaia-X[3] in Europe, the Open Network for Digital Commerce[4] in India and the "*Open innovation platforms*" *for developing AI technology in China*[5].

So, looking forward, although tensions, geopolitical divisions, and security pressures are bound to increase and affect and alter the FOSS ecosystem in unpredictable ways, it is unlikely that the FOSS ownership regime will retreat in favor of a return to proprietary software. Rather, FOSS is likely to become a competitive lever in this new phase of development as well. A competitive lever in public and industrial policies, in growth and development strategies, and in the political and geopolitical struggle to assert a new kind of "sovereignty" and leadership over future techno-economic systems.

Indeed, the first signs have already appeared. And as has happened time and again in key stages of the rise of FOSS adoption in the market, the first to take up the challenge of betting on FOSS are those who have been left behind and are trying to catch up. In this case, China, the European Union and India.

A new phase is opening up in the evolution of the FOSS ecosystem. A third phase for FOSS, in which new governance systems and economic models will emerge to support its further development.

As has been the case so far in hybridisation with the market, different models and configurations are likely to emerge. But, what the trajectory of FOSS suggests is that it would be a mistake to overlook the importance of the innovations that will occur in this area. Part of the future competition between global political, economic and technological systems will depend on them.

REFERENCES

Baldwin, C. Y. (2015). *Bottlenecks, modules and dynamic architectural capabilities.* Harvard Business School Finance Working Paper, (15-028).

Baldwin, C. Y. (2018). *Design Rules, Volume 2: How Technology Shapes Organizations: Chapter 14 Introducing Open Platforms and Business Ecosystems.* Harvard Business School, Harvard Business School Research Paper Series, 19-035.

Baldwin, C. Y., & Woodard, C. J. (2009). The architecture of platforms: A unified view. *Platforms, Markets and Innovation, 32*, 19-44.

Barbrook, R. (1998). The hi-tech gift economy. *First Monday.*

Benkler, Y. (2002). Coase's penguin, or, linux and" the nature of the firm. *The Yale Law Journal*, 369–446.

Benkler, Y. (2006). *The Wealth of Networks: How Social Production Transforms Markets and Freedom.* Yale University Press.

Benkler, Y. (2013). Commons and Growth: The Essential Role of Open Commons in Market Economies. *The University of Chicago Law Review. University of Chicago. Law School.*

Benkler, Y. (2019). De la comunitat imaginada a la comunitat de pràctica, Sharing Cities. *Capítol, 13*, 311–323.

Berlinguer, M. (2016). *Quantifying Value in Commons-based Peer production. Digital Method Winter School.* University of Amsterdam.

Berlinguer, M. (2018). The value of sharing. How commons have become part of informational capitalism and what we can learn from it. The case of FOSS. *Rassegna Italiana di Sociologia, 59*(2), 263–288.

Berlinguer, M. (2019). *Repensar la Smart City: Barcelona: ciudad abierta, colaborativa y democrática.* Icaria.

Berlinguer, M. (2020a). Commons, Markets and Public Policy. *Transform!*

Berlinguer, M. (2020b). New commons: Towards a necessary reappraisal. *Popular Communication, 18*(3), 201–215.

Berlinguer, M. (2021). Digital Commons as new Infrastructure: A new generation of public policy for digital transformation. *Umanistica Digitale*, (11), 5–25.

Blanke, T., & Pybus, J. (2020). The material conditions of platforms: Monopolization through decentralization. *Social Media + Society, 6*(4).

Blind, K. (2004). *The Economics of Standards.* North Hampton.

Blind, K., & Böhm, M. (2019). The Relationship Between Open Source Software and Standard Setting. EUR 29867 EN, Publications Office of the European Union. doi:10.2760/163594

Blind, K., Böhm, M., Grzegorzewska, P., Katz, A., Muto, S., Pätsch, S., & Schubert, T. (2021). The impact of Open Source Software and Hardware on technological independence, competitiveness and innovation in the EU economy. Final Study Report. European Commission.

Blind, K., & Jungmittag, A. (2008). The impact of patents and standards on macroeconomic growth: A panel approach covering four countries and 12 sectors. *Journal of Productivity Analysis, 29*(1), 51–60.

Boltanski, L., & Chiapello, E. (2005). The new spirit of capitalism. *International Journal of Politics Culture and Society, 18*(3), 161–188.

Castells, M. (2004). Informationalism, networks, and the network society: a theoretical blueprint. *The network society: A cross-cultural perspective*, 3-45.

Cennamo, C., Gawer, A., & Jacobides, M. G. (2018). Towards a theory of ecosystems. *Strategic Management Journal, 39*, 2255–2276.

Chandler, A. D. Jr. (1993). *The visible hand*. Harvard University Press.

Cherif, R., & Hasanov, F. (2019). *The return of the policy that shall not be named: Principles of industrial policy*. International Monetary Fund.

Chesbrough, H. (2006). *Open business models: How to thrive in the new innovation landscape*. Harvard Business Press.

Coase, R. H. (1937). The nature of the firm. *Economica, 4*(16), 386-405.

Constantinides, P., Henfridsson, O., & Parker, G. G. (2018). Introduction—Platforms and infrastructures in the digital age. *Information Systems Research, 29*(2), 381–400.

Coriat, B. (2015). *Le retour des communs: & la crise de l'idéologie propriétaire*. Editions Les liens qui libèrent.

Council of the European Union. (2020). *Berlin Declaration on Digital Society and Value-based Digital Government*. Accessed December 15, 2021. https://digital-strategy.ec.europa.eu/en/news/berlin-declaration-digital-society-and-value-based-digital-government

David, P. A. (2001). *Path dependence, its critics and the quest for historical economics*. Evolution and Path Dependence in Economic Ideas.

David, P. A., & Shapiro, J. S. (2008). Community-based production of open-source software: What do we know about the developers who participate? *Information Economics and Policy, 20*(4), 364–398.

De Streel, A., & Ledger, M. (2021). *New ways of oversight for the digital economy.* CERRE Issue Paper.

Dopfer, K., Foster, J., & Potts, J. (2004). Micro-meso-macro. *Journal of Evolutionary Economics, 14*(3), 263–279.

Dosi, G. (1982). Technological paradigms and technological trajectories: A suggested interpretation of the determinants and directions of technical change. *Research Policy, 11*(3), 147–162.

Eghbal, N. (2016). Roads and bridges. In *The Unseen labor behind our digital infrastructure.* Ford Foundation. Retrieved at: https://fordfoundcontent.blob.core. windows.net/media/2976/roads-and-bridges-the-unseen-labor-behind-our-digital-infrastructure.pdf

Farrell, J., & Klemperer, P. (2007). Coordination and lock-in: Competition with switching costs and network effects. Handbook of Industrial Organization, 3, 1967-2072.

Fennell, L. A. (2011). Commons, anticommons, semicommons. In *Research handbook on the economics of property law.* Edward Elgar Publishing.

Fogel, K. (2005). *Producing open source software: How to run a successful free software project.* O'Reilly Media, Inc.

Fraser, N. (2017). A triple movement? Parsing the politics of crisis after Polanyi. In *Beyond neoliberalism* (pp. 29–42). Palgrave Macmillan.

Frischmann, B. M. (2012). *Infrastructure: The social value of shared resources.* Oxford University Press.

Gawer, A. (2014). Bridging differing perspectives on technological platforms: Toward an integrative framework. *Research Policy, 43*(7), 1239–1249.

Gawer, A., & Cusumano, M. A. (2014). Industry platforms and ecosystem innovation. *Journal of Product Innovation Management, 31*(3), 417–433.

Geels, F. W. (2002). Technological transitions as evolutionary reconfiguration processes: A multi-level perspective and a case-study. *Research Policy, 31*(8-9), 1257–1274.

Geels, F. W. (2010). Ontologies, socio-technical transitions (to sustainability), and the multi-level perspective. *Research Policy, 39*(4), 495–510.

Geels, F. W., & Schot, J. (2007). Typology of sociotechnical transition pathways. *Research Policy, 36*(3), 399–417.

Gorwa, R. (2019). What is platform governance? *Information Communication and Society, 22*(6), 854–871.

Hardin, G. (1968). The tragedy of the commons: The population problem has no technical solution; it requires a fundamental extension in morality. *Science, 162*(3859), 1243–1248. PMID:5699198

Herraiz, I., Izquierdo-Cortazar, D., Rivas-Hernández, F., Gonzalez-Barahona, J., Robles, G., Duenas-Dominguez, S., Garcia-Campos, C., Gato, J. F., & Tovar, L. (2009, March). Flossmetrics: Free/libre/open source software metrics. In *2009 13th European Conference on Software Maintenance and Reengineering* (pp. 281-284). IEEE.

Hippel, E. V., & Krogh, G. V. (2003). Open source software and the "private-collective" innovation model: Issues for organization science. *Organization Science, 14*(2), 209–223.

Hughes, T. P. (1987). The evolution of large technological systems: The social construction of technological systems. In W. E. Bijker, T. P. Hughes, & T. J. Pinch (Eds.), *New Directions in the Sociology and History of Technology* (pp. 51–82). MIT Press.

Hunter, P., & Walli, S. (2013). The rise and evolution of the open source software foundation. *IFOSS L. Rev., 5*, 31.

Izquierdo, J. L. C., & Cabot, J. (2018, May). The role of foundations in open source projects. In *Proceedings of the 40th international conference on software engineering: software engineering in society* (pp. 3-12). Academic Press.

Izquierdo, J. L. C., & Cabot, J. (2020). *A Survey of Software Foundations in Open Source.* arXiv preprint arXiv:2005.10063.

Jacobides, M. G., Cennamo, C., & Gawer, A. (2018). Towards a theory of ecosystems. *Strategic Management Journal, 39*(8), 2255–2276.

Jessop, B. (2001). Regulationist and autopoieticist reflections on Polanyi's account of market economies and the market society. *New Political Economy, 6*(2), 213–232.

Jessop, B. (2013). Revisiting the regulation approach: Critical reflections on the contradictions, dilemmas, fixes and crisis dynamics of growth regimes. *Capital and Class, 37*(1), 5–24.

Kattel, R., Drechsler, W., & Reinert, E. S. (2009). Introduction: Carlota Perez and evolutionary economics. Techno-Economic Paradigms: Essays in honour of Carlota Perez, 1-18.

Katz, M., & Sallet, J. (2018). Multisided platforms and antitrust enforcement. *The Yale Law Journal*, 2142–2175.

Katz, M. L., & Shapiro, C. (1994). Systems competition and network effects. *The Journal of Economic Perspectives*, 8(2), 93–115.

Kelly, K. (1999). *New rules for the new economy: 10 radical strategies for a connected world*. Penguin.

Knell, M. (2021). The digital revolution and digitalized network society. *Review of Evolutionary Political Economy*, 2(1), 9–25.

Köhler, J., Geels, F. W., Kern, F., Markard, J., Onsongo, E., Wieczorek, A., ... Wells, P. (2019). An agenda for sustainability transitions research: State of the art and future directions. *Environmental Innovation and Societal Transitions*, 31, 1–32.

Kollock, P. (1999). The economies of online cooperation: Gifts and public goods in cyberspace. *Communities in Cyberspace, 239*.

Kostakis, V. (2019). How to reap the benefits of the "digital revolution"? Modularity and the commons. *Halduskultuur*, 20(1), 4–19.

Kostakis, V., & Bauwens, M. (2014). *Network society and future scenarios for a collaborative economy*. Springer.

Kuhn, T. S. (1974). Second thoughts on paradigms. *The Structure of Scientific Theories, 2*, 459-482.

Lakhani, K. R., & Wolf, R. G. (2003). Why hackers do what they do: Understanding motivation and effort in free/open source software projects. *Open Source Software Projects*.

Lazzarato, M. (1996). Immaterial labor. *Radical thought in Italy: A potential politics*, 133-47.

Lepak, D. P., Smith, K. G., & Taylor, M. S. (2007). Value creation and value capture: A multilevel perspective. *Academy of Management Review*, 32(1), 180–194.

Lerner, J., & Tirole, J. (2002). Some simple economics of open source. *The Journal of Industrial Economics*, 50(2), 197–234.

Lundell, B., Butler, S., Fischer, T., Gamalielsson, J., Brax, C., Feist, J., ... Mattsson, A. (2021). Effective Strategies for Using Open Source Software and Open Standards in Organizational Contexts: Experiences From the Primary and Secondary Software Sectors. *IEEE Software*, 39(1), 84–92.

Martinez-Alier, J., Munda, G., & O'Neill, J. (1998). Weak comparability of values as a foundation for ecological economics. *Ecological Economics, 26*(3), 277–286.

Mauss, M. (2002). *The gift: The form and reason for exchange in archaic societies.* Routledge.

Mazzucato, M., Entsminger, J., & Kattel, R. (2020). Public value and platform governance. *UCL Institute for Innovation and Public Purpose WP, 11.*

Mazzucato, M., Entsminger, J., & Kattel, R. (2021). Reshaping Platform-Driven Digital Markets. *Regulating Big Tech: Policy Responses to Digital Dominance, 17.*

Mazzucato, M., Kattel, R., & Ryan-Collins, J. (2021). Industrial Policy's Comeback. *Boston Review.* https://bostonreview.net/forum/industrial-policys-comeback/

Moore, M. H. (2014). Public value accounting: Establishing the philosophical basis. *Public Administration Review, 74*(4), 465–477.

Morell, M. F., Salcedo, J. L., & Berlinguer, M. (2016, September). Debate about the concept of value in Commons-Based Peer Production. In *International Conference on Internet Science* (pp. 27-41). Springer.

Muegge, S. (2013). Platforms, communities, and business ecosystems: Lessons learned about technology entrepreneurship in an interconnected world. *Technology Innovation Management Review,* 5–15.

O'Mahony, S. (2007). The governance of open source initiatives: What does it mean to be community managed? *The Journal of Management and Governance, 11*(2), 139–150.

O'Neil, M. (2009). *Cyberchiefs: Autonomy and authority in online tribes.* Pluto Press.

O'Neil, M., Cai, X., Muselli, L., Pailler, F., & Zacchiroli, S. (2021). *The coproduction of open source software by volunteers and big tech firms.* News Media Research Centre, University of Canberra.

O'Reilly, T. (2019). *Antitrust regulators are using the wrong tools to break up Big Tech.* https://qz.com/1666863/why-big-tech-keeps-outsmarting-antitrust-regulators

Ostrom, E. (1990). *Governing the commons: The evolution of institutions for collective action.* Cambridge university press.

Parker, G., Van Alstyne, M. W., & Jiang, X. (2016). *Platform ecosystems: How developers invert the firm.* Boston University Questrom School of Business Research Paper, (2861574).

Parker, G. G., & Van Alstyne, M. W. (2005). Two-sided network effects: A theory of information product design. *Management Science, 51*(10), 1494–1504.

Perens, B. (2005). The emerging economic paradigm of open source. *First Monday.*

Perez, C. (2003). *Technological revolutions and financial capital.* Edward Elgar Publishing.

Perez, C. (2010). Technological revolutions and techno-economic paradigms. *Cambridge Journal of Economics, 34*(1), 185–202.

Perez, C. (2012). Technological revolutions and the role of government in unleashing golden ages. *Journal of Globalization Studies, 3*(2), 19–25.

Perez, C. (2013). Unleashing a golden age after the financial collapse: Drawing lessons from history. *Environmental Innovation and Societal Transitions, 6,* 9–23.

Polanyi, K. (1957). Societies and Economic Systems. In *The Great Transformation.* Beacon Press.

Powell, W. W. (1990). Neither market nor hierarchy. *Sociology of organizations: Structures and relationships,* 30-40.

Prattico, L. (2012). Governance of open source software foundations: Who holds the power? *Technology Innovation Management Review, 2*(12).

Raymond, E. (2001). *The Cathedral & the Bazaar* (Revised Edition). O'Reilly.

Raymond, E. S. (1998). Homesteading the noosphere. *First Monday.*

Reichman, J. H., & Uhlir, P. F. (2003). A contractually reconstructed research commons for scientific data in a highly protectionist intellectual property environment. *Law and Contemporary Problems, 66*(1/2), 315–462.

Riehle, D. (2010). The economic case for open source foundations. *Computer, 43*(01), 86–90.

Riehle, D. (2021). The Open Source Distributor Business Model. *Computer, 54*(12), 99–103.

Rose, C. (1986). The comedy of the commons: Custom, commerce, and inherently public property. *The University of Chicago Law Review. University of Chicago. Law School, 53*(3), 711–781.

Rose, C. M. (2003). Romans, roads, and romantic creators: Traditions of public property in the information age. *Law and Contemporary Problems, 66*(1/2), 89–110.

Rullani, E. (2000). Le capitalisme cognitif: Du déjà vu? *Multitudes*, 2(2), 87–94.

Rullani, E. (2009). *I premi Nobel per l'economia anno domini 2009. Ovvero, l'economia dei commons e delle reti, che popolano la Terra di Mezzo tra mercato e piano.* Venice International University. Retrieved at: https://criticalmanagement. uniud.it/fileadmin/user_upload/Rullani_sui_Nobel_Economia_2009.pdf

Sidak, J. G. (2016). The value of a standard versus the value of standardization. *Baylor Law Review*, 68, 59.

Smith, H. E. (2000). Semicommon property rights and scattering in the open fields. *The Journal of Legal Studies*, 29(1), 131–169.

Söderberg, J. (2015). *Hacking capitalism: The free and open source software movement.* Routledge.

Srnicek, N. (2017). *Platform capitalism.* John Wiley & Sons.

Swann, G. P. (2010). *The economics of standardization: An update.* Report for the UK Department of Business, Innovation and Skills (BIS).

Tucker, C. (2018). Network Effects and Market Power: What Have We Learned in the Last Decade? *Antitrust*, 72-79.

Valenduc, G. (2018). *Technological revolutions and societal transitions.* ETUI Research Paper-Foresight Brief.

Vercellone, C., Bria, F., Fumagalli, A., Gentilucci, E., Giuliani, A., Griziotti, G., & Vattimo, P. (2015). D3. 2 Managing the commons in the knowledge economy. *Decentralised Citizens Engagement Technologie.* http://www. nesta. org.uk/sites/ default/files/d-cent_managing_the_commons_in_the_knowledge_economy. pdf

Weber, S. (2000). The Political Economy of Open Source Software. UCAIS Berkeley Roundtable on the International Economy, UC Berkeley.

Weber, S. (2004). *The success of open source.* Harvard University Press.

Winter, S. G., & Nelson, R. R. (1982). *An evolutionary theory of economic change.* University of Illinois at Urbana-Champaign's Academy for Entrepreneurial Leadership Historical Research Reference in Entrepreneurship.

Zeitlyn, D. (2003). Gift economies in the development of open source software: Anthropological reflections. *Research Policy*, 32(7), 1287–1291.

ENDNOTES

[1]   There has been a notable rediscovery of the commons in the past few decades. In part this is due to the work of Nobel prizewinner Elinor Ostrom (1990). Nevertheless, Free and Open Source Software is a kind of commons significantly different from the "traditional commons" studied by Ostrom, which are typically legacies of pre-capitalistic societies. These commons – sometimes called digital commons, information commons or knowledge commons – instead have been pragmatically reinvented on the opposite side of capitalistic modernity: that is, on the new frontier of the digital revolution. One of the most important differences is that these "new commons" - as Ostrom began to name them toward the end of her life (Hess & Ostrom, 2007) - typically flourish around resources that are non-rival. This characteristic makes the governance of this kind of commons different from the characterizations, dilemmas and principles of governance that Ostrom developed in her studies. The most important difference is that they are not threatened by the risk of over-exploitation and depletion, which is the central dilemma in Hardin's 'Tragedy of the Commons' (1968) and in Ostrom's studies. There is here a contradiction between two schools of thought on commons, rarely addressed (Rose, 2003; Benkler, 2013).

[2]   Heartbleed was a security vulnerability found in 2014 in the OpenSSL cryptography library, a FOSS security implementation used by hundreds of thousands of organizations.

[3]   See https://gaia-x.eu/

[4]   See https://en.wikipedia.org/wiki/Open_Network_for_Digital_Commerce

[5]   See https://cset.georgetown.edu/publication/ministry-of-science-and-technology-notice-on-the-publication-of-the-guidance-on-national-new-generation-artificial-intelligence-open-innovation-platform-construction-work/

Chapter 3
Building Open Source Hardware Business Models

Laetitia Marie Thomas
Université Grenoble Alpes, France

Karine Evrard-Samuel
Université Grenoble Alpes, France

Peter Troxler
Hogeschool Rotterdam, The Netherlands

ABSTRACT

Open source hardware (OSH) initiatives are collectively managed projects enabled by the internet and digital fabrication tools. They allow people to create products in a cheaper, faster, and more efficient manner. To date, there is no strategic and actionable framework using the commons theory for analyzing how these hardware initiatives develop economically effective and sustainable business models. Based on an analysis of the business models of 27 community-based and community-oriented OSH initiatives studied over a 3-year period, this chapter presents such a framework. The five-stages spiral framework offers to guide companies and startups involved in OSH to interact with their surrounding innovation ecosystems progressively, enrich their value propositions and grow in impact.

Over the past decade, despite research interest in Digital Commons (Fuster Morell, 2014; Acquier *et al.*, 2016; Benkler, 2017; Raworth, 2017; Litman, 2014), little information exists on how commons-based peer-production open source hardware (OSH) initiatives may monetize their innovations. The aim of this chapter is to investigate the business models used by open-source hardware entrepreneurs and

DOI: 10.4018/978-1-6684-4785-7.ch003

explore the nature of the value created in such initiatives. Question which continue to baffle researchers are:

- How can value creation and capture be based on a collective resource?
- Can a resource arrangement that works in practice work in theory?
- How can design documentation be commercially exploitable, freely editable and available concurrently?

Open Design, identified as critical for spreading the impact of the circular economy, has become the modus operandi for social design. Therefore, understanding it's growth patterns and deviations is important as this addresses the long-term viability in the context of the economic transformation needed to implement circular economy and the UN's SDG goals.

Open source hardware and peer production, both instances of Digital Commons applied to manufacturing, are believed to be the most radical, theoretical and organizational innovations to have emerged from the Internet (Raasch *et al.*, 2009; Van Abel *et al.*, 2010; Bonvoisin, *et al.* 2016; Moritz *et al.*, 2016; Benkler, 2016; Sanguinetti, 2019).

To date, Commons research has focused on how Open Source and Knowledge Commons need to be purposefully protected from enclosure and kept open as raw material for ideas (Hess & Ostrom, 2011; Litman, 2014). Fuster Morell and Espelt, (2018) devised a much-needed holistic framework to assess the knowledge, governance and technological openness of commons-based cooperative platforms. Raworth (2017) explained that distributed and regenerative designs are novel configurations of value creation and capture in Digital Commons. Troxler, (2019) has adapted Ostrom's governance principles (1990) to Open Design.

Yet, to our knowledge, how Digital Knowledge Commons can be monetized, and what growth patterns could be aligned with distributed and generative value, have yet to be developed in literature. Thus, it is interesting to look closely at business models for open source hardware as this concept represents the orchestration of activities surrounding value creation, delivery and capture (Teece, 2010; Zott & Amit, 2010). The purpose of this chapter therefore, is to provide an actionable, strategic framework to help open source entrepreneurs in developing their business models. The 5-stage spiral framework is a creativity tool for brainstorming "what is right for us" solutions. OSH projects may use the modular nature of business model patterns, combining them like building blocks according to an organization's strategic needs. As organizations iterate through the stages, they are enriched from slightly different perspectives.

This chapter is structured as follows: the first section details the implications of OSH, with Digital Knowledge and Innovation Commons, on entrepreneurship and business models. The following section explains how different model types may be strategically used as building blocks depending upon an organization's needs. The authors present a framework showcasing the most frequent to the most daring business model patterns used in OSH initiatives. Lastly, they explain how OSHBMs have the potential of shifting away from linear and extractive production and consumption models to ones where value is generated, appropriated and preserved.

BACKGROUND

Digital Knowledge Commons

The Commons Theory is an intriguing boundary-spanning theory, expressing the transition from hierarchical and proprietary logic based on closed property, to a decentralized, contributive logic of structured openness managed by formal and informal institutional mechanisms. Choosing the Commons theory as a theoretical base offers a feasible construct from which to study how open source hardware initiatives grow while opening up their core innovation to a wider community.

The Theory contends that Digital Commons are a self-organized social system for the long-term stewardship of non-depletable and non-rivalrous resources preserving shared values and community identity, and are subject to social dilemmas. Unlike Natural Commons which are scarce, the particularity of Digital Commons is that the more they are used and shared, the more efficient, cheaper and transparent they become. They furnish raw material for ideas and need to be kept open in order that knowledge circulate (Bollier, 2014; Litman, 2014; Raworth, 2017; Hess & Ostrom, 2011).

In the case of free and libre open source hardware (FLOSH) because the building plans, assembly instructions, and bills of materials are published on a digital platform, such as GitHub, they are *Digital Knowledge Commons*. Eric Von Hippel (2005), in the concluding insights of his book *Democratizing Innovation* writes, "As innovation becomes more user-centered, the information needs to flow more freely and in a more democratic way, thereby creating "rich intellectual commons . . . [and] attacking a major structure of the social division of labor."

Kate Raworth (2017) explains that the Commons theory is powerfully disruptive, as it addresses novel configurations in value creation and capitalism through *distributive* and *regenerative* design. The notion of "distributive" means easy to replicate. Anyone with an Internet connection can entertain, inform, learn and teach worldwide.

Digital fabrication technologies are the essence of distributive design and manufacturing as they blur the line between producers and consumers. Applied to industry, the term distributive manufacturing means democratizing access to manufacturing. The idea is to make technology more robust, more modular and more freely available, globally empowering global citizens to break away from currently unsustainable supply chains (Rifkin, 2014, p.8; Kumar *et al.,* 2020; Rauch *et al.,* 2016).

The other disruption offered by Digital Commons is that of being regenerative by design. The concept of a circular economy is the intention of transforming industrial manufacturing from extractive to regenerative design by using renewable energy and eradicating waste by design. Diverging from the take-make-and-waste mentality, waste becomes "food" as biological and technical materials are never used up and thrown away but circulated again and again through cycles of reuse and renewal. (Raworth, 2017, p. 220). Sustainability as meeting the needs of the present without compromising the needs of future generations to meet their own needs, merely means achieving a neutral point of not doing any more damage to our ecosystem. Regenerative design goes further, restoring, renewing and revitalizing energy sources and materials. Regenerative design integrates the needs of society with those of nature (Orcajada, 2021).

To these novel configurations, generativity is added as the human capacity to problem-solve in a myriad of different ways adapted to a plethora of different contexts. Eglash (2016) refers to generativity as "the bottom-up circulation of unalienated value". Zittrain defines generativity as unintended applications which spontaneously occur when "driven by large, varied, and uncoordinated audiences" (2006, p. 1980). Troxler, (2010) defines it as "fab-lab magic": the satisfaction of going from an idea to a tangible reality and of showing others how to do it. In layman's terms, this means making sure the "apple seed" of an innovation – design plans, bill of materials and assembly instructions – remains open, so as to generate countless new apple trees. Generativity is the basis of the Academany programs, developed by Neil Gershenfeld and Sherry Lassiter, sets the grounds for worldwide educational collaborations offering distributed education on demand, combining local manufacturing and global networking.

Table 1 provides a literature review on the Commons theory covering the history of the Commons (Ostrom 1990), the integration of Commons to growth (Hess & Ostrom, 2011; Benkler, 2017; Litman, 2014); the importance of open governance (Fuster Morell and Espelt, 2018; Troxler, 2019); and the novel configurations of value creation and capture offered through Digital Commons (Raworth, 2017).

Yet, to date and to our knowledge, how Digital Knowledge Commons can be monetized, what growth patterns could be aligned with distributed, regenerative and generative value, has not been treated in literature. Thus, it is interesting to look at business models for open source hardware as this concept has become the means of representing how value is created and captured.

Table 1. Literature review of the commons theory

Themes covered	Topics	Subtopics
History of the commons	Natural Commons	Tragedy, Comedy and Triumph of Commons (Raworth, 2017; Benkler, 2016; Fuster Morell, 2014).
	Digital and Knowledge Commons	Definitions of Digital Commons (Hess & Ostrom, 2011; Raworth, 2017).
		Understanding Knowledge Commons (Hess & Ostrom, 2011).
		Scope of Digital Commons (Benkler, 2006; Benkler, 2016; Litman, 2014).
		Integration of commons to growth (Benkler, 2016)
Novel configurations of value creation and capture in Commons	Distributive Design	Networked information economy (Raworth, 2017)
		Peer Production/Open source hardware/ Open Design (Benkler 2016; Li, Seering and Wallace, 2018; Li and Seering, 2019; Troxler, 2019)
		Drivers and motivations for Digital Commons (Benkler 2016, Li, Seering and Wallace, 2018)
		Challenging the centrality of property to growth (Benkler 2016)
		Integration of open commons to growth (Benkler 2016)
	Regenerative Design	Beyond sustainability to appropriate participation and design as nature (Raworth, 2018, Orcajada, 2021)
	Generative Design	Generative Justice (Eglash, 2016; Troxler, 2010)
	Wealth creation	Money creation and complementary currencies (Raworth, 2018)
Principles for Commons	Principles for common-pool resources	Principles for natural common-pool resources (Hess & Ostrom, 2011)
		Principles for Open design governance (Troxler, 2019)
		Assessment of Commons collaborative platforms (Fuster Morell & Espelt, 2018)
		Digital and Digitally supported Commons and Open Data (Fuster, Carballa Schmikowski, Smorto et al., 2017)
Business Models for OSH	Dimensions of OSHBM	Components (Fjelsted et al., 2012; Bonvoisin et al., 2017
		Typologies (Thomas, 2019; Pierce, 2017; 2012; Decode, 2017; Moritz et al., 2016; Stacey & Pearson, 2015; Tinck & Bénichou, 2014; Wolf & Troxler, 2016)

Open Source Hardware Innovation and Entrepreneurs

Open, collaborative hardware development is a new innovation paradigm. FLOSH – which would stand for Free and Libre Open Source Hardware – in Stallman's terms, as in "free speech not free beer", as an alternative to intellectual property restriction is capable of grounding sustainable innovation ecosystems which, as in the software industry, are also able to leverage scientific and technological development in other industrial sectors.

Open Source Hardware Innovation is a collaborative, product development process, in which building plan designs, assembly instructions and bills of material are made publicly available online for anyone to study, replicate, modify, distribute and sell, including hardware based on those designs (Raasch *et al.*, 2009; Bonvoisin *et al.*, 2016; Bonvoisin *et al.*, 2017). Thus, OSH is characterized by knowledge sharing and decentralization enabled by modern information and communication technologies (ICT) (Moritz *et al.*, 2016). Ideally, OSH uses readily-available components, materials and standard processes, maximizing possibilities of mass participation as well as the means of deviating from conventional business models and a market economy (Troxler, 2019). As such Open Design, and OSH as part of open design, transcend organizational boundaries, blending the traditional innovation categories of product, process, managerial or radical innovations (Sanguinetti, 2019, p.52). OSH, at the crossroads of different innovation categories, represents a disruptive innovation for organizations needing to reconfigure their own business models. OSH, is part of the Design Global Manufacture Local (DG-ML) model described by Kostakis *et al.*, (2015) as a proto-model of production which, for the moment cannot perpetrate itself independently of capitalism. Nonetheless, its complementary components represent a paradigm shift away from "the irrational exploitation of resources and the ecologically destructive magnification of production and consumption".

The open source hardware and peer production phenomena as regards manufacturing force us to reevaluate the centrality of property to growth (Raasch *et al.*, 2009; Bonvoisin, *et al.*, 2016; Moritz *et al.*, 2016; Benkler, 2017). Changes here are disruptive as they lead to changes in the firm-centric business model understanding of how firms seek to create and capture value. They suggest that innovation and manufacturing processes are becoming democratized and that "anyone" may learn and teach each other how to attain energy, food and technological sovereignty, for example.

OSH entrepreneurs are a new entrepreneur type who forgo intellectual property ownership and license their products as open source to run their businesses. They wager that benefits gained from their communities will offset the risks of lowering entry barriers to competitors (Li and Seering, 2019). These entrepreneurs tend to follow the maker ethos and open-source culture of being an actor rather than a spectator in a technological world.

Research has revealed that OSH projects have strong potential for social innovation. Often, with value-driven around notions of making, freedom and collective innovation, they materialize ideals of degrowth imaginary, such as autonomy and conviviality central to the objectives of Transition Towns and the Fab City Collective (Kostakis *et al.*, 2015; Fab City Collective 2018; Hopkins, 2019). These values help in federating support within and beyond their internal communities to include stakeholders in broader, local and global ecosystems. These values also serve to catalyze global and local DG-ML pipelines, implementing objectives such as the Fab City's locally production of 50% of city consumption within forty years, while inspiring citizens to become interested in achieving energy, food and technological sovereignty (Thomas, 2019; Unterfrauner *et al.,* 2017; Acquier *et al.,* 2016)

Business Model Research for Open Source Hardware

If OSH is a proto production model, OSHBM are a proto business models. As Gavras (2019) suggests, the question is whether an alternative, holistic emergent productive model is proposed or if existing corporate infrastructure is reorganized according to design principles primarily native to open source culture. Indeed, at this stage, existing literature on business models for open source hardware remains descriptive but neither strategic enough for either theoretical insight nor for practical application. Fjeldsted *et al.*, (2012), analyze the novel key elements required for commercial OSH initiatives, namely the platform, drive, community, product development process, and business model. Moritz *et al.*, (2016); Li and Seering, (2019) and Mies, *et al.*, (2019), observe the crucial importance of community building in the value creation and capture mechanisms. Menichinelli (2015) and Pearce (2012; 2017) observe that such business models blur the boundaries between consumers and producers, notably for scientific equipment. Troxler and Wolf (2017) analyze such agency in the form of formally appointed functional groups (division of labor), stabilized procedures (rules), and loose networks of people (community).

Tables 2-5 display our conceptual order of the different, current literature streams concerning OSH business models from both academic and practitioner perspectives, as related to four business model design aspects – financing, product and service mix, corporate competences, and the platform model.

While peer production and open source hardware transcend firm-based management theories – they are spreading in practice, but in theory they remain a puzzle. The Commons theory is an interesting lens through which to observe this. Based on the literature review, the research gap identified is that to date there is no strategic and actionable framework using the Commons theory to analyze how open source hardware initiatives monetize their innovations and capture value; how they grow in scope and scale while opening their innovations to a broader community. To fill this gap, we studied how open source hardware initiatives grow while opening their core innovation to a wider community. This study was conducted over a three-year period, from 2016 through 2019 as part of the Franco-German OPEN! Research

Table 2. OSHBM patterns related to financing

Pattern Title	Pattern Description
3rd party funding/Contribution from wide range of actors (Decode, 2017; Moritz *et al.*, 2016)	An institution funds the production/conservation/expansion of a common as part of its own mission, or to pursue its commercial interests.
Reciprocity based voluntary contributions/Direct Donations (Decode, 2017; Stacey & Pearson, 2015)	Where individuals and organizations make voluntary financial contributions to sustain the production of a common on the basis of reciprocity.
Disassociating revenue making strategies/Two-sided market logic (Decode, 2017)	Revenue models in which a positive externality created by the main output is produced and used to create revenue (selling of user data and publicity).
Advertising (Stacey & Pearson, 2015; Moritz et al., 2016)	In this version of multi-sided platforms, advertisers pay for the opportunity to reach the audience of the content creators.

Table 3. OSHBM patterns related to product and service mix

Pattern Title	Pattern Description
Product as a service (Tinck & Bénichou, 2014; Moritz *et al.*, 2016)	Rose to prominence in 1959, when Xerox introduced the "pay per copy" printing model. Now spreading throughout industries via trends such as the sharing economy and the circular economy.
Freemium (Decode, 2017)	The selling of an extended/more performant version of the original digital common.
Shifting revenue making strategies (Decode, 2017)	In order not to charge for the common produced, revenue making is shifted towards the selling of something else.
Digital to Physical (Stacey & Pearson, 2015)	Giving away the bits and selling the atoms (where bits refer to digital content and atoms refer to a physical object).
Novelty (Wolf & Troxler, 2016)	Drawing on the current state of a new technology, such as 3D printing.
Direct sale of objects via web shops (Wolf & Troxler, 2016; Moritz *et al.*, 2016)	Selling designs directly via a web shop of their own, peripheral to the main business of selling

Table 4. OSHBM patterns related to corporate competences

Pattern Title	Pattern Description
Design Centric (Tinck & Bénichou, 2014)	Most common in OSHW. Organization focused on product design and R&D, while manufacturing is handled by another party. In this model brand and community are key strategic assets.
Expertise and Experience base (Tinck & Bénichou, 2014)	Model directly inspired from FLOSS, where most common BM consists in monetizing expertise and services.
Research and educational activities (Wolf & Troxler, 2016)	3D printing courses. Creating physical objects for educational purposes, or improving 3D printing technology. Excluded sharing of knowledge.
Manufacturing Centric (Tinck & Bénichou 2014)	The organization's core value proposition is to manufacture and distribute OSHW for an affordable price.
Customized prototyping for industry or private clients (Wolf & Troxler, 2016; Moritz *et al.*, 2016)	To repair broken objects or to create personal things. May include closed parts and dual licensing.
Standardize and Leverage (Tinck & Bénichou 2014)	Opening up one key product, which can be profitable in itself, but the openness serves to make the associated technology a de facto standard in the industry.

project, and studied 27 different open source mechatronic hardware initiatives. Table 6 displays the research design of the study in which the authors use open source hardware initiatives as a case study to explore how Digital Knowledge Commons can be both monetized and shared with a broader community.

Table 5. OSHBM patterns related to the platform model

Pattern Title	Pattern Description
Membership fees (Stacey & Pearson, 2015)	A traditional nonprofit funding model. In the Made with Creative Commons context, they are directly tied to the reciprocal relationship that is cultivated with the beneficiaries of their work.
Brokerage/ Matchmaking (Decode, 2017; Stacey & Pearson, 2015)	Based on matchmaking two parties such as a driver and rider or host and guest.
Online Brokerage and sales platform (Wolf & Troxler, 2016)	Consists of internet-based infrastructure allowing suppliers to expose themselves to a potential clientele and helping customers to find services and products from a range of suppliers.

Table 6. Research design of study

	Conceptual framework	References
Research gap	"Puzzle" of OSHBMs	(Chesbrough, 2003; Soloviev *et al.*, 2010; Menichinelli, 2015; Wolf & Troxler, 2016; De Filippi, 2018)
Theoretical sampling	tangible, complex, open OSH initiatives	(Bonvoisin et al., 2017; Bonvoisin et al., 2018)
Theoretical foundation	Digital Commons (raw material for ideas)	(Hess & Ostrom, 2011; Benkler, 2013; Raworth; 2017; Fuster-Morell *et al.*, 2017; Fuster-Morell & Espelt, 2018)
Methodology	Qualitative transversal case study analysis of 22 community-based OSH initiatives and 5 community-oriented OSH initiatives	(Eisenhardt and Graebner, 2007; Mantere & Ketokivi, 2013; Gavard-Perret *et al.*, 2012; Ketokivi & Choi, 2014; Avenier & Thomas, 2015, Timmermans & Tavory, 2012; Goffin et *al.*,2019)
Outcome	Framework for Digital Commons to grow in scope	(Saebi & Foss, 2018)

BUILDING OPEN SOURCE HARDWARE BUSINESS MODELS

Business Models as Building Blocks

The study revealed a large spectrum of activated revenue streams. Their range correlated with the community joining process. In essence, the "fat end of value capture" lies in the long tail of products and services around the hardware products (Thomas, 2017, 2019). The heart of value creation, however, lies in the ability to access, replicate, modify and use design files. Such openness factors, together with the potential impact of innovation achieved through network effects, are what fuel the momentum for design collaboration, making the product become better, faster, cheaper and more efficient.

Figure 1. Business models clusters identified in study

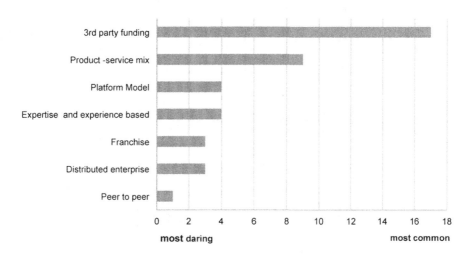

The authors organized the following business model patterns, as idealized examples of business models from the most common to the most daring or unusual (see Figure 1).

The most commonly activated pattern was "3rd party funding" (16 projects), in which projects relied on forms of crowdsourcing, direct donations, or on corporate sponsorships. More mature projects (7 years +) had evolved into a hybrid model where a corporate structure funded the operations of the non-profit. The next cluster of patterns was the "Product-service mix" (9 projects), taking the form of a freemium offer to which kit sales, training, workshops or maintenance packages could be added. The following cluster, "Expertise and experience-based" (4 projects), included corporate competencies relating to design-centric or manufacturing-centric activities such as consulting or customizing offers. The Franchise pattern (3 projects) appeared as a means of ensuring quality and safety standards.

The "Platform model" (4 projects), included more elaborate interaction modes with co-creator communities through subscription, or matchmaking. The OSH initiative thus becomes a platform where customers can browse for designs, download them for a fee and produce them at their local Fab Lab, or be directed (through matchmaking) to the manufacturer most apt to fabricate them. Platforms are mainly about lock-in, monitoring, controlling and monetizing exchanges, "knowing" what people are doing to stimulate behavior that is easy to monetize.

The least used patterns appearing in our findings are the "distributed enterprise" model (3 projects) and the "Peer-to-peer" model (1 project), in which the point is

Table 7. Distribution of business model patterns per initiative

Project	1	2	3	4	5	6	7	8	9	10	11	12	13	14	15	16	17	18	19	20	21	22	23	24	25	26	27	SUM
3rd party funding																												15
Sales																												13
Self-funded																												9
Crowdfunding																												7
Kits																												6
Workshops																												5
Consulting																												3
Subscription																												2
Renting platform																												1
N/A																												1
License																												1

not only is to give other people the opportunity to reproduce the product itself, but also to train people to build a business around it in order for the initiative to scale.

When analyzing which OSH initiative used which business model pattern, what appears noteworthy in all projects is their use of business model pattern combination, also observed by Wolf and Troxler (2016). Table 7 shows the distribution of these patterns. The top row numbers the 27 different OSH projects studied. The left column details the list of business model patterns activated in each initiative. The right column indicates the number of projects using each business model pattern.

Three different clusters of business model pattern bricks can be identified. The 3rd-party-funding cluster builds on the product service mix + corporate competence models. Expertise is either design-centric or manufacturing-centric. This business model pattern directly derived from free and libre open source software (FLOSS) consists in shifting revenue-making strategies from product sales to expertise and services. Offers will take the form of DIY workshops wherein people purchase "the experience of building it yourself". Consulting services may be offered to customize or to build derivatives, such as an aquaponic greenhouse to grow fresh, aromatic plants for a restaurant; or learning to use your processes; or, for instance, the rental of the OSH initiative's collaborative platform for decentralized problem solving.

The distributed enterprise cluster builds upon the above, with the difference that it adds "train the trainer" workshops in order, to not only use OSH for the benefits of decentralized problem solving, but to further diffuse the concept by creating entrepreneurs who will replicate the model. The Peer-to-peer pattern, for transactions between private individuals, is organized by an intermediary responsible for their safe and efficient handling. Eventually this function can be monetized by charging transaction fees or through advertising and donations.

The platform cluster (4 projects) includes the subscription and matchmaking models. These create value via their capacity to orchestrate an ecosystem of industry players (designers, manufacturers, resellers, customers, prosumers) around one key technology or design platform.

The last two clusters, Distributive entreprise and Platform, stand out as the most elaborate in the sense that they articulate the most varied streams of revenues and value offerings.

The modular nature of business model patterns reveals that, depending on an organization's specific context and resources, the patterns can be combined to provide multiple revenue streams. These appear to be used individually, to be regrouped in different categories, and/or to serve as building blocks. The patterns identified build upon one another, compiling "all of the above" solutions. The modular nature of the "bricks" creates both a level of complexity and a facility of use, as the projects can begin from wherever they stand.

Proposal for an Open Source Hardware Business Growth Model

Figure 2 illustrates how OSH initiatives progressively interact with their surrounding innovation ecosystems, enrich their value propositions and grow in impact. This framework is the fruit of many rounds of abductive iterations using data, literature, sessions with entrepreneurs interested in opening up their business models, and experts in OSH with academic and practitioner backgrounds. Through loops of presentations and feedback received, a categorizing began to emerge based on what Gassman *et al.*, (2014) would call a *similarity principle*.

Patterns were organized into a 5-stage framework – from the most commonly used business models to those least commonly used.

Figure 2. Five-stage framework of most commonly to least commonly found OSHBMs

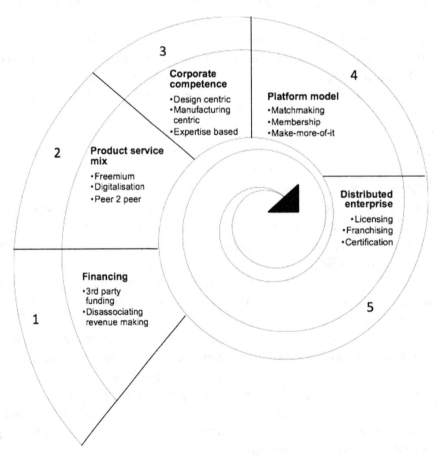

The spiral sense of the framework represents the iterative process projects go through in designing their progressively harder and riskier architecture of activities: first, finding funding sources; next fine-tuning the value proposition; third, leveraging the organization's corporate competence; then orchestrating and monetizing exchanges among actors; and finally, franchising the model to develop its impact. OSH project holders may constantly have to fine-tune the manner in which they create and share value with their stakeholders. These stages reveal the creative concessions observed for revenue making while the core aspects of value propositions remain open. Briefly, like climbing a mountain stages 1 through 3 are easier. Stage 4 represents a struggle for businesses seeking to open their business models. Stages 1 through 4 are in line with what has previously been described in literature. Stage 5, the distributed enterprise, emerged inductively from our empirical findings. This stage would represent the arduous mountain top – hard to reach but fulfilling "the promise of open source", that is, open source enterprises creating open source enterprises, allowing the DNA of an innovation to circulate so that others may creatively adapt it to their own local contexts.

Stage 1: Financing (N=16/27)

The first Stage pertains to external financing modes. OSH initiatives require capital to fund their activities. The cultural difference between an open source approach and the traditional closed model is that OSH initiatives need to be more creative to do so.

This stage also serves to build a consortium, accrue legitimacy, get a feel for what external stakeholders are willing to support and a sense of what public entities are striving for. Two main options are available: 3rd party funding and disassociating revenue-making strategies.

3rd party funding refers to sourcing money from institutions, corporate actors or the general public. The goal being to find institutions willing to fund the production/conservation/expansion of a common, because they have an interest in it. This support may include public funding, grants, or corporate sponsorship. The drawback, of course, is risking a lack of independence as regards the governance or economic model. General public support can take the form of reciprocity-based revenue-making strategies, such as crowdfunding campaigns or direct individual donations. Voluntary financial contributions sustain the production of a common based on reciprocity. The novelty here is the ability to limit influence or professional investors. This category includes memberships, donations, pay now, buy later, becoming a patron or pay-what-you-want, where customers are given a range of price options for a product or service.

The disassociating revenue making strategy is the second mode of tapping into external funding. Here, a positive externality created by the main output is produced to create revenue. For instance, once the community is large enough, the organization may charge third parties for advertising on the community forum, earn income through sponsorships or sell personal data.

Stage 2: Product Service Mix (N=9/27)

Through this Stage, OSH initiatives can experiment with tailoring their value proposition design and their go-to market strategies. Indeed, in the initial stage of a project, most proponents had a vague idea of who their target customers were, and what value proposition would adequately match their needs. The idea here is to move progressively from a product mindset to a service mindset. As one of the OSH entrepreneurs explained, "if we were just interested in selling a final product we might as well sell bidets".

Propositions for this Stage include freemium options, whereby what was collectively developed can be offered for free to establish a large initial customer base but custom add-ons and premium offers are developed for specific needs, or for a more efficient version of the original digital common. The common produced is not charged but revenue making is 'shifted' to the selling of something else related to the common. In the case of OSH, both 'digital-to-physical' and 'experience-selling' make sense. For instance, in the case of the Danish furniture brand, Stykka, (which intends to become the OSH equivalent to furniture design that Spotify is to music), Fab Market or Open Desk, designers are compensated if customers select their designs, and if they choose to manufacture the designs in their local Fab Lab or woodshop. Experience selling comes through selling DIY workshops where users learn how to build, weld and assemble their own machinery, brick press, tractor, or solar power generator. Peer-to-peer refers to transactions between private individuals, such as the case for E-nable: where 3D printing machine owners build prosthetic limbs for children born with agenesia.

Stage 3: Corporate Competence (N=4/27)

During Stage 3, the OSH initiative needs to carefully assess its core strengths in order to build its competitive advantage. If the founders are design-centric, they are most often focused on product design and R&D, and they outsource the manufacturing. In this model, the brand and the community are key strategic assets. If they are manufacturing–centric, the organization's core value proposition is to manufacture and distribute open hardware products for an affordable price. In addition to the brand and customer community, industrial efficiency is a key asset. One noteworthy example is Seeed Studios, the "IOT Hardware enabler" which manufactures electronic products for makers and engineers. Indeed, many parts required for hardware are manufactured in Shenzen, China, "the factory of factories" which, based on its manufacturing might, has developed a synergy with all manufacturers in the world and has become a "hardware accelerator".

Another business model pattern associated with this stage of corporate competence, is customized prototyping for industry or private clients. As the design skills for creating and developing a 3D printed prototype are scarce, therefore still novel, customers can be "locked-in" to a vendor's world, which will make switching to another provider more difficult.

Through the pattern of the integrator model the organization will gain economies of range and efficiency by controlling most or all parts of the supply chain from sourcing to manufacture to distribution. In the case of Baidu and Tesla, this approach fosters innovation and improves efficiency. Tesla, for instance, is using this model to consolidate its position and modify market boundaries from the inside by creating both the demand and the supply of associated products and services, such as electrical batteries, charging stations and Powerwalls.

If the organization chooses to focus on expertise and experience, their revenue models will come from monetizing expertise and services. Consulting services may be offered to customize or build derivatives of a given product (ex: Arduino) or to learn about the processes used. For instance, Local motors and Wikispeed offer the service of renting out their collaborative design platform. Similar to the "make more of it" pattern, knowhow and resources are sold to the third party as a service. Accumulated specialist knowledge and spare capacities are monetized and new expertise built up, all of which can be used to further improve internal processes and revitalize the core business (Gassman *et al.,* 2014).

These design, manufacturing or expertise-based design types, offer the opportunity to "standardize and leverage". The idea being to open-up one key product in order to make the associated technology a de facto standard in the industry as is the case with Tesla's strategy.

Stage 4: The Platform Model (N=4/27)

Inspired by the digital economy, the core of the value proposition in this model is to organize an ecosystem of industry players around one key technology or design platform.

The goal, regrouping a variety of different players: makers, designers, manufacturers, buyers, is to form a multi-sided market. This model opens-up core assets, in order to enable new roles in a firm's organization. Revenue generation, beyond just selling a product, can come from subscription fees, training sessions corresponding to the experience, selling, and make- more-of-it patterns identified by Gassman *et al.,* (2014).

This category includes deriving revenues from brokering strategies. Here revenue is based on matchmaking between two parties such as driver or a rider or a host and a guest. This method is widely used by platform cooperatives and can take the forms of a transaction fee or a subscription. In the case of Kreatize, the value proposition is based on an algorithm matching a manufacturer's requirements with a supplier capable of producing and improving the design. Make Works is another example specific to manufacturing, enabling the sourcing of local manufacturing and materials. This type of competence will become increasingly important through distributed manufacturing, wherein key assets are the ability to map manufacturers and their competencies to reconfigure supply chains. One respondent explained: "what we are trying to do is to create supply chains on the fly, in the sense that depending on the products and the local actors, you organize the supply chain locally".

Stage 5: Distributed Enterprise (N=3/27)

Stage 5, emerged from our empirical data and is the most challenging to implement. Three of our cases were experimenting with either a franchise or a distributed enterprise model. These patterns together form the "distributed enterprise" stage (3/27) which is placed at the end of the process, because although it may not be the starting goal of many OSH initiatives, it is a logical progression.

One OSH entrepreneur explained:

We're training them either to produce the machines you can make in a fabrication shop, or to actually produce them by taking the blueprints to a fabricator and then selling, having them fabricating the product for you. We prefer the idea of the immersion-training workshop in manufacturing, where you organize the workshop. We have twelve people or so, they pay you to build it, they get immersion training and you sell the product. It's a dual revenue model, where you're catching revenue for manufacturing as well as education.

In this schema, revenues can also come from labels and certifications from the host organization, certifying that, after having gone through a certain number of workshops, the resulting product is sufficiently safe. The patterns of licensing or franchising, or of matchmaking are other options if the initial project has developed a superior knowledge of supply chain logistics that makes buying in bulk easier. Another OSH entrepreneur explained: "I'm saving them the trouble of having to find all the materials they need from 25 different places". Franchising is a perfect means of allowing for geographical expansion without having to muster up all the resources and carry all the risk, which is handled by franchised, independent entrepreneurs (Gassman *et al.*, 2014).

SOLUTIONS AND RECOMMENDATIONS

Prerequisites for Building Open Source Hardware Business Models

The main recommendation offered is a mindset shift from a "me" perspective focused on personal interest and scarcity to the "we"/ common good perspective of abundance found in Commons-based peer production. This shift is understood as a means of accelerating a circular economy and empowering individuals and organizations to address problems, such as climate change, that a single entity or company cannot solve alone.

The OSH initiatives studied were value driven. Indeed, the projects carrying a strong social or environmental vision were more likely to receive contributions from community members as well as stakeholder support. Similar values were used to federate a community of contributors. Conversely, when interacting with and within organizations which do not have an organizational culture endorsing these values, at best there is a stasis state, and at worst the values are undermined. These findings are congruent with previous research by Zott *et al.*, (2011) and Breuer & Lüdeke-Freund (2018) attest to the importance of values-based innovation for addressing complex societal problems.

The crux of the matter at this point seems to be the ability to establish participatory governance ensuring the transparency and effectiveness of the initiatives on multiple global and local levels. Here, governance needs to be value-driven in order to promote generative, decentralized, bottom-up innovation processes. This point coincides with the principle of "nested enterprises" with multiple activity layers identified by Ostrom (1990).

Implementing Open Source Hardware Business Models

To date, OSH just has not had the same impact and spread as OSS. Perhaps the simple reason is that hardware is hard. While the marginal cost of producing one unit in software certainly nears zero, the reality in hardware of materials and space will always cost money (Tinck & Bénichou, 2014). While even the development phase of industrially produced goods itself may generate relatively low costs, they bear about 70% the responsibility for the costs in downstream areas through production and sales. Recent work on Open Source Economy and "Open Source Product Life Cycle", integrates the externalities previously borne by society such as waste disposal and or costs due to environmental toxins and pollution, which should be made visible, and ultimately be included in the product price (Rabis, 2019).

Additionally, the sustainability of distributed manufacturing, particularly in constraint-based innovation, relies largely on continued access to affordable materials either imported or, preferably, locally sourced. Indeed, off-the-shelf components can limit the design and customization potential which are inherent to the concept of user-developed hardware and digital fabrication (Erhun, 2018, Gavras, 2019).

Moreover, globally, there are different standards for raw material and parts, electrical wiring, imperial and metric measures. One of the authors experienced this while building an HILO weaving machine and running to the hardware store a number of times because parts specifications in Germany are not the same as in France.

Our findings offer a practical sense for understanding what revenues OSH projects can activate in answer to the "what's right for us?" question. They suggest ways that OSH projects can raise money to get traction for their ideas, and even design the ideas themselves to produce their own revenue. Just as Gassman *et al.*, (2014) suggest with the Business Model Navigator, the idea is to assess the current means of revenue of an OSH initiative, while activating and brainstorming other possibilities. Each stage of our spiral framework (see Figure 2) suggests consecutive steps that may assist in understanding how to create an OSH business model project for an innovation, how to market it and how to position oneself in the market.

The framework displays progressively more challenging steps to implement. OSH initiatives and companies should not be deterred by these sequential steps. Together, they form a logical progression of OSH potential and can be taken separately or grouped, like building blocks. If an OSH initiative explores and applies each of these patterns, together they may have a compounding effect, generating even more value. Most businesses operate on the 1 to 3-stage basis. Stage 4 allows exploring the new roles and revenues created if a given organization opens up its tangible assets, such as fabrication space or its machinery, or its intangible assets, such as building plans, to a wider community (Zimmerman, 2014; Danish Design Center, 2018). This platform stage is difficult to implement in sectors and in industries accustomed to revenue from closed intellectual property. Stage 5, the "Distributed Enterprise", is the most risk-embedded step for enterprises. It enables OSH initiatives to think about how to become the "Mc Donald's" of their own industries and to grow in geographical scale. The distributed enterprise is a means of riding "piggyback" on something that is already in place. In line with FLOSS's philosophy, it permits standing on the shoulders of giants, and is where a real potential for OSH lies.

This phased approach to business model design allows initiatives to progressively reach out for ecosystem support, to gain a broader customer-user base, strengthen their core competencies and to scale for impact. Indeed, business model design is a continual weaving together of activities as organizations gradually discover their ecosystem, find new partners, accumulate experience, and identify new customer needs (Frankenberger *et al.*, 2014; Zott & Amit, 2010, Magretta, 2002). Our framework illustrates the blurring of boundaries between partners and customers as OSHBMs tend to have "fuzzier systems and more units" (Menichinelli, 2015). This occurs at various entry points. One is access to the innovation's blueprints. Another is through crowdfunding, as customers now become investors and partners. The platform stage gives additional ways of blurring lines. Matchmaking provides clear, open-innovation opportunities with key suppliers, who can become partners. Finally, in the last stage, the distributed enterprise further blurs lines, as not only the blueprint for the innovation is shared, but how to build a business as well.

Value Generation, Appropriation, and Preservation

Our findings indicate that the terms value creation and capture may need to be replaced in light of Open Source Economics. The novelty of OSHBM, explained in Figure 3, is that through distributive, regenerative and generative design OSH has the potential to generate, appropriate and preserve value, even to alter positively the current unsustainable and traditional centralized economies of scale and associated extraction of material and labor.

The upper left quadrant represents value generation. The notion of value generation is central to OSH initiatives. The objective is to raise funds giving traction to OSH ideas, or even better to design the ideas themselves to produce their own revenue and outperform existing extractive models. However, value creation is no longer only about bargaining relationships between buyers and sellers; rather, value generation and appropriation, bottom left quadrant has become a function of how often an innovation is downloaded and whether or not it has been appropriated massively, and whether or not it has impacted patterns of consumption or production. Through OSH, value creation becomes a function of how a given technology has been developed to actually meet customer and user needs (Thomson and Jakubowski, 2012; Pearce, 2017; Joyce and Paquin, 2016). In this sense, the most modular and circular designs that are easy to copy and can be applied like Lego parts in a remix of recurring solutions can generate the most value creation (Zimmerman, 2019). Use value goes from being the specific qualities of the product perceived by customers in relation to their needs (Bowman and Ambrosini, 2000), to notions of dignity, mutual support, and social inclusion (Unterfrauner *et al.*, 2017). This occurs, as Li and Seering, (2019) note, because the existence of an active community of developers, mentors and consumers increase the perceived and functional value of OSH products and services through 1) instant feedback on market information; 2) justification of the product's performance; 3) emotional value related to users learning and exploration experiences. Thus, open source can increase customers' perceived value and decrease the cost of running a company.

Figure 3. Building an open source hardware business model

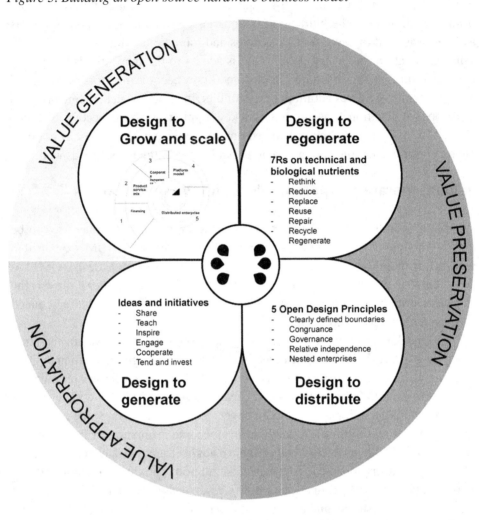

The notion of value appropriation means that peer-to-peer networks of distributive design (Raworth, 2017, p.192) and the capacity to "inform, learn and teach worldwide" enable copying and implementing innovations globally. The concept of OSH to learn globally and make locally enables individuals to share, teach, inspire, engage, cooperate, tend and invest in ideas and initiatives that make a difference. In this sense, the value created by OSH potentially transcends financial value, as well as the 7Rs of rethinking, reducing, replacing, reusing, repairing, recycling and regenerating biological and technical materials, (upper right quadrant in the figure). This unalienated circulation of Digital Knowledge Commons ignites human skill and competence to co-create and adapt local solutions to global problems.

What makes OSH value appropriation crucial to the entrepreneurship potential of achieving circular and generative economy goals, is letting the DNA, or the "seed" of an innovation circulate, enabling others to do the same, or something different, based on the hardware. Just as distributive value is an inside-out process of making an innovation available worldwide, value appropriation is an outside-in process, whereby an individual learns to experiment with OSH technology and adapt it to his or her needs. Just as seeds naturally are fertile, and unnaturally are not, OSHBM have the potential to be built around the generation, appropriation and preservation of Digital Innovation Commons.

The accepted and collective responsibility for the preservation of Digital Innovation Commons is at the crux of Ostrom's legacy, going from Natural to Digital Commons: a self-organized social system for the long-term stewardship of non-depletable and non-rivalrous resources preserving shared values and community identity, which are subject to social dilemmas. Of course, the natural and technical elements of an OSH initiative need to be preserved and tended, but as (bottom right quadrant), any OSH initiative is enriched if it heeds the open design principles of clearly defined boundaries; congruence, open governance, relative independence and nested enterprises (Troxler, 2019; Fuster Morell & Espelt, 2018; Hess and Ostrom, 2011; Ostrom, 1990).

Through distributed manufacturing and distributed enterprises, OSH, in the desire to solve complex problems, helps shift from an ethos focused on personal gain, to one focused on the Common good. As one OSH entrepreneur stated, OSH allows moving "from massively producing average products at a high global cost, to locally producing products that better fit our needs, at a lower cost". This would support the growth and development of regional economic cycles and achieve sustainable production through digitalization, personalization and localization (Rauch *et al.,* 2016; Kumar *et al.,* 2020). This remains an ideal in many cases, for instance OSH scientific equipment (Pearce, 2012, 2017) or other equipment such as aquaponics kits remain too expensive to be appropriated by the general public. However, our research shows the ways that OSH initiatives can craft their business models around these issues.

FUTURE RESEARCH DIRECTIONS

This research opens a number of future avenues, feeding into previous discussions on whether OSH proposes an alternative, holistic emergent and productive model; or if it reorganize existing corporate infrastructure (Gavras, 2019). One example could be to study the decentralized financing forms of monetization available to distributed manufacture in the prism of knowledge, governance and technological and openness.

As extensive research continues to explore emerging sustainable business models (Massa, Breuer and Lüdeke-Freund, 2022; Kopnina and Poldner, 2022); another possible stream of research could entail investigating whether organizations which have experimented with open source hardware initiatives do, or do not, find their business models transformed in the long run. Such research would seek to track the continual adaptation, responsiveness - and resilience-with-variation' 'value' of OSH. Following Røvik's (2011) theory on virus spread and contamination, do OSH initiatives "infect" the host and change operational processes? This theory could be used as a framework for describing 'emergence' as a continual, collaborative, commons-based business model pattern.

However, does such research go deep enough in tackling the cultural entropy underlying humans and organizations' unsustainable current modes of production and consumption? Based on evidence from 27 OSH entrepreneurs we have highlighted how OSHBM's have the potential to positively alter current unsustainable centralized economies of scale and associated material and labor extraction, to generate, appropriate and preserve value. Future research, building on the Transition Town movement could look at how that potential could be imagined, modelized and applied as commons are fundamentally a social process relying on relationships and shared knowledge (Kostakis *et al.,* 2015; Bregman, 2021; Hopkins, 2019, Elworthy, 2020).

CONCLUSION

This chapter explores the implications of FLOSH as a new innovation paradigm introducing novel forms of value creation and capture through distributive, regenerative and generative design.

We propose a 5-stage framework for helping OSH practitioners develop their business models using the full scope of OSH, which is based on three-year of research conducted in the scope of the OPEN! Research project, studying 27 open source hardware initiatives. Apart from providing actionable, strategic steps, the objective of the framework is to reimagine a market economy, and to live in what Kate Raworth calls Doughnut Economics, that is in equilibrium between our social foundations and the ecological ceiling of the planet.

Solving our greatest challenges is not only a matter of smart solutions. These are being developed, and they are amazing. The challenges in today's confusing world are that we need to start working together, better and faster. To this end a number of solutions are being developed using open source hardware to make faster, better, and cheaper innovations that can be deployed worldwide to tackle beehive colony collapse disorder, and oil spills, grow food, and build quicker.

To achieve this intention, the authors provide recommendations for a mindset shift from the "me" perspective focused on personal gain and scarcity to the common good perspective defined by Ostrom as equity, efficiency and sustainability offered by peer-production.

The chapter concludes with suggested avenues for future research to explore to what degree does OSH transform the operational processes of host organizations, and how the disruptive potential of OSH may be further imagined, modelized and applied.

ACKNOWLEDGMENT

This research was jointly funded by the French and German national science agencies ANR (Agence Nationale de la Recherche, grant ANR-15-CE26-0012) and DFG (Deutsche Forschungsgemeinschaft, grants JO 827/8-1 and STA 1112/13-1).

REFERENCES

Acquier, A., Carbone, V., & Massé, D. (2016). L'Economie Collaborative: Fondements théoriques et agenda de recherche. In *2nd International Workshop on the Sharing Economy*. Paris: ESCP Europe.

Benkler, Y. (2017). Peer production, the commons, and the future of the firm. *Strategic Organization*, *15*(2), 264–274. doi:10.1177/1476127016652606

Bollier, D. (2014). *Think like a Commoner. A Short Introduction to the Life of the Commons. Gabriola Island*. New Society Publishers.

Bonvoisin, J., Buchert, T., Preidel, M., & Stark, R. (2018). How participative is open source hardware? Insights from online repository mining. *Design Science*, *4*(4), 1–31. doi:10.1017/dsj.2018.15

Bonvoisin, J., Mies, R., Boujut, J.-F., & Stark, R. (2017). What is the "Source" of Open Source Hardware? *Journal of Open Hardware*, *1*(1), 1–18. doi:10.5334/joh.7

Bonvoisin, J., Thomas, L., Mies, R., Gros, C., Stark, R., Samuel, K., Jochem, R., & Boujut, J.-F. (2017). Current state of practices in open source product development. DS 87-2. In *21st International Conference on Engineering Design (Vol 2)*. Design Processes, Design Organisation and Management.

Bowman, C., & Ambrosini, V. (2000). Value Creation Versus Value Capture: Towards a Coherent Definition of Value in Strategy. *British Journal of Management, 11*(11), 1–15. doi:10.1111/1467-8551.00147

Bregman, R. (2021). *Human Kind a Hopeful History*. Bloomsbury Publishing PLC.

Breuer, H., & Lüdeke-Freund, F. (2018). Values-Based Business Model Innovation: A Toolkit. In Sustainable business models: Principles, Promise, and Practice. Springer. doi:10.1007/978-3-319-73503-0_18

Danish Design Center. (2018). *Remodel, A toolkit for Open Design Business Models*. https://remodel.dk

De Filippi, P. (2018). Blockchain: A global infrastructure for distributed governance and local manufacturing. In Fab City the mass distribution of (almost) anything. Barcelona: IAAC Fab Lab Barcelona.

Dias, S. (2021). *Fabricademy 2021-22 Workshop HILO Machine Part 1*. https://vimeo.com/649695293/dddf9f225d

Eglash, R., Babbitt, W., Bennett, A., & Callahan, B. (2016). *Culturally Situated Design Tools: Generative justice as a foundation for stem diversity (Issue December)*. IGI Global.

Elworthy, S. (2020). *The Mighty Heart. How to transform conflict*. Pureprint Group. E-nable project. https://e-nable.fr/fr/

Erhun, D. (2018). *An ICT4D initiative: FabLabs as a potential catalyst for constraint-based innovation in Rwanda* [Master Thesis]. University of Amsterdam.

Fab City Collective. (2018). Fabcity white paper. In *Fab City the mass distribution of (almost) anything*. Barcelona: IAAC Fablab Barcelona.

Fab Market. (n.d.). https://distributeddesign.eu/talent/

Fjeldsted, A. S., Adalsteinsdottir, G., Howard, T. J., & McAloone, T. (2012). Open Source Development of Tangible Products - from a business perspective. In NordDesign 2012. Creative Commons Netherlands, Premsela: the Netherlands Institute for Design and Fashion and Waag Society.

Foss, N. J., & Saebi, T. (2018). Business models and business model innovation: Between wicked and paradigmatic problems. *Long Range Planning, 51*(1), 9–21. doi:10.1016/j.lrp.2017.07.006

Frankenberger, K., Weiblen, T., & Gassmann, O. (2014). The antecedents of open business models: An exploratory study of incumbent firms. *R & D Management, 44*(2), 173–188. doi:10.1111/radm.12040

Fuster Morell, M. (2014). Governance of online creation communities for the building of digital commons: Viewed through the framework of the institutional analysis and development. In Governing Knowledge Commons. Oxford University Press.

Fuster Morell, M., Carballa Schichowski, B., Smorto, G., Espelt, R., Imperatore, P., Rebordosa, M., Rodriguez, N., Senabre, E., & Ciurcina, M. (2017). Decode. *Decentralised Citizens Owned Data Ecosystem., 1*(3), 1–144.

Fuster Morell, M., & Espelt, R. (2018). A Framework for Assessing Democratic Qualities in Collaborative Economy Platforms: Analysis of 10 Cases in Barcelona. *Urban Science (Basel, Switzerland), 2*(3), 1–13. doi:10.3390/urbansci2030061

Gassmann, O., Frankenberger, K., & Csik, M. (2014). *The business model navigator.* Pearson Education.

Gavras, K. (2019). Open source beyond software: Re-invent open design on the Common's ground. *Journal of Peer Production, 13*, 1–25.

Goffin, K., Åhlström, P., Bianchi, M., & Richtnér, A. (2019). Perspective: State-of-the-Art: The Quality of Case Study Research in Innovation Management. *Journal of Product Innovation Management, 36*(5), 586–615. doi:10.1111/jpim.12492

Hess, C., & Ostrom, E. (2011). *Understanding Knowledge as Commons. From Theory to Practice.* MIT Press.

Hopkins, R. (2019). *From what is to what if: unleashing the power of imagination to create the future we want.* Somerset House.

Joyce, A., & Paquin, R. L. (2016). The triple layered business model canvas: A tool to design more sustainable business models. *Journal of Cleaner Production, 135*, 1474–1486. doi:10.1016/j.jclepro.2016.06.067

Kopnina, H., & Poldner, K. (2022). *Circular Economy. Challenges and opportunities for Ethical and Sustainable Business.* Routledge.

Kostakis, V., Niaros, V., Dafermos, G., & Bauwens, M. (2015). Design global, manufacture local: Exploring the contours of an emerging productive model. *Futures, 73*, 126–135. doi:10.1016/j.futures.2015.09.001

Kumar, M., Tsolakis, N., Agarwal, A., & Srai, J. S. (2020). Developing distributed manufacturing strategies from the perspective of a product-process matrix. *International Journal of Production Economics*, *219*, 1–17. doi:10.1016/j.ijpe.2019.05.005

Li, Z., & Seering, W. (2019). Does open source hardware have a sustainable business model? An analysis of value creation and capture mechanisms in open source hardware companies. *The International Conference on Engineering Design, ICED*. 10.1017/dsi.2019.230

Litman, J. (2014). The public domain. *Emory Law Journal*, *39*(4), 965–1022.

Lüdeke-Freund, F., Breuer, H., & Massa, L. (2022). *Sustainable Business Model Design. 45 Patterns*. Academic Press.

Make Works. (n.d.). https://make.works/companies

Menichinelli, M. (2015). Open Meta-Design. In D. Bihanic (Ed.), *Empowering Users through Design* (pp. 193–212). Springer. doi:10.1007/978-3-319-13018-7_11

Mies, R., Bonvoisin, J., & Jochem, R. (2019). Harnessing the Synergy Potential of Open Source Hardware Communities. In Co-Creation. Management for Professionals (pp. 129–145). Springer Nature Switzerland. doi:10.1007/978-3-319-97788-1_11

Moritz, M., Redlich, T., Grames, P. P., & Wulfsberg, J. P. (2016). Value creation in open-source hardware communities: Case study of Open Source Ecology. In *PICMET 2016 - Portland International Conference on Management of Engineering and Technology: Technology Management For Social Innovation*. Open Desk. https://www.opendesk.cc/

Orcajada, A. (2021). *Material Driven. Fabricademy 2021 Recitation*. https://class.textile-academy.org/classes/2021-22/week06/

Ostrom, E. (1990). *Governing the Commons. The Evolution of Institutions for Collective Action*. Cambridge University Press. doi:10.1017/CBO9780511807763

Pearce, J. M. (2012). Building research equipment with free, open-source hardware. *Science*, *337*(6100), 1303–1304. doi:10.1126cience.1228183 PMID:22984059

Pearce, J. M. (2017). Emerging Business Models for Open Source Hardware. *Journal of Open Hardware*, *1*(1), 1–14. doi:10.5334/joh.4

Raasch, C., Herstatt, C., & Balka, K. (2009). On the open design of tangible goods. *R & D Management*, *39*(4), 382–393. doi:10.1111/j.1467-9310.2009.00567.x

Rabis, F. (2019). *Open Source Ökonomie Diplomarbeit Ehrenwörtliche Erklärung* [PhD]. Technische Universität Dresden.

Rauch, E., Dallasega, P., & Matt, D. T. (2016). Sustainable production in emerging markets through Distributed Manufacturing Systems (DMS). *Journal of Cleaner Production, 135*, 127–138. doi:10.1016/j.jclepro.2016.06.106

Raworth, K. (2017). *Doughnut Economics: Seven ways to think like a 21st century economist*. Random House Business Books.

Rifkin, J. (2014). *Ushering In A Smart Green Digital Global Economy To Address Climate Change And Create A More Ecological And Humane Society*. https://www. troisiemerevolutionindustrielle.lu/wp-content/uploads/2016/01/6-9-2015_Digital-Europe_Ushering-In-A-Smart-Green-Digital-Global-Economy-To-Address-Climate-Change-And-Create-A-More-Ecological-And-Humane-Society-2.pdf

Røvik, K. A. (2011). From Fashion to Virus: An Alternative Theory of Organizations' Handling of Management Ideas. *Organization Studies, 32*(5), 631–653. doi:10.1177/0170840611405426

Sanguinetti, V. (2019). *Adoption de l'Open Source par les organisations: Articuler business model ouvert et implication dans les communautés*. Université Jean Moulin Lyon III.

Stacey, P., & Hinchliff Pearson, S. (2017). *Made with creative commons*. Ctrl-Alt-Delete Books. https://creativecommons.org/use-remix/made-with-cc/

Stykka. (n.d.). https://www.stykka.com/

Teece, D. J. (2010). Business models, business strategy and innovation. *Long Range Planning, 43*(2–3), 172–194. doi:10.1016/j.lrp.2009.07.003

The academy of (almost) anything. (n.d.). https://academany.org/about/

Thomas, L. (2019). *Business models for Open Source Hardware*. Université Grenoble Alpes.

Thomas, L., & Samuel, K. (2017). Characteristics of Open Source Business Models. *XXVIII ISPIM Innovation Conference.*

Thomson, C. C., & Jakubowski, M. (2012). Toward an open source civilization: innovations case narrative: open source ecology. *Innovations: Technology, Governance, Globalization, 7*(3), 53–70. doi:10.1162/INOV_a_00139

Tincq, B., & Bénichou, L. (2014). *Open Hardware Business Models.* Workshop at Open Hardware Summit. https://fr.slideshare.net/btincq/business-models-for-open-source-hardware?fbclid=IwAR1LzRMjs0fHn-0BjeP46G_tD9VyT9nKHZ1saDVJ4Le44h7R7GoTNxGdaEk

Troxler, P. (2010) Commons-based Peer-Production of Physical Goods. Is There Room for a Hybrid Innovation Ecology? *Third Free Culture Research Conference.*

Troxler, P. (2019). Building Open Design as a Commons. In The Critical Makers Reader: (Un) learning Technology. Academic Press.

Unterfrauner, E., Schrammel, M., Voigt, C., & Menichinelli, M. (2017). The Maker Movement and the Disruption of the Producer-Consumer Relation. *Internet Science*, *342*(November), 1–51.

Van Abel, B., Evers, L., Klaassen, R., & Troxler, P. (2010). *Open Design Now. Why Design Cannot Remain Exclusive.* Bis publishers.

Von Hippel, E. (2005). *Democratizing Innovation.* The MIT Press. doi:10.7551/mitpress/2333.001.0001

Wolf, P., & Troxler, P. (2016). Community-based business models Insights from an emerging maker economy. *Interaction Design and Architectures*, *30*(30), 75–94. doi:10.55612-5002-030-005

Zimmerman, L. (2014). *Open Design Platform.* https://larszimmermann.de/Open-platform-design-flowchart-vs-0-2-released

Zimmerman, L. (2019). *Mifactori, what is Open Circular Design.* https://mifactori.de

Zittrain, J. (2006). The Generative Internet. *Harvard Law Review*, *119*, 1974. https://ssrn.com/abstract=847124

Zott, C., & Amit, R. (2010). Business model design: An activity system perspective. *Long Range Planning*, *43*(2–3), 216–226. doi:10.1016/j.lrp.2009.07.004

KEY TERMS AND DEFINITIONS

Business Models: The architecture of activities through which a firm creates, captures and delivers value.

Commons: A shareable resource of nature or society that people choose to use or govern through self-organizing that is vulnerable to social dilemmas.

Digital Commons: Digital Commons are non-depletable and non-rivalrous. The more they are used and shared, the more efficient, cheaper, and transparent they become. They serve as the raw material for ideas, and need to be kept open to allow knowledge to circulate.

FLOSH: Free and libre open source hardware.

FLOSS: Free and libre open source software.

FOSS: Free open source software.

OSH: Open Source Hardware is a collaborative product development process in which building plan designs, assembly instructions and bills of material are made publicly available for anyone to study, replicate, modify, distribute and sell, including hardware created, based on those designs.

Chapter 4
Open Source and Free Software Licenses for Embedded Systems

Renê de Souza Pinto
Zededa GmbH, Germany

ABSTRACT

Several open source operating systems are being used in commercial embedded applications, such as smartphones, set-top boxes, routers, video game consoles, and many other consumer electronics. One of the best examples is the Linux kernel, which is present in millions of different embedded devices. That said, the Linux kernel is licensed under GNU General Public License version 2 (GPLv2), which enforces any derivative work to be licensed under the same terms as the original license. Embedded device manufacturers must be aware of such clauses and understand how to handle the distribution of their systems, including free software and open source operating systems, such as Linux kernel. This chapter covers relevant aspects of different open source licenses regarding operating systems and some common issues faced by developers of commercial applications. The foundation knowledge is presented to guide readers to choose an open source operating system according to its license for embedded commercial applications.

INTRODUCTION

The Operating System (OS) plays a central role in a computational system: it provides an abstraction of the hardware for running applications and manages all machine resources. A few decades back, Operating Systems were evolving along with the

DOI: 10.4018/978-1-6684-4785-7.ch004

PC industry, while embedded systems were still composed of very specialized applications, usually running on microcontrollers with much less computational power than general-purpose systems. However, the rapid growth of microelectronics technologies pushed embedded systems to a new level: embedded platforms emerged on the market using powerful SoCs (System-on-a-Chip) that can run general-purpose OSes with a performance comparable (or in some cases, even better) with PCs. Additionally, the embedded hardware became less expensive and the FOSS and Open Source Hardware community brought to life many open embedded platforms through successful projects, such as the Raspberry PI. Currently, a huge number of embedded platforms running FOSS artifacts (such as the Linux kernel) are inexpensive and available to the general public. This evolution was a key factor to the development of new technologies, such as the development of IoT devices and has changed the embedded industry as well. Manufacturers started to use FOSS in their products (routers, smartphones, TVs, among many others) and several licensing issues arose throughout the years. In 2008, Free Software Foundation (FSF) initiated a lawsuit against Cisco claiming that GNU's GPL (General Public License) and LGPL (Lesser General Public License) were violated in many Linksys (acquired by Cisco) products (Lee, 2008). GNU's tools *binutils*, *coreutils*, *glibc*, among others, were distributed only in binary form along with several Linksys firmwares without meeting all requirements fixed by these licenses. In 2009 the parties announced a joint agreement that included a non-disclosed monetary contribution from Cisco to FSF (Smith, 2009). In 2006 the German programmer Harald Welte prosecuted D-Link (iFross, 2006) claiming that software of his authorship that were part of Linux kernel was distributed along with the firmware of a storage device (Wireless G Network Media Storage DSM G600) without meeting all GPL requirements. The violations were found after a reverse engineering process made by the author, which bought a device. The court ordered the reimbursement of all costs expended by the author with the legal process, purchasing of the device, and reverse engineering work, besides enforcing D-Link to meet all license requirements. The same programmer was also the plaintiff in other cases brought to court in different countries. In 2013, Welte prosecuted the company FANTEC for using his software kernel components (netfilter/iptables) in one of their firmwares (FANTEC 3DFHDL Media Player device) without the release of complete corresponding source code (Welte, 2013), in this case the source code was released but it did not fully match the version present in the firmware. The court decided a penalty fee to FANTEC plus expenses for the lawyers. Additionally, it was requested that the company disclosed the exact information about the media player firmware. These examples show how not following all FOSS license requirements can bring not only image but also financial damages to the companies. Although the source code is open and widely available, there are important differences on license terms across different FOSS licenses. One key term is how derivative works can be licensed by the licensees (the person or entity who is receiving the license from a licensor). For some licenses, it's mandatory to release any derivative work under the same terms of the original license. Although the term "derivative work" can be broadly interpreted, such clauses can impact specially embedded systems, because while in a PC environment the distinction between user applications and the OS might be very clear, and applications usually don't require specific device drivers to work (or when required, they are already provided by the general purpose OS), the components of an embedded system are tied to the hardware and distributed as a whole along with device's firmware. In many cases it also requires device drivers that must be developed and integrated to the running OS. For some processor and microcontroller architectures that don't support different execution modes, application's code is built along with the OS kernel and flashed to the device's memory. These aspects are critical for embedded commercial applications, the license of all third party system components must be considered at the design phase in order to facilitate any licensing decision to be made. There are different approaches that can be followed to make a proprietary embedded application running on an Operating System with a FOSS license and still meet all requirements with no license violation. For instance, running a proprietary application on top of an unmodified FOSS Operating System is in accordance with FOSS license terms. However, eventual changes made to the OS kernel must be released under the same license terms depending on the type of the FOSS license. Thus, stakeholders must know all the terms, the differences and the obligations of licensors and licensees when dealing with FOSS artifacts. The goal of this chapter is to provide the foundation knowledge and cover the main aspects of FOSS licensing focusing on Operating Systems for commercial embedded systems. For the simplicity of understanding, throughout the text the term commercial shall be used interchangeably with the term proprietary in order to define systems, applications and/or any products that contain artifacts commercially developed and/or not licensed under a FOSS license. Note that even if a commercial application releases software artifacts under a FOSS license, the same concerns must be taken into account in order to meet all license requirements.

This chapter is organized as follows: Background section explores the main concepts of Operating Systems and different kernel architectures as well as relevant topics on licensing and naming that are important to understand. Section Main Open Source and Free Software Licenses discusses the main open source and free software licenses used in several Operating Systems and what is the difference between them in respect to distribution of derivative work. The Operating Systems Licensing Use Cases section describes the licensing of some well-known Operating Systems. Licensing Approach for Commercial Applications discusses some real cases of commercial embedded applications and approaches that might be considered for new projects. The Conclusion section summarizes the whole discussion of the chapter and concludes by presenting the outcomes.

BACKGROUND

Operating Systems

Defining an Operating System can be tricky since it can be decomposed into different components. According to (Tanenbaum & Bos, 2015), an Operating System can be seen as an Extended Machine and as a Resource Manager. The first is related to how the OS abstracts the underlying hardware to the applications. For instance, a text editor application writes or reads a file from a storage device without care which type of the device it is dealing with. Usually, the OS will provide some generic system calls, such as *open()*, *close()*, *read()* and *write()* that the application can use to manipulate files across all storage devices available. The OS is responsible for translating the information provided by the applications and communicating directly to the specific storage device according to its interface (SATA, SAS, NVMe, etc) in order to read and write the corresponding device block(s). In the same way, all machine resources will be abstracted to applications through the system calls interface. The set of calls and the abstraction layer presented by the OS to applications can be seen as an extension of the machine, a big advantage of this model is that different OSes can provide the same abstraction layer (system calls, utilities, APIs), making applications portable across OSes. In fact, the POSIX standard (The Open Group Base, 2017) aims to define all important components of an UNIX Operating System, since the system calls up to shell utilities, commands, specific directories and many other properties that in theory, will allow any POSIX application to run unmodified on any POSIX Operating System. Although many Unix-like OSes are not 100% compliant with POSIX, those similarities still provide a reasonable degree of portability across applications.

An Operating System can also be seen as a Resource Manager because it's responsible to handling all machine resources, from processing and memory allocation to control disks, video and input devices, network and Wi-Fi cards, clocks or any other hardware resource that requires a specific operation and shall be offered to applications in a safe and organized way, orchestrated by the OS. At the OS side, device drivers are the entities in charge of controlling a certain type of device(s). On big and/or general purpose systems, all device drivers required by the machine hardware are usually provided by the OS. However, embedded systems act on dedicated devices, running in specific hardware that many times are not fully supported by the embedded Operating System. In such cases, device drivers must be developed and integrated.

In order to run several programs inside the same OS execution instance and protect them from each other, i.e., insulate each part of the memory where programs reside (also providing address translation), most processor architectures provide two (or eventually more) execution modes: the kernel mode and the user mode. The kernel mode (or kernel space) is a privilege mode where the code running inside it has direct access to the whole machine resources: it can access and map the whole memory, program DMA and other hardware controllers, receive processor interrupts, it can even completely power off the machine. The kernel is the core of the Operating System, it contains the main interface between the hardware and the software and depending on the architecture design it can contain all device drivers and system components. The user mode (or user space) has much less privileges than kernel mode. It can only access the memory that was mapped for, it has no direct hardware access, it cannot receive interrupts directly and it should access system resources only through the abstraction layer provided by the OS and/or through auxiliary system libraries.

As the ancient adage says *"with great power there must also come great responsibility"*, at the same time that the code running in kernel mode has direct access to all machine resources and it can reach very good performance (since there is almost no overhead for communication), it can also crash the whole system if does something wrong, such as forbidden memory accesses, get stuck on spin locks or any other error that could be fixed in user mode by killing and restarting the user space application. These are some of the reasons that take system designers to develop different architectures of Operating Systems, that in summary differ on how the system components are split between kernel and user mode.

Figure 1 shows a Monolithic architecture for an Operating System. In this architecture, the OS kernel, which runs entirely in kernel mode, contains all device drivers and components to control all machine resources and implement the system calls for user space applications. Some of the advantages of this architecture are the performance (since kernel components, such as device drivers, can interact between them without restrictions and intermediary layers), direct hardware access, the whole kernel can be seen (many times built) as a single image requiring less API interfaces and the kernel can still be modularized. Only user applications, such as system daemons, interfaces, utilities and general user applications will run in user mode (no kernel components are running in this unprivileged execution level). The main drawback for this architecture is that one single failure, for instance, from a bugged device driver, can compromise the whole system. However, modern monolithic kernels, such as the Linux kernel, are able to load/unload kernel components during runtime and protect themselves at a certain level against driver failures.

Figure 1. A monolithic architecture for an operating system

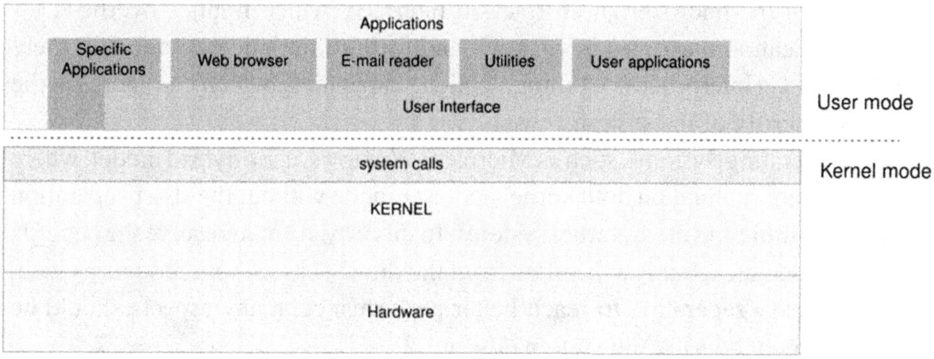

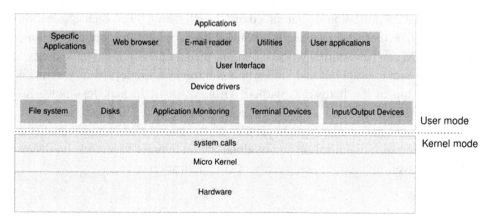

An opposite approach to monolithic design is the microkernel architecture, illustrated in Figure 2. In this architecture, the microkernel is composed only by the fundamental components of the Operating System, such as the interrupt and clock device drivers. Other services and device drivers: file system and disk servers, terminal devices, application monitoring, input/output device controllers and other OS components run in user mode, which means they are under the same privilege level of user space applications, i.e., cannot access hardware directly but only through the abstraction interface with the microkernel. On the one hand, if some device driver or other component running on user space fails, the microkernel is not directly compromised, and it has a chance to perform recovery procedures or in the worst case, a gracefully reset.

The code of a microkernel can be kept simpler and smaller when compared with monolithic kernels, it can also be very modularized as components will be

Figure 2. A microkernel architecture for an operating system

implemented as user space processes. However, all access to the hardware shall be made through the microkernel abstraction interface, which implies overhead for the communication messages going back and forth to the microkernel, i.e., there are a lot of IPC (Interprocess Communication) happening, which can increase the overall complexity of the system.

Some Operating Systems, such as Microsoft Windows, use a hybrid model, where components are running on both kernel and user mode without the strict separation seen in monolithic and microkernel systems. In this way, it could receive the benefits of both architectures, but it will suffer from the drawbacks of both models as well. There is no easy separation to reach better performance, many aspects should be taken into account during the system design.

Another different approach is the Library Operating Systems (Porter et al., 2011), an old and simple design that has been specialized into a new approach called Unikernel (Madhavapeddy et al., 2013), a topic that has been researched and used more frequently in the last few years, generally with the focus on cloud environments (Kuenzer et al., 2021; Chen et al., 2022; Cha et al., 2022). As illustrated by Figure 3, in such designs, the Operating System, system libraries, application libraries and the user application run as a single entity in kernel mode. Every piece of software that is needed to support an application is provided in a single image. This particular setup can be interesting for Virtualized environments. As the hardware became more powerful, maintenance complexity and security hazards issues have also increased. Virtualization technologies have emerged to address these issues (Laadan & Nieh, 2010). Processor architectures have been updated in order to allow different Virtual Machines (VMs), with different Operating Systems, running on the same system. This environment is particularly interesting for servers and cloud systems but it has been used in embedded systems as well (Tiburski et al., 2021). Instead of running several applications on top of a complex (and big) Operating System, several VMs can be deployed, each one running a single application as a specialized Unikernel image. Only the components needed by the corresponding application will be part of the Unikernel and the insulation is guaranteed by Virtualization. Since each application is running alone, there is no need to run it inside user space. If the application fails, the whole VM can be restarted without compromising other system applications.

It's important to point out that Unikernels can run as a single VM or baremetal (directly on top of the hardware, without virtualization). In fact, less powerful embedded systems also use a single image (Library OS) when protection is not available, i.e., when there is only one privileged execution level. Nevertheless, it is desired to keep such organization and modularization in order to provide hardware abstraction layers and reduce complexity of the application code.

Figure 3. A Unikernel architecture for an operating system

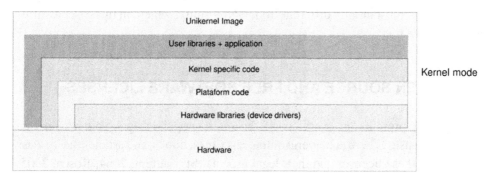

Licensing and Naming

A solid knowledge of Operating System architectures is a key factor for the understanding of the licensing processing. The way that the OS is structured can directly impact licensing obligations depending on the terms of the respective license. In microkernel architecture, for instance, a third-party device driver could run as a user space application without requiring the source code or any changes of the microkernel. However, in a monolithic architecture, a third-party device driver should be loaded and run along with the kernel (inside kernel space). Sources of the kernel might be needed to build the third-party code. In a Unikernel, the third-party and the kernel codes will be linked together into a single image. The dependency between third-party applications and the kernel will represent a key factor when addressing issues regarding derivative work.

There is another important topic regarding the definition of Operating Systems. Besides providing hardware abstraction and resourcing management, the overall goal of an Operating System is to allow applications to run and use the hardware resources besides giving usability of the system to users. The kernel is the core, an essential component of the Operating System. However, it's useless to the user by itself (Stallman, 2021). A set of system utilities, libraries and programs are required to provide the full functionality of an OS. Although the term Operating System has been used undistinguished to refer to the kernel and to the whole OS, knowing these nuances is essential to avoid confusion and misusing names, such as Linux vs. GNU/Linux. Linux refers to the Linux kernel, and GNU/Linux refers to the Operating System composed by a Linux kernel plus a set of programs developed by the GNU project, which is the case for almost every so-called "Linux distribution", which in fact, should be called GNU/Linux distribution, since is an Operating System composed by the Linux kernel and the GNU artifacts. Another interesting case is the Android Operating System, which also uses a Linux kernel, but is followed by a set of libraries and tools majorly developed by the Android project. The architecture of Android is substantially different from GNU/Linux, which, in this case, justifies different naming.

MAIN OPEN SOURCE AND FREE SOFTWARE LICENSES

This section presents an overview of the main (popular) open source and free software licenses. There are several online resources, books, and articles that discuss in detail all these licenses and their legal aspects (St. Laurent, 2004; Rosen, 2005; Gérman et al., 2007; Gérman & Hassan, 2009; Gérman et al., 2010). Websites of organizations, such as the FSF - Free Software Foundation (http://www.fsf.org) and the Open Source Initiative (https://opensource.org/) provide licenses in their full contents along with frequently asked questions, guides and information for licensors and licensees. The licenses covered by this section are:

- **MIT (*The MIT License*, n.d.)**
- **BSD (*The 3-Clause BSD License*, n.d.)**
- **Apache 2.0 (*Apache License, Version 2.0*, n.d.)**
- **GPL (*The GNU General Public License v2.0*, n.d.)**
- **LGPL (*GNU Lesser General Public License v2.1*, n.d.)**

Before discussing each one of these licenses, it's important mentioning about the SPDX (Software Package Data Exchange) specification(Stewart et al., 2010; O'Neall, n.d.), released in 2010 with the goal to develop and promote open standards in order to facilitate compliance with free software and open source licenses, it is defined as a standard format for communicating the components, licenses and copyrights associated with software packages. For instance, this specification defines unique short identifiers for conformant FOSS licenses, which can be used along with software packages to enable efficient and reliable identification of such licenses. Thus, by using these unique identifiers, there are no doubts on which license it is referring to.

The MIT License

The MIT license (SPDX short identifier: MIT), along with the BSD license, is one of the earliest open source licenses. It was created at the Massachusetts Institute of Technology in the late 1980s with the development of the X Window System, that's why sometimes it is also referred to as X or X11 license (with some small variations). The license itself it's straightforward and has the following contents:

Copyright <YEAR> <COPYRIGHT HOLDER>

Permission is hereby granted, free of charge, to any person obtaining a copy of this software and associated documentation files (the "Software"), to deal in the Software without restriction, including without limitation the rights to use, copy, modify, merge, publish, distribute, sublicense, and/or sell copies of the Software, and to permit persons to whom the Software is furnished to do so, subject to the following conditions:

The above copyright notice and this permission notice shall be included in all copies or substantial portions of the Software.

THE SOFTWARE IS PROVIDED "AS IS", WITHOUT WARRANTY OF ANY KIND, EXPRESS OR IMPLIED, INCLUDING BUT NOT LIMITED TO THE WARRANTIES OF MERCHANTABILITY, FITNESS FOR A PARTICULAR PURPOSE AND NONINFRINGEMENT. IN NO EVENT SHALL THE AUTHORS OR COPYRIGHT HOLDERS BE LIABLE FOR ANY CLAIM, DAMAGES OR OTHER LIABILITY, WHETHER IN AN ACTION OF CONTRACT, TORT OR OTHERWISE, ARISING FROM, OUT OF OR IN CONNECTION WITH THE SOFTWARE OR THE USE OR OTHER DEALINGS IN THE SOFTWARE.

The first sentence of the license is the copyright notice, where the author (or authors) claims the authorship of the respective work. The second paragraph states the terms of the license: the licensee (the person and or entity who is receiving the work) has no restrictions or limitations to use, copy, modify, merge, publish, i.e., make any derivative work and distribute it under (or not) the terms of the same license. It can also sublicense and sell the Software without the release of the source code. All these terms make MIT a permissive license. There is only one condition stated by the third paragraph: The original copyright notice and the permission notice shall be kept in all copies or substation portions of the software. A variation of the MIT license, called MIT No Attribution (SPDX short identifier: MIT-0) removes the third paragraph.

The fourth paragraph is present in almost all FOSS licenses and states about the lack of absolutely any kind of warranty by the copyright holders, who cannot be liable for any claim, damages or other liability. It's important to point out, nonetheless, that in most cases warranty can still be provided via an agreement (unless explicitly forbidden by the license). For example, a company selling a support service for a FOSS licensed software, can sell warranty as part of its services, the license doesn't change, but the liability will rely on the company and not on the copyright holders (unless in case they are the same).

The BSD License

The BSD license originated at University of Berkley, California, with the Berkeley Software Distribution (BSD), an Operating System developed by the Computer Systems Research Group (CSRG) that was based on earlier versions of Unix. Like the MIT, the BSD license is also a permissive license and it was the foundation for several BSD license variants, usually differing by small variations in the text and number of main clauses. The original version, nowadays called as the BSD 4-clause license, contained a clause stating:

All advertising materials mentioning features or use of this software must display the following acknowledgement: This product includes software developed by the <copyright holder>.

This clause sometimes causes problems with the commercial exploration of the software. The name of copyright holders can be used deliberately to promote the software instead of acknowledging the original authors. In the case of BSD OS, the name of University of Berkeley started to be used in advertising materials on purpose to potentially endorse a derivative proprietary work. The license was changed in 1999 and this clause was removed. This section will cover the BSD 3-Clause license (SPDX short identifier: BSD-3-Clause), also known as the "New" or "Revised" license. The full contents of this license are:

Copyright <YEAR> <COPYRIGHT HOLDER>

Redistribution and use in source and binary forms, with or without modification, are permitted provided that the following conditions are met:

1. Redistributions of source code must retain the above copyright notice, this list of conditions and the following disclaimer.

2. Redistributions in binary form must reproduce the above copyright notice, this list of conditions and the following disclaimer in the documentation and/or other materials provided with the distribution.

3. Neither the name of the copyright holder nor the names of its contributors may be used to endorse or promote products derived from this software without specific prior written permission.

THIS SOFTWARE IS PROVIDED BY THE COPYRIGHT HOLDERS AND CONTRIBUTORS "AS IS" AND ANY EXPRESS OR IMPLIED WARRANTIES, INCLUDING, BUT NOT LIMITED TO, THE IMPLIED WARRANTIES OF

MERCHANTABILITY AND FITNESS FOR A PARTICULAR PURPOSE ARE DISCLAIMED. IN NO EVENT SHALL THE COPYRIGHT HOLDER OR CONTRIBUTORS BE LIABLE FOR ANY DIRECT, INDIRECT, INCIDENTAL, SPECIAL, EXEMPLARY, OR CONSEQUENTIAL DAMAGES (INCLUDING, BUT NOT LIMITED TO, PROCUREMENT OF SUBSTITUTE GOODS OR SERVICES; LOSS OF USE, DATA, OR PROFITS; OR BUSINESS INTERRUPTION) HOWEVER CAUSED AND ON ANY THEORY OF LIABILITY, WHETHER IN CONTRACT, STRICT LIABILITY, OR TORT (INCLUDING NEGLIGENCE OR OTHERWISE) ARISING IN ANY WAY OUT OF THE USE OF THIS SOFTWARE, EVEN IF ADVISED OF THE POSSIBILITY OF SUCH DAMAGE.

The first sentence is the copyright notice. The second paragraph states that the software can be used in source and binary forms, with or without modification as long as the conditions pointed in the license are met. Then, clauses 1. and 2. ask for basically the same conditions as in MIT license: redistributions of source code or binary form must retain the copyright notice, the clauses and the license disclaimer. This information must be present in sources, documentation and/or other materials provided by the distribution. However, it differs from the MIT license in Clause 3., that states that the name of copyright holder and contributors may not be used to endorse or promote derivative works without specific prior written permission. This clause protects the original licensors from having their image or reputation used (and even affected) by derivative works that could take advantage of their names in order to make self-promotion.

The last paragraph is the disclaimer of warranties, which is similar to the MIT license. The software is provided expressly without any kind of warranties.

The Apache License

The Apache license, like MIT and BSD, is a permissive license that was created by the ASF - Apache Software Foundation (https://www.apache.org/) in order to license the Apache Web Server. Its first version (Apache 1.0) was released in 1995 and was very similar to the BSD license, including the clause about the obligation to cite the Apache Group (former ASF's name) in advertising materials. In 1999, ASF followed the BSD license removing this clause and releasing the Apache 1.1 version. In 2004, a revised and more complete version of the license was approved and published by ASF as the Apache 2.0 (SPDX short identifier: Apache-2.0). This is still the current version of the license and has the following contents:

TERMS AND CONDITIONS FOR USE, REPRODUCTION, AND DISTRIBUTION

1. Definitions.

*"**License**" shall mean the terms and conditions for use, reproduction, and distribution as defined by Sections 1 through 9 of this document.*

*"**Licensor**" shall mean the copyright owner or entity authorized by the copyright owner that is granting the License.*

*"**Legal Entity**" shall mean the union of the acting entity and all other entities that control, are controlled by, or are under common control with that entity. For the purposes of this definition, "**control**" means (i) the power, direct or indirect, to cause the direction or management of such entity, whether by contract or otherwise, or (ii) ownership of fifty percent (50%) or more of the outstanding shares, or (iii) beneficial ownership of such entity.*

*"**You**" (or "**Your**") shall mean an individual or Legal Entity exercising permissions granted by this License.*

*"**Source**" form shall mean the preferred form for making modifications, including but not limited to software source code, documentation source, and configuration files.*

*"**Object**" form shall mean any form resulting from mechanical transformation or translation of a Source form, including but not limited to compiled object code, generated documentation, and conversions to other media types.*

*"**Work**" shall mean the work of authorship, whether in Source or Object form, made available under the License, as indicated by a copyright notice that is included in or attached to the work (an example is provided in the Appendix below).*

*"**Derivative Works**" shall mean any work, whether in Source or Object form, that is based on (or derived from) the Work and for which the editorial revisions, annotations, elaborations, or other modifications represent, as a whole, an original work of authorship. For the purposes of this License, Derivative Works shall not include works that remain separable from, or merely link (or bind by name) to the interfaces of, the Work and Derivative Works thereof.*

*"**Contribution**" shall mean any work of authorship, including the original version of the Work and any modifications or additions to that Work or Derivative Works thereof, that is intentionally submitted to Licensor for inclusion in the Work by the copyright owner or by an individual or Legal Entity authorized to submit on behalf*

*of the copyright owner. For the purposes of this definition, "**submitted**" means any form of electronic, verbal, or written communication sent to the Licensor or its representatives, including but not limited to communication on electronic mailing lists, source code control systems, and issue tracking systems that are managed by, or on behalf of, the Licensor for the purpose of discussing and improving the Work, but excluding communication that is conspicuously marked or otherwise designated in writing by the copyright owner as "**Not a Contribution.**"*

*"**Contributor**" shall mean Licensor and any individual or Legal Entity on behalf of whom a Contribution has been received by Licensor and subsequently incorporated within the Work.*

2. Grant of Copyright License. *Subject to the terms and conditions of this License, each Contributor hereby grants to You a perpetual, worldwide, non-exclusive, no-charge, royalty-free, irrevocable copyright license to reproduce, prepare Derivative Works of, publicly display, publicly perform, sublicense, and distribute the Work and such Derivative Works in Source or Object form.*

3. Grant of Patent License. *Subject to the terms and conditions of this License, each Contributor hereby grants to You a perpetual, worldwide, non-exclusive, no-charge, royalty-free, irrevocable (except as stated in this section) patent license to make, have made, use, offer to sell, sell, import, and otherwise transfer the Work, where such license applies only to those patent claims licensable by such Contributor that are necessarily infringed by their Contribution(s) alone or by combination of their Contribution(s) with the Work to which such Contribution(s) was submitted. If You institute patent litigation against any entity (including a cross-claim or counterclaim in a lawsuit) alleging that the Work or a Contribution incorporated within the Work constitutes direct or contributory patent infringement, then any patent licenses granted to You under this License for that Work shall terminate as of the date such litigation is filed.*

4. Redistribution. *You may reproduce and distribute copies of the Work or Derivative Works thereof in any medium, with or without modifications, and in Source or Object form, provided that You meet the following conditions:*

1. You must give any other recipients of the Work or Derivative Works a copy of this License; and

2. You must cause any modified files to carry prominent notices stating that You changed the files; and

3. You must retain, in the Source form of any Derivative Works that You distribute, all copyright, patent, trademark, and attribution notices from the Source form of the Work, excluding those notices that do not pertain to any part of the Derivative Works; and

*4. If the Work includes a "***NOTICE***" text file as part of its distribution, then any Derivative Works that You distribute must include a readable copy of the attribution notices contained within such NOTICE file, excluding those notices that do not pertain to any part of the Derivative Works, in at least one of the following places: within a NOTICE text file distributed as part of the Derivative Works; within the Source form or documentation, if provided along with the Derivative Works; or, within a display generated by the Derivative Works, if and wherever such third-party notices normally appear. The contents of the NOTICE file are for informational purposes only and do not modify the License. You may add Your own attribution notices within Derivative Works that You distribute, alongside or as an addendum to the NOTICE text from the Work, provided that such additional attribution notices cannot be construed as modifying the License.*

You may add Your own copyright statement to Your modifications and may provide additional or different license terms and conditions for use, reproduction, or distribution of Your modifications, or for any such Derivative Works as a whole, provided Your use, reproduction, and distribution of the Work otherwise complies with the conditions stated in this License.

5. Submission of Contributions. *Unless You explicitly state otherwise, any Contribution intentionally submitted for inclusion in the Work by You to the Licensor shall be under the terms and conditions of this License, without any additional terms or conditions. Notwithstanding the above, nothing herein shall supersede or modify the terms of any separate license agreement you may have executed with Licensor regarding such Contributions.*

6. Trademarks. *This License does not grant permission to use the trade names, trademarks, service marks, or product names of the Licensor, except as required for reasonable and customary use in describing the origin of the Work and reproducing the content of the NOTICE file.*

7. Disclaimer of Warranty. *Unless required by applicable law or agreed to in writing, Licensor provides the Work (and each Contributor provides its Contributions) on an "AS IS" BASIS, WITHOUT WARRANTIES OR CONDITIONS OF ANY KIND, either express or implied, including, without limitation, any warranties or* *conditions of TITLE, NON-INFRINGEMENT, MERCHANTABILITY, or FITNESS FOR A PARTICULAR PURPOSE. You are solely responsible for determining the appropriateness of using or redistributing the Work and assume any risks associated with Your exercise of permissions under this License.*

8. Limitation of Liability. *In no event and under no legal theory, whether in tort (including negligence), contract, or otherwise, unless required by applicable law (such as deliberate and grossly negligent acts) or agreed to in writing, shall any Contributor be liable to You for damages, including any direct, indirect, special, incidental, or consequential damages of any character arising as a result of this License or out of the use or inability to use the Work (including but not limited to damages for loss of goodwill, work stoppage, computer failure or malfunction, or any and all other commercial damages or losses), even if such Contributor has been advised of the possibility of such damages.*

9. Accepting Warranty or Additional Liability. *While redistributing the Work or Derivative Works thereof, You may choose to offer, and charge a fee for, acceptance of support, warranty, indemnity, or other liability obligations and/or rights consistent with this License. However, in accepting such obligations, You may act only on Your own behalf and on Your sole responsibility, not on behalf of any other Contributor, and only if You agree to indemnify, defend, and hold each Contributor harmless for any liability incurred by, or claims asserted against, such Contributor by reason of your accepting any such warranty or additional liability.*

END OF TERMS AND CONDITIONS

The license is composed by nine sections:

- Section 1: It defines all important terms used throughout the license. Some definitions are straightforward (what is a License, Licensor, Sources, Object, etc). However, two terms are worth it to be discussed: Derivative Works and Contribution. According to the license, "Derivative Works" shall mean any work (either in Sources or Object form) that includes modifications, revisions, annotations and any elaborations that represent, as a whole, an original work of authorship. If the work can remain separated from the original work or be only linked or have names changed in the original interfaces, then it is not considered a derivative work. The term "Contribution" shall mean any derivative work (modifications, additions, fixes) that is sent to the original licensor in order to be integrated into the original work, under the control (and copyright) of the licensor and under the same license.

- Section 2: States the grant of copyright license. It basically grants to licensees the rights to reproduce, prepare derivative works of, sublicense, and distribute the work and derivative works in source or object format.
- Section 3: It grants to licensees a perpetual, worldwide, non-exclusive, no-charge, royalty-free, irrevocable patent license to those patents that are needed to use the original work. It doesn't cover patents that could eventually be issued separated from the work. If the licensee institutes a patent litigation against any entity (licensors, contributors, etc) any patent licenses granted for that work shall terminate as of the date such litigation is filed.
- Section 4: States all the terms for redistribution of the work or derivative works, such as providing the copy of the license, noticing about changed files (when applicable) and instructions about attribution notices for derivative works.
- Section 5: Any contribution sent to the licensors in order to be integrated to the original work shall be licensed under the same terms of the original license and under control of the licensor, unless an specific agreement with other terms is made with the licensor.
- Section 6: Explicitly forbids the use of the name of the licensor to promote or endorse derivative works, unless when the name is used to describe the origin of the derivative work.
- Sections 7 and 8: States about the lack of warranties and liability working in the same way as in MIT and BSD licenses.
- Section 9: States about the permission for derivative works to provide warranties through some agreement (with a charge of a fee, for instance) as long as it stays consistent with the license, which means that the limitation of liability of copyright holders must still be satisfied.

In summary, the Apache 2.0 license works in the same way as MIT and BSD licenses. However, some terms that are implicit in BSD and MIT, are explicitly defined in Apache 2.0, which can avoid misunderstanding or violations of the license. The section about the Grant of Patent License explicitly grants all permissions regarding patents rights that must be required to use the work. Also, the license explicitly defines all the terms for contributions and derivative works. On one hand, contributions sent to be integrated to the original work shall be licensed under the same terms of the original license. On the other hand, submitting contributions is not mandatory; licensees are also free to release their derivative work under another license.

Table 1. Versions of the GNU general public license

License Name and Version	SPDX Short Identifier
GNU General Public License v1.0 only	GPL-1.0-only
GNU General Public License v1.0 or later	GPL-1.0-or-later
GNU General Public License v2.0 only	GPL-2.0-only
GNU General Public License v2.0 or later	GPL-2.0-or-later
GNU General Public License v3.0 only	GPL-3.0-only
GNU General Public License v3.0 or later	GPL-3.0-or-later

The GNU General Public License (GPL)

The original GNU General Public License (GPL) was written by Richard M. Stallman, published in 1989 with the goal to be used with the software from the GNU project (created by him in 1983) and guarantee freedom to users to use, share, modify and redistribute modified versions of free software. Three versions of the license were released throughout the years; all of them can be used through two small variations, as listed by Table 1.

In contrast with the licenses discussed so far (MIT, BSD and Apache), the GNU GPL is not a permissive license. Instead, it enforces what is so called nowadays as Copyleft, i.e., copyright holder uses his or her rights granted by the copyright law to grant to licensees the right to use, share, change and redistribute modifications of the original software. However, any derivative work must be released under the terms of the same license, which means that the source code must be available - particularly, a licensee cannot make a commercial (closed source) application derived from a GPL software and release it under another license.

There are two small variations on how each version can be used by licensor(s): one states that the software is licensed exclusively on the terms of that particular version of the license; the other one states that the software is licensed under the terms of the current version, or any later version. There is a clause on the license provisioning this option and the changes rely only on the declaration of the license in the sources and corresponding artifacts of the software.

GPL version 1 and version 2 are very similar. Version 3.0 introduced important changes related to patents, free software compatibility and hardware restrictions against derivative works. The main discussion presented here will be made over the GPL version 2, which includes all the core terms of GPL licensing and is the license used by many embedded projects, specially the Linux kernel, present in millions of embedded devices around the globe. The differences of version 3 will be discussed further, though. The GPL version 2.0 has the following contents:

GNU GENERAL PUBLIC LICENSE

Version 2, June 1991

Copyright (C) 1989, 1991 Free Software Foundation, Inc.

51 Franklin Street, Fifth Floor, Boston, MA 02110-1301, USA

Everyone is permitted to copy and distribute verbatim copies of this license document, but changing it is not allowed.

Preamble

The licenses for most software are designed to take away your freedom to share and change it. By contrast, the GNU General Public License is intended to guarantee your freedom to share and change free software--to make sure the software is free for all its users. This General Public License applies to most of the Free Software Foundation's software and to any other program whose authors commit to using it. (Some other Free Software Foundation software is covered by the GNU Lesser General Public License instead.) You can apply it to your programs, too.

When we speak of free software, we are referring to freedom, not price. Our General Public Licenses are designed to make sure that you have the freedom to distribute copies of free software (and charge for this service if you wish), that you receive source code or can get it if you want it, that you can change the software or use pieces of it in new free programs; and that you know you can do these things.

To protect your rights, we need to make restrictions that forbid anyone to deny you these rights or to ask you to surrender the rights. These restrictions translate to certain responsibilities for you if you distribute copies of the software, or if you modify it.

For example, if you distribute copies of such a program, whether gratis or for a fee, you must give the recipients all the rights that you have. You must make sure that they, too, receive or can get the source code. And you must show them these terms so they know their rights.

We protect your rights with two steps: (1) copyright the software, and (2) offer you this license which gives you legal permission to copy, distribute and/or modify the software.

Also, for each author's protection and ours, we want to make certain that everyone understands that there is no warranty for this free software. If the software is modified by someone else and passed on, we want its recipients to know that what they have is not the original, so that any problems introduced by others will not reflect on the original authors' reputations.

Finally, any free program is threatened constantly by software patents. We wish to avoid the danger that redistributors of a free program will individually obtain patent licenses, in effect making the program proprietary. To prevent this, we have made it clear that any patent must be licensed for everyone's free use or not licensed at all.

The precise terms and conditions for copying, distribution and modification follow.

TERMS AND CONDITIONS FOR COPYING, DISTRIBUTION AND MODIFICATION

0. This License applies to any program or other work which contains a notice placed by the copyright holder saying it may be distributed under the terms of this General Public License. The "Program", below, refers to any such program or work, and a "work based on the Program" means either the Program or any derivative work under copyright law: that is to say, a work containing the Program or a portion of it, either verbatim or with modifications and/or translated into another language. (Hereinafter, translation is included without limitation in the term "modification".) Each licensee is addressed as "you".

Activities other than copying, distribution and modification are not covered by this License; they are outside its scope. The act of running the Program is not restricted, and the output from the Program is covered only if its contents constitute a work based on the Program (independent of having been made by running the Program). Whether that is true depends on what the Program does.

1. You may copy and distribute verbatim copies of the Program's source code as you receive it, in any medium, provided that you conspicuously and appropriately publish on each copy an appropriate copyright notice and disclaimer of warranty; keep intact all the notices that refer to this License and to the absence of any warranty; and give any other recipients of the Program a copy of this License along with the Program.

You may charge a fee for the physical act of transferring a copy, and you may at your option offer warranty protection in exchange for a fee.

2. You may modify your copy or copies of the Program or any portion of it, thus forming a work based on the Program, and copy and distribute such modifications or work under the terms of Section 1 above, provided that you also meet all of these conditions:

a) You must cause the modified files to carry prominent notices stating that you changed the files and the date of any change.

b) You must cause any work that you distribute or publish, that in whole or in part contains or is derived from the Program or any part thereof, to be licensed as a whole at no charge to all third parties under the terms of this License.

c) If the modified program normally reads commands interactively when run, you must cause it, when started running for such interactive use in the most ordinary way, to print or display an announcement including an appropriate copyright notice and a notice that there is no warranty (or else, saying that you provide a warranty) and that users may redistribute the program under these conditions, and telling the user how to view a copy of this License. (Exception: if the Program itself is interactive but does not normally print such an announcement, your work based on the Program is not required to print an announcement.)

These requirements apply to the modified work as a whole. If identifiable sections of that work are not derived from the Program, and can be reasonably considered independent and separate works in themselves, then this License, and its terms, do not apply to those sections when you distribute them as separate works. But when you distribute the same sections as part of a whole which is a work based on the Program, the distribution of the whole must be on the terms of this License, whose permissions for other licensees extend to the entire whole, and thus to each and every part regardless of who wrote it.

Thus, it is not the intent of this section to claim rights or contest your rights to work written entirely by you; rather, the intent is to exercise the right to control the distribution of derivative or collective works based on the Program.

In addition, mere aggregation of another work not based on the Program with the Program (or with a work based on the Program) on a volume of a storage or distribution medium does not bring the other work under the scope of this License.

3. You may copy and distribute the Program (or a work based on it, under Section 2) in object code or executable form under the terms of Sections 1 and 2 above provided that you also do one of the following:

a) Accompany it with the complete corresponding machine-readable source code, which must be distributed under the terms of Sections 1 and 2 above on a medium customarily used for software interchange; or,

b) Accompany it with a written offer, valid for at least three years, to give any third party, for a charge no more than your cost of physically performing source distribution, a complete machine-readable copy of the corresponding source code, to be distributed under the terms of Sections 1 and 2 above on a medium customarily used for software interchange; or,

c) Accompany it with the information you received as to the offer to distribute corresponding source code. (This alternative is allowed only for noncommercial distribution and only if you received the program in object code or executable form with such an offer, in accord with Subsection b above.)

The source code for a work means the preferred form of the work for making modifications to it. For an executable work, complete source code means all the source code for all modules it contains, plus any associated interface definition files, plus the scripts used to control compilation and installation of the executable. However, as a special exception, the source code distributed need not include anything that is normally distributed (in either source or binary form) with the major components (compiler, kernel, and so on) of the operating system on which the executable runs, unless that component itself accompanies the executable.

If distribution of executable or object code is made by offering access to copy from a designated place, then offering equivalent access to copy the source code from the same place counts as distribution of the source code, even though third parties are not compelled to copy the source along with the object code.

4. You may not copy, modify, sublicense, or distribute the Program except as expressly provided under this License. Any attempt otherwise to copy, modify, sublicense or distribute the Program is void, and will automatically terminate your rights under this License. However, parties who have received copies, or rights, from you under this License will not have their licenses terminated so long as such parties remain in full compliance.

5. You are not required to accept this License, since you have not signed it. However, nothing else grants you permission to modify or distribute the Program or its derivative works. These actions are prohibited by law if you do not accept this License. Therefore, by modifying or distributing the Program (or any work based on the Program), you indicate your acceptance of this License to do so, and all its terms and conditions for copying, distributing or modifying the Program or works based on it.

6. Each time you redistribute the Program (or any work based on the Program), the recipient automatically receives a license from the original licensor to copy, distribute or modify the Program subject to these terms and conditions. You may not impose any further restrictions on the recipients' exercise of the rights granted herein. You are not responsible for enforcing compliance by third parties to this License.

7. If, as a consequence of a court judgment or allegation of patent infringement or for any other reason (not limited to patent issues), conditions are imposed on you (whether by court order, agreement or otherwise) that contradict the conditions of this License, they do not excuse you from the conditions of this License. If you cannot distribute so as to satisfy simultaneously your obligations under this License and any other pertinent obligations, then as a consequence you may not distribute the Program at all. For example, if a patent license would not permit royalty-free redistribution of the Program by all those who receive copies directly or indirectly through you, then the only way you could satisfy both it and this License would be to refrain entirely from distribution of the Program.

If any portion of this section is held invalid or unenforceable under any particular circumstance, the balance of the section is intended to apply and the section as a whole is intended to apply in other circumstances.

It is not the purpose of this section to induce you to infringe any patents or other property right claims or to contest validity of any such claims; this section has the sole purpose of protecting the integrity of the free software distribution system, which is implemented by public license practices. Many people have made generous contributions to the wide range of software distributed through that system in reliance on consistent application of that system; it is up to the author/donor to decide if he or she is willing to distribute software through any other system and a licensee cannot impose that choice.

This section is intended to make thoroughly clear what is believed to be a consequence of the rest of this License.

8. If the distribution and/or use of the Program is restricted in certain countries either by patents or by copyrighted interfaces, the original copyright holder who places the Program under this License may add an explicit geographical distribution limitation excluding those countries, so that distribution is permitted only in or among countries not thus excluded. In such case, this License incorporates the limitation as if written in the body of this License.

9. The Free Software Foundation may publish revised and/or new versions of the General Public License from time to time. Such new versions will be similar in spirit to the present version, but may differ in detail to address new problems or concerns.

Each version is given a distinguishing version number. If the Program specifies a version number of this License which applies to it and "any later version", you have the option of following the terms and conditions either of that version or of any later version published by the Free Software Foundation. If the Program does not specify a version number of this License, you may choose any version ever published by the Free Software Foundation.

10. If you wish to incorporate parts of the Program into other free programs whose distribution conditions are different, write to the author to ask for permission. For software which is copyrighted by the Free Software Foundation, write to the Free Software Foundation; we sometimes make exceptions for this. Our decision will be guided by the two goals of preserving the free status of all derivatives of our free software and of promoting the sharing and reuse of software generally.

NO WARRANTY

11. BECAUSE THE PROGRAM IS LICENSED FREE OF CHARGE, THERE IS NO WARRANTY FOR THE PROGRAM, TO THE EXTENT PERMITTED BY APPLICABLE LAW. EXCEPT WHEN OTHERWISE STATED IN WRITING THE COPYRIGHT HOLDERS AND/OR OTHER PARTIES PROVIDE THE PROGRAM "AS IS" WITHOUT WARRANTY OF ANY KIND, EITHER EXPRESSED OR IMPLIED, INCLUDING, BUT NOT LIMITED TO, THE IMPLIED WARRANTIES OF MERCHANTABILITY AND FITNESS FOR A PARTICULAR PURPOSE. THE ENTIRE RISK AS TO THE QUALITY AND PERFORMANCE OF THE PROGRAM IS WITH YOU. SHOULD THE PROGRAM PROVE DEFECTIVE, YOU ASSUME THE COST OF ALL NECESSARY SERVICING, REPAIR OR CORRECTION.

12. IN NO EVENT UNLESS REQUIRED BY APPLICABLE LAW OR AGREED TO IN WRITING WILL ANY COPYRIGHT HOLDER, OR ANY OTHER PARTY

WHO MAY MODIFY AND/OR REDISTRIBUTE THE PROGRAM AS PERMITTED ABOVE, BE LIABLE TO YOU FOR DAMAGES, INCLUDING ANY GENERAL, SPECIAL, INCIDENTAL OR CONSEQUENTIAL DAMAGES ARISING OUT OF THE USE OR INABILITY TO USE THE PROGRAM (INCLUDING BUT NOT LIMITED TO LOSS OF DATA OR DATA BEING RENDERED INACCURATE OR LOSSES SUSTAINED BY YOU OR THIRD PARTIES OR A FAILURE OF THE PROGRAM TO OPERATE WITH ANY OTHER PROGRAMS), EVEN IF SUCH HOLDER OR OTHER PARTY HAS BEEN ADVISED OF THE POSSIBILITY OF SUCH DAMAGES.

END OF TERMS AND CONDITIONS

The license is composed by a preamble, which gives an overview and goals of license terms, followed by 13 clauses (enumerated from 0 to 12): each one of them states in detail all terms and conditions applied on copying, modifying and distributing the licensed software. It ends with clauses about lack of warranty and no liability of copyright holders. The GNU GPL guarantees freedom to licensees to use (as they want), share, modify and distribute modified versions of the work under the same terms of the license. It emphasizes that free doesn't mean free of charge, but free as a freedom. Licensees can sell copies of the software within a media source and charge a fee for the media, for instance, but not for the software itself. Also, making source code available is a requirement to meet all terms of the license.

Regarding derivative works, the license states that its terms applies on any modified work as a whole, i.e., if a new portion that was included in the software, is not derived from it, and can be reasonably considered independent and separate work, then the license doesn't apply to this portion when distributing as a separate work. However, any modification or additions (no matter how big or even translations to another language) that are derived from or dependent on the software to work, are considered as derivative work and must be under the terms of the license. For example, any code added and distributed along with the GPL software must be under the same license terms. In the beginning, this condition created an issue specially for users that would like to use GNU libraries (licensed under the GPL) with proprietary software. Although the libraries can be used without any modification or additional piece of code, linking (statically) a proprietary code with a GPL software library would combine GPL and proprietary code in the same binary, which can be seen (legally) as a derivative work. In such a case, the combined work would be released under the proprietary license, violating the GPL. In order to eliminate any ambiguity or wangle about these cases, and allow the spread of the use of GNU libraries, the GNU LGPL, initially called GNU Library General Public License was released in 1991 along with the GPL version 2. In 1999, a revised version was released under a slightly different acronym, the GNU Lesser General Public License. In general the LGPL preserves many of the rights of the GPL license. However, it allows proprietary code to be linked with non-GPL programs.

The GNU GPL Version 3

The version 3 of GNU GPL (SPDX short identifier GPL-3.0-only for attribution only or GPL-3.0-or-later for no version attribution) was released on June 29 in 2007. A very good quick guide to the main differences in the license compared with older versions can be found at (Smith, 2008). The version 3 keeps all rights (and freedom) of former versions, it revises the text changing some terms, and most notable, it introduces some important terms that are worth of discussing:

- Protecting Users' Legal Rights From Anti-Circumvention Law: A new clause was added to protect users against a process sometimes called "Tivoization". This term was coined by Richard Stallman in allusion to Tivo Corporation, a manufacturer of DVRs (digital video recorders) that used GPLed code in their equipment (specially the Linux kernel), but incorporated hardware mechanisms to allow only signed firmware to be booted and run by the machine. Therefore, only firmwares released by TiVo could be executed in their equipment. In this way, even releasing the source code and being in conformance with all GPL (up version 2) terms, the manufacturer was able to block users from using the available source code to develop custom firmware that could run in their equipment. The GPLv3 explicitly forbids this practice.
- Besides "Tivoization", GPLv3 also guarantees users the freedom to write and distribute GPLv3 software that can bypass restriction mechanisms, such as DRM (Digital Rights Management), without being threatened by laws that make it illegal to write such type of software (like the DMCA - Digital Millennium Copyright Act). This is an interesting clause because it doesn't prohibit DRM mechanisms to be developed with GPLv3 code. However, if any code released under GPLv3 is used to develop such a mechanism, the license states that this mechanism will not count as an effective technological "protection" measure. Thus, any code that breaks and/or bypasses this mechanism can be distributed unhindered by the DMCA and similar laws.
- Refined terms against patent threats: Version 3 enforces that any patent license necessary to exercise the rights given by the GPLed work must be provided. Therefore, it protects licensees from being sued later by a contributor of the GPLed work.
- Changes the term "distribution" to "convey": The term "distribution" can be treated differently by Copyright laws of other countries outside the United

States. Version 3 explicitly defines the term "convey" and uses it throughout the license to indicate all different ways that licensees can distribute the GPLed software.

It's important to point out that GPL version 2 is still in use by many projects, most notably by the Linux kernel, which is licensed under the GPL-2.0-only. Linus Torvalds, the creator and principal maintainer, several times made public criticisms of GPLv3, especially regarding the Anti-Tivoization terms. Nevertheless, GPLv3 has been widely adopted. In 2015, it represented the fifth most used license in GitHub repositories(*Open Source License Usage on GitHub.com*, 2015).

The GNU Lesser General Public License (LGPL)

The GNU LGPL was originally released in 1991 as the GNU Library General Public License (*GNU Library General Public License V2.0*, n.d.) by the Free Software Foundation. In 1999 it was released as the GNU Lesser General Public License under the version 2.1. The main goal of this license is to give to the users all rights provided by the GNU GPL, but it makes an exception that allows proprietary programs to be linked to LGPL libraries without obligating them to be under the terms of the same license. The LGPL version 2.1 has the following contents:

GNU LESSER GENERAL PUBLIC LICENSE

Version 2.1, February 1999

Copyright (C) 1991, 1999 Free Software Foundation, Inc.

51 Franklin Street, Fifth Floor, Boston, MA 02110-1301 USA

Everyone is permitted to copy and distribute verbatim copies of this license document, but changing it is not allowed.

[This is the first released version of the Lesser GPL. It also counts as the successor of the GNU Library Public License, version 2, hence the version number 2.1.]

Preamble

The licenses for most software are designed to take away your freedom to share and change it. By contrast, the GNU General Public Licenses are intended to guarantee your freedom to share and change free software--to make sure the software is free for all its users.

This license, the Lesser General Public License, applies to some specially designated software packages--typically libraries--of the Free Software Foundation and other authors who decide to use it. You can use it too, but we suggest you first think carefully about whether this license or the ordinary General Public License is the better strategy to use in any particular case, based on the explanations below.

When we speak of free software, we are referring to freedom of use, not price. Our General Public Licenses are designed to make sure that you have the freedom to distribute copies of free software (and charge for this service if you wish); that you receive source code or can get it if you want it; that you can change the software and use pieces of it in new free programs; and that you are informed that you can do these things.

To protect your rights, we need to make restrictions that forbid distributors to deny you these rights or to ask you to surrender these rights. These restrictions translate to certain responsibilities for you if you distribute copies of the library or if you modify it.

For example, if you distribute copies of the library, whether gratis or for a fee, you must give the recipients all the rights that we gave you. You must make sure that they, too, receive or can get the source code. If you link other code with the library, you must provide complete object files to the recipients, so that they can relink them with the library after making changes to the library and recompiling it. And you must show them these terms so they know their rights.

We protect your rights with a two-step method: (1) we copyright the library, and (2) we offer you this license, which gives you legal permission to copy, distribute and/or modify the library.

To protect each distributor, we want to make it very clear that there is no warranty for the free library. Also, if the library is modified by someone else and passed on, the recipients should know that what they have is not the original version, so that the original author's reputation will not be affected by problems that might be introduced by others.

Finally, software patents pose a constant threat to the existence of any free program. We wish to make sure that a company cannot effectively restrict the users of a free program by obtaining a restrictive license from a patent holder. Therefore, we insist that any patent license obtained for a version of the library must be consistent with the full freedom of use specified in this license.

Most GNU software, including some libraries, is covered by the ordinary GNU General Public License. This license, the GNU Lesser General Public License, applies to certain designated libraries, and is quite different from the ordinary General Public License. We use this license for certain libraries in order to permit linking those libraries into non-free programs.

When a program is linked with a library, whether statically or using a shared library, the combination of the two is legally speaking a combined work, a derivative of the original library. The ordinary General Public License therefore permits such linking only if the entire combination fits its criteria of freedom. The Lesser General Public License permits more lax criteria for linking other code with the library.

We call this license the "Lesser" General Public License because it does Less to protect the user's freedom than the ordinary General Public License. It also provides other free software developers Less of an advantage over competing non-free programs. These disadvantages are the reason we use the ordinary General Public License for many libraries. However, the Lesser license provides advantages in certain special circumstances.

For example, on rare occasions, there may be a special need to encourage the widest possible use of a certain library, so that it becomes a de-facto standard. To achieve this, non-free programs must be allowed to use the library. A more frequent case is that a free library does the same job as widely used non-free libraries. In this case, there is little to gain by limiting the free library to free software only, so we use the Lesser General Public License.

In other cases, permission to use a particular library in non-free programs enables a greater number of people to use a large body of free software. For example, permission to use the GNU C Library in non-free programs enables many more people to use the whole GNU operating system, as well as its variant, the GNU/ Linux operating system.

Although the Lesser General Public License is Less protective of the users' freedom, it does ensure that the user of a program that is linked with the Library has the freedom and the wherewithal to run that program using a modified version of the Library.

The precise terms and conditions for copying, distribution and modification follow. Pay close attention to the difference between a "work based on the library" and a "work that uses the library". The former contains code derived from the library, whereas the latter must be combined with the library in order to run.

TERMS AND CONDITIONS FOR COPYING, DISTRIBUTION AND MODIFICATION

0. This License Agreement applies to any software library or other program which contains a notice placed by the copyright holder or other authorized party saying it may be distributed under the terms of this Lesser General Public License (also called "this License"). Each licensee is addressed as "you".

A "library" means a collection of software functions and/or data prepared so as to be conveniently linked with application programs (which use some of those functions and data) to form executables.

The "Library", below, refers to any such software library or work which has been distributed under these terms. A "work based on the Library" means either the Library or any derivative work under copyright law: that is to say, a work containing the Library or a portion of it, either verbatim or with modifications and/or translated straightforwardly into another language. (Hereinafter, translation is included without limitation in the term "modification".)

"Source code" for a work means the preferred form of the work for making modifications to it. For a library, complete source code means all the source code for all modules it contains, plus any associated interface definition files, plus the scripts used to control compilation and installation of the library.

Activities other than copying, distribution and modification are not covered by this License; they are outside its scope. The act of running a program using the Library is not restricted, and output from such a program is covered only if its contents constitute a work based on the Library (independent of the use of the Library in a tool for writing it). Whether that is true depends on what the Library does and what the program that uses the Library does.

1. You may copy and distribute verbatim copies of the Library's complete source code as you receive it, in any medium, provided that you conspicuously and appropriately publish on each copy an appropriate copyright notice and disclaimer of warranty;

keep intact all the notices that refer to this License and to the absence of any warranty; and distribute a copy of this License along with the Library.

You may charge a fee for the physical act of transferring a copy, and you may at your option offer warranty protection in exchange for a fee.

2. You may modify your copy or copies of the Library or any portion of it, thus forming a work based on the Library, and copy and distribute such modifications or work under the terms of Section 1 above, provided that you also meet all of these conditions:

a) The modified work must itself be a software library.

b) You must cause the files modified to carry prominent notices stating that you changed the files and the date of any change.

c) You must cause the whole of the work to be licensed at no charge to all third parties under the terms of this License.

d) If a facility in the modified Library refers to a function or a table of data to be supplied by an application program that uses the facility, other than as an argument passed when the facility is invoked, then you must make a good faith effort to ensure that, in the event an application does not supply such function or table, the facility still operates, and performs whatever part of its purpose remains meaningful.

(For example, a function in a library to compute square roots has a purpose that is entirely well-defined independent of the application. Therefore, Subsection 2d requires that any application-supplied function or table used by this function must be optional: if the application does not supply it, the square root function must still compute square roots.)

These requirements apply to the modified work as a whole. If identifiable sections of that work are not derived from the Library, and can be reasonably considered independent and separate works in themselves, then this License, and its terms, do not apply to those sections when you distribute them as separate works. But when you distribute the same sections as part of a whole which is a work based on the Library, the distribution of the whole must be on the terms of this License, whose permissions for other licensees extend to the entire whole, and thus to each and every part regardless of who wrote it.

Thus, it is not the intent of this section to claim rights or contest your rights to work written entirely by you; rather, the intent is to exercise the right to control the distribution of derivative or collective works based on the Library.

In addition, mere aggregation of another work not based on the Library with the Library (or with a work based on the Library) on a volume of a storage or distribution medium does not bring the other work under the scope of this License.

3. You may opt to apply the terms of the ordinary GNU General Public License instead of this License to a given copy of the Library. To do this, you must alter all the notices that refer to this License, so that they refer to the ordinary GNU General Public License, version 2, instead of to this License. (If a newer version than version 2 of the ordinary GNU General Public License has appeared, then you can specify that version instead if you wish.) Do not make any other change in these notices.

Once this change is made in a given copy, it is irreversible for that copy, so the ordinary GNU General Public License applies to all subsequent copies and derivative works made from that copy.

This option is useful when you wish to copy part of the code of the Library into a program that is not a library.

4. You may copy and distribute the Library (or a portion or derivative of it, under Section 2) in object code or executable form under the terms of Sections 1 and 2 above provided that you accompany it with the complete corresponding machine-readable source code, which must be distributed under the terms of Sections 1 and 2 above on a medium customarily used for software interchange.

If distribution of object code is made by offering access to copy from a designated place, then offering equivalent access to copy the source code from the same place satisfies the requirement to distribute the source code, even though third parties are not compelled to copy the source along with the object code.

5. A program that contains no derivative of any portion of the Library, but is designed to work with the Library by being compiled or linked with it, is called a "work that uses the Library". Such a work, in isolation, is not a derivative work of the Library, and therefore falls outside the scope of this License.

However, linking a "work that uses the Library" with the Library creates an executable that is a derivative of the Library (because it contains portions of the

111

Library), rather than a "work that uses the library". The executable is therefore covered by this License. Section 6 states terms for distribution of such executables.

When a "work that uses the Library" uses material from a header file that is part of the Library, the object code for the work may be a derivative work of the Library even though the source code is not. Whether this is true is especially significant if the work can be linked without the Library, or if the work is itself a library. The threshold for this to be true is not precisely defined by law.

If such an object file uses only numerical parameters, data structure layouts and accessors, and small macros and small inline functions (ten lines or less in length), then the use of the object file is unrestricted, regardless of whether it is legally a derivative work. (Executables containing this object code plus portions of the Library will still fall under Section 6.)

Otherwise, if the work is a derivative of the Library, you may distribute the object code for the work under the terms of Section 6. Any executables containing that work also fall under Section 6, whether or not they are linked directly with the Library itself.

6. As an exception to the Sections above, you may also combine or link a "work that uses the Library" with the Library to produce a work containing portions of the Library, and distribute that work under terms of your choice, provided that the terms permit modification of the work for the customer's own use and reverse engineering for debugging such modifications.

You must give prominent notice with each copy of the work that the Library is used in it and that the Library and its use are covered by this License. You must supply a copy of this License. If the work during execution displays copyright notices, you must include the copyright notice for the Library among them, as well as a reference directing the user to the copy of this License. Also, you must do one of these things:

a) Accompany the work with the complete corresponding machine-readable source code for the Library including whatever changes were used in the work (which must be distributed under Sections 1 and 2 above); and, if the work is an executable linked with the Library, with the complete machine-readable "work that uses the Library", as object code and/or source code, so that the user can modify the Library and then relink to produce a modified executable containing the modified Library. (It is understood that the user who changes the contents of definitions files in the Library will not necessarily be able to recompile the application to use the modified definitions.)

b) Use a suitable shared library mechanism for linking with the Library. A suitable mechanism is one that (1) uses at run time a copy of the library already present on the user's computer system, rather than copying library functions into the executable, and (2) will operate properly with a modified version of the library, if the user installs one, as long as the modified version is interface-compatible with the version that the work was made with.

c) Accompany the work with a written offer, valid for at least three years, to give the same user the materials specified in Subsection 6a, above, for a charge no more than the cost of performing this distribution.

d) If distribution of the work is made by offering access to copy from a designated place, offer equivalent access to copy the above specified materials from the same place.

e) Verify that the user has already received a copy of these materials or that you have already sent this user a copy.

For an executable, the required form of the "work that uses the Library" must include any data and utility programs needed for reproducing the executable from it. However, as a special exception, the materials to be distributed need not include anything that is normally distributed (in either source or binary form) with the major components (compiler, kernel, and so on) of the operating system on which the executable runs, unless that component itself accompanies the executable.

It may happen that this requirement contradicts the license restrictions of other proprietary libraries that do not normally accompany the operating system. Such a contradiction means you cannot use both them and the Library together in an executable that you distribute.

7. You may place library facilities that are a work based on the Library side-by-side in a single library together with other library facilities not covered by this License, and distribute such a combined library, provided that the separate distribution of the work based on the Library and of the other library facilities is otherwise permitted, and provided that you do these two things:

a) Accompany the combined library with a copy of the same work based on the Library, uncombined with any other library facilities. This must be distributed under the terms of the Sections above.

b) Give prominent notice with the combined library of the fact that part of it is a work based on the Library, and explaining where to find the accompanying uncombined form of the same work.

8. You may not copy, modify, sublicense, link with, or distribute the Library except as expressly provided under this License. Any attempt otherwise to copy, modify, sublicense, link with, or distribute the Library is void, and will automatically terminate your rights under this License. However, parties who have received copies, or rights, from you under this License will not have their licenses terminated so long as such parties remain in full compliance.

9. You are not required to accept this License, since you have not signed it. However, nothing else grants you permission to modify or distribute the Library or its derivative works. These actions are prohibited by law if you do not accept this License. Therefore, by modifying or distributing the Library (or any work based on the Library), you indicate your acceptance of this License to do so, and all its terms and conditions for copying, distributing or modifying the Library or works based on it.

10. Each time you redistribute the Library (or any work based on the Library), the recipient automatically receives a license from the original licensor to copy, distribute, link with or modify the Library subject to these terms and conditions. You may not impose any further restrictions on the recipients' exercise of the rights granted herein. You are not responsible for enforcing compliance by third parties with this License.

11. If, as a consequence of a court judgment or allegation of patent infringement or for any other reason (not limited to patent issues), conditions are imposed on you (whether by court order, agreement or otherwise) that contradict the conditions of this License, they do not excuse you from the conditions of this License. If you cannot distribute so as to satisfy simultaneously your obligations under this License and any other pertinent obligations, then as a consequence you may not distribute the Library at all. For example, if a patent license would not permit royalty-free redistribution of the Library by all those who receive copies directly or indirectly through you, then the only way you could satisfy both it and this License would be to refrain entirely from distribution of the Library.

If any portion of this section is held invalid or unenforceable under any particular circumstance, the balance of the section is intended to apply, and the section as a whole is intended to apply in other circumstances.

It is not the purpose of this section to induce you to infringe any patents or other property right claims or to contest validity of any such claims; this section has the sole purpose of protecting the integrity of the free software distribution system which is implemented by public license practices. Many people have made generous contributions to the wide range of software distributed through that system in reliance on consistent application of that system; it is up to the author/donor to decide if he or she is willing to distribute software through any other system and a licensee cannot impose that choice.

This section is intended to make thoroughly clear what is believed to be a consequence of the rest of this License.

12. If the distribution and/or use of the Library is restricted in certain countries either by patents or by copyrighted interfaces, the original copyright holder who places the Library under this License may add an explicit geographical distribution limitation excluding those countries, so that distribution is permitted only in or among countries not thus excluded. In such case, this License incorporates the limitation as if written in the body of this License.

13. The Free Software Foundation may publish revised and/or new versions of the Lesser General Public License from time to time. Such new versions will be similar in spirit to the present version, but may differ in detail to address new problems or concerns.

Each version is given a distinguishing version number. If the Library specifies a version number of this License which applies to it and "any later version", you have the option of following the terms and conditions either of that version or of any later version published by the Free Software Foundation. If the Library does not specify a license version number, you may choose any version ever published by the Free Software Foundation.

14. If you wish to incorporate parts of the Library into other free programs whose distribution conditions are incompatible with these, write to the author to ask for permission. For software which is copyrighted by the Free Software Foundation, write to the Free Software Foundation; we sometimes make exceptions for this. Our decision will be guided by the two goals of preserving the free status of all derivatives of our free software and of promoting the sharing and reuse of software generally.

NO WARRANTY

15. BECAUSE THE LIBRARY IS LICENSED FREE OF CHARGE, THERE IS NO WARRANTY FOR THE LIBRARY, TO THE EXTENT PERMITTED BY APPLICABLE LAW. EXCEPT WHEN OTHERWISE STATED IN WRITING THE COPYRIGHT HOLDERS AND/OR OTHER PARTIES PROVIDE THE LIBRARY "AS IS" WITHOUT WARRANTY OF ANY KIND, EITHER EXPRESSED OR IMPLIED, INCLUDING, BUT NOT LIMITED TO, THE IMPLIED WARRANTIES OF MERCHANTABILITY AND FITNESS FOR A PARTICULAR PURPOSE. THE ENTIRE RISK AS TO THE QUALITY AND PERFORMANCE OF THE LIBRARY IS WITH YOU. SHOULD THE LIBRARY PROVE DEFECTIVE, YOU ASSUME THE COST OF ALL NECESSARY SERVICING, REPAIR OR CORRECTION.

16. IN NO EVENT UNLESS REQUIRED BY APPLICABLE LAW OR AGREED TO IN WRITING WILL ANY COPYRIGHT HOLDER, OR ANY OTHER PARTY WHO MAY MODIFY AND/OR REDISTRIBUTE THE LIBRARY AS PERMITTED ABOVE, BE LIABLE TO YOU FOR DAMAGES, INCLUDING ANY GENERAL, SPECIAL, INCIDENTAL OR CONSEQUENTIAL DAMAGES ARISING OUT OF THE USE OR INABILITY TO USE THE LIBRARY (INCLUDING BUT NOT LIMITED TO LOSS OF DATA OR DATA BEING RENDERED INACCURATE OR LOSSES SUSTAINED BY YOU OR THIRD PARTIES OR A FAILURE OF THE LIBRARY TO OPERATE WITH ANY OTHER SOFTWARE), EVEN IF SUCH HOLDER OR OTHER PARTY HAS BEEN ADVISED OF THE POSSIBILITY OF SUCH DAMAGES.

END OF TERMS AND CONDITIONS

The LGPL is structured in the same way as the GPL license. It starts with a preamble that gives an overview and the main goals of the license, followed by 17 clauses (enumerated from 0 to 16) that make provisions very similar to the GPL. However, LGPL makes an important distinction between "derivative work" and "work that uses the Library". Like in GPL, any modification, addition, or customization of the source code of the Library (even if only for translation purposes) shall be considered as a derivative work, and must be distributed under the terms of the license. These terms guarantee the freedom to use, share, modify and distribute the modified work, making the same provisions of GPL. On the other hand, a "work that uses the Library" it's a program that contains no derivative of any portion of the Library, but it's compiled or linked with it, i.e., it uses the Library to work, but it doesn't change the code of the Library itself. It's important to point out that if a "work that uses the Library" includes material which is part of the Library (from header files, for instance), then, the program should be considered as a "derivative work" and shall be under the terms of the license unless only numerical parameters, data structure layouts and assessor, small macros and/or inline functions, with ten lines or less in length are used. In such a case the use is unrestricted. The clause 6 of the license makes an exception for "works that use the library", allowing them to be released under any license terms provided that the terms permit modification of the work for the customer's own use and reverse engineering for debugging such modifications (release source code is not mandatory). In summary, proprietary applications are allowed to use, be linked and combined with LGPL code without the need to follow the same terms of the LGPL license, as long as the LGPL code is not changed and made a derivative work. Additionally, it gives to the users the permission to perform reverse engineering and even binary changes for their own use. The creation of LGPL brought more people to use many libraries of the GNU project, such as the GNU C Library and have helped the use of GNU software to spread and grow at the same time that also protects LGPL code by guaranteeing the same rights as in GPL for derived works. One last comment worthy of mention, the LGPL allows a certain copy of a LGPL Library to be promoted to regular GPL. This clause makes it easy to distribute LGPL Libraries along with GPL software.

Operating Systems Licensing Use Cases

This section describes a few use cases of well-known Operating Systems that are licensed under the licenses previously discussed.

FreeRTOS

FreeRTOS(*FreeRTOS Website*, n.d.) is a Real Time Operating System created in 2003 by Richard Barry with the goal to be easy to use, small and real time capable. It can run on several microcontrollers and processors of more than 35 different architectures. The development was maintained by Richard's company, Real Time Engineers Ltd. until 2017, when the company passed stewardship of the FreeRTOS project to Amazon Web Services (AWS), which now offers the Amazon FreeRTOS, with IoT capabilities that help devices to connect to the cloud.

FreeRTOS is composed of a kernel and several libraries that implement different functionalities. It's a Library OS, which means that the kernel, libraries and user application are built all together to form a single image that will run on the device. The FreeRTOS kernel and FreeRTOS libraries are licensed under the MIT license (SPDX short identifier: MIT). A partner company, WITTENSTEIN high integrity systems, offers two commercial versions of the FreeRTOS:

- OpenRTOS™: is a commercially licensed version of FreeRTOS. Both share the same code base, but OpenRTOS™ is relicensed with professional support and warranty; preparation for BSP (board support package) and porting to new processors service.

- SafeRTOS® it's also based on FreeRTOS. However, it's a pre-certified safety RTOS to meet requirements of industrial, medical, automotive and other international safety standards (IEC 61508 SIL 3, IEC 62304, ISO 26262, etc).

Since FreeRTOS is provided as a Library OS, the licensing model (using a permissive license), allows proprietary applications to use and distribute it without the need to share the source code of their application. Also, it allows commercial versions to be re-licensed and sold offering support, warranty, pre-certified code and/or other services.

FreeBSD

FreeBSD(*The FreeBSD Project Website*, n.d.) it's a Unix-like Operating System originated from the BSD OS (4.4BSD-Lite release) developed by the Computer Systems Research Group (CSRG) at the University of Berkley. It was first released in 1993 and it's licensed under the BSD 2-Clause license, also called FreeBSD license. Currently ported to several architectures and with a huge number of applications available, it has been a successful project, widely used in different applications and products, such as routers, firewalls, NAS devices, web servers and cloud systems. Adopted by big companies, such as Netflix and Sony (firmware of PlayStation 3, 4 and Vita game consoles are based on FreeBSD), it's also based on a monolithic kernel architecture, like the Linux kernel. However, since it's licensed under a permissive license, it can be commercially explored and distributed without the availability of source code.

Unikraft

Unikraft (*Unikraft Website*, n.d.) it's a unikernel provided as a whole ecosystem for building specialized POSIX-Compliant unikernel images with extremely modularization, so several system functionalities are provided as libraries, which can be built according to the application that will run along with the unikernel. It supports x86 and ARM architectures and multiple hypervisors. Unikraft is licensed under the terms of BSD 3-Clause license. Since all application code is linked together with kernel code to form a single image, a non-permissive license would not allow a closed source application to be distributed with unikernel. By using BSD licensing, proprietary applications can be linked along with Unikraft without the need of release source code.

Linux kernel

The Linux kernel (*The Linux Kernel Website*, n.d.) has reached more than 27 million lines of code as one of the most successful FOSS projects around the world. According to its creator, Linus Torvalds, one of the key factors that collaborated with the growth of the project and avoided its fragmentation was the GPL license(Bhartiya, 2016). The Linux kernel it's licensed under the GPL version 2 (GPL-2.0-only), any code contribution submitted to be included in the kernel must be licensed under this license or under a compatible one. It can also be licensed under a dual license, being one of compatible GPL version 2 variants and alternatively under a permissive license, such as MIT and BSD, for instance. An exception is made for header files that describe the kernel User-space API (UAPI), which is the interface between the kernel API (for example, APIs for video capture devices, input devices, etc) and user-space programs; these files are allowed to be included in non-GPL applications.

Linux kernel supports loadable modules, i.e., binary kernel modules (usually device drivers) that can be loaded during runtime and will run inside the kernel space. The license for the module must be informed to the module loader using the macro MODULE_LICENSE() with one of the following arguments: "GPL", "GPL v2", "GPL and additional rights", "Dual MIT/GPL", "Dual BSD/GPL", "Dual MPL/GPL" or "Proprietary". When "Proprietary" is specified, the module will not be able to access any of the kernel symbols exported as GPL through the macro EXPORT_GPL_SYMBOL(). Although this restriction mechanism is provided by the kernel, it doesn't mean that the module will meet all license requirements. In fact, there is a recurring discussion on whether a module can be seen as a derived work (of the kernel) or not. It's important to point out that even a kernel module can be distributed separately from the kernel, it depends on kernel to run and it runs on kernel space along with it. On the other hand, there are still discussions about some cases where the module was not originally developed for the Linux kernel, so some controversy whether it is or not derivative work might exist. Nevertheless, the Linux kernel community has repeatedly reinforced that no GPL exception is made by them in favor of proprietary kernel modules (Moglen & Choudhary, 2016).

Licensing Approach for Commercial Applications

The manufacturers of a commercial application (whether embedded or not) must be always aware of implications of the licenses when dealing with FOSS artifacts in their systems. A general approach towards the licensing of a commercial application starts with a detailed overview of the system. The licenses of all system components must be checked: Operating System kernel, user space system libraries, user space programs, such as system utilities and all dependencies of proprietary applications.

For those components licensed under permissive licenses, the obligations for commercial distribution are, in general, straightforward to meet. The manufacturer must guarantee to include the right copyright disclaimer (as and when requested by the license) in manuals, application's menu, etc. Nowadays it's very common to find such disclaimers in the manuals and menus of TVs, Smartphones and other consumer electronics products. All related disclaimers can be shown at once through a dedicated menu option about open source licensing, as done by Android OS, for instance.

The actions to be taken by manufacturers in order to be in conformance with non-permissive FOSS licenses are more complex, especially when dealing with derivative works. A top down approach for check, design and decide about licensing can be taken going through the following general items:

- Application's code: If the application is internally using, it's dependent or it's based on any non-permissive FOSS code, then it should be considered as a derivative work, and its sources shall be available to users under the terms of the FOSS license. For instance, a program that uses GPL code, cannot be (never) released under a proprietary license. In a nutshell, the rights of GPL cannot be reduced, in any instance, by licensees.

- Application's dependency libraries: It must be guaranteed that all libraries used by the application are under permissive licenses, or at least, under LGPL (which allows proprietary code to be linked with LGPLed libraries). Otherwise, the application can also be considered derivative work and shall conform to the terms of the non-permissive license. For instance, a library licensed under the GPL cannot be linked with a proprietary application.

- User space programs and system libraries: When dealing with general purpose systems, such as PCs, manufacturers will usually only distribute the final proprietary application binary that will run on the user's Operating System. However, for embedded systems, the device's firmware will usually contain not only the specific application, but also the whole Operating System, which includes system utilities and libraries. By doing so, the manufacturer is distributing these applications as well. Thus, it must be in conformance with all respective licenses. In case of GPL, distributing proprietary programs along with GPLed software in the same package does not violate the license, but the corresponding source code of all GPLed binaries within the package must be available. Manufacturers can release the source code on their website, as it has been done by several companies, such as D-Link (*D-Link GPL Source Code Support*, n.d.), Huawei (*Huawei Open Source Release Center*, n.d.), Sony (*Sony Linux Technical Information*, n.d.) and many others.

- Operating System kernel and device drivers: Especially important for embedded systems, that distributes the kernel along with the device's firmware and many times requires specific device drivers to work, either third parties or developed by the manufacturer. If the kernel it's licensed under a permissive license, the manufacturer will have those usual obligations of such licenses, like providing the copyright disclaimer. However, the manufacturer is allowed to use, modify the kernel, create proprietary device drivers and will not have the obligation to release the source code of any customization. On the other hand, if the kernel is licensed under a non-permissive license, such as GPL, then the manufacturer must pay close attention when dealing with device drivers. Linux Kernel, for instance, is licensed under the GPL version 2, which means that any modification made on the kernel and distributed within the firmware (in binary form), must also be available in the source code form. The easiest way is to provide an URL at the manufacturer's website pointing to the corresponding source code package of the firmware. Note that the source code must correspond exactly to the version of the binary form. Providing an outdated or non-corresponding source code will violate the license. Regarding loadable kernel modules, even if some device driver is developed as a kernel module and can be distributed independently, when it is bound to the kernel, it runs along with the binary kernel code, and it depends on the kernel to run, so it can fall in the category of derivative works (although some corner cases can be matter of discussion). In case of Linux kernel modules, the best options for commercial manufacturers are:
  - license all their Linux kernel modules under GPL version 2 (even better if they can push their changes upstream);
  - do not use third party kernel modules that are not 100% in conformance with GPLv2;
  - choose another kernel (with a permissive license, such as BSD) when custom device drivers cannot be open sourced;
  - avoid any device driver that uses binary blobs to circumvent GPL license terms;
  - keep track and release exactly the source code corresponding to the binaries;
- For microkernels and hybrid architectures: if a device driver can run entirely as a separated user space application, then it cannot be considered a derivative work of the kernel and should follow the same approach for regular user space applications licensing. This approach can be found in some projects, such as the seL4 microkernel (*What Does SeL4's License Imply?*, 2019).
- Check the license of other types of sources: Not only source code, but other files such as icons, text fonts and documentation might be licensed under the

terms of FOSS licenses, such as the Creative Commons (*Creative Commons Website*, n.d.) or the GNU Free Documentation License (*GNU Free Documentation License V1.3*, n.d.). These licenses also have specific clauses and terms considering work distribution that must be followed by licensees.

Although guaranteeing the conformance with the licenses of all components of a complex system might demand big efforts, it can also avoid big problems in the future. Manufacturers shall not neglect licensing conformance checking. Specialized lawyer consulting can be contracted if necessary and the copyright holders can also be contacted when doubts about any license term arises. Knowing the terms and the foundation of the main FOSS licenses are indispensable for those who are working, developing and distributing commercial software.

CONCLUSION

Free Software and Open Source projects are now driving a massive number of complex, critical and important systems throughout the world. The main FOSS licenses are mature and have evolved throughout the years following all technological advances. They protect not only the copyright holders but also the licensees, giving to them the freedom to use, share, modify and redistribute the modified work without being treated by law loopholes or weak license clauses. They can help to build a fair ecosystem where proprietary applications can coexist with FOSS components without harming any of the sides. However, manufacturers of commercial applications must be aware and follow all license terms of all FOSS artifacts included in their systems in order to reach a final product completely in conformance with all involved licenses. Regarding commercial embedded applications, the Operating System might have a high impact on the application's license model depending on how it's licensed. This Chapter covered:

- The foundational knowledge regarding embedded systems and Operating Systems
- Relevant aspects and terms of the main Free Software and Open Source licenses
- Differences between permissive and non-permissive licenses, such as the MIT, BSD and GNU GPL
- Use cases on Operating Systems licensing
- Presented a top-down approach that can help and guide manufacturers of commercial embedded applications to meet all requirements of FOSS components involved in their systems

Non-permissive licenses, such as GPL, have more specific obligations and do not allow the reduction of the license rights, which implies that any derivative work must also follow the license terms and have the source code available. Embedded systems using the Linux kernel (licensed under GPL version 2) must have the sources available of any device driver (running along with the kernel, as a module or built-in) as well as any kernel modification(s) made by the manufacturer. GPL applications distributed in binary form within firmware or any other software package must also be available through the corresponding sources by the distributor.

Manufacturers of commercial applications must ensure that all components of their systems are in conformance with the corresponding licenses and, when required, the right version of the source code corresponding to the compiled binaries are available. The best way to avoid license violations is to know the foundation of FOSS licensing, terms and differences across main (popular) licenses, talk to copyright holders, ask lawyer support when required, and have a clean and transparent process to distribute their software.

REFERENCES

Apache License. Version 2.0. (n.d.). *The Apache Software Foundation!* Retrieved August 20, 2022, from https://www.apache.org/licenses/LICENSE-2.0

Bhartiya, S. (2016, August 27). *CIO. Linus Torvalds says GPL was defining factor in Linux's success.* Retrieved September 3, 2022, from https://www.cio.com/article/238985/linus-torvalds-says-gpl-was-defining-factor-in-linuxs-success.html

Cha, S.-J., Jeon, S. H., Jeong, Y. J., Kim, J. M., & Jung, S. (2022). OS noise Analysis on Azalea-unikernel. *2022 24th International Conference on Advanced Communication Technology (ICACT),* 81-84. 10.23919/ICACT53585.2022.9728776

Chen, K.-H., Günzel, M., Jablkowski, B., Buschhoff, M., & Chen, J.-J. (2022). Unikernel-Based Real-Time Virtualization Under Deferrable Servers: Analysis and Realization. *34th Euromicro Conference on Real-Time Systems (ECRTS 2022),* 231. 10.4230/LIPIcs.ECRTS.2022.6

Creative Commons website. (n.d.). *Creative Commons: When we share, everyone wins.* Retrieved August 28, 2022, from https://creativecommons.org/

D-Link GPL source code support. (n.d.). *D-Link | Technical Support | Downloads.* Retrieved August 28, 2022, from https://tsd.dlink.com.tw/dlist?OS=GPL

Free Documentation License, G. N. U. v1.3. (n.d.). *GNU.org.* Retrieved August 28, 2022, from https://www.gnu.org/licenses/fdl-1.3.html

FreeRTOS website. (n.d.). *FreeRTOS - Market leading RTOS (Real Time Operating System) for embedded systems with Internet of Things extensions*. Retrieved August 31, 2022, from https://www.freertos.org/index.html

Gérman, D., Gonzalez-Barahona, J., & Robles, G. (2007). A Model to Understand the Building and Running Inter-Dependencies of Software. *14th Working Conference on Reverse Engineering (WCRE 2007)*, 140-149. 10.1109/WCRE.2007.5

Gérman, D., & Hassan, A. (2009). License integration patterns: Addressing license mismatches in component-based development. *2009 IEEE 31st international conference on software engineering*, 188-198.

Gérman, D., Penta, M. D., & Davies, J. (2010). Understanding and auditing the licensing of open source software distributions. *2010 IEEE 18th International Conference on Program Comprehension*, 84-93.

GNU Lesser General Public License v2.1. (n.d.). *GNU.org*. Retrieved August 20, 2022, from https://www.gnu.org/licenses/old-licenses/lgpl-2.1.html

GNU Library General Public License v2.0. (n.d.). *GNU.org*. Retrieved August 29, 2022, from https://www.gnu.org/licenses/old-licenses/lgpl-2.0.html

Huawei Open Source Release Center. (n.d.). *HUAWEI Consumer*. Retrieved August 28, 2022, from https://consumer.huawei.com/en/opensource/

iFross. (2006). *LG Frankfurt a.M., Urteil v. 06.09.2006, Az. 2-6 O 224/06*. Institut für Rechtsfragen der Freien und Open Source Software. https://www.ifross.org/Fremdartikel/urteil_lg_frankfurt_gpl.pdf

Kuenzer, S., Bădoiu, V.-A., Lefeuvre, H., Santhanam, S., Jung, A., Gain, G., Soldani, C., Lupu, C., Teodorescu, Ș., Răducanu, C., Banu, C., Mathy, L., Deaconescu, R., Raiciu, C., & Huici, F. (2021). Unikraft: Fast, Specialized Unikernels the Easy Way. *Proceedings of the Sixteenth European Conference on Computer Systems*, 376-394. 10.1145/3447786.3456248

Laadan, O., & Nieh, J. (2010, May). Operating system virtualization: practice and experience. *Proceedings of the 3rd Annual Haifa Experimental Systems Conference*, 1-12.

Lee, M. (2008, December 11). *Free Software Foundation Files Suit Against Cisco For GPL Violations — Free Software Foundation — Working together for free software*. Free Software Foundation. Retrieved August 13, 2022, from https://www.fsf.org/news/2008-12-cisco-suit

Madhavapeddy, A., Mortier, R., Rotsos, C., Scott, D., Singh, B., Gazagnaire, T., Smith, S., Hand, S., & Crowcroft, J. (2013). Unikernels: Library operating systems for the cloud. *Computer Architecture News*, *41*(1), 461–472. doi:10.1145/2490301.2451167

Moglen, E., & Choudhary, M. (2016, February 26). *The Linux Kernel, CDDL and Related Issues*. Software Freedom Law Center. Retrieved September 3, 2022, from https://softwarefreedom.org/resources/2016/linux-kernel-cddl.html

O'Neall, G. (n.d.). *spdx/spdx-spec: The SPDX specification in MarkDown and HTML formats*. GitHub repository. Retrieved August 21, 2022, from https://github.com/spdx/spdx-spec

Open source license usage on GitHub.com. (2015, March 9). *The GitHub Blog*. Retrieved August 27, 2022, from https://github.blog/2015-03-09-open-source-license-usage-on-github-com

Porter, D. E., Boyd-Wickizer, S., Howell, J., Olinsky, R., & Hunt, G. C. (2011, March). Rethinking the Library OS from the Top Down. *SIGPLAN Notices*, *46*(3), 291–304. doi:10.1145/1961296.1950399

Rosen, L. E. (2005). *Open source licensing: software freedom and intellectual property law*. Prentice Hall PTR.

Smith, B. (2008). *A Quick Guide to GPLv3*. GNU.org. Retrieved August 27, 2022, from https://www.gnu.org/licenses/quick-guide-gplv3.html#neutralizing-laws-that-prohibit-free-software-but-not-forbidding-drm

Smith, B. (2009, May 20). *FSF Settles Suit Against Cisco — Free Software Foundation — Working together for free software*. Free Software Foundation. Retrieved August 13, 2022, from https://www.fsf.org/news/2009-05-cisco-settlement.html

Sony Linux Technical Information. (n.d.). *Sony Global - Source Code Distribution Service*. Retrieved August 28, 2022, from https://oss.sony.net/Products/Linux/common/search.html

St. Laurent, A. M. (2004). *Understanding Open Source and Free Software Licensing*. O'Reilly Media.

Stallman, R. (2021). *Linux and GNU*. GNU.org. Retrieved August 18, 2022, from https://www.gnu.org/gnu/linux-and-gnu.html

Stewart, K., Odence, P., & Rockett, E. (2010). Software package data exchange (SPDX) specification. *IFOSS L. Rev., 2*.

Tanenbaum, A. S., & Bos, H. (2015). *Modern Operating Systems*. Pearson.

The 3-Clause BSD License. (n.d.). *Open Source Initiative*. Retrieved August 20, 2022, from https://opensource.org/licenses/BSD-3-Clause

The FreeBSD Project website. (n.d.). *The FreeBSD Project*. Retrieved September 2, 2022, from https://www.freebsd.org/

The GNU General Public License v2.0. (n.d.). *GNU.org*. Retrieved August 20, 2022, from https://www.gnu.org/licenses/old-licenses/gpl-2.0.html

The Linux Kernel website. (n.d.). *The Linux Kernel Archives*. Retrieved September 2, 2022, from https://kernel.org/

The MIT License. (n.d.). *Open Source Initiative*. Retrieved August 20, 2022, from https://opensource.org/licenses/MIT

The Open Group Base. (2017). *POSIX.1-2017*. The Open Group Base Specifications Issue 7, 2018 edition. Retrieved August 15, 2022, from https://pubs.opengroup.org/onlinepubs/9699919799.2018edition/

Tiburski, R. T., Moratelli, C. R., Johann, S. F., Matos, E., & Hessel, F. (2021, March). A lightweight virtualization model to enable edge computing in deeply embedded systems. *Software, Practice & Experience*, *51*(9), 1964–1981. doi:10.1002pe.2968

Unikraft website. (n.d.). *Unikraft*. Retrieved September 2, 2022, from https://unikraft.org/

Welte, H. (2013, June 26). *Regional court Hamburg judgement against FANTEC*. gpl-violations.org. Retrieved August 15, 2022, from https://gpl-violations.org/news/20130626-fantec_judgement/

What does seL4's license imply? (2019, December 9). *microkerneldude*. Retrieved August 28, 2022, from https://microkerneldude.org/2019/12/09/what-does-sel4s-license-imply/

KEY TERMS AND DEFINITIONS

Commercial Application: An application developed from a commercial context, it might usually involve proprietary solutions sold to one or more customers and distributed through a closed source form.

Derivative Work: A work made from an original work through modifications and/or additions that cannot be functional without the original work, both are very tied to each other.

Embedded System: A system designed for a specific functionality that usually is encapsulated into another computer system and/or device. In contrast to general-purpose systems, it is tied to the hardware where it runs.

FOSS: Stands for Free and Open Source Software.

Microkernel: An OS architecture where the kernel running in kernel mode only contains essential features, such as basic device drivers and IPC mechanisms. Other functionalities are implemented as user space applications, which communicate with the microkernel in order to access the hardware and other resources of the machine.

Monolithic: An OS architecture where the whole kernel runs in kernel mode, including device drivers, kernel services, etc.

Operating System: Software that acts as a resource manager, handling all hardware resources of the machine and abstracting them to user space applications, being the fundamental layer between the hardware and the software.

Chapter 5
Coherent Synergy:
Fostering Innovation in Open Source Ecosystems

Francisco Jose Monaco
iD https://orcid.org/0000-0001-6172-2689
Universidade de Sao Paulo, Brazil

ABSTRACT

The open-source paradigm has evolved from the early enthusiasts' circles to enter the agenda of the mainstream industry, while related initiatives have been extending the idea of open, collaborative development to other kinds of intellectual artifacts. Against this background, it is pertinent to ask how an innovation-based business that deliberately renounces the exclusive prerogatives endowed by intellectual property can foster continuous innovation. In order to shed light on those questions, this article addresses the open-source model as a new paradigm of innovation fostering that does not rely on the IP-enforcement model. The investigation brings up a comprehensive conceptual framework to understand different kinds of open-source business models in a unified and systematic way. By introducing a broader definition of open-source innovation, the study formulates the notion of coherent synergy: a property that determines the roles of the intellectual creation and the different stakeholders in innovation ecosystems.

INTRODUCTION

Brought to the fore in the 80s by way of an organized initiative, the contemporary notion of freely sharable, cooperatively developed technology was first systematically

DOI: 10.4018/978-1-6684-4785-7.ch005

formulated in the context of the software industry. The term *free,* as in *Free Software*, endorsed by the Free Software Foundation[1] (FSF), the pioneer catalyst of the concept and founder of the hugely influential GNU Project, conveys the initiative's driving motivation (Stallman, 2002) towards the moral principles of individual freedom and the ethics of sharing and collaboration. The related qualifier *open*, as in *Open Source Software*, has been later proposed (Perens, 1999) by the Open Source Initiative[2] (OSI), another authoritative source backed by prominent organizations and practitioner communities, as a label to highlight the methodological aspect of open, collaborative development. Apropos terminology, while both standpoints converge with respect to technical aspects of open development, their scope differ to some extent — with FSF, on the one hand, criticizing the usage of the alternative term "open" as detrimental to its agenda of raising public awareness about user freedom, and the OSI, on the other, arguing in favor of separating the moral and methodological concerns. In response, the conciliatory expression *free and open source*, as in *Free and Open Source Software,* by acronym FOSS[3], has been suggested to refer to both perspectives collectively, focusing on their elements of convergence.

Through the volunteer efforts of multiple seminal undertakings, the central idea of free open collaboration has flourished into the prominent achievements of influential open-source projects such as GNU, Linux, FreeBSD, Wikipedia, Mozilla, Apache, PostgreSQL, and Python, to name only a little few of the growing number of remarkably successful examples. While varying in philosophical grounds and strategic approaches, open-source supporter communities regard the idea of unrestricted equal rights to intellectual creations as a key condition for ensuring people's control over the technology they use, promoting essential privacy and security guarantees, and leveraging agile technological development. And although formal definitions proposed by leading organizations differ in terminology and rationalization of principles, all of them essentially agree on the conditions required for a product to be considered free and open in the sense mentioned earlier: the non-exclusive rights to freely *use, modify* and *redistribute* the item without restrictions on field of endeavor, or discrimination of people or groups.

Now, being around for nearly 40 years, the open-source paradigm has evolved from the early enthusiasts' inner circles to enter the agenda of the mainstream industry. Concomitantly, related concepts of open-source hardware, open educational resources, and open science, among others, expand the idea of collaborative construction of publicly accessible knowledge to encompass other intellectual products made available under the same free and open status. So as to embrace this broadened, more generic notion, we herein will use the term *open source* to refer to open-source systems in general when addressing the matter from a technical perspective[4].

With all being said about the impact of the open-source approach on the several segments of the industry where its influence has been felt, this article calls attention to the fact that the relevance of the open-source model, however, is due not only to the way it has been reshaping the industry but also, and above all, to how it defies the conventional notion of *intellectual property* (IP) as fundamental to the purpose of fostering innovation. For nearly half a century, IP enforcement has been the cornerstone for encouraging invention in industry, existing so intrinsically in the practice of science, technology, and art business fields, that IP is often tacitly taken as imperative, almost inseparable from the very concept of innovation. From commercial enterprises to public research institutions, organizations aim to be agile in formalizing the registry of copyrights, patents, or other forms of intellectual property, as a means to ensure either a competitive advantage or direct profits from licensing contracts.

Given the *status quo*, it is not without surprise that the startling emergence of successful commercial open-source projects has been received, to some extent, with a certain skepticism, or even sharp opposition in some cases — while in extreme events, free software licensing would be likened to a deadly insidious disease (Sun-Times, 2001) that sickens the otherwise healthy intellectual property instrument[5]. While perhaps overstated, the distrust was not a rare occurrence within an industry perplexed by the radical contrast brought up by the open-source experience. How come an innovation-based business that deliberately renounces the exclusive prerogatives endowed by the IP expedient could gain momentum as a system capable of fostering continuous innovation progress? What explains how some community-run open-source ventures have evolved from volunteer undertakings into long-standing, economically sustainable projects? Why have major commercial enterprises been increasingly engaging in developing open-source products? Even today, to a large extent, some of these questions remain not satisfactorily answered for many newcomers and even experienced open technology developers.

Some attempts to grasp the success of open-source enterprises have customarily approached it as a tactical device to boost the marketing strategy of companion closed-source proprietary products. The present article, differently, argues that, in order to shed light on this seeming paradox, it is helpful to contemplate the open-source model beyond the role as a smart deviant maneuver designed for a still orthodox business context, and comprehend open-source as an entirely new paradigm of innovation fostering that is alternative to the traditional IP-enforcement model. The advent of the open-source industry brings into the open the evidence that there is more than one way to foment continuous innovation, and that while IP enforcement is one of such ways, it is not the sole possibility. Unconventional as it may sound, this standpoint may help to unveil the inner mechanisms driving the open-source economic ecosystem[6], and understand how it can encourage continuous innovation by means other than the traditional access-right reservation on intellectual creations.

Interestingly, this alternate system is not at all new, and both — the IP-enforcement and the open-source approaches — have been around together for a long time, and uncountable examples may be evoked in varying segments of the industry. It just so happens that the contrast has been made particularly evident since the 1990s in the software field and, perhaps more recently, in the computer hardware sector.

True, several essays about open-source business models have been written during the last decade. Still, the literature is predominantly focused on case studies of commercial subsidiary services, such as support, consulting, training, customization, and so on. While legitimate approaches, those possibilities only hold because the open-source product exists in the first place. The sole description of profitable ancillary services around open-source products does not address why people and organizations finance the development of such products and how this strategic decision would meet their business goals. A more general and systematic insight of the principles underlying the open-source ecosystem is in order to understand how, even not relying on IP enforcement, open-source may uphold continuous innovation. This knowledge may also help to comprehend the positive and negative factors influencing the sustainability of an open-source project, and offer a conceptual ground for the design of business strategies for commercial open-source development.

That said, in exploring this domain, the present article does not seek to enumerate well-known open-source business models, nor is it committed to specifying methods to profit from particular products or services. Rather, the study aims at examining the foundational mechanisms that underlie economically sustainable open-source enterprises and abstract the theoretical rationales that maintain the consistent self-coordinated interaction in development.

The investigation brings up a comprehensive conceptual framework to understand, in a unified and systematic way, the workings of different kinds of open-source business models. Introducing a broader definition of *open-source innovation*, which encompasses software, hardware, artwork and other kinds of intellectual creations, the study formulates the notion of *coherent synergy*: a property that determines the roles of the intellectual creation and the different stakeholders in open-source continuous innovation ecosystems.

THE CASE OF OPEN SOURCE SOFTWARE

As this article argues, the open-source perspective, as we examine it here, is not restricted to software, nor is it particular to the domain of computational systems. Instead, it is generalizable to all kinds of intellectual creations and may be found present in varying sectors. Nevertheless, since the free and open source software experience is so expressive and yields so many auspicious examples, it is appealing to explore the software industry as a study case to illustrate some abstract notions through more concrete examples.

There are several formal definitions of open-source, proposed by varying supporting organizations. The Free Software Foundation (FSF), pioneering the organized open-source movement, states that a piece of software is *free software* if it is published in such a way as to guarantee four essential freedoms[7], aimed at endowing anyone that receives the software with full control over it, and the means to help oneself and one's community (Stallman, 2001). With extensive wording, the basic freedoms are numbered from 0 to 3, and expressed as the ability to use, inspect, modify and distribute the software without discrimination of purpose, person or group. The Open Source Initiative (OSI), in turn, defines that a piece of software is open source if its distribution license fulfills a set of requirements (Perens, 1999) which includes: public availability of the source code; free and gratuitous (re)distribution of the software under the equivalent terms; creation and distribution of derivative works; no discrimination of people, group or field of endeavor; and product and technology neutral license — the specific 10 criteria specified by OSI should be consulted for the precise definition. Some of the world's largest open-source software contributors[8] abide by the OSI definition. Consistently, the glossary of Software Freedom Conservancy, another leading organization in the open-source scenario, defines (SFC, 2022) *software freedom* as the liberty to run, study, (re)distribute, and (re)install (modified) versions of a piece of software, with emphasis on the idea that there should be equal protections for privacy and redistribution. In the same strain, the Wikipedia[9] entry for the term open-source alludes to the free license to use, copy, study, and change the software, and to openly share source code as a means to encourage people and organizations to improve the software. The spirit of those definitions mentioned above is reflected in both the *de facto* understanding and the official vocabulary of national and international governance instances.

Notwithstanding wording differences and implied motivations, all referenced formulations converge in the fundamental criteria defining open-source, which may be summarized, without loss of generality, as the concomitant fulfillment of the rights to use, modify and distribute the software. More specifically, free and open source licenses must specify that the right to use be guaranteed to any user and for any purpose; that the right of modification be readily ensured without the need for complementary authorization request; and that the right of distribution allow one to share the software in its original or modified form, and either free-of-charge or commercially. As it will be further explained in the next sections of the present study, the latter condition is fundamental to ensuring the economic sustainability of the open-source ecosystem.

Seeing that the open-source model literally resigns over some exclusive advantages allowed by the intellectual-property status, the antonym of both *free* and *open* source is, accordingly, *proprietary* source. Caution should be exercised not to use the adjective *commercial* as opposed to open-source, precisely because an open-source license must, by definition, allow for the commercialization of the item. Likewise, free software, or open source, should not be mistakenly referred to as *freeware* or *shareware,* seen that in the software licensing's lingo, those words are loosely employed to identify proprietary software whose use terms allow for free (in the sense of gratuitous) utilization, but do not guarantee the liberties of modification or distribution. Also, using the term *public domain* in place of open-source is a misnomer, as a piece of free and open source creation may be — and often is — copyrighted, as long as its license ensures their users the rights of use, modification, and distribution required by the open-source definition.

Why Do Individuals and Organizations Use Open-Source Software?

When asked why they have adopted open-source-based solutions, individuals and organizations bring forth several reasons. Naturally, one of the first criteria to come up is the cost factor. An essential requisite of the open-source denomination is that the source code be made publicly available unconditionally to the payment of any fee. While not preventing commercial distribution, the specification requires that a company that sells open-source software disclose a well-known alternate form through which anyone can obtain the source code gratuitously. Consequently, there is always the possibility of acquiring open-source products at very low or even no cost. That is in itself a self-evident compelling argument to explain the adoption of open-source technology, especially by individuals and small enterprises that administer limited budgets.

Money-saving, nevertheless, is not the only reason organizations look after the dissemination of open-source technology. A direct consequence of cost reduction is eliminating the economic barrier against access to state-of-art technology. An ordinary desktop or laptop computer intended for home, office, or school use typically contains a modern operating system, office tools like a text editor and an electronic spreadsheet, Internet access software, media playing application, and other customary tools for daily needs. If we consider only proprietary software, several of those pieces must either be purchased or will come as pre-installed items whose cost is indirectly embedded in the bundle's sell price. Among other possibly gratuitous utilities, there may be trial-only samples whose full-featured versions will also be paid for. This simple setup already adds to the cost of ownership. Yet, the cost of tools required for applications in science, engineering, medicine, and akin areas is notoriously more expressive. Programs for computational simulation, professional media editing, computer-aided design, medical image processing, production planning, structural analysis, process optimization, and other highly specialized tasks are commercialized — either as permanent licenses or periodic subscriptions — at much higher prices. It is not unusual that such dedicated tools cost several times the value of the computer hardware, with prices reaching amounts inaccessible for most users other than large companies, well-funded research institutions, banks, and other wealthy corporations. In contrast, open source imposes no economic obstacles to the adoption of cutting-edge technology. With the advent of GNU and Linux open-source projects, for instance, the operating system used by big tech companies in developed nations is the same operating system at the reach of small entrepreneurs in developing countries. The Linux that runs in the International Space Station, is the same software used in public schools of socially disfavored communities. By virtue of its egalitarian benefit, the adoption of open-source products has also been encouraged by public policymakers (EU Commission, 2021) as a resource to promote digital inclusion and social justice.

Neither cost reduction nor social inclusion, nonetheless, necessarily account for the primary motivation for open-source adoption by large enterprises. Another reason the decision makers in those environments claim is the pursuit of flexibility. It is intuitive and well understood that, in the ambit of the proprietary industry, the design of a new product should consider a trade-off between quality excellence and development cost: the more significant the investment in adding value to the product, the more the product becomes attractive to customers. However, that comes at the expense of higher selling prices, which contrarily disfavors the product's attractiveness. For instance, if a given set of features is thought to make a piece of software well suited for a large portion of the potential users, then attempting to meet the needs of the remaining customers may prove not strategically advantageous, as the cost to augment the slice of the potential consumers may actually end up reducing the product's viability. The same applies to deciding how much to spend on perfecting performance, reliability, usability, and other quality attributes. In some sense, proprietary products are arguably generic, and the end user has no resort but to adapt to the features they are allowed. Some organizations then opt for open-source solutions motivated by the possibility of adapting the technology to their process and not the other way around, and to be in control of the development of the technology that is pivotal for their business. That is a relevant capability for ensuring autonomy in strategic planning.

Regarding autonomy, a fourth related motive for adopting open-source technology arises from concerns about the reliability of the critical components of the organizational strategy. An unsettling collection of "what-ifs" often occurs to planners and decision-makers when it comes to considering the risk posed by the selection of one or another solution that will compose the essential business infrastructure. What if the unique supplier of a proprietary software framework, upon which a crucial industry process relies, decides to discontinue the product's development along with support and regular updates? Or, even more drastically, what if it ceases business? Those worries may suggest opting for a safer, yet technically inferior, solution over the available optimal alternatives. Even with the most conservative choice of supplier, there is also the inevitable fact that the direction and pace of the technology development will be driven by the supplier's own business goals, which may not coincide with the customers' strategic interests. For instance, it is not uncommon for a closed-source technology provider to not adhere to an emerging open standard to the detriment of a proprietary alternative it wants to enforce as a *de facto* industry norm. The manufacturer's own plans condition the implementation of new features, and the releases of updates and improvements may follow a schedule subordinate to the supplier's commercial strategies — for example, to delay the release of a new product capability in the function of the competitors' moves. In this aspect, open-source users may more safely depend on collaboratively developed technology. If the open-source project has an active community of contributors, there is more than one single supplier capable of sustaining long-term development, providing support, and offering on-demand contracts to implement customizations. If the priorities of the project's governance board, or the contributor community, ever diverge too much from those of the user, then it is feasible to *fork* — *i.e.,* split — the project and start to work in a parallel undertaking. Even in the less likely event that the whole community is eventually dissolved for any reason, it is always possible to take over the development and proceed from there.

Yet another concern regarding the open-source model is the guarantee of transparency, an essential concept in the context of security and privacy. Contrary to a closed-source technology —- whose guard against security violations must be trusted by claim, and is only experimentally proven to the extent that black-box testing allows to ascertain — open-source technology is auditable at the very design and implementation level. Fully exposed, the internal mechanisms can be inspected for both accidental defects and malicious injections. The longer the source code is publicly available and the larger the contributor community, the more likely that hidden bugs be detected, breaches for unauthorized access spotted, and performance and dependability bottlenecks identified. Moreover, aligned to the concerns endorsed by national and international legislations, the display of the source code allows for public assessment of the product's compliance with privacy policies, and for the society more easily detect abuses against the user rights related to the treatment of personal data and ethical use of private information. Not only an issue of individual rights, but in several other circumstances, especially in the ambit of government affairs, transparency may also play a critical concern in matters of national security and state sovereignty.

Why Do People and Organizations Produce Open-Source Software?

The five cases mentioned above do not exhaust all the conceivable forms in which free and open technology may represent a strategic choice in varying contexts. Nevertheless, even though the advantages from the users' perspective can be sensibly related to the increasing adoption of open-source technology in both public and private sectors, such perception does not explain, however, the complementary question of why individuals and organizations engage in open-source development. That is to say, while there are arguably obvious advantages to *using* open-source products, the reason why people and organizations invest time, labor, and financial resources in *creating* open-source products may not be so self-evident.

Again, an attempt to grasp possible answers to those questions may come up with some tentative propositions. Some may sound like partial clues; others may regard myths and misconceptions.

It is a widespread belief among lay narratives that open-source development is primarily a hobby, a form of entertainment beloved and practiced mostly within geek circles. It is undeniable that there are community-run projects that did start under that motivation. Indeed, by far one of the most prominent examples in this domain, the notable Linux project, lends itself to a practical illustration. In 1991, a young undergraduate student of the Computer Science course at the University of Helsinki made the anthological public call (Hasan, 2002) inviting people worldwide to contribute to his personal project:

I'm doing a (free) operating system (just a hobby, won't be big and professional like gnu) for 386(486) AT clones" — later adding: "Do you pine for the nice days of minix-1.1, when men were men and wrote their own device drivers? Are you without a nice project and just dying to cut your teeth on an OS you can try to modify for your needs? (...) Then this post might be just for you:-)

Ten years later, Linus would publish his book *"Just for Fun"*, whose title demonstrates the nature of the project's original motivations (Diamond and Torvalds, 2001). Several known free and open-source works, as well as many lesser-known initiatives by countless computer science and programming enthusiasts, share the same origin. It is noteworthy, though, that Linux, like those other originally pastime undertakings, evolved to become a world-class mainstream operating system, attracting substantial investment from many of the leading companies in the software and hardware segments. Those major commercial enterprises are not likely to seek hobby activities.

Another supposition about open-source development is that most work is carried out under the motivation of philanthropy or political idealism. If not selfless volunteers aimed at the common good, who else would design and implement technological creations for free? This assumption is not entirely without grounds. The utmost influential GNU Project, which brought about the foundational framework for the subsequent open-source prosperity, is deeply inspired by thoughtful considerations on the moral implications of freedom in the context of collaboration, sovereignty, and knowledge dissemination. In the project's inaugural document, the GNU Manifesto, the author Richard Stallman, declares (Stallman, 1985):

I consider that the Golden Rule requires that if I like a program, I must share it with other people who like it. Software sellers want to divide the users and conquer them, making each user agree not to share with others. I refuse to break solidarity with other users in this way. I cannot in good conscience sign a nondisclosure agreement or a software license agreement. . . . So that I can continue to use computers without dishonor, I have decided to put together a sufficient body of free software so that I will be able to get along without any software that is not free.

The GNU Project produced a vital part of the infrastructural components that enabled the flourishing of today's open-source systems, including much of the software that Linux relies on. While ethics is undoubtedly a thematic pertinent to all fields of human activity — and conceivably of interest to the organizations that benefit from the GNU legacy — the recount of historical events that led to the founding of successful open-source-based enterprises[10], however, reveals that volunteer solidarity alone can not account for the economic viability of those enterprises in the long run.

Although progressively dissolved by overwhelming counterevidence, a myth persists in the lay common sense that open-source is a second-line product, as empirical observation suggests that quality goes pairwise with price. Under this reasoning, low-cost would be synonymous with inferior, and "cheap product" is immediately understood as mediocre. This condition might result from either deficient competence or else the intentional stratagem of downgrading an open-source trial sample with the objective of promoting a full-featured closed-source release. Although low-quality open-source software undoubtedly does exist — and in large quantities — there is no plausible evidence that closed-source development is inherently more capable of yielding superior quality than the open-source model. The rise of first-rate open-source products has helped this misconception gradually fade away.

Naturally, there are also developers who publish open-source artifacts not aiming at a profit, but at building a portfolio. Large *software forges* — SaaS[11] based source management platforms for collaborative software development[12] — that provide version control systems, issue tracking tools, and other useful functionality, usually offer a free entrance-level subscription for open-source projects. An ever-growing number of software developers publish their work under open-source licenses seeking professional exposition and network building. It is widely known that hiring companies, especially in the information technology segment, value engagement in the open-source community as a worthy entry in the curriculum vitae of aspiring programmers and software engineers.

The Open-Source Economic Sustainability

The above overview outlines a few hypotheses that might arguably be evoked as motivations for people and organizations to invest in open-source development. Despite their non-neglectable contribution to the continuous production of open-source resources, it is pertinent to observe that hobby, philanthropy, low commercial prospect, advertisement, portfolio building, and possibly other comparable interests, neither individually nor collectively, can be arguably accounted for the large, long-lasting, world-class open-source projects existing today. Such a phenomenon calls for a more sound explanation capable of justifying individuals' and organizations' massive investments and the impressive amount of effort dedicated by community-driven ventures and large companies to deliver ambitious open-source resources. And a clue to that question may be found in the very definition of open-source, more specifically in the clause of distribution.

Recalling, the denomination open-source is based on the rights to use, modify and distribute the software, with its formulation prescribing that those three privileges be not restricted to purpose, person, group, or additional permission request. The last clause, in particular, states that the user must be free to distribute the software *either in its original or modified form, and either free-of-charge or commercially*. The "original or modified form" specification is intended to allow the distribution of derivative works. The "free-of-charge or commercially" part, in turn, is meant to ensure that the creation of derivative works can support productive professional activity. Together, those two requirements lay the groundwork for enabling the open-source paradigm as an economically-sustainable model of continuous innovation fostering.

In the next section, we break down such a model into its fundamental principles and explore how it functions from a systemic perspective. A word is in order, though, as historically, the open-source movements did not emerge from this rationalization, nor the formulation of open-source itself was derived from the theoretical treatment we herein outline. Instead, the present study is carried out as a *post facto* analysis. In it, we abstract a conceptual innovation fostering model of which the open-source case is a realization. It is not argued that this instantiation was designed under the rationales of the introduced approach; instead, the open-source movement is a spontaneous phenomenon that seems to have naturally evolved around the mechanisms we identify, even if in an unplanned, organic manner, as unproductive strategies faded out and effective ones converged to a consistent system.

INNOVATION ECOSYSTEMS

For the sake of laying out a conceptual ground upon which to develop the discussion, let us consider the common notion of *innovation* as meaning, without prejudice to strict domain-specific definitions and different legal interpretations, any kind of intellectual creation artifact — irrespective of its nature whether technological, artistic, scientific, or other — having implied the virtues of novelty and value delivery. Under this perspective, the term may refer, for instance, to technical, literary, musical innovation, and so on, and may apply to ideas — such as a chemical formula or industrial process — or their tangible expressions — such as a book's textual material or a piece of software's source code.

While the ability to innovate in the implementation of inner processes is widely recognized as a vital competence for the modern industry, the present discussion applies to the enterprise — either an organization or an individual entrepreneur — that delivers innovation as a product, and to which the text will refer as *innovation enterprise*, or *innovation industry*. The software industry, whose core business is the development of novel software applications, is an example of an innovation enterprise, as are those in the computer hardware, pharmaceutical, digital entertainment, music, cinema, biotechnology segments, and so forth.

Regarding the context of the traditional, *i.e.*, proprietary, innovation industry, Figure 1 brings a very abstract depiction of the mechanics through which stakeholders exploit the innovation artifacts, and how knowledge sharing impacts the development dynamics. The whole scheme is here termed an *innovation ecosystem* — and again, it is a very simplified intuitive description suited for the purpose of the present analysis.

The system represents the perspective of the innovation creator, referred to as the *developer* of the *innovation* item — be this some technology, artwork, educational content, or any other intellectual artifact. The arrow connecting the two respective blocks denotes that the developer *invests* resources — money, labor, time etc. — to produce the item of innovation. The diagram symbolizes that the developer invests also in the development of new products (including services) enabled by the innovation. Those products, in turn, deliver value to the consumer, here labeled *user*, who finances the development by resorting to some *fund* source, and ultimately generates revenue for the developer. The funding source may represent the user itself, by employing its own capital to contract the developer, or else the developer

Figure 1. Partial view of the traditional innovation ecosystem

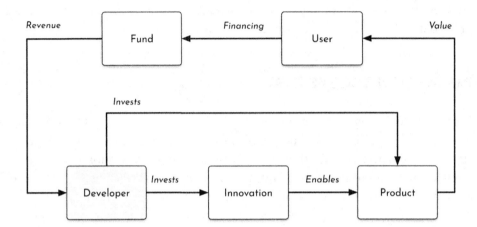

by its own initiative. The fund may yet refer to an external instance such as a public or private funding agency with a mission of fostering innovation.

For the sake of illustration, suppose a software company that, financed either by own capital or by a contracting customer, invests its development resources to create a novel computational method (innovation). The invention, implemented as a programming library, is aimed at enabling cutting-edge performance and functionality attributes for a computer-simulation program (product) targeted at the building industry (user) — say, for the segment of bridge construction. The software company works in the product's development and gets financially compensated by the construction company — or, alternatively, by a public funding agent in the scope of a technological development program. In any case, the first two stakeholders, the developer and the user, have their business purposes fulfilled through the interaction: the former accomplishes its profit goals, and the latter has its needs met by the new specialized software. The third stakeholder, the funding instance, if present, is as well satisfied.

Closed-Source Innovation Ecosystem

The diagram of Figure 2 completes the partial representation depicted in the former schematic (Figure 1) by introducing an additional stakeholder, collectively representing the developer's *peers*.

The arrow descending from the innovation block portrays the intuitive notion that, if competitors have free access to the intellectual artifact, then, by making some extra investment to create an *enhanced* version of the product — say with a better user

Figure 2. Closed-source innovation ecosystem

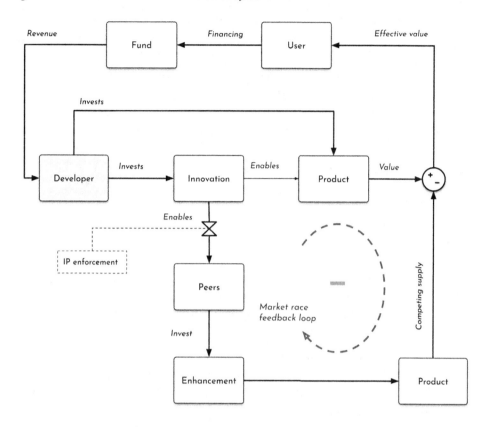

interface — then a rival company may introduce a *competing supply* in the system. In the present framework, the effect of such competition is modeled as a decrease in the value that the consumer attributes to the original product — that is, other possibly more attractive alternatives are available. This reduction may negatively impact the customer's initial disposition to finance the developer (recalling, the model describes the perspective of the innovation creator) and, ultimately, in a loss of revenue. Such an effect may be conceptually interpreted as the occurrence of a *market-race feedback loop*: the higher the developer's investment in the innovation development, the more accessible for the competition to seize the targeted market share; the more the developer's profit is so challenged, the less incentive for continuing the development. The result is a negative feedback loop because the competition's effect acts against the developer's interest — indeed a very elementary principle that can be grasped even by common sense. And seeing that the competitor does not incur the development costs borne by the original developer, the rival company enjoys an unfair advantage by being able to either negotiate lower selling prices, or afford significant improvements to make the product more attractive.

It has long been recognized that one way to intervene in this ecosystem, so as to foster innovation, is by limiting the competition's capability of exploiting the innovation in ways that discourage the creator's investment. That is precisely the justification for introducing the *intellectual property* (IP) instrument — alluded to in the diagram by the schematic valve symbol. Its objective is to encourage the inventor to devote effort and resources to the intellectual creation by offering it a certain degree of protection against unfair competition, should the creator intend to exploit the intellectual artifact commercially in a way that would be otherwise harmed by competition. The IP mechanism can be used to secure the creator's advantage or to directly profit by licensing the creation.

The IP mechanism works by artificially conferring intangible creations the temporary status of a property. The attribution is said to be artificial because, concerning the legal concept of regular (tangible) property, and despite competing theoretical doctrines and the specificities of varying national jurisdictions, in most developed nations, the premise of property is tied with the promise of a few elementary property rights. Notwithstanding the different terms used to enumerate them in diverse contexts, the idea is that the property owner can control how others are allowed to access its property, and exert the privileges of use, fruition, and disposal. The right to use entitles the owner with the dues of enjoying the property, *e.g.*, living in their house or driving his car. The right of fruition grants the owner the exclusive prerogative of earning the benefits derived from the property, *e.g.*, collecting the profits from the rental of their car or the income resulting from the selling of crops grown in their lands. The right of disposal empowers the owner with the authority of ceasing the ownership by transferring or relinquishing the property, *e.g.*, by donating their real estate or selling their car. To fully enjoy the rights of use, fruition and disposal, the owner must be able to claim possession of the property, and be ensured the means to enforce the fulfillment of their ownership benefits. Also, as the holder of the property rights, the owner is the only one entitled to decide how others may enjoy the property. That is implemented by way of a license that specifies certain conditions under which third parties can exert some of the property rights. For instance, a license may allow one to use an item either commercially or complimentary; or it may permit one to profit from the property.

While it may be argued that the same conceptual framework of regular property can be naturally extended to intellectual creations, some experts reason that intrinsic differences between tangible and intangible items pose theoretical and practical challenges to that viewpoint. For example, if one takes unauthorized possession of a book volume, then its owner is deprived of the opportunity to read it (right of use), rent it (right of fruition), or make it a gift (disposal). On the other hand, if one makes an unauthorized copy of the same book, the owner remains in possession of its volume to fully enjoy all of their presumed property rights. The only disadvantage the owner could possibly perceive in this circumstance is the disfavoring of the commercial exploitation of the book, should they envisage a business model in which the exclusive ability to make copies of the item is paramount for the success of their enterprise. And this is what the intellectual property expedient serves to: the enabling of a particular kind of business model for exploiting intellectual creations.

Under this perspective, the IP instrument provides another legal device, supplementary to the regular property, to claim the alikeness of tangible and intangible things. Essentially, the IP legislation enacts the equivalence between subtracting and multiplying an intangible asset. Considering separately both the material manifestation of the book with its pages and cover on the one hand, and on the other the abstract nature of the story and visual depictions it conveys, it is only under the force of such artificial arrangement that reproducing the intellectual content of the book can be likened to stealing the physical volume. To the question "who owns a poem", prior to the advent of IP, the answer would appoint the humanity rather than the poet; now, since IP is in force, the only one who has no need of worrying about the legal conditions under which it is safe to recite the verses in public — or it in the social media for that matter — is the poet themselves. Should the author elect a different kind of business model to profit from the creation that do not depend of rights reservation — or else be driven by the sake of art solely — there would be no inherent reason to restrict the public enjoyment of the piece of art — a subtle hint revealing the distinct philosophical rationales grounding the notion of property and intellectual property. Those who abide by this doctrine understand that the IP instrument is a concession conferred by the society, through which it surrenders its otherwise natural right to use the intangible intellectual asset, as a way to allow the creator secure the economic viability of their intended business model. The legal apparatus of patents and copyright serve this purpose, and the fact that they expire after a determined time duration, as opposed, for instance, to real estate ownership that does not expire, is a clue of the distinct character of those two types of property.

In any case, the IP device is not only a sensible measure but also a necessary agency to enable the innovation ecosystem represented in Figure 1. Regarding the running example of the editorial industry, if any competitor is allowed to print and sell copies of a book, then fewer readers might be convinced to purchase the item from the original publisher. And since this publisher is the one who pays professional writers, the competition will have an unfair advantage right from the beginning. The issue becomes even more critical when considering digital publishing: making copies and distributing eBooks is so easy that not even the competing publisher can cope. Some industrial segments use to tackle this problem by guarding valuable intellectual assets under strict industrial secrecy. In contrast, the patent mechanism is proposed as an alternative to encourage the company to disclose its creations for the benefit of scientific and technological development, in exchange for the guarantees ensured by the IP contract. In other circumstances, though, keeping secrets is not even practical or possible, such as with artwork products that are inherently intended to be exposed.

Apropos, there exists a vigorous debate about the ethical implications of the IP thesis and its merit in boosting or restraining the pace of innovation, with some questioning the idea of selectively denying access to knowledge and its application. In the free and open-source movements, for instance, there is much discussion about how rapidly technology and science can evolve with and without IP enforcement and how fast could equitable access to new medicines, educational content, information technology, and other benefits propagate. Be it as it may, and through an unbiased and purely technical perspective, the fact remains that, in order to implement a sustainable innovation ecosystem like the one being examined, the source needs to be closed, and the IP approach emerges as a realistic strategy.

Open-Source Innovation Ecosystem

It is opportune to compare the previously outlined traditional, closed-source innovation ecosystem with the alternate model schematically illustrated in Figure 3.

The upper part of the diagram does not change: the developer invests in the creation of the innovation artifact, which enables the development of new products. Those products deliver value to the user and provide the motivation for financing the developer's revenue. Attention should be drawn to the absence of the mechanism to prevent the developer's peers from taking advantage of the innovation item, as was the case in the proprietary model. And this is not without reason: under this approach, the developer deliberately abdicates from the exclusive prerogative to explore the innovation, under the prospect that the enhancements that the peers come to implement will also be made available under the same unrestrictive conditions — thereby returning to the original developer. In the present framework, such retribution is modeled as compensation paid to the user in the form of value added to the innovation.

Many software developers release their projects under open-source licenses upon this motivation. To draw a picture, let us recall the illustration previously mentioned about the software company that produces computational tools for the building industry — but now, rather than bridge construction, say it operates in the design of dams for hydroelectric power generation. Let us suppose it decides to embrace an open-source business model.

First, a basic premise of this system is the availability of an ample framework of open-source resources with the quality and versatility required to yield an effective

Figure 3. The open-source innovation ecosystem

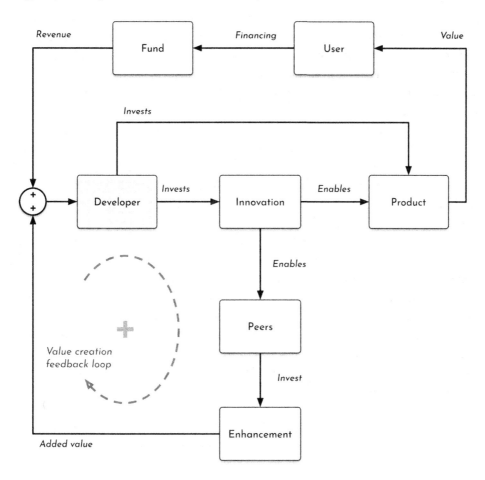

collaborative infrastructure. Thus, if the condition is fulfilled, the software company in the example would not start the development of its product from scratch but, rather, would build onto the existing foundation. It is enough to consider that this developer also plays the role of a peer in an already existing ecosystem. Software reuse is a widely recognized industrial practice capable of accelerating the development and incorporating the quality of the base components into the product. Second, be it bound to the terms of the licenses associated with the selected open-source tools, or by way of a calculated strategy, the company will release its own enhancements also in the form of open-source resources. What might sound like a wrong move from the perspective of the proprietary innovation ecosystem becomes the winning ploy in the alternate open-source model.

Suppose, for instance, another company — let us call it the peer — which also needs a software tool for itself or one of its clients in the building industry. Suppose it decides on the same strategy as the developer did. In that case, it will also conduct some research to identify suitable resources in the open-source infrastructure and, lukely, find the same framework, but now with the enhancements added by the former developer. Under the same reasoning it is likely that the peer will be motivated to pick the piece of software and use it as a base for further development. Indeed, the larger the number of peers participating in this process, the more intensive the development of the shared resource — and the more likely this resource will become increasingly attractive. It may even evolve into a mainstream solution, not unlike the many word-class pieces of open-source software that have established themselves as *de facto* standards in the industry, lending themselves as concrete examples of how this kind of ecosystem works.

One thing to note is that, in this interaction, by making the innovation freely available for third parties, the developer invites its peers as contributors — and, importantly, the contributors finance themselves through their own undertakings. The self-funded contributor community lays the major cornerstone of this innovation ecosystem model. It is through that mechanism that the *value-creation feedback* of Figure 3 emerges. It is denoted positive feedback because the more the community invests in enhancing the common resource infrastructure, the more the infrastructure becomes attractive for new contributors. The shared framework serves as a reservoir of innovation commons which each stakeholder benefits from and adds value to in a self-sustaining collaborative enterprise.

The software industry has plenty of factual instances of this configuration. Linux is again the canonical example. Some of the world's leading computer hardware manufacturers today do not sell Linux distributions. Still, they hire personnel to work in the development of Linux or donate funds to other projects in charge of Linux development because they want that operating system to run on their CPUs and support their peripherals. That is not only strategic to reach the market of Linux users, but also to reduce the cost of desktop and notebook computers that would otherwise need a preinstalled proprietary operating system. Many manufacturers of home appliances contribute software to the Linux project because they are interested in using an open-source embedded operating system to power their devices. Big tech companies back the Linux project because they want to use Linux as part of their cloud infrastructure, or as a platform for their corporate products, or as a development environment, among other reasons. The Linux Foundation, the non-profit consortium to promote Linux development, is endorsed by several of the giant players[13] in the software and hardware industry, all of them engaged as peers in the value creation feedback loop of the Linux ecosystem. Other outstanding examples may be found among communities that contribute to major Web application frameworks and microservices architectures, some of which support much of the Internet experience nowadays, including technologies for virtualization, containers, artificial intelligence packages, compilers, scrip interpreters, data analysis, and others[14].

COHERENT SYNERGY

Figure 4 depicts, side by side, both types of innovation ecosystems examined in the previous sections.

Figure 4. Synergy coherence in innovation ecosystems

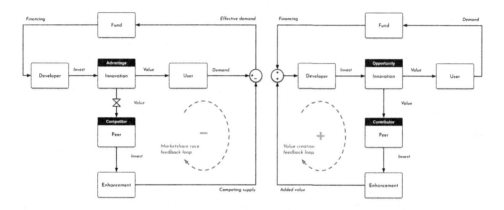

Which approach is more applicable is a natural, perhaps unavoidable, consequence of the business model in operation. As for the system on the left, that is the traditional scenario found in the proprietary innovation industry. For example, suppose a pharmaceutical company which employs its own reserves to finance the development of a new drug formula. In that case, it is reasonable that the company will be unwilling to allow other peer corporations competing for the same market to exploit the innovation. Likewise, for a software development company that intends to profit from a given product based on the number of copies sold, its business goals would be severely threatened if customers were allowed to reproduce and distribute those copies freely. There is hence an inherent contradiction between the interests of the developer, on one hand, and those of the peers and the users, on the other, concerning the ability to make free use of the innovation. Under these circumstances, electing to license the innovation as open source would be will-advised, and that is why IP enforcement is a central element in the proprietary approach.

Let this system be contrasted with the open-source innovation ecosystem depicted on the figure's right. This may be the case of cloud-computing infrastructure providers that actively contribute to the development of an open-source virtualization platform. There is no conflict of interest if another company in the same business also contributes to the same piece of software. Both use the platform to build their products, and therefore both make benefit of the improvements added to the innovation item by each other. While some customers may prefer to implement their own on-premises infrastructure using the referred open-source platform, others will readily opt for paying a trouble-free subscription plan to have their systems hosted in the cloud. The cost of development of the platform is shared between all contributors, and hence an open-source model is feasible and arguably advantageous in this case.

The purposeful contrast between both cases brings up a hint to distinguish when either a proprietary or open-source approach is suitable, as it draws attention to how the synergy between stakeholders emerges in both ecosystems with respect to whether their strategies concur in contention or in congruence. In the latter case, where peers collaborate to foster innovation as a result of their congruent interests, we will refer to the system as operating in *coherent synergy*. In the alternate case, where some peers take advantage of other peers being denied access to the innovation as a result of conflicting business goals, we will refer to the system as operating in *non-coherent synergy*. Notice that in both cases, each peer acts in its self-interest and coordinates its decisions accordingly; what determines the unfolding of a coherent or non-coherent synergy is the kind of business model each ecosystem operates.

The examples are specific, but it is possible to recognize some more fundamental features underlying the described cases, which account for their innovation ecosystem being coherent or non-coherent. Two factors, one concerning the innovation and another the product, are relevant for this distinction: the strategic function of innovation, and the convenience of the value delivered by products.

Strategic Function of Innovation

Recalling the example of the pharmaceutical industry and the proprietary software company, the non-coherent synergy yielded by their ecosystems is a direct consequence of their business models attributing to innovation the function of *competitive advantage* — a resource that the creator needs to reserve for its exclusive control in order to secure its goals. It is through the privileged control of innovation that the company can stay ahead of its rivals in the market. In a system where innovation plays such a role, the creator's peers function as *competitors*.

Differently, in the alternate case of the cloud computing providers that collaborate to develop an operating system, neither sees the innovation item as a competitive advantage; rather, the innovation is part of a collaboration infrastructure and functions as an *opportunity creation* resource for new products and services. Similarly, the widespread adoption of an open-source enterprise-quality database benefits all stakeholders that make use of it, including companies that develop products and services that need a world-class database component — hence their disposition to contribute to the collaborative development of large community-driven projects in this category. In such a system, the creator's peers function not as competitors but as *contributors*, and so as to boost the value-creation feedback, no steps are taken to prevent peer developers from using the innovation item in their own products.

Attention should be drawn to remark that the distinction between the functions of innovation in each system is not intrinsic to the nature of the intellectual artifact itself. Instead, as pointed out, it derives from the business model design. There are, for instance, software companies operating in either the proprietary or open-source modes. The decisive factor is how they treat innovation either as a competitive advantage or opportunity creation resource.

It is also worthy of note that while synergy coherence as a concept is formalized in the present discussion, the positive properties of a coherently synergic innovation ecosystem are not completely unheard of. The notion of Open Innovation (OI), for instance, has been proposed (Huizingh, 2011) to raise the awareness about the ways in which companies can benefit from the use of external ideas in their innovation, by intentionally allowing knowledge sharing with other organizations and communities of users. Sponsored hackathons[15], public API releases, distribution of free development kits are among increasingly applied strategies to invite customers and other organizations into open innovation environments. Through this collaboration the company prospects new demands, learns new use cases, probes customers' satisfaction, reduces cost of research and incorporates methods and best practices. Observe, however, that the intersection between Open Innovation and the herein introduced Open-Source Innovation is partial and limited. OI does not imply open source and is mainly discussed in the context of the proprietary industry. It is not uncommon that OI strategies involve the distribution of closed-source development kits and the release of public APIs under exclusive restrictive licenses.

The widespread practice of releasing proprietary products in incomplete form for the purpose of providing a platform upon which users can build creative additions does not necessarily ground a synergically coherent system. First, some OI models support approaches in which the development of new products is controlled by the company that owns the platform — which is a source of potential conflict between the developer and the contributor's community. Second, the proprietary status of the platform does not encourage the user community to freely recreate it, and possibly perfect it, to suit their own business goals — which would be a condition to drive a spontaneous, sustainable continuous innovation process. Moreover, unless the platform is made available under licensing terms that allow all users to make equal

Figure 5. Coherent and non-coherent synergies

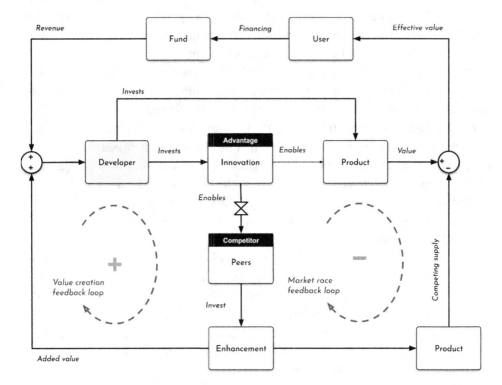

use of it, the discrimination of groups, or the conditioning of access to subscription fees or request of selective permission, are factors restraining the value-creation feedback loop.

In view of those aspects, and resorting to the illustration of Figure 5, the OI approach addresses how partially opening the valve of IP enforcement can be strategically beneficial to the company business model, even if such a model is predominantly competitive, and the property of the innovation is pivotal to secure an advantage in the market. Coherent synergy, conversely, is about designing or reengineering the company business model such that it does not depend on IP enforcement — with the valve fully open, *i.e.,* eliminated from the circuit. This requires that innovation be one hundred percent open source and that collaboration not be bounded by a deliberate strategy of the developer. The mention of a deliberate strategy is relevant here, as it rules out unavoidable technical impediments, and highlights that the synergy coherence concerns the ambit of decision-making. Put short, coherent synergy implies intended unrestrained collaboration.

At this point, it is probably opportune to address the notion of *competitiveness* as a mechanism of evolution in the innovation process. If presented as an alternative to competition, the view of an exclusively collaborative environment may seem to neglect the well-established understanding that selective pressure to outperform rivals under the environment's constraints is the driving force of the evolution phenomenon. That is a known fact in the natural selection theory and likewise in the business framework. In this regard, coherent synergy does not actually avoid competition; instead, it determines the ambit in which competition should unfold. The competition between two proprietary innovation companies happens both at the level of products and the level of the organizations themselves — inasmuch as if one product becomes less successful than the other in the market, its developer company is less successful as well. Differently, in a coherent-synergy ecosystem, as in the case of many open-source products, competition occurs only in the ambit of the innovation artifact; peer developers themselves still collaborate. If one product proves to be less effective than the other, then, in that case, its developer company is free to incorporate features of the competing innovation or even to completely merge into its development process.

One valid point about competitiveness that might arise from this discussion is that even when collaborating peers see a benefit in contributing to the development of shared innovation resources, they may eventually find themselves competing for the market share of the products enabled by the innovation. On that matter, unless some peer is seeking after some real monopoly in the segment — and then there is no room for cooperation whatsoever — there comes the second requirement for a coherently synergic ecosystem, concerning the value delivery by the product.

Convenience of the Value Delivery by Products

The proprietary innovation system has become so commonplace in modern industry that, even for the average lay individual, it is pretty straightforward to identify the primary characteristic of its business models. The developer exploits the competitive advantage ensured by the IP enforcement to profit from the innovation artifact. It can do so either indirectly, by enjoying the exclusive service of the innovation so as to be ahead of the competition, or directly, by licensing, selling, or allowing the IP rights — *e.g.,* patents or copyrights — in exchange for enjoying third parties' IP assets. Now, concerning open-source innovation, if not by offering exclusive advantages ensured by IP enforcement, how can the innovation aggregate competitive value to the product?

In order to answer this question, it may be opportune to resort to a concrete example. Let us consider that the founders of a new software development company are in the process of designing a business model for their future enterprise. One of the options they analyze is to release their software products as open source. On this possibility, one might reasonably raise two genuine questions: "who would purchase our products if potential customers can just serve themselves by copying our source code and compiling it themselves?"; and "what if another company takes possession of our source code, enhances it, and starts to sell a similar, possibly more attractive product?".

Before going through the possible answers to those questions, let us consider an analogous example in a radically different industry segment that traditionally produces a ubiquitous open-source product: bread. With perhaps a few exceptions, bread is primarily open source, insofar as its recipe — which by analogy stands for the bread's source code — is not subject to IP restrictions. Anyone can use, modify and distribute bread recipes for profit or not. The illustration is for sure nonorthodox and admittedly picturesque, but the contrast is purposeful to highlight some aspects that might hide under the tacit premises of the more conventional examples. Let us consider, for instance, the founder of a new bakery raising the same questions regarding its new business: "who would purchase our products if potential customers can just serve themselves by copying our recipes and baking bread themselves?" and "what if another company takes possession of our recipe, enhances it, and starts to sell a similar, possibly more attractive product?"

Those latter questions should be easier to respond to, given the usual real-world experience. To the first inquiry — who will purchase our products — the natural answer would point to almost everyone in the foreseen market share. It is not because people can make bread in their homes that they will gladly wake up early in the morning, mix the ingredients and bake the dough for breakfast, all before leaving for work or school. Most will naturally prefer to expend some extra money to buy freshly made bread at the local bakery, or else get a portion of industrialized loaf from a grocery store. To the second inquiry — what if another company gets our recipes — the solid, long-standing success of the bakery industry speaks for itself. Moreover, when a new kind of bread, pastry, or confectionery becomes a trending product, it is often possible for bakeries to incorporate their recipes into their portfolio, and even to add some differential customization.

Prior to returning to the software company case, it may be worth comparing the bakery industry with yet another unorthodox and likewise picturesque example: shoelace knots. Although used since antiquity, as revealed by archeological findings dating back to the bronze age, and later evolved through ancient Greeks' and Romans' sandals, shoelaces as we know them today became popular in the 19th century. Out of the many ways in which shoelaces can be tied, the classic bow knot is by far the most common. Bow knot is open source. Unlike other fasteners such as zippers and velcro, which were patented, the shoelace bow knot remained free for use, modification, and distribution, allowing the shoe industry to freely take advantage of such technology in the design of new products. Awkward as it may sound, what would be the prospect of a new commercial enterprise whose business consisted of fastening customers' shoes with well-tied quality bow knots? The oddity of the example is intended, and the answer to it is probably obvious: likely not promising. However, in comparing the bakery and the shoe-fastening business, if both offer open-source products, why are their prospects so divergent? The explanation comes quite intuitively: customers find purchasing bread from a commercial supplier convenient, more than getting their shoes fastened by a hypothetical knot shop.

In the framework of synergy coherence, it is useful to draw a distinction between the value of a product and the vehicle through which this value is distributed. The value is always some form of *convenience:* the convenience of having pre-prepared food when needed; the convenience of using a sophisticated word processor. The piece of bread is the vehicle through which the food convenience is delivered; the physical media or online repository through which the word processor is obtained accounts for its distribution vehicle. True, bread is a tangible object, and software is an immaterial product easy to multiply. However, the comparison drawn here likens bread and the software media as distribution vehicles; and likens the benefit of prepared food and the computer application to the convenience aspect. With this in mind, the model considers that the bakery is delivering an *elective convenience* to customers, meaning that users are spontaneously predisposed, and indeed prefer, to expend resources to acquire the product. Contrarily, because it is not delivering elective convenience, the shoe fastening shop would only justify optimism if it could create convenience artificially, for instance, by holding privileged IP rights over the shoelace bow knot and then demanding customers to pay a bow knot utilization fee — or charging shoemakers for a commercial license to incorporate bow knots in their products. Customers might be compelled to pay the compulsory charge to pass the access barrier, but that would not be by way of their natural willingness.

Now, finally getting back to the original illustration of the software development company, we can address the questions in light of this conceptualization. "Who would purchase our products if potential customers can just serve themselves by copying our source code and compiling it themselves?" "What if another company takes possession of our source code, enhances it, and starts to sell a similar, possibly more attractive product?". Perhaps the answer to the first query is that only customers who prefer the pre-compiled software, or would like to have it in physical media, would purchase copies. The second inquiry is a bit more challenging, as nothing is being done to prevent competition. And there lies the problem because a business model that foresees profiting from selling copies of software products is not delivering elective convenience. Judging by the extension of digital piracy[16] worldwide, one might infer that a great deal of the market would rather copy than purchase those products — indeed in the same way that people would not want to pay for shoelace knots. In a non-coherent innovation ecosystem, IP enforcement is employed to secure the market share. In the coherent-synergy approach, instead, it is the business model that should be reviewed. For instance, profiting from the sales of copies of digital work is not suitable for a coherently synergic ecosystem. Instead, leading companies such as Suse and Canonical, responsible for two of the most prominent Linux distributions, publish their respective products under open-source licenses, whereas designing their business models based on services and supplementary products that operate on top of Linux platforms. Software support, maintenance, consulting, customization, integration, and porting are among services offered by these and other companies operating with coherent-synergy business models.

The principle applies to domains beyond the software field. In the music industry, for instance, most professional singers and bands today rely on the sales of artistic albums for a substantial fraction of their revenue. Such a business model is non-coherent, seeing that the expectation of the artist disagrees with that of the customers, and as a result, the former struggles against piracy. Professional theater companies, on the other hand, usually base their revenues on the commercial execution of public performances. Should music artists implement an analogous business model and base their profits on live public exhibitions as well, piracy would not be a matter of concern. On the contrary, the more the pieces of digital music are copied and shared, the larger their potential to increase the fan base, and hence the larger the prospective public in the live concerts. Imitating the artist's performance is possible under an open-source model, but the elective convenience delivered by the artist lies in the authenticity of the performance. A cover artist's presentation has its place but it does not substitute for the original — as copies of digital work do — and likewise for original pieces of art and their alternative counterfeits.

In summary, the applicability of the coherent-synergy innovation ecosystem paradigm requires the design of an appropriate business model in which the product effectively delivers an elective convenience for customers. By elective convenience, the statement means that the product must address a customer's genuine need, offering a solution that they are spontaneously willing to pay for. For instance, copying digital work is so easy and inexpensive nowadays that most customers do not have the real need to purchase physical or digital copies of software or artistic works; people can effortlessly serve themselves to obtain those items. Digital work copies as a product, therefore, do not deliver elective convenience. The need to purchase the items is then artificially imposed through IP enforcement. Attending concerts, accessing support for software systems, and subscribing to online services do account for elective conveniences.

COHERENT ECOSYSTEMS

Summarizing the previous discussion, Figure 6 represents the notion of a coherent-synergy innovation ecosystem schematically.

Figure 6. Coherent-synergy ecosystem

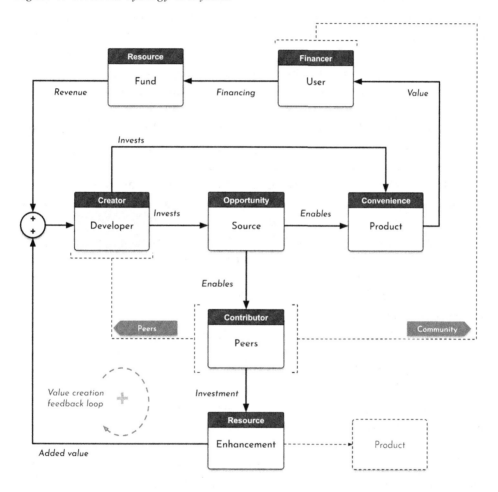

The diagram highlights all the aspects relevant to the discussion, now translated into the core elements of the coherent-synergy model. The scheme expresses the perspective of the *developer*, the individual or the organization *investing* in the innovation creation process. The innovation enables *products* and services that deliver value to the user who, ultimately, generates revenue for the developer. The innovation development may be *financed* either by the customer upon contract, by the developer through its own initiative, or by interested third parties. The picture highlights the notion of *community*, in which peer developers and *users* take part. A distinctive feature of such an ecosystem is that it relies on the perspective that the community collectively contributes to the development process in return for the value it receives from the freely available innovation. The community is, therefore, self-financed through the products and services it is capable of implementing based on the shared intellectual resources. This latter point is central to the concept of coherent synergy and, ultimately to the open-source ecosystem: the community collaborates spontaneously with the developer in the continuous improvement of the creation without requiring direct expenditure; the community funds itself by means of the economic advantage it derives from products and services built upon the common infrastructure.

Generically, the block *innovation* represents any kind of original intellectual creation with the potential for enabling new *products*, including services, regardless of its nature, whether technological, educational, artistic, managerial, scientific, or other. In this framework, the substantial artifact corresponding to the innovation item is represented by the concept of *source* — herein referring to the *description of an innovation artifact in an appropriate form and sufficient details such that competent third parties are capable of effectively implementing and adapting the item for their own purposes.* This broader definition extends beyond the usual strict meaning assumed in the computer software domain, where the preferred form to describe the item so as to allow developers to implement and modify the program is its source code, written in a given programming language. In the more comprehensive sense, the source of a piece of hardware corresponds to its technical specification, including schematics, lists of electronic parts, ensembling directions, and other technical instructions required for modifying and building the equipment. In the same vein, the source of a book encompasses the text, graphical elements, and other features needed to transform and reproduce the volume; the source of a piece of music comprehends the scores and lyrics; the source of a piece of research work covers its experimental design and empirical data, and so on. Moreover, the extended meaning of the term *source* comprises not only the tangible expression of the intellectual creation — as in the sense understood by copyright legislation — but also the abstract ideas corresponding to an invention — in the sense assumed by the patent legislation. Objectively, this means that source refers not only to the program source code but also to the algorithm it implements; and not only to the textual elements of a literary work but also to the story it tells along with the characters and other narrative elements. With the exception of some limited aspects of trademarks that concern more about product and developer identification than about innovation value, the concept extends to other types of intellectual properties such as industrial design and plant breeders' rights.

In order for the innovation ecosystem to be synergically coherent, every peer needs to abide by an appropriate business model that aligns itself with the congruent interest of the community. To that end, such a business model should meet two essential criteria:

a) innovation must function as a strategic resource to create opportunities for products and services — as opposed to the role of competitive advantage — such that peers have compatible interests concerning the exploitation of the intellectual creation;

b) products enabled by the innovation must convey elective convenience to the users so that consumers are genuinely and spontaneously disposed to expend funds for the delivered value, and that the steady demand be not dependent on access restriction measures.

The first requirement aims at ensuring that the community is committed to wholly sharing contributions to the innovation so as to encourage effective, unrestrained collaborations among peers, and unleash the full potential of the value-creation feedback circuit. The second provision is a requirement to uphold an economically sustainable innovation business. Collectively both strategic elements provide the conditions to foster a continuous innovation process not reliant on IP enforcement, and to allow for the community of peers to indirectly finance the innovation development by means of its reciprocal contributions.

Open-Source Innovation

It is a natural consequence of the above rationale that, at the technical level, two factors are paramount for the success of a synergically-coherent ecosystem. First, the innovation must be open source; otherwise, fully unrestrained collaboration is inherently not possible. In this essay, we will use the term *open-source innovation* to distinguish the present context from the already existing, non-synonym expression "open innovation". In the same vein that the notion of "source" is here generalized, the definition of *open* should also be correspondingly adjusted. For the sake of synthetic formulation, *open-source innovation* herein refers to *the concurrent fulfillment of equal non-exclusive rights of use, modification, and distribution of the innovation artifact.*

By "concurrent fulfillment", the statement declares the three requisites as necessary conditions that must be met simultaneously. By "equal non-exclusive rights," the definition asserts that the guarantees must be fairly ensured to all users, with no discrimination of field of endeavor, people, group, or any other criteria. Public availability of the source code is naturally indispensable. Special attention should be drawn with respect to the explicit conditional "equal," which, in a strictly literal sense, does not yield any exception nor even to the IP rights holder. Equal rights, therefore, implies that all users must be granted the same liberties to use, modify and distribute the intellectual creation, and therefore enjoy, to the full extent, the same prerogatives that the property owner. Such prerogatives include even the right to use and distribute the artifact in its original or modified form, and either free of charge or commercially — which is absolutely essential for the economic sustainability of the coherent ecosystem. This subtle yet crucial point is arguably the heart of the matter when it comes to understanding the open-source paradigm — even in the more restricted, traditional context of open-source software. While the conventional usage of IP enforcement aims at restricting the users' access to the property rights associated with the innovation, the open-source perspective deliberately relinquishes those privileges such that *all users are set in equitable positions with regard to the fruition of intellectual creation.* The diametrical opposition between the open-source and the proprietary approaches stems from the distinct strategy that each one relies upon to foster continuous innovation.

BUSINESS DESIGN

The role of innovation as a resource for enabling opportunities for new products and services, and the delivery of elective convenience for users, are both at the core of the open-source innovation model. And as both features become central in the design of the business model of any enterprise electing such a path, it is worthy to examine a few aspects pertinent to the strategic ambit and analyze how they may either promote or hinder those two features.

Open-Source Licensing

Public domain is the status of an intellectual creation that is not a property because either authorship has never been claimed, or property rights have been waived by the creator, or else the maximum embargo period allowed by the respective type of IP instrument has expired. If not in the public domain, the creation is intellectual property.

Whilst an intellectual creation in the public domain bears some equivalence with open source, given that it does not restrict the essential rights to make use of the item, its application for open-source release is not usually endorsed, as the validity of public domain status may differ in distinct jurisdictions. The expiration times of varying types of IP may be different among countries, and local legislations may have different interpretations of which mechanisms, if any, are available for the author to officially disclaim property rights. In general, it is strongly recommended that an open-source creation be claimed as intellectual property, and then concomitantly released under a proper open-source license.

A license is an instrument that the IP holder uses to allow third parties to enjoy one or more of the IP rights associated with a proprietary intellectual creation, and that set the conditions under which such permission applies. In order for a license to be considered an open-source innovation license, as previously discussed, it must grant the user the concurrent fulfillment of equal non-exclusive rights of use, modification, and distribution of the intellectual artifact. That means the right to take advantage of the innovation and incorporate it into products for any purpose, without discrimination of people, group, or field of endeavor; the right to modify the item and produce derivative works; and the right to distribute products enabled by the innovation either in its original or modified form, and either complimentary of commercially. A derivative work, in this context, is any product that incorporates innovation.

In the case of software, the tree requisites boil down to the commonly understood definition of open-source software, namely the autonomy to freely use, modify and distribute copies of the software. In the case of a drug formula, this translates into the right to produce the chemical, create new compounds derived from the base formula, and distribute products based on the original or extended formula. In case of an artistic drawing, the condition implies the right to exhibit and reproduce the image in any media, create artworks based on the drawing, and distribute copies of the original or derivative work, and so on.

As earlier mentioned, *freeware* and *shareware* licenses are not open-source licenses, seeing that they allow one to use and sometimes share the item but not to change it or distribute modifications. Notice that the availability of the source code is a necessary but not sufficient condition for an intellectual creation to be considered open source. Some companies make the source code of their proprietary products publicly available under a so-called Source Availability License (SLA), a distribution term that allows third parties to inspect the source code but does not authorize them to incorporate it into their own products — and in doing so SLA is therefore not open-source. There are also some licenses aimed at making the creation's source code publicly accessible and even allowing derivative works, but whose terms forbid the commercial use of the intellectual artifact. For example, the Creative Commons' licenses that include the ND or NC conditions — no derivative works, or no commercial use — belong to this category. The non-commercial use clause is sometimes considered by independent artists or researchers of public universities as result of their intention to produce knowledge for the common good rather than for profit. Those licenses by definition do not qualify as open-source, seeing that they do not allow for the economical sustainability of the continuous innovation ecosystem. Other related terms include *open access*, an emerging business model in the scientific publishing industry, in which authors are charged publication fees while readers have free access to the articles. Open access is seen as a positive change capable of making scientific communication more widely accessible both for researchers and the public in general. Nevertheless, open access is not the same as open source; indeed most implementations today still rely on proprietary business models, and licensing terms do not necessarily allow commercial derivative works to their full extent.

The fields of software and hardware are replete with examples of open-source compatible licenses. Samples vary in the specific terms and additional conditions, but in essence, all agree with the three essential rights of use, modification, and distribution. The Open-Source Initiative, for instance, publishes a list of requirements that a license must fulfill so that it can be classified as an open-source license. The Free Software Foundation, likewise, has another specification to determine if a license is a free-software license. A systematic list of provisions for Open-Source Hardware (OSH) is perhaps not as well systematized as in the software area but is also present in varying existing OSH licenses (Pearce, 2017).

One crucial aspect of open-innovation licenses that impacts not only the viability of the business model but also the whole ecosystem's synergy is how the license terms extend to derivative works. The possibilities divide open-innovation licenses into two main categories, one which requires derivative works to abide by a license no more restrictive than the license of the original work, and one that allows derivative works to be distributed under more restrictive terms. In the domain of open-source software, the former is known as *copyleft*. The term is a pun on the mechanism of copyright, originally meant to reserve the proprietary rights on derivative works exclusively for its author. In the reverse direction, copyleft subverts the use of the copyright expedient to compel the publication of derivative works under the same open-source status. The General Public License (GPL) created by the GNU Project is an example of a copyleft license (GNU, 2007). Several important projects in the open-source landscape adopt the GPL. Linux, for instance, is currently distributed under the GPL version 2. Git, MySQL, and WordPress are other examples of GPLed software. Other copyleft licenses include OpenSSH License, Eclipse Public License and Open Software License (SDPX, 2022).

The alternative to copyleft is commonly referred to as non-copyleft, as the licenses in this category allow derivative works to be distributed under terms that are more restrictive than those imposed by the original work's license. The Lesser General Public License, LGPL, is a non-copyleft version of the GPL published by the Free Software Foundation (GNU 2007b). Its main purpose is to allow the use of open-source software in circumstances where a copyleft license would not be practical or possible. For instance, that happens when the computer program in question is meant to be linked against an already existing proprietary piece of software. In the terminology of the area, linking may be generically explained as the process by which two programs are combined into one larger program, with one referencing variables and functions from the other. It so happens that in many jurisdictions, computer source code is treated similarly to regular literary works under copyright laws. By analogy, then, the latter program produced by linking two programs together may be seen as a derivative work, since the larger program encompasses both former programs. This may result in a conflict for the proprietary software owner, as the copyleft licensed software would require the derivative work to be released under an open-source license, and the whole source code of the final product would have to be disclosed and made available for free use, modification and redistribution. A common scenario where this problem occurs is in the development of device drivers, which are the components of an operating system responsible for its interface with hardware. In order to implement this interaction, the hardware manufacturer may make available device-specific *firmware*, small pieces of embedded software that directly control the device's electronics. More often than not, this firmware is proprietary and linking it against a copylefted device driver is not allowed. The LGPL is also suggested as an alternative for software libraries in specific cases where allowing the library to be used in non-free software development is considered strategic for creating new opportunities for open source. The GNU C library, GTK, and FFmpeg are examples of software released under the LGPL. Other non-copyleft licenses include BSD License, Apache License and MIT License (SDPX, 2022). Even allowing that a piece of open-source software be incorporated into a proprietary product, a non-copyleft open-source compliant license still must require that the distribution of the product discloses the utilization of the open-source item, and explicitly inform where the source code of that item can be obtained from.

Copyleft is sometimes subject to criticism within the free and open-source community under the claim that it is overly restrictive, and that it is ethically contradictory in restraining the developer's freedom to decide whether to release their derivative works as open source or not. In response, some copyleft advocates counter argue that restricting the restriction of freedom is intrinsically promoting freedom. Independently of philosophical perspectives, though, the choice between copyleft and non-copyleft licenses has also a very concrete impact on the innovation ecosystem synergy. As discussed, the central rationale for the open-source innovation model is to foster the value creation feedback, which presupposes a pact among peers settling that all parties are disposed to return their contributions back to the community. Copyleft is a form of securing the collaboration covenant, and in this sense, ensuring that derivative works remain open-source is a technically sensible strategy to guarantee the sustainability of the innovation ecosystem. From this standpoint, non-copyleft should be regarded as a secondary option for when there is an explicit and well-reasoned argument for opting for a non-copyleft license. This may be the case, for instance, of a library that needs to be linked against proprietary software so that the latter can interact with other open-source software. Furthermore, becoming irremediably bound to a copyleft license with no possibility of regrets should not be a concern, as it is possible to change the license in the next public releases, as well as to publish the software under a different license to handle special circumstances.

All this discussion about open-source software may be analogously extended to open-source innovation in general.

Product's Value Design

While the open-source paradigm gains relevance in industry, many different business models have been experimented with varying degrees of success. Nevertheless, even if producing open-source artifacts, not all examples are instances of coherently synergic innovation ecosystems. Some are truly open collaborative environments supported by the congruent interests of the community; others are essentially competitive proprietary innovation businesses that exploit open-source as a strategic maneuver. Between the two extremes there are some business models laying midway. An exhaustive enumeration of examples is beyond the scope of the present study. Nonetheless, a few well-known cases are worth mentioning for the sake of illustration.

Ancillary Services

Among many real-world examples, one widely applied business model is the type based on *ancillary services*. The software industry has plenty of examples of companies that build their business on commercial services enabled by the open-source software projects they contribute to. Technical support is one of the best-known products. There is a faint myth still wandering amid the lay observers, which presumes that because no single company can be held responsible for a piece of open-source software, then there is no one to back users in need of support. Such a misconception is brought about by the assumption that the product support must be provided by the product manufacturer — as it is in fact often the case in the proprietary industry. Seeing through the perspective of the coherent-synergy model; however, support service is decoupled from the manufacturing service, so acquiring both products from the same supplier is unnecessary. One is not bound to a unique support provider and may choose among options segmented to different niches.

Another example, especially in the embedded systems segment, is porting products to different software and hardware platforms. Yet other ancillary services include product customization, technical consulting, professional training, technical advice for deployment and integration, and other specialized forms of assistance. Sometimes ancillary services are offered independently of the software product as on-demand contracts or periodic subscriptions. Very often, however, services are commercialized as accessory contracts. In this mode, the supplier, either the developer or a third party, makes the software available under two distinctive terms, one complimentary and another for purchase. The latter, offered in return for monetary compensation — either as a one-time fee or subscription plan — offers the same piece of software under the same license, but implies the acquisition of a companion package of services.

Dual-Licensing

A caveat is in order for another kind of multi-term distribution commonly referred to as multi-licensing. As the IP owner, one has the discretionary prerogative to choose which rights each third-party user is allowed to enjoy, and this capability may be used to make the same innovation item available to different users under distinct licenses — often one copyleft and another proprietary. This approach is utilized, for instance, by some companies that develop copylefted open-source software but want offer the item for third parties interested in incorporating it into proprietary solutions. Despite being relatively common and commercially appealing, such an expedient exploits the copyleft device not to guarantee the consistent openness of the derivative works, but as a tactic to gain bargain power over a given product. While from the merely technical point of view, the software remains open-source, and no one is deprived of their rights to make use of the item, from the business model perspective, this is not a synergically coherent system. First, it was not designed to deliver elective convenience; the copyleft license is used to prevent the user from being able to serve themself from the open-source creation and hence need to purchase the proprietary version. In this sense, the result is not essentially different from using IP enforcement to secure a competitive advantage. Second, it violates the principle of non-exclusive equal rights to use and adapt the item that pertains to the very definition of open-source innovation: users that purchase the alternate proprietary license have privilege over the others in the open-source community. That is not a minor conceptual detail, but it has a tangible impact on the innovation ecosystem, as it is prone to discourage peers from standing by the pact of the unrestrained reciprocal contribution that is the basis to unleash the value creation feedback circuit in a coherent-synergy ecosystem. Furthermore, selective privilege does not agree with the benefits of fairness and inclusive power that account for key features praised by open-source innovation users. Upon this rationale, dual-licensing as a primary business model is incompatible with the open-source innovation model. Instead, it is best suited as a contingent resort to handle special events when it is eventually considered strategic for the collaborative project, rather than for the commercial goals of IP holders alone. Moreover, it is adequate that the dual-licensing policy foresees an open-source non-copyleft license, rather than a proprietary one, as an alternative to the standard copyleft contract. In any case, it is advisable to discuss the decision on a per-case basis with the community since, as stakeholders, the contributing peers are indissociable from the project governance and should be heard to avoid disrupting the collaborative covenant.

Online Deployment

Other than ancillary services, another business model compatible with the coherent-synergy model is the approach practiced by companies deploying open-source software in the Internet cloud. Under the infrastructure-as-a-service (IaaS) version, there are several large companies that rent resources in their data centers in the form of virtual machines running a GNU/Linux-based operating system, which can be accessed remotely by the user to deploy its own online applications. Platform-as-a-service (PaaS) is a similar business model in which the supplier offers online access to development frameworks such as interpreters, libraries and reusable components. Yet, Software-as-a-service (SaaS)[17] is an increasingly popular business model based on the deployment of ready-to-use instances of software applications such as office suites, games and project management software. The services may be commercialized as one-time fees, but the monthly or yearly subscription forms are becoming increasingly popular.

Online deployment is a valid business model for coherent-synergy innovation ecosystems. It delivers elective convenience to the user who prefers to access the software from their web browsers or mobile devices, more than to incur the costs and technical work to deploy a local instance.

Open Core

Another increasingly popular business model that has been gaining traction in the open-source software industry is the so-called *open-core* model. Essentially, the idea consists of making the base software available under compatible open-source licensing and offering proprietary additions under a different license. The open-source version is sometimes referred to as the community edition (CE), while the full-featured version is called the enterprise edition (EE). Although several companies have successfully collected revenue through this method, open-core should not be misleadingly taken for a coherent-synergy model. The fundamental assumption in this approach is that the CE delivers less value than the EE products. That by itself prevents the unrestrained collaborative circuit, seeing that the EE owner exploits the contribution added to the CE by the community to promote its proprietary product. In contrast, the improvements on the EE are not fully returned to the shared infrastructure. Practitioners of the open-core approach find themselves permanently in an inevitable dilemma of deciding which features should be exclusive of the proprietary version and which should be made available to the community. That is an actual issue to which readers may be familiarized and, indeed, a brief search on the Internet may bring up discussions on this matter — some even explaining why the community edition should be purposely not too good. Such conflict between the developer's and its peers' interests is, by definition, non-coherent and can negatively affect the perception of reciprocal collaboration attitude in the community.

Tardy Liberation

Still another known approach to profit from open-source software consists in making the product initially available under a proprietary license for a given time and then making a second release later on, now under an open-source license. During the embargo period, the developer company can collect the revenue it estimates worthy of the investment; after the business goals have been reached, the software is fully open-sourced. The strategy is often suggested as an expedient to finance the initial development of open-source projects, at the expense of delaying the free public release. While less contradictory than the open-core solution regarding the conflicts between the developer and the community, tardy liberation is unsuitable for a coherent synergy innovation ecosystem. For one thing, that approach creates an advantage for those who can afford early access relatively to those who need to wait for the tardy release. Even temporarily, this is a conflicting situation and, essentially, the method is definitely not different from the non-coherent innovation model based on IP enforcement — copyrights and patents also expire after some time when the innovation becomes public domain. The main reason, however, why tardy liberation is not a suitable business model for a coherent-synergy ecosystem is that it is not economically sustainable in the long term, as there is no provision for continuing the development after the embargo period. In this sense, it is not even properly an open-innovation business model at all; it may be better seen as a transient proprietary model that does not foresee the community participation in the continuous innovation process.

Companion Products

There is yet another business model for open-source innovation along the lines of ancillary services and online deployment that, like those, is based on delivering complementary value. It is the case of companies that invest in developing open-source software that enables other products, such as computer hardware and electronic appliances. The Android operating system, for instance, provides an open-source platform for smartphone manufacturers to power their devices and support a large base of user applications, which drives the interest of the user community in contributing to Android development. Google, the company behind the project, commercially licenses the trademark Android for manufacturers that want to advertise the compatibility of their mobile devices with the operating system. Another revenue stream comes from the operation of the online store where official applications are distributed with added values such as online commerce functionality, integrity check, and secure downloading. Android itself is currently based on Linux, another open-source operating system. Linux and Android are also used as embedded operating systems by manufacturers of home appliances such as network routers, smart TVs, media players, and countless other equipment.

Commissioned Development

Perhaps one of the most versatile financing models for open-source innovation is commissioned development. The provision for this modality was included in the innovation ecosystem model of Figure 6, by indicating the funding resource as an independent component. The entity may represent a public funding agency, industrial consortium, crowdfunding enterprise, or non-governmental organization interested in fostering innovation in a given area. That may be a viable open-source innovation business model, for instance, for the pharmaceutical industry and other sectors traditionally based on proprietary innovation. Instead of spending its own resources on the development of new drug formulae and subsequently pursuing the investment return through patent licensing, in this model, the commissioning agent — *e.g.,* a governmental institution in the scope of a public policy program, or an international organization aimed at world health promotion — finances the company to create and publish the formulae under open-source terms. Much of the regular research work developed in academic institutions around the world is carried out under this perspective. The public or private research institution is hired to solve problems and make the so-created open-source innovations available to society. The same model applies to art, education, entertainment, and other segments.

Summary

In summary, ancillary services, companion products, online deployment, and commissioned development are three examples of business models compatible with the concept of a coherent-synergy innovation ecosystem and its rationales concerning continuous innovation fostering. Dual-licensing, tardy liberation, and open core, on the other hand, are not compatible, seeing that those models do not comply with the fundamental requirement of a synergically coherent innovation ecosystem, namely the congruent interests regarding the exploitation of the intellectual creation, and delivery of elective convenience, both aiming at the unrestrained collaboration among community members.

The coherent-synergy paradigm and the open-source innovation model are not necessarily explicit choices in all areas. In many circumstances, they represent only the tacit way of organizing business in that given segment. Examples in the industries of food, engineering, and artistic business have been mentioned throughout the former passages of this article. In the open-source field — and possibly also the rising open hardware movement — we find both the coherent and non-coherent models coexisting vigorously, offering a remarkable contrast for comparative analysis. The non-coherent proprietary approach hegemonically dominates other industry domains. Devising feasible, economically sustainable open-source business models for these different fields constitutes perhaps the most crucial challenge to unleashing the emergence of coherent-synergy innovation ecosystems in those segments. Actually, even in the already auspicious open-source software area, while we see successful ecosystems in subdomains such as operating systems, web servers and browsers, frontend and backend microservices frameworks, database servers, and machine learning technology, the same is not witnessed in several other areas. For instance, the segments of professional media editions and digital games are still largely monopolized by the proprietary industry. The envisaging of novel economically sustainable business models for open-source innovation is still a challenge in demand of research to enable the development of coherent-synergy innovation ecosystems in several sectors.

Project Governance

One of the aspects in which open-source innovation development differs from the corresponding process in the proprietary environment is that the latter is mostly carried out within the boundaries of an organization and steered toward its business goals. There is a centralized decision-making instance that finances the development and determines what should be done, when, and how. In contrast, open-source innovation is collaboratively developed in a coherent-synergy ecosystem, by a self-funded community in which peers work independently in pursuit of their own goals. It is the fact that the shared open-source resources benefit all parties that binds the community together, and coherently engaged in continuous innovation development. Nurturing an active and harmonious community is therefore paramount for the success of the cooperative ecosystem, which brings up the crucial role of project governance.

There are several concerns worthy of mention regarding this topic. Among them is the project scope. While the creator that initiates the innovation development may have a vision regarding its potential uses to enable products and services, other peers will voluntarily join the community if they also find uses for the creations according to their own goals. It is, therefore, beneficial for the ecosystem to consider that the creation can be exploited beyond the original scope, and regard flexibility among the primary concerns when making design decisions. For instance, if some effort is required to implement some extra feature or structural pattern that may broaden the field of applicability of the project, this additional investment may be decidedly worthwhile.

Open-source leverages the idea of "hive development": instead of large monopoly companies creating the software we all use, open-source foresees a much more decentralized structure, where individuals and organizations engage independently and decide on the course of the development. The way such a self-organization process works in practice has spontaneously emerged from empirical exercises. Usually, the original creator of the innovation artifact, *e.g.,* an open-source software, who is also the holder of the item's IP rights, is regarded by the community as the official authoritative maintainer of the project. This can be an individual, a private company, or, as it's common for large projects, a foundation created to manage the development resources. The community, in turn, contributes to the project in different forms. Additions to the source are either transferred to the project owner, or are released under compatible open-source licenses. Influent members of the community may be invited or elected to compose a governance board geared toward the community's needs and views. The community's representativity does not correspond exactly to a democratic decision structure: neither the project owner needs to abide by the community demands, nor is the community obliged to accept the owner's decision. The project owner, who controls the intellectual rights on the artifact, cannot be coerced to implement the community requests. On the other hand, the community is free to fork the project into another instance, and proceed with the development from there on under a new governance entity. Successful projects have learned the skills of conciliation and trustworthiness.

THE ETHICS OF OPEN-SOURCE

One concern that assumes primary relevance in the open-source domain is ethics. Sustaining the community's cohesion requires maintaining an environment in which peers feel ethically and morally comfortable. Ethics is undoubtedly essential in any context, but in a proprietary development ecosystem, an individual's principles can — even if not ideally — coexist not perfectly aligned with the organizational ethos. Employees are expected to abide by the values endorsed by the company and, since perfect conformity is not to be sensibly expected, some tension between individual beliefs and corporate views is plausible and bearable to some reasonable extent. In an open community, differently, peers are not bound by contracts, and ethical issues are more prone to discourage spontaneous engagement. Disagreements may easily result in fierce contends, dissension of contributors, and ultimately the disruption of the collaboration ecosystem. Project administrators should have an eye on ensuring a healthy community. This implies acknowledging that some peers take part motivated by economic goals, while others may contribute driven by the interest in science and technology development, or yet aiming at humanitarian causes, or personal interest whether in skill development, art appreciation, portfolio and network building, or amusement activities. Listening to the community's expectations and providing comprehensive feedback are of key importance.

Yet on the subject of ethics, it is important to bear in mind the intrinsic differences between the open-source and proprietary environments with respect to the nature of the interaction among peers. In a non-coherent system, the synergy between the developer and its peers occurs in the context of competition, and success is inherently a matter of ensuring an advantage over rival undertakings. There may certainly be room for forms of inter-organizational cooperation, as conceived by modern economic views that incorporate the principles of the game theory, but the fundamental tenor of the relations among counterparts is of permanent contention. It is completely admissible that a participant takes any opportunity to overcome competitors, and corporate ethics is geared towards legitimating tough tactics to beat opponents. More often than not, any second thoughts about benevolence and commiseration, whether upon moral convictions or philosophical views, may feel awkwardly alien and deemed out of context when it comes to critical decision-making. Although not an explicit code of conduct, the motto "business is business" works as a conventional permit to disregard foreign moral constraints that might otherwise interfere in a corporate member's capability to take objective, yet arguably unempathetic, actions in favor of the company's goals, even those that might sound harsh and unconcerned under the ethos of other social extents.

Such a concession for an impersonal, strictly-business attitude is in blunt contrast to what applies to a coherent innovation ecosystem, where interaction among peers is of a collaborative nature. While competition calls forth a mere-professional relationship as a way to accommodate personal's and professional's dissonant conducts, cooperation, on the other hand, depends on trust and on the conviction that the other parties are committed to the pact of reciprocity. Formal cooperation agreements are good enough to warrant joint initiatives legally, but the need for a contract derives from the lack of confidence in the first place. Moreover, collaboration in a coherent ecosystem is spontaneous, and formal subscription agreements violate the requirement of the open-innovation definition with regard to universal rights to access the creation without further permission. Unrestrained collaboration in a coherently synergic ecosystem is not attainable unless all parties are confident that their peers are equally resolute to contributing to the enterprise without reservations. If each contributor fears that its counterparts will hold back their most promising ideas for a planned proprietary competing innovation, it is less likely that collaborative development will fulfill its potential, as every party will be cautious to ensure an advantage, or a defensive warranty, in an eventual conflict of interests. The net result of the converging efforts will tend to bring about an outcome consisting of what no one considers good enough to be retained for privileged use. Signed documents may serve to demand compensation for contract violations but those can neither cover all risks nor eliminate the tension arising in a competitive environment. Instead, it is worthwhile that community members recognize themselves as sharing moral values upon which they can rely to build trust. Rather than the impersonality and impartiality that are useful to mitigate ethical dilemmas in a competitive system, values such as loyalty and empathy are not only viable in a coherent collaborative environment but also required.

For a successful, fully unrestrained collaboration, it is important that the ecosystem's participants reorient the traditional advantage-oriented corporate mindset to align it with the ethics of the open-source model, grounded on trustworthiness and a sense of community. This implies, for instance, comprehending that the open-source phenomenon is not only of a technical and economic character but also of socio-cultural nature, driven by the ambition of provoking changes in how society organizes itself. Open source is seen by many of its advocates as a paradigm shift from a more competitive toward a more cooperative civilization, where personal values such as kindness, altruism, and generosity do not contradict the urges of professional conduct. Against this background, the plight of choosing between the enforcement of intellectual property, on the one hand, and the promotion of universal knowledge sharing, on the other, is viewed as a consequence of the conflictuous synergy of closed-source innovation. Some opinions in the open-source and free-software communities strongly criticize the very idea of IP enforcement (Rideau, 2004) and its collateral effect restraining inclusive access to humanity's intellectual production. In sustaining their view, they make the point that the technical advantages proposed by the open-source model are indeed the practical result of the principles of freedom and transparency, and the underlying virtues of cooperation over competition, sharing over denying, and community over monopoly. By providing concrete examples of open, collaborative development of freely usable and sharable knowledge, the free software and open-source movements have admittedly done a good job settling the scene for laying out those ideas up for discussion. Individuals and organizations willing to get involved in open-source innovation should be encouraged to get acquainted with those ideas and consider appropriate approaches to engineer ethically consistent business models.

Before concluding this topic, it may be opportune to note another ethic-related aspect of the coherent-synergy model. In the proprietary innovation business, creators rely on IP enforcement to secure a competitive advantage or to implement long-term profits in the form of license fees. Once produced, the intellectual creation can ensure a steady revenue stream for as long as the maximum embargo period allows. Such a revenue model, which accounts for the logic underlying the open-core business approach, is common, for instance, in the chemical, electronics, and aerospace industries, to name a few. In other segments, such as building engineering and healthcare, most companies operate through a different revenue model, in which the return on labor investment occurs in response to new value generation. When an engineering firm is hired to design a new structure such as a bridge, it is compensated by the contractor for creating the project, rather than by tolls installed in the passage. Likewise, private hospitals are paid to deliver customized medical treatments; there is no such thing as collecting royalties due to the patient's recovery based on the prescribed treatment. The coherent-synergy innovation ecosystem model exchanges the passive license-based revenue stream for an active continuous innovation exercise — sometimes, this has been referred to as a development-centric model. Individuals and organizations operating with open-source innovation are better equipped if their vocations are consistent with the will to create novel solutions, overcome new challenges, and innovate constantly. One consequence of this proactive mode of performing is that the full intellectual potential of people and organizations can be employed to always tackle new issues, advance knowledge and unleash development in all areas. It is unlikely that coherent-synergy ecosystems will run out of demands to fulfill, and if we as a society are committed to solving the most concerning troubles of humanity, then the determination to permanently mobilize all existing competencies and talents to address new challenges is something worth considering.

REFERENCES

Comission, E. U. (2021). *Study about the impact of open source software and hardware on technological independence, competitiveness and innovation in the EU economy.* https://digital-strategy.ec.europa.eu/en/library/study-about-impact-open-source-software-and-hardware-technological-independence-competitiveness-and

GNU. (2007a). *Gnu general public license.* https://www.gnu.org/licenses/gpl-3.0.html

GNU. (2007b). *Gnu general public license.* https://www.gnu.org/licenses/lgpl-3.0.html

Hasan, R. (2002). *History of linux.* https://www.cs.cmu.edu/~awb/linux.history.html

Huizingh, E. K. (2011). Open innovation: State of the art and future perspectives. *Technovation, 31*(1), 2–9. doi:10.1016/j.technovation.2010.10.002

Pearce, J. M. (2017). Emerging business models for open source hardware. *Journal of Open Hardware, 1*(1), 2. doi:10.5334/joh.4

Perens, B. (1999). The open source definition. *Open Sources: Voices From the Open Source Revolution, 1*, 171-188.

Rideau. (2004). Patents are an Economic Absurdity. *A Journal for Western Man, 28.*

SFC. (2022). *The Glossary of terms by Software Freedom Conservancy.* https://sfconservancy.org/copyleft-compliance/glossary.html

SPDX. (2022). *SPDX License.* List Software Package Data Exchange, Linux Foundation.

Stallman, R. (1985). *The GNU Manifesto.* https://www.gnu.org/gnu/manifesto.en.html

Stallman, R. (2002). *Free software, free society: Selected essays of Richard M. Stallman.* Lulu. Com.

Sun-Times. Chicago. (2001). *Steve Ballmer's interview to Chicago Sun-Times on June 1 2001.* Author.

Torvalds, L., & Diamond, D. (2001). *Just for fun.* Harper Audio.

ENDNOTES

[1] Free Software Foundation: http://www.fsf.org.

[2] Open Source Initiative: https://opensource.org.

[3] Another surrogate term FLOSS is also in common use, with the letter *"L"* standing for *Libre*, the equivalent of *free* in some romance languages like in Spanish and French. The expedient is an attempt to make up for the ambiguity of the word "free" in English, explicitly highlighting the connotation of "freedom" or "liberty" rather than "gratis". A famous quote by Richard Stallman, author

of the term Free Software, reads: "Free as in free speech, not free beer". That said, neither FOSS nor FLOSS have reached unanimity in the broad community.

4   The usage of the term *open-source* is not meant in prejudice of other proposed denominations such as *free software* or *open-source software*, or of related ethical discussion — and this essay does address this dimension. The term is used because the study is not restricted to software, but extends to other kinds of intellectual creations such as hardware, art and science.

5   The note refers to the historical long-lasting hostility of Microsoft to the open-source model, exemplified in the quote by its former CEO, Steve Ballmer, who in 2001 famously decried Linux as "a cancer that attaches itself in an intellectual property sense to everything it touches".

6   Amid FOSS supporters, some groups criticize the usage of the expression "ecosystem" to refer to the community, as the former might convey halfhearted indifference to socio-ethical concerns regarded by many advocates. In this article the author uses both terms, community and ecosystem, to distinguish two aspects pertaining to the discussion, respectively the body of individuals sharing common goals and values, and the systematic model describing the mechanics of the collaboration process.

7   Perhaps an allegorical reference to *The Four Freedom Speech* by Roosevelt at the 1941 State of the Union address?

8   Including Debian, Drupal Association, FreeBSD Foundation, Linux Foundation, OpenSUSE Foundation, Mozilla Foundation, Wikimedia Foundation, WordPress Foundation.

9   Wikipedia's entry for the term FOSS, as of August 2022.

10   Some historical and noticeable examples of companies that contribute to open-source development include the Mozilla Foundation, RedHat Inc., SUSE Linux GmbH, Canonical ltd., among others.

11   Software as a Service, a business model for online software deployment in which consumers access remote cloud-hosted applications through a local user interface, usually via Web.

12   For example, GitHub, GitLab, Bitbucket, Source Forge and GNU Savannah, to name a few.

13   Companies such as AT&T, Cisco, Fujitsu, Google, Hitachi, Huawei, IBM, Intel, Meta, Microsoft, NEC, Oracle, Orange S.A., Qualcomm, Samsung, Tencent, and VMware are among LF supporting members.

14   Brands such as Mozilla, Apache, Docker, Python, TensorFlow should be easily recognizable.

15   A competition event where software developers team up to design and implement a software solution to address a proposed challenge.

16   The term "piracy" referring to unauthorized copying and distribution of software and digital arts is criticized by some segments of the FOSS community as embodying a biased moral judgment. For advocates of this view, multiplying and distributing knowledge is not morally akin to assaulting ships; it is the ethics of preventing third parties from enjoying and spreading intellectual creations that should be revised, in their opinion.

17   Amazon's EC2 (elastic cloud) product is an example of IaaS. Google's Collab is an example of PaaS. GitLab's online version is an example of SaaS.

Chapter 6
Trusting Critical Open Source Components:
The Linux Case Study

Marcelo Schmitt
Universidade de Sao Paulo, Brazil

Paulo Meirelles
iD https://orcid.org/0000-0002-8923-2814
Universidade de Sao Paulo, Brazil

ABSTRACT

Device drivers are an elementary part of the Linux kernel and comprise roughly 2/3 of the project's lines of code. Even though the fraction of device driver code in a conventional operating system (OS) can vary, some of these components are essential for system functioning. In addition, the Linux kernel is used in a wide range of applications, from cloud service providers to embedded systems and supercomputers. If GNU/Linux systems should be trustworthy to justify running them in those environments, then testing the kernel is fundamental. However, since device drivers are designed to interface with hardware, conventional test approaches may not suit the occasions when devices are unavailable at test time. This raises the question: How are device drivers tested?

DOI: 10.4018/978-1-6684-4785-7.ch006

INTRODUCTION

Trusting Critical FOSS Components

The present chapter revolves around the theme of dependability in Free and Open Source Software (FOSS) systems, with a specific focus on Linux. The study highlights the significance of the FOSS infrastructure that underpins a substantial portion of the software and online systems we rely on for both business and personal purposes. The examination centers on Linux device drivers, serving as a representative case study to raise questions about the level of trust that can be placed in the FOSS ecosystem. The material conducts an exhaustive analysis of the software testing methodologies utilized by the Linux project to assess the quality and reliability of device drivers. This discussion sheds light on the transparency inherent in the FOSS model, as it offers a unique opportunity to inspect and scrutinize the internal workings of the software. This openness stands in contrast to the limited ability to examine proprietary products that drive mission-critical systems, which lack similar transparency.

Linux, as an enduring project, forms the foundation of a substantial portion of today's modern computational infrastructure, a fact that underscores its importance and widespread adoption. The success of Linux is attributed, in part, to the implementation of innovative business models that facilitate collaboration between individuals and organizations with diverse perspectives. This collaborative environment enables stakeholders to leverage shared resources while being actively encouraged to contribute back to the community through money investments and technological enhancements. The chapter presents a valuable exploration of the factors contributing to the positive reputation and resilience of the Linux ecosystem, underscoring the significance of effective strategies that foster cooperation and mutual support within the FOSS community.

Device Drivers

Device drivers are an elementary part of the Linux kernel and comprise roughly 2/3[1] of the project's lines of code. Even though the fraction of device driver code in a conventional operating system (OS) can vary, some of these components are essential for system functioning. In addition, the Linux kernel is used in a wide range of applications, from cloud service providers to embedded systems and supercomputers (Corbet and Kroah-Hartman, 2017). If GNU/Linux systems should be trustworthy to justify running them in those environments, then testing the kernel is fundamental. However, since device drivers are designed to interface with hardware, conventional test approaches may not suit the occasions when devices are unavailable at test time. This bares the question: how are device drivers tested?

This chapter presents an introduction to Linux kernel device drivers, the Linux kernel development process, software test concepts, and popular [2] test tools for assessing device driver functionality.

Linux Kernel Device Drivers

The Linux kernel is accounted for many essential operating system tasks such as memory management, process scheduling, data storage, network communication, and many others (*About Linux Kernel* 2021). The kernel must operate several devices with highly distinct characteristics and complexity to provide fundamental system functionality. Moreover, it is reasonable to avoid mixing the control logic of different devices with one another and with core system logic. Thus, it is usual to encapsulate code for managing a device (or a family of related devices) into a device driver. "A driver is a piece of software whose aim is to control and manage a particular hardware device, hence the name device driver" (Madieu, 2017). For a more objective definition, let's consider that a device driver is characterized by a well-delimited piece of code (usually a file or a few files) whose purpose is to control the operation of a hardware design (or a set of related hardware designs). Usually, hardware designs are described in documents called datasheets or blueprints, which in turn describe the components and operation of a hardware device.

Entire subsystems and kernel portions not restricted to the operation of a single device (or set of devices), e.g., file systems, network stack, process scheduler, memory manager, etc., are not device drivers. Although these components may contain device drivers, they are not device drivers.

Linux Kernel Development Process

The Linux kernel source code is logically divided into several subsystems. "A subsystem is a representation for a high-level portion of the kernel as a whole (A. R. Jonathan Corbet and Kroah-Hartman, 2005)." A subsystem may also be understood as an abstraction to refer to some part of the kernel responsible for some system functionality, such as process scheduling, memory management, networking, etc. Most subsystems have one or more developers who take the overall responsibility for the code on that subsystem. These developers are known as subsystem maintainers (*How the development process works* 2021).

At each release, Linux incorporates changes from hundreds of developers worldwide. These developers may contribute to the project in many ways, such as by improving the documentation, fixing bugs, introducing new features, and providing support for new device drivers. The contributions to Linux (often called patches) are sent through email to appropriate mailing lists. There are several mailing lists at which Linux developers and maintainers review and discuss changes to the kernel.

When a maintainer accepts a patch, they include it in their development repository. Many (if not all) Linux maintainers have their development repositories (or trees) hosted at Kernel.org[3]. Since development trees are publicly accessible, test rings may perform tests on early phases of Linux kernel development. Moreover, Linux kernel developers and maintainers may request test ring administrators to add their repositories to the test infrastructure. After a repository is added to a test ring, it gets periodically pulled for testing (Khan, 2021b; Kroah-Hartman, 2022). Thus, after a patch gets into a development tree, it may be subjected to many tests from Linux kernel test systems.

The development process may be seen as a tree in which the nodes are subsystem development trees and the root is Linus Torvalds' kernel tree (known as the mainline kernel). Mainteiners closer to the root trust maintainers that are farther to review patches and only send good quality code upstream. At the beginning of each development cycle, Linus Torvalds declares he will accept new features for the Linux kernel throughout a period known as the merge window. Then, during a typically two-week span, subsystem maintainers ask Linus (or an upstream maintainer) to add (pull) changes from their trees into his repository. The flow of patches goes up from development trees into Linus Torvalds' mainline. After pulling patches during those couple of weeks,

LINUX KERNEL DEVELOPMENT PROCESS

Linus declares the merge window closed and stops merging new features for the next Linux release. The kernel produced by Linus at the end of a merge window is an artifact that urges testing since it is the bedrock for the upcoming Linux release.

The weeks that follow the merge window are known as a stabilization period during which Linus and many other kernel developers try to fix as many bugs and regressions as possible. That is as also a time of intense testing by robots, automated test systems, and test rings. The testing and bug-hunting season usually lasts six to eight weeks until Linus declares the release candidate to be the new Linux kernel (stable) release (*How the development process works* 2021). After that, Linus opens a new merge window and the process repeats for a newer Linux release.

In addition to the mainline Linux development process described above, there is an effort to provide support and maintenance for stable kernels. The kernels released at the end of each mainline development cycle are considered stable and maintained separately thereafter. The stable kernel maintainers, Greg Kroah-Hartman and Sasha Levin, backport bugfixes from the mainline tree and apply them to designated stable

Figure 1. Linux release process. Original figure from Linux Foundation Mentorship Series - August 9 by Greg Kroah-Hartman. CC BY-NC-SA 4.0. https://www. linuxfoundation.org/webinars/trust-and-the-linux-kernel-development-model

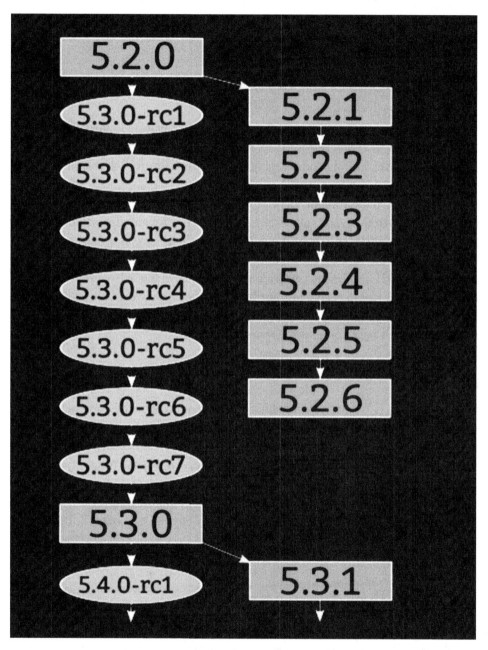

kernels on an as- needed basis. New stable kernel versions are provided until the next mainline (stable) kernel is released. At that point, the stable kernel release cycle rebegins with the newer stable kernel as base (see Figure 1).

Next Trees

Reviewers, testers, maintainers, and developers alike may want to view the changes queued for the next kernel release in an integrated form so they can avoid merging conflicts. However, pulling and merging patches from several subsystem trees is a cumbersome and error-prone task.

To overcome this problem, the community provides next trees, which bring together patches from several subsystems. The main tree for merging patches queued for the next Linux release is linux-next. By design, linux-next is a snapshot of how the mainline should be after the next merge window closes (*How the development process works* 2021). Since linux-next comprises changes intended for the forthcoming Linux kernel, the tree may enable contributions to be tested weeks ahead they reach the mainline. Refer to *How the development process works* (2021) for a detailed reference on the Linux kernel development process.

Software Test

Software testing is "an activity in which a system or component is executed under specified conditions, the results are observed or recorded, and an evaluation is made of some aspect of the system or component" ("IEEE Standard Glossary of Software Engineering Terminology" 1990). There is a variety of ways to test software. One may provide a program with all possible inputs (random testing / fuzzing), run only a few parts of the program (unit testing, integration testing), run a program under extreme conditions (stress testing), or apply any other of many software test techniques.

SOFTWARE TEST

Some authors go further and relax the concept of software test to encompass a larger set of activities in this category. According to Mathur, "*code walkthrough, also known as peer code review, is used to review code and may be considered as a static testing technique.*" (Mathur, 2013) The idea behind this notion of software test is that sometimes one don't even need to run a program to estimate if it's going to work as desired. This concept better aligns with complementary definitions of software testing. For instance, Claudi and Dragoni (2011) stated that "in software engineering, testing is the process of validation, verification and reliability measurement that ensures the software to work as expected and to meet requirements". Likewise, Mathur (2013) suggests that software testing "is the process of determining if a program behaves as expected."

Your authors understand that analyzing the structures and properties of the source code may provide insight into whether a program will function as desired, thus possibly making part of a software testing activity. In this text, the Linux code peer review process will not be approached. Yet, some attention will be given to static analysis tools because they are popular among the Linux development community and are run by automatic test robots that watch over Linux kernel repositories.

Regardless of the program under test, it is intrinsic to the software testing activity to compare measured behavior with the desired behavior described by formal or informal re- quirements (Mathur, 2013). Moreover, many hardware manufacturers provide datasheets describing the components and the functioning of the devices they supply. Therefore, one may think of device driver testing as the act of evaluating, validating, or verifying whether a device driver (or parts of it) operates the hardware it supports as described by its design. However, the reality is more complicated than the theory, meaning not all hardware devices work precisely as their datasheets describe or even come with accessible blueprints. In such cases, device drivers must also deal with nonconforming behavior or resort to reverse engineering.

Mathur (2013) proposed a comprehensive categorization of software testing techniques based on four classifiers. The classifiers ponder the resources for generating the tests, the development phase in which the tests are carried out, the objective of the test activity, and the characteristics of the artifact under test. However, those classifiers are not well suited for distinguishing between Linux kernel test practices for a few reasons.

First, Linux is a free software project, so the source code is accessible to everyone. Therefore, the kernel source can be used as an inspiration for any testing practice. Thus, testing techniques usually classified as black-box could be considered black-box and white- box. For instance, Andrey Konovalov advises reading the code to understand what types of input the system expects and to identify which parts of it can be targeted in the context of fuzzing the Linux kernel (Konovalov, 2021b).

In addition, a kernel developer has access to all phases of the project's lifecycle. One may run tests on the initial versions of the developed code. After making the desired changes, developers may compile and install the kernel for integration testing. At this testing phase, subsystem code can be exercised manually or with the help of additional testing tools. Also, kernel developers often work on improvements to existing functionality. In such cases, the tests performed can be considered regression tests. Since GNU/Linux distributions use or adapt the mainline or stable kernels to make up an operating system, testing against any of these trees is also a form of beta-testing (*Fedora Linux Kernel Overview* 2021; *Kernel-Fedora Project Wiki* 2021; *About Debian* 2021).

Also, developers are interested in testing the Linux kernel to identify regressions. When responding to a bugfix rollback, Torvalds (2007) says why regressions are particularly unwanted in the kernel:

Because it is much more important to make slow, but steady progress and have people know things improve (or at least not "deprove"). We do not want any kind of "brownian motion development".

Other reasons to test the kernel may include checking the behavior under invalid inputs or high workloads, verifying compatibility with external components, investigating security aspects, and more. Thus, robustness testing, stress testing, interface testing, and security testing are examples of tests to which the Linux kernel can be submitted. There are no graphical user interface (GUI) tests since Linux does not contain GUI components.

Finally, considering the artifact under test classifier, testing techniques applied over Linux can be classified as operating system testing or merely code testing. That said, much of the testing over the Linux kernel would be classified as black-and-white-box regression OS testing according to Mathur's classifiers. A different perspective of Linux kernel test tools may be favored if one renounces Mathur's classifiers to examine the means used to perform kernel tests. Instead of trying to classify tests according to the development phase or test goal, let's focus on what is done to test X, where X is the Linux kernel or some of its device drivers. For instance, someone could decide to test a device driver by feeding random values to its interface (fuzzing), creating a model of it and using properties of that model to perform tests (model-based testing), instrumenting the code to measure runtime activity (performance testing, stress testing), etc.

This chapter provides an introduction to 13 Linux kernel test tools. With that, the authors hope to provide a sound perspective on how Linux device drivers are tested. Some test tools are distributed along the Linux kernel itself which can be obtained from https://git.kernel.org/pub/scm/linux/kernel/git/torvalds/lin ux.git. Practical test instructions and advice are provided for many of the tools covered. Yet, the content presented here do not portray all solutions available for kernel testing, nor do they encompass all the possible approaches for driver testing.

Linux Kernel Test Tools

Kselftest

Kernel selftests (kselftest) is a unit and regression test suite distributed with the Linux kernel tree under the *tools/testing/selftests/* directory (*Linux Kernel Selftests* 2021; Khan, 2021a; *Kernel self-test* 2019). Kselftest contains tests for various kernel features and sub- systems such as breakpoints, cpu-hotplug, efivarfs, ipc, kcmp, memory-hotplug, mqueue, net, powerpc, ptrace, rcutorture, timers, and vm sub-systems (Khan, 2014). These tests are intended to be small developer-focused tests that target individual code paths and short- running units supposed to terminate in a timely fashion of 20 minutes (*Linux Kernel Selftests* 2021; *Kernel self-test* 2019) Kselftest consists of shell scripts and user-space programs that test kernel API and features. Test cases may span kernel and use-space programs working in conjunction with a kernel module to test (Khan, 2021a). Even though kselftest's main purpose is to provide kernel developers and end-users a quick method of running tests against the Linux kernel, the test suite is run every day on several Linux kernel integration test rings such as the 0-Day robot and Linaro Test Farm (*Kernel self-test* 2019). It is stated that someday Kselftest will be a comprehensive test suite for the Linux kernel (*Linux Kernel Developer: Shuah Khan* 2017; G. K.-H. Jonathan Corbet, 2017).

To build Kselftest tests, go to the root of the Linux kernel source repository and call the Makefile under selftests directory:

```
$ make -C tools/testing/selftests
```

Some kselftest tests require additional libraries to build. If some test you would like to execute did not compile, try running Kselftest's dependancy script:

```
$ cd tools/testing/selftests && ./kselftest_deps.sh gcc Run
tests target for a single subsystem with:
$ make -C tools/testing/selftests/ TARGETS=drivers/dma-buf run_
tests Quote targets together to build and run multiple tests:
$ make —silent TARGETS="size breakpoints" kselftest Call
kselftest with an empty target list to run all tests:
$ make -C tools/testing/selftests —silent run_tests Note that
some tests require root privileges.
```

See the Linux Kernel Selftests documentation page (*Linux Kernel Selftests* 2021) for more details and examples on how to run and develop Kselftest tests.

Sparse

Sparse (semantic parser) is a semantic checker for C programs originally written by Linus Torvalds to support his work on the Linux kernel. Sparse does semantic parsing of source code files in a few phases summarized as full-file tokenization, pre-processing, semantic parsing, lazy type evaluation, inline function expansion, and syntax tree sim- plification (*Brown, 2016*). The semantic parser can help test C programs by performing type-checking, lock checking, value range checking, as well as reporting various errors and warnings while examining the code (*Sparse 2022*; *Brown, 2016*). In fact, Sparse also comprises a compiler frontend capable of parsing most ANSI C programs as well as a collection of compiler backends, one of which, is a static analyzer that takes the same name (*Welcome to sparse's documentation 2022*).

The kernel build system has a couple of make options that support checking code with static analyzers, and it uses Sparse as the default checker (Khan, 2014). Also, autotest robots such as 0-day and Hulk Robot run Sparse on kernel trees they test (*2020 Linux Kernel History Report* 2020).

Sparse tarballs can be downloaded from https://www.kernel.org/pub/software/ devel/sparse/dist/. Some Linux distributions also provide Sparse as a package through their package management systems. The development version of Sparse may be cloned from git://git.kernel.org/pub/scm/devel/sparse/sparse.git.

Installation should be a matter of running 'make' then 'make install' inside the project's root directory.

When building the kernel, Add "C=1" to the command line to have the re-compiled files checked with a static analyser (Sparse by default).

```
$ make C=1
```

Use C=2 to force all files targeted for compilation to be checked with Sparse. As usual, you may also specify the files for compilation (and static check).

```
$ make C=2 drivers/iio/adc/ad7292.o
```

Note that static analysis checks are made at compilation time and that the program under test (Linux) is not run. This has the benefit of keeping the test setup and workflow simple. No need to install and run the kernel in your machine or in a virtual environment. However, static analysis tools suffer from false positives, i.e., they may issue errors and warnings for good code. So, evaluate the output of static checkers carefully before attempting to fix anything (*Kernel Testing Guide* 2022).

Smatch

Smatch (the source matcher) is a static analyzer developed to detect programming logic errors. For instance, Smatch can detect errors such as attempts to unlock an already unlocked spinlock. It is written in C and uses Sparse as its C parser. Also, the static analyzer is run on Linux kernel trees by autotest bots such as 0-day and Hulk robot (Khan, 2014; *Smatch The Source Matcher* 2021; *2020 Linux Kernel History Report* 2020).

Smatch can be cloned from git://repo.or.cz/smatch.git. The project's documentation (*Smatch The Source Matcher* 2023) lists the software required to build the checker.

To run Smatch checks agains a single device driver you may do:

```
$ make C=2 CHECK="/path/to/smatch/smatch -p=kernel" drivers/
iio/adc/ad7292.o 2> smatch_warns.txt
```

Alternatively, you may check kernel source code by calling Smatch scripts. The follow- ing example runs Smatch over a directory with additional endianess checks enabled.

```
$ /path/to/smatch/smatch_scripts/kchecker -endian drivers/iio/
adc/ 2> smatch_adc_warrns.txt For (re)building the whole kernel
you may use the test_kernel script:
$ /path/to/smatch/smatch_scripts/test_kernel.sh
```

Coccinelle/Coccicheck

Coccinelle is a static analyzer engine that provides a language for specifying matches and transformations in C code. Coccinelle is used to aid the collateral evolution of source code and to help catch specific bugs that have been expressed semantically. Collateral evolution is needed when client code has to be updated due to development in API code. Renaming a function, adding function parameters, and reorganizing data structures are examples of changes that may lead to collateral evolution. For instance, coccicheck, a collection of semantic patches that uses the Coccinelle engine, aids developers in chasing and fixing bugs. coccicheck is available in the Linux kernel under a make target with the same name (*Coccinelle: A Program Matching and Transformation Tool for Systems Code* 2022; N. P. Luis R. Rodriguez, 2016; V. R. Luis R. Rodriguez T. B., 2016). Moreover, coccicheck is run on Linux kernel trees by automated test robots such as 0-day and Hulk robots (*2020 Linux Kernel History Report* 2020; N. P. Luis R. Rodriguez, 2016).

Coccinelle can be obtained through the package manager of many GNU/Linux distri- butions, as a compressed tar.gz file from the project's web page, or through it's GitHub repository.

Run Coccinelle checks over a directory with:

```
make coccicheck M=drivers/iio/adc/
```

Use the C option to run Coccinelle checks over a single device driver:

```
$ make C=2 CHECK=scripts/coccicheck drivers/iio/adc/ad7292.o 1>
cocci.log
```

Coccinelle has a "patch" mode in which it generates patches to fix the suspect code patterns whenever possible.

```
$ make coccicheck MODE=patch M=drivers/iio/temperature/ 1>
cocci.log
```

See the Coccinelle Linux documentation page (*Coccinelle - The Kernel Documentation* 2023) for details on Coccinelle usage.

See the Kernel Testing Guide [4] documentation page for advice on the cases one can make best use of each kernel static analyser.

LTP

The Linux Test Project (LTP) is a test suite that contains a collection of automated and semi-automated tests to validate the reliability, robustness, and stability of Linux and related features (Khan, 2014; Iyer, 2012). By default, the LTP run script includes tests for filesystems, disk I/O, memory management, inter process communication (IPC), process scheduler, and system call interfaces. Moreover, the test suite can be customized by adding new tests, and the LTP project welcomes contributions (Khan, 2014).

Some Linux testing projects are built on top of LTP or incorporate it somewhat. For example, LTP was chosen as a starting point for Lachesis, whereas the Linaro Automation and Validation Architecture (LAVA) framework provides commands to run LTP tests from within it (Khan, 2014). Another test suite that runs LTP is LKFT (*2020 Linux Kernel History Report* 2020; *Tests in LKFT* 2021).

The Linux Test Project (LTP) is available at GitHub [5]. The project has a build. sh script to help compile the test suite.

Before running any test though, be aware that some LTP stress tests are intended to find (or cause) problems in functioning systems. Thus, it's recommended to not run those tests in production environments(*LTP README* 2022). Running LTP inside a virtual machine (VM) may mitigate the risk of messing up your development environment.

To run LTP a test case, one must compile the modules associated with it then run the user space program inside the test's directory. For instance, to run LTP tests for ACPI support:

```
$  cd  testcases/kernel/device-drivers/acpi/
$  make
$  PATH=$PATH:$PWD./ltp_acpi
```

To build, install, and run all tests, do:

```
$ make
$ make install
$ cd /opt/ltp
$ ./runltp
```

The completion time of each test tends to be short, and the results (pass or fail) are very clear. For example, it takes about 30 minutes to run the entire collection of system call tests.

```
$ ./runltp -f syscalls
```

Trinity

Trinity is a random tester (fuzzer) specialized in testing the system call interfaces that the Linux kernel presents to user space (Kerrisk, 2013). Trinity employs some techniques to pass semi-intelligent arguments to the syscalls being called. For instance, it accepts a directory argument from which it will open files and pass the corresponding file descriptors to system calls under test. This feature can be helpful for discovering failures in filesystems. Thus, Trinity can find bugs in parts of the kernel other than the system call interface. Some areas where people used Trinity to find bugs include the networking stack, virtual memory code, and drivers (Jones, 2017; Kerrisk, 2013).

Trinity may be downloaded from its repository on GitHub[6].

Your authors suggest running Trinity inside a virtual machine to mitigate the risk of breaking your development environment. The fuzzer may corrupt data files, including those mounted in network file shares. It is recommened to be careful with network setup and configuration because Trinity can generate sequences of syscalls that send random network packets to other hosts (Jones, 2017).

Build and install Trinity:

```
$ ./configure
$ make
$ make install
```

Start the fuzzer to stress a specific system call (or run withouth the -c option to stress them all):

```
./trinity -c splice
```

As described by Konovalov (2021a), *"trinity is a kernel fuzzer that keeps making system calls in an infinite loop."*. There is no precise number of tests to run and no time limit for their completion. After being interrupted, the program shows the number of executed system calls, how many ended successfully, and how many terminated with failures.

jstest

jstest is a user space utility program that displays joystick information such as device status and incoming events. One can use jstest to test the Linux joystick API's features and a joystick driver's functionality (*xpad - Linux USB driver for Xbox compatible controllers* 2021; *Linux Joystick support - Introduction* 2021; Kitt, 2009).

jstest is part of the Linux Console Project and can be obtained from Source Forge[7] or through the package manager of some GNU/Linux distributions.

To use jstest, one must start the application with the path to a joystick or gamepad device. jstest then displays the inputs obtained from joysticks and gamepads and thus might be helpful to test the functioning of drivers for these devices.

```
$ jstest /dev/input/js0
```

You will be able to see the data captured by your joystick driver in the terminal.

ktest

ktest provides an automated test suite that can build, install, and boot-test Linux on a target machine. It can also run post-boot scripts on the target system to perform further testing (Khan, 2014; Jordan, 2021). ktest has been included in the Linux kernel repository under the *tools/testing/ktest* directory. The tool consists of a perl script (ktest.pl) and a set of configuration files containing test setup properties. In addition to the build and boot tests, ktest also supports git bisect, config bisect, randconfig, and patch check as additional types of tests. If a cross-compiler is installed, ktest can also run cross-compile tests (*Ktest* 2017; Khan, 2014).

ktet documentation (*Linux Joystick support - Introduction* 2023) contains example configuration files for various tasks ktest may perform. However, seting up everything needed to run ktest is a several step procedure. Jordan (2021) provides some guidelines to set ktest up. By default, ktest uses QEMU and libvirt. Further, since many libvirt features are used, one may need to install several system packages. On debian-like systems, one would install them with:

```
$ sudo apt-get install qemu qemu-kvm libvirt-clients libvirt-
daemon-system bridge- utils virtinst libvirt-daemon virt-
manager libguestfs-tools diffstat
```

An OS image will also be needed to test the kernels produced. You may create a virtual disk and do a fresh installation or download a disk image from the Internet. Many Linux distributions provide minimal disk images for download, some of them are Debian [8], Ubuntu [9], Fedora [10], and Suse [11].

Create the virsh virtual machine:

```
$ sudo virt-install -name virt-ktest -description "ktest
virtual machine" -ram=2048 -vcpus=2 -os-variant=debianbullseye
-import -disk path=`pwd`/debian-ktest.qcow2 -graphics none -
network bridge:virbr0
```

Start the VM and login:

```
$ sudo virsh start virt-ktest
$ sudo virsh console virt-ktest Inside the VM, install packages
needed by ktest: vm$ sudo apt-get install bzip2 dra-
```

cut
Inside the VM, enable ssh server:

```
vm$ ssh-keygen -A vm$ systemctl start sshd
```

Inside the VM, edit /etc/ssh/sshd_config file:

```
PasswordAuthentication yes
PermitEmp-
tyPasswords yes
PermitRootLogin yes
```

Inside of the VM, configure custom grub menu entry as explained by Jordan (2021).

Disconnect the VM and generate a ssh-key:

```
$ ssh-keygen -f /.ssh/id_rsa_ktets_virt.id_rsa
-t rsa -N ""
```

Copy the ssh key to the VM:

```
$ sudo virt-sysprep -a debian-ktest.qcow2 -ssh-inject
centos:file:/home/$USER/.ssh/id_rsa_ktets_virt.pub
Start virsh network:
$ sudo virsh net-start default
```

Create a ktest.conf file specifying virtual machine name and additional parameters. Look at *tools/testing/ktest/sample.conf* for inspiration. Then run ktest passing the config file for your setup:

```
$ ./tools/testing/ktest/ktest.pl ktest_virsh.conf
```

After started, ktest will automatically build the Linux kernel, install the kernel image and modules into the virtual machine, update the boot configuration to use the newly installed kernel, boot the virtual machine, and run custom scripts listed in the conf file inside the VM after it boots.

Syzkaller

Syzkaller is said to be a state-of-the-art Linux kernel fuzzer (Konovalov, 2021a). The syzbot system is a robot developed as part of the syzkaller project that continuously fuzzes main Linux kernel branches and automatically reports found bugs to kernel mailing lists. Syzbot can test patches against bug reproducers. A feature that may be useful for testing bug fix patches, debugging, or checking if the bug still happens. While syzbot can test patches that fix bugs, it does not support applying custom patches during fuzzing. It always tests vanilla unmodified git trees. Nonetheless, one can always run syzkaller locally on any kernel to better test a particular subsystem or patch (Vyukov *et al.*, 2021). Syzbot is receiving increasing attention from kernel developers. For instance, Sasha Levin said he hoped that failure reproducers from syzbot fuzz testing could be added as part of testing for the stable tree at some point (Edge, 2020).

Syzkaller source code is hosted on GitHub [12]. The project's documentation (al., 2023) provides instructions on how to set up Syzkaller to perform tests on a few particular kernel architectures. Whatever architecture you choose, the list of steps the set up the fuzzer is long. In summary, one will need to download or build an OS image, set up QEMU, install a supported Go[13] version, and build the kernel for the particular target architecture.

When run, Syzkaller prints execution environment information to the terminal and activates an HTTP server. The server pages display detailed test information such as execution logs, code coverage, the number of syscall sequences executed, and the number of crashes.

TuxMake

TuxMake, by Linaro, is a command line tool and Python library designed to make building the Linux kernel easier. It seeks to simplify Linux kernel building by providing a consistent command line interface to build the kernel across various architectures, toolchains, kernel configurations, and make targets. By removing the friction of dealing with different build requirements, TuxMake assists developers, especially newcomers, to build the kernel for uncommon toolchain/architecture combinations. Moreover, TuxMake comes with a set of curated portable build environments distributed as container images. These versioned and hermetic filesystem images make it easier to describe and reproduce builds and build problems. Although it does not support every Linux make target, the TuxMake team plans to add support for additional targets such as kselftest, cpupower, perf, and documentation. TuxMake is part of TuxSuite, which in turn makes part of Linaro's main Linux testing effort (Rue, 2021; Dan Rue, 2021; *Rapid Operating System Build and Test* 2021).

TuxMake is available from its GitLab repository[14] and can also be downloaded as a package for many GNU/Linux distros.

To build the Linux kernel with TuxMake do:

```
$ tuxmake
$ tuxmake -o /KernelLinux/tuxmake_build/
```

Note that TuxMake focuses on building the kernel and thus only builds the artifacts bound to make targets, not triggering the execution of test cases even when those targets would do so by default.

LKFT

Linaro's LKFT (Linux Kernel Functional Testing) is an automated test infrastructure that builds and tests Linux release candidates on the arm and arm64 hardware architec- tures (*2020 Linux Kernel History Report* 2020). The mission of LKFT is to improve the quality of Linux by performing functional testing on real and emulated hardware targets. Weekly, LKFT runs tests over 350 release-architecture-target combinations on every git-branch push made to the latest 6 Linux long-term-stable releases, linux-next, and the mainline tree. In addition, Linaro claims that their test system can consistently report results from nearly 40 of these test setup combinations in under 48 hours (*Rapid Operating System Build and Test* 2021; *Linaro's Linux Kernel Functional Test framework* 2021). LKFT incorporates and runs tests from several test suites such as LTP, kselftest, libhugetlbfs, perf, v4l2-compliance tests, KVM-unit-tests, SI/O Benchmark Suite, and KUnit (*Tests in LKFT* 2021).

0-Day Test Robot

The 0-day test robot is a test framework and infrastructure that runs several tests over the Linux kernel, covering core components such as virtual memory management, I/O subsystem, process scheduler, file system, network, device drivers, and more (*Linux Kernel Performance* 2021). Static analysis tools such as Sparse, Smatch, and Coccicheck are run by 0-day as well (*2020 Linux Kernel History Report* 2020). These tests are provided by Intel as a service that picks up patches from the mailing lists and tests them, often before they are accepted for inclusion (G. K.-H. Jonathan Corbet, 2017). 0-day also tests key developers' trees before patches move forward in the development process. The robot is accounted for finding 223 bugs during a development period of about 14 months from Linux release 4.8 to Linux 4.13 (which came out September 3, 2017). With that, the 0-day robot achieved the rank of top bug reporter for that period (G. K.-H. Jonathan Corbet, 2017).

Table 1. Summary of test tools and test types.

Tools	Test Types
Kselftest	Unit test, regression test, stress test, functional test, performance test
Sparse	Static analysis
Smatch	Static analysis
Coccinelle	Static analysis
LTP	Functional test, reliability test, robustness test, stability test, stress test
Trinity	Fuzz test
jstest	Functional test
ktest	Build test
Syzkaller/Syzbot	Fuzz test
TuxMake	Build test
LKFT	Regression test, functional test, build test
0-day	Regression test, functional test, build test, performance test
KernelCI	Build test

KernelCI

KernelCI is an effort to test upstream Linux kernels in a continuous integration (CI) fashion. The project's main goal is to improve the quality, stability, and long-term main- tenance of the Linux kernel. It is a community-led test system that follows an open philosophy to enable the same collaboration to happen with testing as open source does to the code itself (*Distributed Linux Testing Platform KernelCI Secures Funding and Long-Term Sustainability as New Linux Foundation Project 2019; Welcome to KernelCI 2021*). KernelCI generates various configurations for different kernel trees, submits boot jobs to several labs worldwide, collects, and stores test results into a database. The test database kept by KernelCI includes tests run natively by KernelCI, but also Red Hat's CKI, Google's syzbot, and many others (Vizoso, 2016; *Welcome to KernelCI 2021*).

SUMMARY

To some extent, several tools can facilitate device driver testing. It is nearly impossible to analyze them all. Yet, this chapter covered 13 Linux kernel testing tools identified as being either focused on driver testing or popular among online publications. These tools make up a heterogeneous group of test solutions comprising various features and test techniques. From unit testing to end-to-end testing, dynamic or static analysis, many ways of putting Linux to the test have been conceived.

Table 1.1 matches test types and test tools. Note that some test types overlap with each other. For instance, one may submmit a host to an elevated number of network packets and measure the time it takes to process each of them (performance test). Since the behaviour (continue to work or not) of the system under the stress condition can also be observed, this is a stress test too. Fuzz testing is sometimes called robustness test and functional tests may be considered a sort of regression testing. Thus, it is more than possible that some test tools are not matched with all types of tests they can provide.

Final Remarks

Device drivers play a critical role in the proper functioning of computer systems, acting as a bridge between the hardware and the software. Their importance cannot be overstated, as they enable communication and facilitate the interaction between various components. In this context, the transparency provided by the open-source model becomes crucial. Unlike proprietary software, which often operates behind closed doors, the open-source approach allows for greater visibility and scrutiny of the inner workings of device drivers. This transparency holds significant implications for trust. Trust built upon promises and assurances can be fragile and uncertain, as it relies on blind faith in the claims made by software vendors. On the other hand, trust built upon transparency, where the source code is open for examination and verification, provides a solid foundation for reliability and dependability. By allowing individuals and organizations to inspect the code, identify vulnerabilities, and contribute to improvements, the open-source model fosters a culture of trust that is based on tangible evidence rather than mere promises.

From a business perspective, the transparency offered by the open-source model encourages innovation and collaboration. Companies can leverage the collective intelligence of the community to identify and address issues, enhance features, and drive continuous improvement. Moreover, the open-source model provides opportunities for businesses to contribute back to the community, creating a virtuous cycle of knowledge sharing and value creation.

REFERENCES

About Debian 2021 *About Debian*. (2021). https://www.debian.org/intro/about.en.html

About Linux Kernel. (2021). The Linux Kernel Organization. https://www.kernel.org/linux.html.

Alessandro, Corbet & Kroah-Hartman. (2005). *Linux Device Drivers* (3ʳᵈ ed.). O'Reilly.

Brown, N. (2016). *Sparse: a look under the hood*. https://lwn.net/Articles/689907/

Claudi, A., & Dragoni, A. F. (2011). Testing linux- based real-time systems: lachesis. *2011 IEEE International Conference on Service- Oriented Computing and Applications (SOCA)*, 1–8. doi: .2011.616624410.1109/SOCA

Coccinelle: A Program Matching and Transformation Tool for Systems Code. (2022). https://coccinelle.gitlabpages.inria.fr/website/

Coccinelle - The Kernel Documentation. (2023). The kernel development community. https://www.kernel.org/doc/html/ latest/dev-tools/coccinelle.html

Corbet, J., & Kroah-Hartman, G. (2017). *2017 Linux Kernel Development Report*. https://www.linuxfoundation. org/wp-content/uploads/linux-kernel-report-2017.pdf

Distributed Linux Testing Platform KernelCI Secures Funding and Long-Term Sustainability as New Lin Distributed Linux Testing Platform KernelCI Secures Funding and Long-Term Sustainability as New Linux Foundation Project. (2019). reTHINKit Media. https: / / www. prnewswire . com / news - releases / distributed - linux - testing - platform-kernelci-secures-funding-and-long-term-sustainability-as-new-linux-foundation-project-300945978.html

Edge, J. (2020). *Maintaining stable stability*. https://lwn.net/ Articles/825536/

Fedora Linux Kernel Overview. (2021). *Fedora Linux Kernel Overview*. https: / / docs . fedoraproject . org /en - US /quick - docs /kernel /overview/

Greg, K.-H. J. C. (2017). *2017 Linux Kernel Development Report*. LWN.net, The Linux Foundation. https://www.linuxfoundation.org/wp-content/uploads/linux-kernel-report- 2017.pdf

How the development process works. (2021). The kernel development community. https://www.kernel.org/doc/html/latest/ process/2.Process.html

IEEE standard glossary of software engineering terminology. (1990). *IEEE Std 610.12-1990.* doi:10.1109/IEEESTD.1990.101064

IyerM. (2012). http: / / ltp . sourceforge . net / documentation/how-to/ltp.php

Jones, D. (2017). *Linux system call fuzzer - README.* https://github. com/ kernelslacker/trinity

Jordan, D. (2021). *So, you are a Linux kernel programmer and you want to do some automated testing...* Oracle. https://blogs.oracle.com/linux/ktest

Kernel - Fedora Project Wiki. (2021). The Fedora Project. https://fedoraproject. org/wiki/Kernel

Kernel self-test. start. (2019). The kernel development community. https://kselftest. wiki.kernel.org/

Kernel Testing Guide. (2022). The kernel development community. https://www. kernel.org/doc/html/latest/dev-tools/testing-overview. html

Kerrisk, M. (2013). *LCA: The Trinity fuzz tester.* https: //lwn.net/Articles/536173/

Khan, S. (2014). *Linux Kernel Testing and Debugging.* https: //www.linuxjournal. com/content/linux-kernel-testing-and-debugging

Khan, S. (2021a). *Kernel Validation With Kselftest.* https: / / linuxfoundation.org/ webinars/kernel- validation- with- kselftest/

Khan, S. (2021b). *Mentorship Session: Kernel Validation With Kselftest.* The Linux Foundation. https: / /www. youtube . com /watch ? v = mpO _ iDEMqWQ

Kitt, S. (2009). *jstest - joystick test program.* https: / / sourceforge.net/p/linuxconsole/ code/ci/master/tree/docs/jstest.1

Konovalov, A. (2021a). *Fuzzing Linux Kernel.* https: / / linuxfoundation.org/webinars/ fuzzing- linux- kernel/

Konovalov, A. (2021b). *Mentorship Session: Fuzzing the Linux Kernel.* https: / / www. youtube . com / watch ? v = 4IBWj21tg

Konovalov, A. (2023). *How to set up syzkaller.* The kernel development community. https://github.com/google/syzkaller/blob/master/docs/linux/setup.md

Kroah-Hartman, G. (2022). *Mentorship Session: Trust and the Linux Kernel Development Model*. The Linux Foundation. https://www. youtube.com/ watch?v=YhDVC7-QgkI

Ktest. (2017). Embedded Linux Wiki. https://elinux.org/Ktest

Linaro's Linux Kernel Func- tional Test framework. (2021). Linaro. https: / / lkft . linaro . org/

Linux Joystick support - Introduction. (2021). The kernel development community. https://www.kernel.org/doc/ html/latest/input/joydev/joystick.html

Linux Joystick support - Introduction. (2023). The kernel development community. https://git.kernel.org/pub/scm/linux/kernel/ git/torvalds/linux.git/tree/tools/testing/ ktest/examples/README?h=v6.2

Linux Kernel Developer: Shuah Khan. (2017). The Linux Foundation. https:// linuxfoundation.org/blog/linux-kernel- developer-shuah-khan/.

Linux Kernel History Report. (2020). The Linux Foundation. https://linuxfoundation. org/wp-content/uploads/2020_ kernel_history_report_082720.pdf

Linux Kernel Performance. (2021). https://01.org/lkp

Linux Kernel Selftests. (2021). The kernel development community. https://www. kernel.org/doc/html/latest/dev-tools/kselftest.html

LTP README. (2022). The Linux Test Project. https://github. com/linux-test-project/ ltp/blob/master/README.md

Madieu, J. (2017). *Linux Device Drivers Development*. Packt Publishing.

Mathur. (2013). *Foundations of Software Testing* (2nd ed.). Pearson India.

Nicolas Palix Luis, R. (2016). *coccicheck* [Wiki]. https://bottest.wiki.kernel.org/ coccicheck.

Rapid Operating System Build and Test. (2021). Linaro. https: / /www. linaro . org /os - build - and - test/

Rue, D. (2011). *Portable and reproducible kernel builds with TuxMake*. https://lwn. net/Articles/841624/

Smatch The Source Matcher. (2021). http://smatch. sourceforge.net/

Smatch The Source Matcher. (2023). https://repo. or. cz/smatch.git/blob/HEAD:/ Documentation/smatch.txt

Sparse. (2022). The kernel development community. https://git.kernel.org/pub/ scm/linux/kernel/git/torvalds/linux.git/tree/Documentation/dev-tools/sparse. rst?h=v5.17-rc7

Tests in LKFT. (2021). Linaro. https://lkft.linaro.org/tests/

Torvalds, L. (2007). *Re: [patch] revert: [NET]: Fix races in net_rx_action vs netpoll*. https://lwn.net/Articles/243460/

Valentin Rothberg Luis, R. (2016). *linux-kernel-bot-tests - start* [Wiki]. https:// bottest.wiki.kernel.org/

Vizoso, T. (2016). *How Continuous Integration Can Help You Keep Pace With the Linux Kernel*. https://www.linux.com/audience/enterprise/how- continuous-integration- can- help- you- keep- pace- linux- kernel/.

Vyukov, D., Konovalov, A., & Elver, M. (2021). *syzbot*. https://github.com/google/ syzkaller/blob/master/docs/syzbot.md

Welcome to KernelCI. (2021). KernelCI. https://kernelci. org/

Welcome to sparse's documentation. (2022). https://sparse.docs.kernel.org/en/latest/

xpad - Linux USB driver for Xbox compatible controllers. (2021). The kernel development community. https://www.kernel.org/doc/html/latest/input/devices/ xpad.html

ENDNOTES

[1]   Estimate calculated with data from cloc tool: https://github.com/AlDanial/cloc

[2]   According to our research on Linux kernel device driver test tools: https:// www.teses.usp.br/teses/disponiveis/45/45134/tde-30112022-152524/

[3]   https://git.kernel.org/

[4]   https://www.kernel.org/doc/html/latest/dev-tools/testing-overview.html

[5]   https://github.com/linux-test-project/ltp

[6]   https://github.com/kernelslacker/trinity

[7]   https://sourceforge.net/projects/linuxconsole/

[8]   http://cdimage.debian.org/cdimage/cloud/

[9]   http://cloud-images.ubuntu.com/

[10]   https://alt.fedoraproject.org/cloud/

[11]   https://download.opensuse.org/tumbleweed/appliances/

[12]   https://github.com/google/syzkaller

[13]   https://golang.org/

[14]   https://gitlab.com/Linaro/tuxmake

Chapter 7
Fostering FOSS Communities:
A Guide for Newcomers

Hillary Nyakundi
freeCodeCamp, Kenya

Cesar Henrique De Souza
Universidade de Sao Paulo, Brazil

ABSTRACT

In this chapter, the authors explore the importance of creating a welcoming and supportive community for new contributors trying to venture into the field of open-source. They cover the best practices for creating a positive and inclusive environment, such as clear documentation, accessible communication channels, and active mentorship programs. Additionally, they delve into some of the key challenges that new contributors often face and also offer strategies for overcoming these obstacles. By promoting a supportive and welcoming community, open-source projects can encourage more people to participate, thereby increasing their overall impact and diversity in society.

INTRODUCTION

The relevance of the concept of community in the FOSS context can not be overemphasized. While the publication of a technological asset — be it a piece of software, hardware design, or another kind of intellectual creation — under an open-source compatible license is sufficient to technically characterize the item as an open-source product itself, from a strategic point of view this is only part of the way. Sure, one may make one's work openly accessible as a means to gain visibility or to

DOI: 10.4018/978-1-6684-4785-7.ch007

fulfill knowledge dissemination goals. However, regarding long-term sustainability, the key point of publishing open-source technology is to promote collaboration. As a business model, FOSS implies a reciprocity deal through which one relinquishes privileged access to one's own intellectual property in exchange for the contribution from those who use it — the community.

Forming a community around a FOSS product is thus not only about creating a fan base to celebrate the project or establishing a relationship channel to cultivate customer fidelity. All these are well enough and make sense in the proprietary and open-source industries. Regarding FOSS, though, building a community means nurturing a network of users capable and willing to contribute back to the project. The community is a critical component of the FOSS ecosystem and can be considered intrinsic to the very paradigm of open source.

In order to boost the community contribution, delivering good technology is not enough. Users must be empowered with the means to take part in the product development, which includes encouraging individuals to experiment, criticize and propose changes.

The FOSS movement has come a long way and the real-world experience demonstrates that an interested and capable community can drive long-lasting, sustainable projects. If allowed, many users will find motivations to improve the product. If endowed with the technical requisites, they will be willing to dedicate time and expertise to contribute. The large, active communities around prominent FOSS projects yield practical evidence for this expectative. That said, it is well known that even those extensive communities do not fully reflect the entire potential of the collaboration ecosystem. Anyone who ventured to contribute to existing FOSS projects will likely recognize the perils that face most newcomers, from difficulties in understanding the technical details, and setting up the development environment, to getting acquainted with the management workflow and interacting with other contributors. Such negative factors have a significant influence on the maintenance of the community, and there is plenty of evidence that many potential collaborators give up before even concluding their first contribution. This chapter addresses the challenges and corresponding mitigation strategies that can help newcomers to have an enjoyable and productive experience contributing to a FOSS project.

THE NEWCOMER'S PERSPECTIVE

Free Open Source Software (FOSS) projects heavily rely on the involvement of volunteers from various locations and depend on a consistent influx of fresh contributors to ensure their long-term success and continuity. In order to maintain a sustainable number of developers, it is crucial to inspire, engage, and retain new participants within a project. Studies suggest that newcomers bring valuable innovation by introducing novel ideas and work methods that benefit the entire group (Kraut et al., 2012). However, the reality is that newcomers often encounter numerous difficulties when attempting to make their initial contribution to a project. FOSS project newcomers are typically expected to independently familiarize themselves with the project (Scacchi, 2002), resembling explorers navigating an inhospitable environment, in dire need of guidance (Dagenais et al., 2010). Consequently, a significant challenge for FOSS projects lies in providing adequate support for these newcomers.

The extensive body of scientific literature delves into various aspects of newcomers joining open-source software (OSS) projects. These studies primarily focus on exploring the underlying dynamics that drive individuals to become FOSS contributors, mapping out the pathways to becoming core developers, and identifying indicators of sustained commitment over time (Hars and Ou, 2001; Ye and Kishida, 2003; Jergensen et al., 2011; Schilling et al., 2012; Zhou and Mockus, 2012). However, there remains a relatively unexplored dimension of the FOSS joining process that revolves around the timeframe between a newcomer's decision to participate and the acceptance of their initial code contribution into the shared repository.

This transient period holds significant importance for FOSS projects since many newcomers intend to join or stay involved in a project solely to make a single contribution, such as fixing a bug or introducing a new feature. The events that unfold during this period have implications for diverse individuals, including users willing to support a new feature and professional developers who come across bugs or seek to customize specific software products. Throughout this learning phase, newcomers encounter obstacles that may influence their decision to discontinue their contributions. As a result, a project's failure to establish a positive initial impression may lead newcomers to hesitate before giving it another chance (Fogel, 2013).

Profiles of newcomers entering the realm of FOSS encompass a diverse range, with varying motivations, backgrounds, and available time for contribution. These distinctions significantly influence the level of effort newcomers invest in overcoming the barriers they encounter. In the face of obstacles, an individual's motivation plays a crucial role in determining their behavior, level of effort, and persistence (Kanfer, 1990). Newcomers driven by stronger motivations, such as earning a grade in an academic setting or receiving payment for their contributions, tend to exhibit greater determination compared to individuals who are driven by their own issues or have a transient interest in the community. Furthermore, developers who have limited time available to contribute to FOSS projects may opt to abandon their efforts if they cannot swiftly overcome the barriers they face.

The present study concentrates on identifying the barriers that newcomers confront when endeavoring to make their inaugural contributions to FOSS projects.

By comprehensively understanding these barriers, researchers and the community at large can channel their efforts toward constructing or refining tools and processes that foster increased contributions, including "drive-by commits" (Pham et al., 2013). Such small changes are made by developers who possess temporary or passing interest in a project, without the intention of prolonged engagement.

Adopting this perspective allows for the identification and comprehension of the barriers that impede newcomers from making their initial contributions to FOSS projects, ultimately leading to the proposal of effective practices aimed at aiding newcomers in overcoming some of these hurdles. The central inquiry at hand revolves around the means to support newcomers in making their first contributions to Open Source projects. So as to delve into this matter, it is imperative to grasp the barriers that newcomers face when embarking on their maiden FOSS project contributions and explore the tools that can alleviate these difficulties.

In the context of proprietary industrial environments, developers are hired under contractual obligations, benefiting from mentorship, formal training sessions, and specific strategies implemented by company human resources to support their development and retention (Burke et al., 2009). Conversely, open collaboration communities rely on voluntary contributions, creating a situation where members find it easier to disengage from their groups (Choi et al., 2010; Choi, 2012). Additionally, the limited awareness of information, lack of trust, and relatively weak interpersonal connections among online group members pose challenges in attracting and retaining participants compared to face-to-face groups (Tidwell and Walther, 2002).

These differences contribute to lower group commitment in online communities compared to traditional offline groups, making it more susceptible for volunteers to withdraw (Wang et al., 2012). The study of newcomers and the obstacles they encounter in online open collaboration communities remains a contemporary issue that warrants further investigation. A crucial challenge for many online communities lies in enhancing members' contributions over time (Zhu et al., 2013). Online communities serve as digital spaces where individuals with shared interests come together, unrestricted by time and space, to exchange self-generated content (Preece, 2001; Jin et al., 2010). Numerous online communities operate on the principles of "open collaboration," relying on voluntary contributions to sustain their existence. Therefore, the vitality and success of these communities depend on the active participation and content contribution of their members, as well as the continuous influx of new members (Lee et al., 2014). Consequently, researchers have been motivated to investigate the process of joining online communities in order to address the ongoing challenge of attracting and engaging new collaborators.

Scientific research has provided valuable insights into various aspects of newcomer behavior in different online communities. For instance, a study conducted by Burke et al. (2009) focused on Facebook users and found that those who witnessed their friends contributing content were more likely to share their own. Another investigation by Tsai and Pai (2014) delved into the mediating effects of psychological factors on newcomers' participation in virtual communities, highlighting the influence of needs fulfillment and cognitive social identity. Fugelstad et al. (2012) examined factors that predict long-term contribution in MovieLens, while Hsieh et al. (2013) explored predictors of contribution in Reddit, emphasizing the role of social interaction and community-specific motivations.

Wikipedia, in particular, has been the subject of significant scientific scrutiny. The decline in new contributors and the challenges of retention have prompted extensive research. Bryant et al. (2005) analyzed the motivations and role perceptions of Wikipedia editors, highlighting how newcomers start with minor contributions based on personal knowledge and interests. Lampe et al. (2012) studied students' engagement in Wikipedia as part of their coursework, emphasizing the impact of language familiarity and technical skills on participation. Farzan and Kraut (2013) examined the participation of psychology students in Wikipedia and highlighted the demotivating effect of hostile editor behavior.

Furthermore, research has explored the influence of feedback and joining experiences on newcomers. Zhu et al. (2013) conducted a field experiment on Wikipedia, studying the impact of different types of feedback on newcomers' contributions. Vora and Komura (2010) investigated the challenges faced by newcomers, particularly related to learning how to use the wiki editor. Halfaker et al. (2011) examined the effect of reverts on editors' motivation and retention, while Halfaker et al. (2013a) explored the rejection of newcomers' contributions as a negative predictor of retention.

In terms of interventions, researchers have proposed tools and strategies to support newcomers in online communities. Choi et al. (2010) identified socialization tactics used in Wikipedia, highlighting the positive influence of welcome messages, assistance, and constructive criticism. Morgan et al. (2013) introduced "Teahouse," a supportive space for new Wikipedia editors, which demonstrated higher satisfaction and increased engagement. Other tools, such as the Article Feedback Tool (Halfaker et al., 2013b) and modified warning messages (Faulkner et al., 2012) have also shown the potential to enhance newcomers' participation.

These studies collectively contribute to a better understanding of newcomer behavior, motivations, and challenges in online communities. By uncovering these insights, researchers aim to improve the design of interventions, foster a sense of belonging, and enhance newcomers' experiences to promote long-term engagement and contribution.

THE DYNAMICS OF JOINING

Considering the already acquired knowledge regarding the experiences and behaviors of newcomers in collaborative online communities, it is pertinent to make note of a few observations, under the light of the scientific literature.

Newcomers typically commence by contributing value to a familiar subject, sometimes unaware of their involvement in a community and the accompanying set of rules (Steinmacher, 2015). The provision of welcome messages, assistance, and constructive criticism has been observed to slow down the natural decline in newcomers' contributions over time. Personalized and polite messages have been shown to enhance retention rates. Increasing participation can be achieved by highlighting the means of contribution, and employing simple and straightforward methods such as comments and feedback. Receiving feedback serves as a stimulus for newcomers to enhance their contributions. The inclination to learn from friends (lurking), receive feedback, and gain a receptive audience are indicators of future contributions.

The cognitive social identity of newcomers is influenced by autonomy, relatedness, and competence, subsequently impacting their participation behavior through affective commitment and collective self-esteem. General volunteer motivation, pro-social behavioral history, and community-specific motivation are reliable predictors of the level of engagement and specific activities that users undertake after joining a community. Membership, influence, and immersion are crucial factors for establishing a central social identification with the community, with users who have received assistance from fellow members and individuals who uphold prosocial values displaying a higher likelihood of supporting newcomers.

The aforementioned examples collectively underscore the complexity of joining an open-source software (OSS) project. A proposed conceptual model (Steinmacher, 2015) aims to dissect this complexity by identifying the various actors interacting within the FOSS ecosystem: the "outsider" represents a potential contributor who has not yet engaged with the project's development, "newcomers" refer to individuals making their initial code contributions, "developers" already contribute to the project but lack formal recognition and commit privileges, and "core developers" are individuals acknowledged by the community as official contributors or those with commit privileges to the repository. This comprehensive model delineates the different pressures that influence the progress of development. Motivation and project attractiveness serve as catalysts that encourage outsiders to contribute. Motivation forces encompass both internal factors (e.g., learning, self-promotion, and recognition) and external factors (e.g., scholarships, course assignments, and specific feature requirements) that drive developers to join and sustain their contributions to a project. Consequently, motivation forces remain integral throughout the joining process, as a lack of motivation often leads to drop-offs. Importantly, these forces can evolve and change during the development process. For instance, some developers initially join a project due to short-term scholarships like those offered by Google Summer of Code or for university course credits, but subsequently continue contributing to learn and promote themselves. Attractiveness forces encompass the characteristics and actions exhibited by the project to attract new users and developers (Santos et al., 2013). These forces may encompass factors such as the project's license type, visibility, age, and the number of developers involved. Attractiveness and motivation work in tandem to entice outsiders towards projects. In certain cases, attractiveness forces play a particularly influential role, drawing in motivated developers who may otherwise struggle to decide which project to support.

The transition from an outsider to a newcomer occurs when a developer decides to contribute to a project and begins the onboarding process. During this stage, motivation continues to drive the developer's commitment to the project. However, opposing presures referred to as "onboarding barriers," can hinder this joining process. These barriers encompass both technical and non-technical obstacles, including the learning curve, lack of community support, and difficulties in initiating contributions. Given their potential to dissuade developers from contributing to the project, it becomes imperative to understand how to address these barriers in order to facilitate the joining process. It is worth noting that these barriers affect both developers aiming to make a single contribution and those aspiring to ascend and become full-fledged project members.

On the other hand, factors that aid retention can encourage newcomers to remain committed to contributing. Retention forces encompass the characteristics and actions employed by a project to attract and retain developers. These forces may include support initiatives designed to help newcomers overcome barriers, such as providing tools for understanding code or suggesting suitable tasks or code snippets to begin with. Other forces encompass mechanisms that support existing developers to contribute more, which, in turn, can lead to a change in motivation, e.g., granting commit rights or implementing gamification elements (Steinmacher, 2015).

Several studies have examined successful cases of developers joining FOSS projects and have analyzed the dynamics of the joining process. The onion model (Nakakoji et al., 2002; Ye and Kishida, 2003), for instance, presents a layered structure that categorizes the roles of FOSS members. Studies of various FOSS projects have shown that members can assume one of eight roles organized hierarchically: passive users, readers, bug reporters, bug fixers, peripheral developers, active developers, core members, and project leaders. However, it is important to acknowledge that not all members aspire to become core contributors. Nonetheless, the model outlines the process that developers ideally undergo to contribute to a project, recognizing that individual paths may vary. Jergensen et al. (2011) investigated the validity of the onion model within large project ecosystems and explored potential modifications in such settings. Analyzing data from the GNOME project spanning a ten-year period (1997-2007), they found limited evidence supporting the onion model's depiction of a gradual participation and socialization process wherein individuals progress from the project's periphery to its core. When considering contributions within the context of ecosystems, the onion model gained slightly more support. Conversely, Herraiz et al. (2006) also examined the onion model by studying the seven-year history of over 1,000 developers in the GNOME project. Their findings provided empirical evidence suggesting that hired and volunteer developers may follow distinct paths, supporting the notion that joining a community is a multifaceted process.

Beyond the onion model, other studies have endeavored to map the joining process in FOSS projects. For example, Krogh et al. (2003) introduced the concept of a "joining script" after analyzing interviews with developers, emails, source code repositories, and documents from the FreeNet project. The joining script outlines the levels and types of activities that newcomers progress through to become community members. Similarly, Ducheneaut (2005) conducted "computer-aided ethnography" by analyzing the Python project's mailing list archives. Through an in-depth analysis of a successful newcomer's socialization journey, the author identified a set of socialization activities that contributed to their success, highlighting the project's size and the existence of specific rites of passage throughout the trajectory.

Existing literature often presents the joining process as a series of steps and activities that newcomers must undertake to become project members. While most studies focus on the path to becoming a core member, the present investigation delves into why newcomers join a project and why they either remain committed or leave the community. As mentioned earlier, four key aspects are emphasized by Steinmacher et al. (2015)

Motivation

The concept of "motivation" encompasses the driving forces behind developers' contributions to open-source software (OSS) projects, encompassing both initial and ongoing motivations. In a study by Lakhani and Wolf (2005), 684 FOSS developers were surveyed to examine their motivations for contributing. The findings revealed that external factors, such as extrinsic benefits and career advancement, emerged as primary motivators. However, the study also highlighted personal enjoyment, the challenge of coding, and the opportunity to improve programming skills as significant contributors to motivation. Hars and Ou (2001) conducted a similar survey to explore the internal and external motives that drive developers' participation in FOSS projects. While their findings aligned with Lakhani and Wolf's study to some extent, they emphasized the role of internal motivators, including intrinsic motivation, fun, and community identification, although external factors still held greater weight. The study underscored the importance of building human capital and personal needs for software solutions as primary external motivations.

In a survey conducted by Hertel et al. (2003) with Linux kernel developers, the authors employed sociological models to explain social movement and virtual team participation. The results indicated that engagement stemmed from developers' identification as Linux developers, their desire to enhance their own software and career prospects, and the time invested in Linux-related tasks.

Shah (2006) conducted a broader study aiming to understand developers' motivations by analyzing interviews, mailing list archives, and documentation from two FOSS projects. Rather than identifying primary motivational forces, the study classified contributors into two types: need-driven participants and hobbyists. Need-driven participants exhibited varying motives, including the necessity of specific features, project reciprocity, the desire to integrate their own source code, career concerns, and the opportunity to receive feedback and improvements on their solutions. Hobbyists, on the other hand, contributed for the sake of fun and entertainment.

These studies provide a glimpse into the vast body of research dedicated to investigating motivation in the context of FOSS. Numerous other studies have explored intrinsic and extrinsic motivational factors, such as those conducted by Bonaccorsi and Rossi (2004), Roberts et al. (2006), Jergensen (2007), David and Shapiro (2008), Oreg and Nov (2008), Ke and Zhang (2010), and Krogh et al. (2012).

It is worth noting that motivation is a widely studied topic in software engineering as a whole, with several studies delving into this subject. For instance, Beecham et al. (2008) conducted a systematic review of 92 studies up until 2006, while França and Silva (2009, 2010), Sharp et al. (2009), Yu and Ming (2009), and França et al. (2011, 2014b) have also contributed to the understanding of motivation in software engineering. Importantly, these reviews encompass studies related to FOSS as well.

Attractiveness

The concept of "attractiveness" encompasses the strategies employed by projects to cultivate the involvement of new developers. Understanding the tactics and policies that attract volunteers to open-source software (OSS) projects is crucial, as the success of a project often hinges on its ability to attract a substantial number of developers (Capiluppi and Michlmayr, 2007). In this section, we delve into studies exploring the attractiveness of FOSS projects.

Santos et al. (2013) presented a comprehensive theoretical model that elucidates the cause-effect relationship of attractiveness as a fundamental construct in FOSS projects. They identified typical causes of attractiveness, such as the project's license type, intended audience, project type, and development status. Indicators of attractiveness, such as website hits, downloads, and the number of project members, were also considered. The consequences of attractiveness, including the number of open tasks and the time required for task completion, were examined. The researchers tested their model using data from over 4000 projects and discovered that the project itself directly influences its attractiveness. Notably, they found that projects catering to end-users and developers tend to be more attractive. Additionally, the application domain of a project impacts its attractiveness, with projects in multimedia, printing, security, and system domains being more appealing, while projects in database, education, science, and sociology domains are less enticing. The study further revealed that mature projects and project licenses also significantly affect attractiveness. These findings align with those presented by Stewart et al. (2006), although there is no complete consensus on the matter (Colazo and Fang, 2009).

Taking a different perspective, Meirelles et al. (2010) expanded upon Santos' model by introducing source code as a typical factor influencing attractiveness. They examined the impact of structural complexity and software size (measured by lines of code and the number of modules) on attractiveness. The study revealed that increased structural complexity has a negative influence on attractiveness, while larger software size has a positive effect. Furthermore, Chengalur-Smith et al. (2010) investigated whether codebase size, project age, and niche size (a concept borrowed from ecology) affect project attractiveness. The findings confirmed that these three characteristics indeed influence a project's ability to attract and retain developers. In a similar vein, Ververs et al. (2011) mapped the influential factors determining developers' participation in the Debian project. By analyzing significant project events and commits spanning 11 years, the authors discovered that specific events such as CeBIT, Debian Day, new or frozen releases, incidents, dependency issues, and the introduction of new developer services exerted the strongest influence.

Onboarding Barrier

"Barriers" encompass the forces that pose obstacles to newcomers and contributors who are eager to make their project contributions. These forces have the potential to delay or even discourage contributions. While existing literature primarily focuses on motivation and factors that attract developers to the core of a project, it often overlooks newcomers who do not envision long-term engagement or those who seek to make a single contribution. However, there are counterexamples such as the studies by Hannebauer et al. (2014), Steinmacher et al. (2014a), Steinmacher et al. (2014d), Steinmacher et al. (2015a), and Steinmacher et al. (2015b), which specifically examine the barriers that influence newcomers' initial contributions.

Jensen et al. (2011) conducted an analysis of mailing lists in FOSS projects to investigate whether emails from newcomers received prompt responses and if factors like gender and nationality influenced the nature of the response. They discovered a positive correlation between receiving timely responses and future participation. While instances of impolite replies to newcomers were few, they noted that such flaming behavior could have a chilling effect, particularly since mailing lists are public. Similarly, Steinmacher et al. (2013b) examined mailing lists and issue trackers to explore the influence of receptivity on newcomer onboarding. They identified factors such as receiving inadequate answers and the experience of the respondent as influences on newcomers' decisions to abandon the project.

Tsay et al. (2014) quantitatively analyzed the association between technical and social factors and the likelihood of accepting contributions. Their findings indicated that both the demonstration of good technical contribution practices in a pull request and strong social connections influenced the decision to accept contributions.

Shifting focus to the technical aspects of projects, Midha et al. (2010) discovered that an increase in cognitive complexity hindered newcomers from making contributions. Thus, code complexity was identified as a barrier to onboarding. Addressing technical barriers, Wolff-Marting et al. (2013) proposed two patterns to help newcomers overcome onboarding challenges. The first pattern aimed to assist newcomers in understanding the project's source code, while the second pattern sought to reduce the fear of introducing new bugs and encouraged newcomers to submit their modifications to the main development branch.

Numerous other studies have proposed approaches to support newcomers in making their first contributions. For example, Cubranic et al. (2005) introduced Hipikat, a tool that constructs a collective memory comprising source code, email discussions, and bug trackers. This tool enables newcomers to seek recommendations based on existing artifacts. Similarly, Wang and Sarma (2011) presented a tool that allows newcomers to identify bugs of interest and explore relevant resources and socio-technical dependencies in a visual and interactive manner.

Park and Jensen (2009) demonstrated that the use of visualization tools facilitated the initial steps of newcomers in FOSS projects. Their research revealed that such tools helped newcomers locate artifacts more efficiently and familiarize themselves with the project's architecture and code structure.

Canfora et al. (2012) proposed and evaluated an approach for identifying and recommending mentors for open-source project newcomers by mining data from mailing lists and source code versioning systems. In a similar vein, Steinmacher et al. (2012b) developed a recommendation approach to assist newcomers in finding the most suitable project member to mentor them in a specific technical task. Fagerholm et al. (2014) conducted a case study to assess the impact of mentoring support on developers and discovered that mentoring significantly influenced newcomer onboarding, enabling them to become more active participants.

Retention

"Retention" forces encompass the project's capacity and characteristics to facilitate newcomers' onboarding and sustain their contributions over time.

In their study on retention, Schilling et al. (2012) examined the longevity of former Google Summer of Code (GSoC) students' involvement in the KDE project. They discovered that the retention of students was strongly influenced by their development experience and familiarity with project coordination practices. Interestingly, they noted that students did not significantly prolong their engagement based on their underutilized abilities within the project or higher academic education.

Zhou and Mockus (2012, 2015) focused on identifying newcomers who were more likely to remain as project contributors, aiming to provide active support to facilitate their continued participation. They found that the interaction between an individual's attitude and the project's climate played a crucial role in determining the likelihood of becoming a valuable contributor.

Building upon the Legitimate Peripheral Participation (LPP) theory by Lave and Wenger (1991), Fang and Neufeld (2009) sought to understand developers' motivations for sustaining their contributions in a sustainable manner. Through qualitative analyses, they revealed that initial participation conditions did not effectively predict long-term involvement. Instead, they found that behaviors related to situated learning and identity construction were positively associated with sustained participation.

Lastly, Qureshi and Fang (2011) employed social resource theory to analyze the trajectories of 133 newcomers across 40 projects. By considering the initial level of interactions and subsequent growth with core members, they identified distinct classes of newcomer behavior, shedding light on the factors that influenced their retention in the projects.

THE NEWCOMER'S STRUGGLE

An interesting examination of the obstacles impeding newcomers was conducted by Steinmacher et al. (2015). The authors undertook a qualitative investigation based on empirical evidence and constructed a model to systematize the identified hindrances, mapping and categorizing them as a taxonomy of barriers faced by newcomers to FOSS projects. The resulting model encompasses 58 hindrances arranged into six categories (Steinmacher et al., 2014c), (Steinmacher et al., 2015c), (Steinmacher et al., 2014d),(Steinmacher et al., 2014a), and (Steinmacher et al., 2015b). The initial data set was obtained from students who contributed to FOSS projects. Through their feedback and recurring reports of barriers, the study compared the findings with existing literature and conducted semi-structured interviews with a small group of FOSS developers. Inputs from members of various FOSS communities, including Apache, LibreOffice, aTunes, Audacity, Cogroo, Etherpad, GNU Emacs, FReePlane, jEdit, Mozilla Firefox, OpenVPN, Moodle, and Noosfero, among others, were considered.

As an initial step, the research collected feedback from both postgraduate and undergraduate students who participated in FOSS projects as part of a regular course. All participants were newcomers between the ages of 21 and 30. The students were assigned to contribute to an existing FOSS project, and upon completing the assignment, their feedback was collected through an open-ended questionnaire. This questionnaire allowed students to reflect and explain the challenges they encountered while attempting to make their first code contribution. Another empirical data set consisted of answers to a questionnaire distributed to volunteer FOSS project developers via their respective mailing lists and forums. The questionnaire included questions designed to profile the contributors (project and contribution time), as well as an open-ended question regarding the main difficulties newcomers face when initiating their contributions to the respective projects. Respondents were categorized as follows: a) experienced members, referring to project owners, managers, or developers who directly commit code to the software repository; b) successful newcomers, including participants who began contributing to the project less than a year before the interview; c) dropout newcomers, indicating volunteers who attempted to contribute but gave up; d) onboarding newcomers, representing volunteers attempting to make their first contribution.

Mapping the hindrances based on the responses, the authors identified a set of shared impediments that affect newcomers.

Some of these challenges immediately manifest when newcomers engage with the project for the first time, encountering unfamiliar and rugged terrains. Novices often confront uncharted landscapes and struggle to navigate and make their contributions effectively. Finding a mentor is frequently cited as an initial barrier, along with selecting an appropriate task to begin with, reproducing issues, identifying the relevant artifacts to resolve an issue, and comprehending the development workflow.

There are also factors pertaining to community members' behavior, encompassing traits such as proactivity, patience, and commitment. Lack of recognition for their work, inadequate gratitude for their answers, shyness, proficiency in English, making irrelevant comments in mailing lists/forums, unresponsiveness, and related issues are also mentioned.

Social interaction emerges as a significant factor. This category encompasses barriers related to newcomers' interactions with the community, including issues related to whom they communicate with, the size of their network, communication styles, and how community members communicate with them. The receptivity of FOSS communities is highlighted as a barrier that can cause newcomers to become disheartened. Problems within this category can take various forms, from a lack of social interaction with project members to receiving untimely or inappropriate answers. The use of intimidating terminology by the community, either overly technical or potentially threatening, is another source of discouragement, as well as misunderstandings resulting from cultural differences.

Naturally, technical challenges also play a role. This type of obstacle encompasses difficulties related to newcomers' experience with the project and how they convey this experience when joining. It includes domain knowledge, familiarity with processes, and technical skills. Barriers may arise due to a lack of technical experience, domain expertise, or understanding of project practices. Adequate knowledge of the programming language, familiarity with technologies and tools used, version control systems, unit testing, and choosing the appropriate development tools are all listed as concerns. Practical factors within the technical category also include poor project design or code quality, code complexity or instability, codebase size, complex architecture or code structure, and delays in accepting contributions. Library dependencies, platform dependencies, among other aspects, are also mentioned.

Documentation represents yet another critical factor. Comprehensive and up-to-date documentation is crucial for newcomers trying to comprehend a project. However, an excessive amount of documentation can lead to information overload. Encountering outdated documentation or becoming overwhelmed by a vast amount of information can result in demotivation. Specific examples include a lack of documentation, outdated documentation, scattered pieces of information, insufficient details about the project structure, setting up a workspace, the contribution process, and project policies.

By combining frameworks proposed in the literature with the empirical results of the experiment conducted, the authors identified a set of common barriers organized into several categories and subcategories (Steinmacher, 2015), as follows.

- Newcomers' orientation
  - **Finding a task to start with**
  - **Finding a mentor**
  - **Finding the correct artifacts to fix an issue**
  - **Outdated list of bugs**
  - **Reproducing issues**
  - **Newcomers don't know what the contribution flow is**
- Newcomer's characteristics
  - Newcomers behavior
    - **Lack of proactivity**
    - **Lack of commitment**
    - **Some newcomers need to contact a real person**

- • Underestimating the challenge
- • Lack of patience
  - ○ Newcomers previous knowledge
    - • **Lack of domain expertise**
    - • **Lack of knowledge of project process and practices**
    - • Lack of technical background
- • **Knowledge of technologies and tools used**
- • **Proper knowledge of the programming language**
- • **Knowledge of versioning control systems**
- • **Choosing the right development tools**
- • **Experience in unit testing**
- • Communication
  - ○ Reception issues
    - • **Not receiving an answer**
    - • **Delayed answers**
    - • **Send a message that can be considered impolite**
    - • **Receiving answers with too advanced/complex contents**
  - ○ Newcomers' communication
    - • **Not sending a meaningful/correct message**
    - • **English level**
    - • **Shyness**
    - • **Making useless comments in the mailing list/forum**
    - • **Low responsiveness**
    - • **Not acknowledging/thanking answers**
- • Documentation problems
  - ○ **Outdated documentation**
  - ○ **Information overload**
  - ○ **Unclear documentation**
  - ○ **Spread documentation**
  - ○ **Lack of documentation**
- • Local environment setup hurdles
  - ○ **Building workspace locally**
  - ○ **Platform dependency**
  - ○ **Lack of documentation on setting up workspace**
  - ○ **Lack of information on required disk space**
  - ○ **Library dependency**
  - ○ **Finding the correct source**
- • Code/architecture hurdles
  - ○ Code characteristics
    - • **Bad code quality**

- **Code complexity/instability**
- **Codebase size**
- **Lack of code comments**
- **Code comments not clear**
- **Bad design quality**
- **Lack of code standards**
- **Outdated code**
  - Code documentation
    - **Lack of design documentation**
    - **Lack of code documentation**
    - **Lack of documentation on project structure**
  - Cognitive problems
    - **Understanding the code**
    - **Understanding architecture**
    - **Understanding the flow of information**
- Change request hurdles
  - **Lack of information on how to send a contribution**
  - **Delay in getting contribution accepted/reviewed**
  - **Getting contribution accepted**
  - **Not raising an issue to create a patch**

Mitigating the barriers

Based on the categorization of barriers, Steinmacher et al. (2015) devised an online platform aimed at assisting newcomers to FOSS projects in making their initial contributions. This platform offers valuable information and relevant links to help newcomers overcome barriers associated with specific categories. To evaluate the effectiveness of this initiative, the researchers conducted a study utilizing various methods, including qualitative data from diaries, a self-efficacy questionnaire, and the Technology Acceptance Model (TAM). The findings revealed that the portal played a crucial role in supporting newcomers by enhancing their understanding of the process and providing guidance through available resources, ultimately bolstering their self-confidence.

The platform suggests a protocol to aid newcomers, encompassing the following actions:

- Presenting a step-by-step suggested contribution flow.
- Providing a list of tasks specifically identified as suitable for newcomers.
- Encouraging communication through mailing lists or Internet Relay Chat (IRC).

- Facilitating the identification of volunteer mentors.
- Clarifying the required knowledge to contribute to the project.
- Including links to tutorials and training materials on relevant technologies.

The roadmap also emphasizes that newcomers should introduce themselves politely, exhibit proactivity and objectivity in their communication, and clearly express their understanding of a problem. Conversely, the project documentation should specify the soft skills expected from newcomers. In the face of difficulties, newcomers are encouraged to explore project resources such as web pages, archives, and mailing lists before seeking assistance. By sending courteous and meaningful messages, many barriers can be alleviated. Additionally, projects should maintain comprehensive and clear documentation, including diagrams and figures that illustrate code structure and flow, as well as links to tutorials covering workspace setup, presentations about the project, code conventions, and style, protocols for submitting pull requests, and information about code licensing.

In the second phase of the experiment, participants were invited to utilize the portal while making contributions to selected projects, with the relevant project information entered into the platform. Participants had the freedom to work at their own convenience, choosing their preferred time and location. The only requirement was that they diligently documented their progress in a diary, which was then shared with the research team. At the conclusion of the experiment, the authors conducted a brief post-study debriefing session with the participants. This session aimed to supplement the information provided by the diaries and address any questions regarding the participants' overall experience, assessment of the activity outcome, barriers encountered during participation, and how they were overcome. The annotations from the participants were then compared to those of another group who did not have access to the portal, providing valuable insights for further analysis.

"I opened my browser and typed the website address (...) I will need to contribute to LibreOffice but I don't have any clue on how to do it" — wrote one of the participants of the latter (control) group.

"... I am a little lost, so I will try a bug that I think I can work with... " — annotated another control participant.

Others mentioned:

"It seems that there is no place centralizing all the commands or information, to enable the developers to integrate quickly"

"I don't know what I was supposed to do after finishing the compilation process. I will watch the video tutorial once again to find it out. I need to define my next steps, I don't know what these steps are".

"I am feeling the necessity of finding something that will be my guide during this process, because until this moment I had to search different solutions and information in different places"

"It seems that there are many ways to gather information about the project. I am searching more and more pages and losing the focus of what I was looking for: how to download the code and develop for the project"

"I decided to organize and search for information once again. I noticed that I had too many pages opened and some of them were obsolete."

In contrast, participants that could obtain systematized information about the project through the online platform reported a substantially different experience.

"The tool seems to be good, because it solves doubts that range from the skills needed to start to pointing how to submit a contribution."

"I could check what newcomers need to know regarding the development environment, accessing the links to documentation and relevant guidelines, understanding how to search for help and who to talk to in case of problems and, mainly, accessing the newcomer guide showing the flow and offering support to each step of the process."

"...the tool helped me a lot, because it gave me an outstanding guidance about what I needed to do and, consequently, made me spend less time and made me more confident"

No participant who used the tool in the contribution process reported barriers related to newcomers' orientation, what are the next steps, or feeling lost. The participants reported on the portal's organization, and highlighted the role of the "contribution flow" in overcoming the barrier of not knowing "how to start." For example:

"I (...) read the 'How to start', and followed the steps of the suggested flow. Then, I accessed the 'setup your workspace'..."

"The flow was great. I always used it, and from here I accessed the other information. It is easy"

"That timeline [the flow] is very good. I really liked it. I think that for those who are contributing the first time it is very good, because the person thinks 'what should I do now?' and the answer is there"

"... the 'How to start', the information about workspace setup and the contribution flow were really helpful."

"checking the skills that newcomers needed to know about the development, either technical – like language, versioning control system and preferable operating system – and behavior – respect, commitment and proactivity... I don't know the code review tool, Gerrit, so I will need to know more about it..."

"I clicked 'check your skills' and the skills needed to contribute to the project were shown. Among them there was the languages C, C++, Java and Python, and the tool Git, that I never used before, and needed to learn how to use..."

"I decided to take a look at the bugs listed as easy at FLOSScoach (...) because it seemed something simple and that I would handle..."

"As it [the platform] suggested, I will seek for help in the community. I will write a comment at the Bugzilla, to confirm my understanding about the bug and ask if I can assign the task to me."

Among the obstacles encountered by the newcomers examined, technical challenges emerged as the most significant barriers. These challenges proved to be the primary cause for the majority of students failing to submit their contributions within the specified timeframe. From this analysis, valuable insights can be gleaned: (i) newcomers should begin by engaging with smaller and more recent projects, as these tend to have simpler setups and code that is easier to comprehend; (ii) communities should prioritize addressing workspace setup problems and offer clear instructions in the form of easy hacks, thereby assisting newcomers in locating the specific elements that require modification.

PRACTICAL TIPS TO BUILDING A COMMUNITY

Creating a friendly environment is crucial for a FOSS community to thrive, and for this to happen, having some ground rules for people to follow will most definitely ensure a community that is comfortable for everyone. In order to achieve this, there are a few things that must be put in place:

Code of Conduct and Community Guidelines

Having a set of community guidelines in place is the first step to having a friendly and inclusive community. Those guidelines help to set expectations and behaviors within a group, as they ensure that everyone feels equal, safe, and respected. While working on those guidelines, it is important to keep this in mind:

- the guidelines should clearly define the accepted and unaccepted behaviors;
- there should be clear guidance on how to report any cases of misconduct;
- a team that enforces the community guidelines should also be mentioned;
- consequences to be taken in case of misconduct should be listed too.

In addition to this, the guidelines should outline best practices for communication and collaboration and the necessary steps that should be followed. This will make it easier for newcomers and existing contributors to easily work together.

Encouraging Diversity and Inclusion

Diversity and inclusion definitely play a role in the growth and success of FOSS projects. The first encounter one will have with their colleague can determine their success in anything one sets out to do. Open-source communities can be intimidating to newcomers who may feel like they do not belong or lack the necessary skills to make a meaningful contribution. It is important to have a welcoming and supportive environment that caters to everyone regardless of their background, skill, and experience.

One strategy that always seems to work, not only in tech but in any other career, is promoting inclusivity. In open-source communities, this can be achieved by providing guidelines and resources for inclusive communication and behavior. This could involve creating a code of conduct that outlines clear policies for respectful communication and behavior. It is likely that, at some point during sign-up into social media rooms, we are all familiar with different moderators requiring our consent that we will abide by the community guidelines and policies. These rules are set to ensure that all community members can understand what behavior is expected of them and feel safe and included in the community.

In a similar fashion, we all have seen how big tech companies, like Google and Microsoft, organize cultural celebrations and educational workshops or invite guest speakers from diverse backgrounds. Such activities provide opportunities for community members to learn from one another and develop a deeper understanding and appreciation of different perspectives and experiences.

Mentorship and Onboarding Programs

Mentorship and onboarding programs help newcomers feel supported. Experienced community members can play a key role in guiding and supporting newcomers as they navigate the complex and often daunting process of open-source contribution.

Mentorship programs can offer a range of benefits to both newcomers and mentors. As a newcomer, having the advice of an experienced mentor will mean that they will get the needed guidance and support they need. This will often range from getting insight on how to correctly choose projects to contribute to getting feedback for your work, getting the right connections within the community, and navigating the social dynamics of the community.

To ensure that mentorship programs are beneficial, providing resources and training to mentors will help them support and guide new contributors in the right direction. This can include providing recommendations on effective mentoring strategies, offering resources and training on open-source contribution processes and tools, and establishing mechanisms for mentors to share best practices and collaborate with one another.

Encouraging Collaboration and Innovation

Providing newcomers with collaboration and innovation opportunities ensures that the projects continue to grow and remain relevant among the community members.

Having the community members involved in the decision-making process establishes transparency and allows contributors to voice their opinions and ideas in shaping the direction of the project.

By encouraging contributors to collaborate with other projects, share ideas, and learn from one another, FOSS communities can collectively tackle challenges and push the boundaries of what is possible. This can be achieved through cross-project hackathons, shared communication channels, and partnerships with other open-source organizations.

In addition to this, rewarding contribution is important to maintaining motivation among the community members. Appreciating contributor efforts can be either through public recognition, giving awards, or even simple thank-you messages — this can go a long way in creating a positive atmosphere and encouraging continued engagement. By creating an environment where collaboration and innovation are valued, FOSS communities can thrive, and drive projects towards success.

Ensuring Long-Term Sustainability

The sustainability of FOSS projects is furthered by establishing transparent governance structures. A well-defined governance scheme helps the community's leadership bodies create clear guidelines and processes for decision-making, conflict resolution, and community management at large. Creating a community based on accountability and transparency will help maintain an engaged and motivated community.

A culture of continuous improvement and innovation is essential for the success of any FOSS project. By continuously encouraging the community members to assess the project's goals and technologies will help promote an adaptable environment. The encouragement can range from different forms, including welcoming new ideas, embracing change, and being up to date with the industry's trends. That should help the communities maintain their relevance and ensure they continue to provide value to their members.

Another key point is encouraging ownership and succession planning. Most open-source project roles are volunteer-based, and the unpredictability of a person leaving is not certain. By nurturing a sense of shared responsibility and pride among community members, projects can avoid stagnation and single points of failure. Creating opportunities for new contributors to assume leadership roles and preparing for the eventual transition of key positions can help to preserve the project's momentum and ensure that it continues to thrive well into the future.

Challenges Faced by FOSS Communities

Building and maintaining a thriving FOSS community is challenging and, at the same time, a rewarding endeavor. As the rise of FOSS projects continues to extend in popularity, it's important to understand the challenges that may arise when trying to create a community of contributors. Some of the major challenges include funding, governance, and sustainability, to name a few of the relevant aspects. Without proper planning, those difficulties can limit the potential of the community and hinder its ability to evolve. By clearly understanding the potential hardships, the group can better understand how capable they need become, and then develop strategies to build stronger and more sustainable communities.

i. Funding

This is a common challenge facing not only FOSS projects but also any form of business out there. Failure to secure adequate funds to support the community's growth and sustainability may lead to its collapse before you even know it. This can negatively impact the ability of the community and project to attract new contributors, hindering its growth potential. A good way to come across such a problem is by applying for grants, seeking sponsorship, and joining incubator programs.

ii. Governance

The governance structure is another matter. Just like in any other venture, governance should evolve and adapt over time, so as to cope with eventual changes. Establishing a clear decision-making process will help not only the community management but also the flow of contributions from the members. Governance issues can lead to conflicts among contributors, which in turn may affect collaboration between the members.

iii. Sustainability

Projects need to be able to survive and evolve in the long-run as a way to ensure that they remain able to meet the needs of the users and contributors. Such success can be threatened by lack of resources and poor governance, hence failure in attracting new contributors.

iv. Lack of Diversity and Inclusion

When talking about communities that comprise many individuals, diversity and inclusion becomes critical components for their success; FOSS communities are no different. Despite this being a major concern, many FOSS communities and projects still struggle with the lack of diversity and inclusion, which at some point, may hinder the growth of the communities. A community that is built by members who all share similar backgrounds, experiences, and perspectives may become inefficient regarding its ability to incorporate different perspectives and adapt to etic and sociocultural demands. But with a diverse community, different people can bring a range of ideas to the table leading to more creative and innovative solutions. Some common benefits that may be championed by diversity include:

- A wide range of perspectives and alternative ideas;
- Increased innovation and creativity capability;
- Better representation of groups and cultural variety;
- Improved community engagement and participation;
- Enhanced awareness of global issues and how they impact FOSS projects.

Some effective strategies to handle the diversity and inclusion challenges include:

- Outreach and recruitment programs;
- Creating inclusive environments;
- Mentorship and support programs;
- Addressing bias and discrimination.

v. Communication Barrier

Effective communication is crucial for the success of a FOSS community. However, in many communities, achieving effective communication remains a challenge, specially with respect to language barriers and cultural differences. As we all know, communities comprise people from different backgrounds and regions, meaning we all speak different languages and have different beliefs, and even if there is a lingua franca, this does not eliminates communication noise. Another common challenge is the difference in time zones. This makes it hard to schedule meetings and collaborate in real-time. As a result, a lack of face-to-face interactions can make it harder to build relationships and trust among community members. In addition to these physical challenges, we may also be faced with technical communication barriers such as communication network dependability and limited bandwidth

— especially in underdeveloped regions — which might also pose a challenge to interaction and inclusivity.

To overcome these communication-related challenges, communities can opt to try out a few practices, such as having clear and detailed documentation and guide that ensure that developer members from different backgrounds understand the project guidelines and requirements. Another solution would be choosing the appropriate and easily accessible communication channels. This might vary with the type of meeting or information being shared. Some possible solutions can be email, chat, and video conferencing.

Establishing a clear communication pattern might also come in handy. This should involve having a set response time, providing regular updates and feedback, encouraging open and transparent communication, and having regular check-up calls or standup meetings — that not only ensures that the community members are on the same page and up to date but also helps build trust and promote collaboration among the community members.

Another idea that has proven to work is the localization of community project resources, such as documentation and guide pages, into different languages. This not only helps create awareness of the project but also promotes diversity in a manner that even those who are not familiar with a certain language are able to contribute to the project. A good example of such implementation is the freeCodeCamp[1] organization which is translating their entire learning process and articles into different world languages.

Remember that by prioritizing effective communication, transparency, and collaboration the FOSS projects and communities will be able to increase their reach and impact in greater percentages.

vi. Maintaining Contributor Motivation and Engagement

Contributors are the main force behind the success of any open-source project, and keeping them motivated and engaged is important. Some of the major reasons why motivation and rewarding of contributors is important include:

- They feel valued and appreciated;
- These rewards may come in different forms such as verbal or written recognition like "thank" notes or social media posts; sending of branded swags or any other form of merchandise; giving contributors opportunities to attend conferences, meetups, or other events to share their experience and journey; giving financial compensation or other forms of incentives such as access to pro plans for different services.

All those motivations might seem small, but they do play a huge impact on the communities, as they highlight that good contribution is acknowledged.

In a FOSS community, for one to be able to pull these acts together, some strategies to be put together include:

- First, one must understand that creating a welcoming and inclusive community is key to keeping contributors engaged;
- Next, understand that providing community members and contributors with the opportunity to learn new skills and grow their knowledge will come in handy — and can be achieved through conducting regular workshops and training sessions; encouraging collaborations and mentoring between the community members; organizing hackathons and other self-development challenges;
- Encouraging collaboration between the community members, which can be achieved by having clear communication channels and timely responses;
- Having clear pathways set to promote contributor growth and advancement through outlining clear expectations and end goals for different contributor levels, providing opportunities for leadership and mentorship within the communities.

Generally, recognizing each effort made by any contributor is a great way of ensuring engagement and long-term commitment.

vii. Managing Conflict and Maintaining a Positive Community Culture

Conflict and negativity in a community can create roadblocks that might affect the progress of the community, while having positive community culture can help attract new members and promote innovation. It's important to understand the possible sources of community conflict and come up with strategies to mitigate them.

Some common sources of community conflict in communities include:

- Differences in opinion and approaches to solving problems.
- Power dynamics within the community – most communities comprise of volunteers; this can create power imbalances and tension within the community.
- Misunderstandings caused by cultural or language barriers, some of them including
    - Encouraging respectful communication and active listening, leading to a more positive and productive discussion and outcome;

○ Having a facilitator to mediate and conduct open discussions that encourage multiple perspectives, thence uncovering underlying issues and finding possible solutions that satisfy all parties;

○ Seeking third-party mediation and arbitration in a case where a conflict escalates, seeking assistance can help resolve the conflict;

○ Implementing conflict resolution guidelines and procedures, which can be developed and documented to help contributors navigate how to handle disagreements in a constructive and productive way.

As much as managing community conflict is important, so is fostering a positive community culture. Some strategies to achieve this include:

- Establish community guidelines and a code of conduct;
- Encouraging and recognizing positive contributions and behaviors;
- Providing resources and support to community members to expand their knowledge;
- Teaching and training members how to handle burnout and stress;
- Creating a culture of collaboration, inclusivity, and transparency.

By understanding these common sources of conflict and how to resolve them, one can more effectively build a community that encourages collaboration, innovation, and inclusivity.

Case Studies: Successful Contributor Communities

To illustrate the importance of having newcomer-friendly and supportive communities, let's examine some of the most thriving open-source projects and their contributors base and get a grasp of what exactly counts to their success. This can offer valuable lessons that one can adapt to their local reality.

Linux Kernel

Linux might be considered one of the most successful and long-lasting FOSS communities. With thousands of developers collaborating worldwide, the project has maintained its relevance and growth over the decades. Some of the notable pointing towards its success include:

- Clear governance structure;
- An open contribution system;

- Transparent funding system mostly supported by corporate sponsorship and individual donors.

The Linux kernel development has a well-known governance model that ensures its undeniable success. To begin with, The Linux Foundation oversees the development of the project and provides support to the community.

The project has developed a strong culture of inclusivity and diversity, which has helped attract a diverse community of contributors from different parts of the world, regardless of their variety of native languages, as the project documentation is widely translated. Such diversity has promoted innovation and given the community power to drive the development of different projects.

Python

Python aggregates another community widely known for its inclusivity and accessibility, which has helped the project attract and retain a diverse community of contributors. The project was first released in the 90s, and since then, it has grown into one of the most used programming languages in the world. The community has been able to promote an environment that welcomes newcomers through mentorship programs, comprehensive documentation, and a friendly culture. Some of the key strategies that led to its success are:

Python has a well-defined and organized governance system. The Python Software Foundation is responsible for the development and promotion of the language. The PSF provides oversight of the projects, and it's mandated to make decisions about various aspects of the project.

Another key strategy is the source of funding. Python is primarily funded through sponsorship, donations, and merch sales.

Mozilla

Mozilla Foundation is responsible for projects such as Firefox and Thunderbird. The organization has been able to build a robust open-source community maintaining its principles and commitment to transparency, user privacy, and web accessibility. The organization is structured in a manner that there is a group of leaders whose focus is on community development which has made the organization attract and retain contributors from different backgrounds.

OpenStack

OpenStack is another good example that shows how when all the strategies discussed in the sections above can lead to the success of a community. The project has begun in 2010 with only a few contributors on board, but since then, it has grown into a massive community of more than 100,000 contributors and organizations, making it one of the largest FOSS projects to exist.

The success of the project and community was because of several factors. To begin with, OpenStack has a well-established governance structure that ensures the project is managed effectively. The governance structure is as follows: the project is overseen by the OpenStack foundation, which is made up of representatives from the different contributing companies, individual members, and the OpenStack Technical Committee. The committee oversees the development of the project, ensuring they are on track and keep up with the project's goals and values.

In terms of finances, the organization has a diverse model of funding that supports its sustainability. The project is funded by different cooperate sponsors, individuals, and donations. That has enabled the project to grow, ensuring its long-term sustainability.

As stated earlier, the success of an open-source project is strongly connected to an active community. OpenStack emphasizes collaboration and innovation. The project has clear guidelines set in place which encourage contributors to collaborate and share knowledge. In addition to this, they also offer mentoring that supports newcomers to the project, ensuring they are able to make meaningful contributions. OpenStack prioritizes diversity and inclusion; this has helped the program attract more contributors over time, and also ensures that the community is a safe place and welcoming new contributors.

FINAL NOTES

Open source software (OSS) projects consist of online communities of developers who collaborate on a shared collection of source code elements to create specific software products. These communities typically consist of geographically dispersed developers who work together through the Internet. The source code for these software products is generally distributed under licenses approved by organizations such as the Free Software Foundation or the Open Source Initiative.

The supposed advantages of OSS stem from the fact that the source code is freely shared. As highlighted by Eric Raymond in 1999, the involvement of a larger number of users and developers in the OSS process leads to an improvement in the quality of the code. Continuous feedback contributes to making the software more robust as many people contribute to identifying, reporting, and fixing bugs. Raymond encapsulates this idea with what he calls "Linux Law": "given enough eyeballs, all bugs are shallow."

For the purpose of this thesis, the most significant advantage of a shared and public codebase is that any developer who wishes to contribute can access the code, work on it, and submit changes. Raymond (1999) compares this development model to a bustling bazaar, where visitors have the freedom to observe, interact, modify, and remove what they desire.

In community-based OSS projects, the bazaar-like (Raymond in 1999) structure relies on the efforts of volunteers. The growth and sustainability of a project depend on a continuous influx of newcomers. Newcomers contribute to the project by correcting software defects and introducing new features. Therefore, the success of an OSS project is often linked to the steady arrival of newcomers.

Certain aspects of newcomers joining OSS projects are relevant to productivity. The integration of newcomers into a project may require additional coordination efforts, as a larger team necessitates more coordination. Communication efforts may also increase due to the greater number of messages exchanged among team members. These challenges align with the two key factors addressed by Brooks' Law: productivity (the ramp-up problem) and the overhead of communication and coordination (Brooks, 1995). Brooks' Law states that "adding manpower to a late project makes it later." While community-based OSS projects do not always adhere to strict release schedules, the concept of being "late" can be interpreted from the perspectives of sponsors, users, and participants.

In summary, we can draw valuable lessons for the success of FOSS projects. Establishing a clear governance structure is critical to managing and running a project. Having a diverse finance model will ensure the project's long-term sustainability. Building a welcoming and inclusive environment that supports newcomers, having set standards to solve conflicts, and acknowledging contributions, all these factors add to enabled many projects to maintain their relevance, attract new contributors, and foster continued innovation.

With all this in mind, promoting and advocating for a welcoming and inclusive environment should be one of the priorities of FOSS project managers. Well-supported and engaged communities will drive innovation, increase project adoption, and ultimately lead to a more robust and sustainable open-source ecosystem. With the advancement in technology, open-source software continues to shape contributor communities, making them become part of the development cycle. An encouraging word is to continually participate in open-source contributions, whether by reporting issues, submitting code changes, writing documentation, or by helping others in the community. The more we get involved, the more we grow and the greater there are advancements in technology and collaboration.

REFERENCES

Adler, A., Gujar, A., Harrison, B. L., O'Hara, K., & Sellen, A. (1998). A Diary Study of Work-related Reading: Design Implications for Digital Reading Devices. *Proceedings of the SIGCHI Conference on Human Factors in Computing Systems*, 241–248. 10.1145/274644.274679

Bonaccorsi, A., & Rossi, C. (2004, January). Altruistic individuals, selfish firms? The structure of motivation in Open Source software. *First Monday, 9*(1), 1. doi:10.5210/fm.v9i1.1113

Brooks, F. P. (1995). *The Mythical Man-Month: Essays on Software Engineering*. Addison-Wesley Professional.

Bryant, S. L., Forte, A., & Bruckman, A. (2005). Becoming Wikipedian: Transformation of Participation in a Collaborative Online Encyclopedia. *Proceedings of the 2005 International ACM SIGGROUP Conference on Supporting Group Work*, 1–10. 10.1145/1099203.1099205

Burke, M., Marlow, C., & Lento, T. (2009). Feed Me: Motivating Newcomer Contribution in Social Network Sites. *Proceedings of the SIGCHI Conference on Human Factors in Computing Systems*, 945–954. 10.1145/1518701.1518847

Canfora, G., di Penta, M., Oliveto, R., & Panichella, S. (2012). Who is Going to Mentor Newcomers in Open Source Projects? *Proceedings of the ACM SIGSOFT 20th International Symposium on the Foundations of Software Engineering*, 44:1–44:11. 10.1145/2393596.2393647

Capiluppi, A., & Michlmayr, M.F. (2007). From the Cathedral to the Bazaar: An Empirical Study of the Lifecycle of Volunteer Community Projects. In *Open Source Development, Adoption and Innovation*. Springer-Verlag Boston.

Chengalur-Smith, I. N., Sidorova, A., & Daniel, S. L. (2010, November). Sustainability of Free/Libre Open Source Projects: A Longitudinal Study. *Journal of the Association for Information Systems, 11*(11), 657–683. doi:10.17705/1jais.00244

Choi, B., Alexander, K., Kraut, R. E., & Levine, J. M. (2010). Socialization Tactics in Wikipedia and Their Effects. *Proceedings of the 2010 ACM Conference on Computer Supported Cooperative Work*, 107–116. 10.1145/1718918.1718940

Choi, B. R. (2012). *Essays on Socialization in Online Groups*. Tepper School of Business - Carneggie Mellon University.

Colazo, J., & Fang, Y. (2009, May). Impact of License Choice on Open Source Software Development Activity. *Journal of the American Society for Information Science and Technology*, *60*(5), 997–1011. doi:10.1002/asi.21039

Cubranic, D., Murphy, G. C., Singer, J., & Booth, K. S. (2005, June). Hipikat: A project memory for software development. *IEEE Transactions on Software Engineering*, *31*(6), 446–465. doi:10.1109/TSE.2005.71

Dagenais, B., Ossher, H., Bellamy, R. K. E., Robillard, M. P., & de Vries, J. P. 2010. Moving into a new software project landscape. *Proceedings of the 2010 ACM/IEEE 32nd International Conference on Software Engineering*, 275–284. 10.1145/1806799.1806842

David, P. A., & Shapiro, J. S. (2008, December). Community-based production of open-source software: What do we know about the developers who participate? *Information Economics and Policy*, *20*(4), 364–398. doi:10.1016/j.infoecopol.2008.10.001

Ducheneaut, N. (2005, August). Socialization in an Open Source Software Community: A Socio-Technical Analysis. *Computer Supported Cooperative Work*, *14*(4), 323–368. doi:10.100710606-005-9000-1

Fagerholm, F., Johnson, P., Guinea, A. S., Borenstein, J., & Münch, J. (2014, November). Onboarding in Open Source Projects. *IEEE Software*, *31*(6), 54–61. doi:10.1109/MS.2014.107

Fang, Y., & Neufeld, D. (2009, April). Understanding Sustained Participation in Open Source Software Projects. *Journal of Management Information Systems*, *25*(4), 9–50. doi:10.2753/MIS0742-1222250401

Faulkner, R., Walling, S., & Pinchuk, M. (2012). Etiquette in Wikipedia: Weening New Editors into Productive Ones. *Proceedings of the Eighth Annual International Symposium on Wikis and Open Collaboration*. 10.1145/2462932.2462939

Fogel, K. (2013). *Producing Open Source Software: How to Run a Successful Free Software Project*. O'Reilly Media.

França, A. C. C. (2009). An Empirical Study on Software Engineers Motivational Factors. *Proceedings of the 2009 3rd International Symposium on Empirical Software Engineering and Measurement*, 405–409. 10.1109/ESEM.2009.5316011

França, A. C. C., & da Silva, F. Q. B. (2010). Designing Motivation Strategies for Software Engineering Teams: An Empirical Study. *Proceedings of the 2010 ICSE Workshop on Cooperative and Human Aspects of Software Engineering*, 84–91. 10.1145/1833310.1833324

França, A. C. C., da Silva, F. Q. B., Felix, L. C., & Carneiro, D. E. S. (2014, January). A. de, Carneiro, D.E.S. 2014b. Motivation in software engineering industrial practice: A cross-case analysis of two software organisations. *Information and Software Technology, 56*(1), 79–101. doi:10.1016/j.infsof.2013.06.006

França, A. C. C., Gouveia, T. B., Santos, P. C. F., Santana, C. A., & da Silva, F. Q. B. (2011). Motivation in software engineering: A systematic review update. *Proceedings of the 15th Annual Conference on Evaluation Assessment in Software Engineering,* 154–163. 10.1049/ic.2011.0019

Fugelstad, P., Dwyer, P., Moses, J. F., Kim, J., Mannino, C. A., Terveen, L., & Snyder, M. (2012). What Makes Users Rate (Share, Tag, Edit...)?: Predicting Patterns of Participation in Online Communities. *Proceedings of the ACM 2012 Conference on Computer Supported Cooperative Work,* 969–978. 10.1145/2145204.2145349

Halfaker, A., Geiger, R. S., Morgan, J., & Riedl, J. (2013a, May). The Rise and Decline of an Open Collaboration System: How Wikipedia's reaction to sudden popularity is causing its decline. *The American Behavioral Scientist, 57*(5), 664–688. doi:10.1177/0002764212469365

Halfaker, A., Keyes, O., & Taraborelli, D. (2013b). Making Peripheral Participation Legitimate: Reader Engagement Experiments in Wikipedia. *Proceedings of the 2013 Conference on Computer Supported Cooperative Work,* 849–860. 10.1145/2441776.2441872

Halfaker, A., Kittur, A., & Riedl, J. (2011). Don't Bite the Newbies: How Reverts Affect the Quantity and Quality of Wikipedia Work. *Proceedings of the 7th International Symposium on Wikis and Open Collaboration,* 163–172. 10.1145/2038558.2038585

Hannebauer, C., Book, M., & Gruhn, V. (2014). An Exploratory Study of Contribution Barriers Experienced by Newcomers to Open Source Software Projects. *Proceedings of the First International Workshop on CrowdSourcing in Software Engineering,* 11–14. 10.1145/2593728.2593732

Herraiz, I., Robles, G., Amor, J. J., Romera, T., Barahona, J. M. G., & Carlos, J. (2006). The processes of joining in global distributed software projects. *Proceedings of the 2006 International Workshop on Global Software Development for the Practitioners,* 27–33. 10.1145/1138506.1138513

Hertel, G., Niedner, S., & Herrmann, S. (2003, July). Motivation of software developers in Open Source projects: An Internet-based survey of contributors to the Linux kernel. *Research Policy, 32*(7), 1159–1177. doi:10.1016/S0048-7333(03)00047-7

Hsieh, G., Hou, Y., Chen, I., & Truong, K. N. (2013). Welcome! Social and Psychological Predictors of Volunteer Socializers in Online Communities. *Proceedings of the 2013 Conference on Computer Supported Cooperative Work*, 827–838. 10.1145/2441776.2441870

Jensen, C., King, S., & Kuechler, V. (2011). Joining Free/Open Source Software Communities: An Analysis of Newbies' First Interactions on Project Mailing Lists. *Proceedings of the 44th Hawaii International Conference on System Sciences*, 1–10. 10.1109/HICSS.2011.264

Jergensen, C., Sarma, A., & Wagstrom, P. (2011). The Onion Patch: Migration in Open Source Ecosystems. *Proceedings of the 19th ACM SIGSOFT Symposium and the 13th European Conf. on Foundations of Software Engineering*, 70–80.

Jergensen, N. (2007, May). Developer autonomy in the FreeBSD open source project. *The Journal of Management and Governance*, *11*(2), 119–128. doi:10.100710997-007-9026-5

Kanfer, R. (1990). Motivation Theory and Industrial and Organizational Psychology. In Handbook of Psychology, Industrial and Organizational Psychology. Counsulting Psychologist Press.

Ke, W., & Zhang, P. (2010, December). The Effects of Extrinsic Motivations and Satisfaction in Open Source Software Development. *Journal of the Association for Information Systems*, *11*(12), 784–808. doi:10.17705/1jais.00251

Kraut, R. E., Burke, M., Riedl, J., & Resnick, P. (2012). The Challenges of Dealing with Newcomers. In Building Successful Online Communities: Evidence-Based Social Design. MIT Press. doi:10.7551/mitpress/8472.003.0006

Lakhani, K. R., & Wolf, R. G. (2005). *Perspectives on Free and Open Source Software.* The MIT Press.

Lampe, C., Obar, J., Ozkaya, E., Zube, P., & Velasquez, A. (2012). Classroom Wikipedia Participation Effects on Future Intentions to Contribute. *Proceedings of the ACM 2012 Conference on Computer Supported Cooperative Work*, 403–406. 10.1145/2145204.2145267

Lave, J., & Wenger, E. (1991). *Situated Learning : Legitimate Peripheral Participation.* Cambridge University Press. doi:10.1017/CBO9780511815355

Lee, S., Park, D.-H., & Han, I. (2014, January). New members' online socialization in online communities: The effects of content quality and feedback on new members' content-sharing intentions. *Computers in Human Behavior*, *30*, 344–354. doi:10.1016/j.chb.2013.09.015

Meirelles, P., Santos, C., Miranda, J., Kon, F., Terceiro, A., & Chavez, C. (2010). A study of the relationships between source code metrics and attractiveness in free software projects. *Proceedings of the 2010 Brazilian Symposium on Software Engineering*, 11–20. 10.1109/SBES.2010.27

Midha, V., Palvia, P., Singh, R., & Kshetri, N. (2010). Improving open source software maintenance. *Journal of Computer Information Systems*, *50*(3), 81–90.

Morgan, J. T., Bouterse, S., Walls, H., & Stierch, S. (2013). Tea and Sympathy: Crafting Positive New User Experiences on Wikipedia. *Proceedings of the 2013 Conference on Computer Supported Cooperative Work*, 839–848. 10.1145/2441776.2441871

Nakakoji, K., Yamamoto, Y., Nishinaka, Y., Kishida, K., & Ye, Y. (2002). Evolution Patterns of Open- source Software Systems and Communities. *Proceedings of the International Workshop on Principles of Software Evolution*, 76–85. 10.1145/512035.512055

Oreg, S., & Nov, O. (2008, September). Exploring motivations for contributing to open source initiatives: The roles of contribution context and personal values. *Computers in Human Behavior*, *24*(5), 2055–2073. doi:10.1016/j.chb.2007.09.007

Park, Y., & Jensen, C. (2009). Beyond pretty pictures: Examining the benefits of code visualization for open source newcomers. *Proceedings of the 5th IEEE International Workshop on Visualizing Software for Understanding and Analysis*, 3–10. 10.1109/VISSOF.2009.5336433

Pham, R., Singer, L., Liskin, O., Filho, F. F., & Schneider, K. (2013). Creating a Shared Understanding of Testing Culture on a Social Coding Site. *Proceedings of the 2013 International Conference on Software Engineering*, 112–121. 10.1109/ICSE.2013.6606557

Preece, J. (2001). Sociability and usability in online communities: Determining and measuring success. *Behaviour & Information Technology*, *20*(5), 347–356. doi:10.1080/01449290110084683

Qureshi, I., & Fang, Y. (2011, January). Socialization in Open Source Software Projects: A Growth Mixture Modeling Approach. *Organizational Research Methods*, *14*(1), 208–238. doi:10.1177/1094428110375002

Raymond, E. S. (1999). *The Cathedral and the Bazaar*. O'Reilly & Associates, Inc. doi:10.100712130-999-1026-0

Roberts, J. A., Hann, I.-H., & Slaughter, S. A. (2006, July). Understanding the Motivations, Participation, and Performance of Open Source Software Developers: A Longitudinal Study of the Apache Projects. *Management Science, 52*(7), 984–999. doi:10.1287/mnsc.1060.0554

Santos, C., Kuk, G., Kon, F., & Pearson, J. (2013, March). The Attraction of Contributors in Free and Open Source Software Projects. *The Journal of Strategic Information Systems, 22*(1), 26–45. doi:10.1016/j.jsis.2012.07.004

Scacchi, W. (2002, February). Understanding the requirements for developing open source software systems. *IEE Proceedings. Software, 149*(1), 24–39. doi:10.1049/ip-sen:20020202

Schilling, A., Laumer, S., & Weitzel, T. (2012). Who Will Remain? An Evaluation of Actual Person-Job and Person-Team Fit to Predict Developer Retention in FLOSS Projects. *Proceedings of the 2012 45th Hawaii International Conference on System Sciences*, 3446–3455. 10.1109/HICSS.2012.644

Shah, S. K. (2006, July). Motivation, Governance, and the Viability of Hybrid Forms in Open Source Software Development. *Management Science, 52*(7), 1000–1014. doi:10.1287/mnsc.1060.0553

Sharp, H., Baddoo, N., Beecham, S., Hall, T., & Robinson, H. (2009, January). Models of motivation in software engineering. *Information and Software Technology, 51*(1), 219–233. doi:10.1016/j.infsof.2008.05.009

Steinmacher, I., Chaves, A. P., Conte, T., & Gerosa, M. A. (2014a). Preliminary empirical identification of barriers faced by newcomers to Open Source Software projects. *Proceedings of the 28th Brazilian Symposium on Software Engineering*, 1–10.

Steinmacher, I., Chaves, A. P., & Gerosa, M. A. (2010). Awareness support in global software development: a systematic review based on the 3C collaboration model. *Proceedings of the 16th international conference on Collaboration and technology*, 185–201. 10.1007/978-3-642-15714-1_15

Steinmacher, I., Chaves, A.P., & Gerosa, M.A. (2013a). Awareness Support in Distributed Software Development: A Systematic Review and Mapping of the Literature. *Computer Supported Cooperative Work (CSCW), 22*(2-3), 113–158.

Steinmacher, I., Conte, T., & Gerosa, M. A. (2015a). Understanding and Supporting the Choice of an Appropriate Task to Start With In Open Source Software Communities. *Proceedings of the 48th Hawaiian International Conference in Software Systems*, 1–10.

Steinmacher, I., Conte, T., Gerosa, M. A., & Redmiles, D. F. (2015b). Social Barriers Faced by Newcomers Placing Their First Contribution in Open Source Software Projects. *Proceedings of the 18th ACM Conference on Computer Supported Cooperative Work & Social Computing*, 1–13. 10.1145/2675133.2675215

Steinmacher, I., Gerosa, M. A., & Redmiles, D. (2014b). Attracting, Onboarding, and Retaining Newcomer Developers in Open Source Software Projects. *Proceedings of the Workshop on Global Software Development in a CSCW Perspective*.

Steinmacher, I., Silva, M. A. G., & Gerosa, M. A. (2014c). Barriers Faced by Newcomers to Open Source Projects: A Systematic Review. In Open Source Software: Mobile Open Source Technologies. Springer.

Steinmacher, I., Silva, M. A. G., Gerosa, M. A., & Redmiles, D. F. (2015, March). A systematic literature review on the barriers faced by newcomers to open source software projects. *Information and Software Technology*, *59*, 67–85. doi:10.1016/j. infsof.2014.11.001

Steinmacher, I., Wiese, I. S., Chaves, A. P., & Gerosa, M. A. (2012a). Newcomers Withdrawal in Open Source Software Projects: Analysis of Hadoop Common Project. *Proceedings of the 2012 Brazilian Symposium on Collaborative Systems*, 65–74. 10.1109/SBSC.2012.16

Steinmacher, I., Wiese, I. S., Chaves, A. P., & Gerosa, M. A. (2013b). Why do newcomers abandon open source software projects? *Proceedings of the 2013 6th International Workshop on Cooperative and Human Aspects of Software Engineering*, 25–32.

Steinmacher, I., Wiese, I. S., Conte, T., Gerosa, M. A., & Redmiles, D. (2014d). The Hard Life of Open Source Software Project Newcomers. *Proceedings of the International Workshop on Cooperative and Human Aspects of Software Engineering*, 72–78. 10.1145/2593702.2593704

Steinmacher, I., Wiese, I. S., & Gerosa, M. A. (2012b). Recommending mentors to software project newcomers. *Proceedings of the Third International Workshop on Recommendation Systems for Software Engineering*, 63–67.

Stewart, K. J., Ammeter, A. P., & Maruping, L. M. (2006, June). Impacts of License Choice and Organizational Sponsorship on User Interest and Development Activity in Open Source Software Projects. *Information Systems Research, 17*(2), 126–144. doi:10.1287/isre.1060.0082

Tidwell, L. C., & Walther, J. B. (2002). Computer-Mediated Communication Effects on Disclosure, Impressions, and Interpersonal Evaluations: Getting to Know One Another a Bit at a Time. *Human Communication Research, 28*(3), 317–348. doi:10.1111/j.1468-2958.2002.tb00811.x

Tsay, J., Dabbish, L., & Herbsleb, J. (2014). Influence of social and technical factors for evaluating contribution in GitHub. *Proceedings of the 36th International Conference on Software Engineering*, 356–366. 10.1145/2568225.2568315

Ververs, E., van Bommel, R., & Jansen, S. (2011). Influences on Developer Participation in the Debian Software Ecosystem. *Proceedings of the International Conference on Management of Emergent Digital EcoSystems*, 89–93. 10.1145/2077489.2077505

von Krogh, G., Haefliger, S., Spaeth, S., & Wallin, M. W. (2012, June). Carrots and Rainbows: Motivation and Social Practice in Open Source Software Development. *Management Information Systems Quarterly, 36*(2), 649–676. doi:10.2307/41703471

von Krogh, G., Spaeth, S., & Lakhani, K. R. (2003). Community, joining, and specialization in open source software innovation: A case study. *Research Policy, 32*(7), 1217–1241. doi:10.1016/S0048-7333(03)00050-7

von Krogh, G., & von Hippel, E. (2003, July). Editorial: Special issue on open source software development. *Research Policy, 32*(7), 1149–1157. doi:10.1016/S0048-7333(03)00054-4

Vora, P., & Komura, N. (2010). The n00b Wikipedia Editing Experience. *Proceedings of the 6th International Symposium on Wikis and Open Collaboration*, Article 36. 10.1145/1832772.1841393

Wang, J., & Sarma, A. (2011). Which bug should I fix: helping new developers onboard a new project. *Proceedings of the 4th International Workshop on Cooperative and Human Aspects of Software Engineering*, 76–79. 10.1145/1984642.1984661

Wang, L. S., Chen, J., Ren, Y., & Riedl, J. (2012). Searching for the Goldilocks Zone: Trade-offs in Managing Online Volunteer Groups. *Proceedings of the ACM 2012 Conference on Computer Supported Cooperative Work*, 989–998. 10.1145/2145204.2145351

Wolff-Marting, V., Hannebauer, C., & Gruhn, V. (2013). Patterns for tearing down contribution barriers to FLOSS projects. *Proceedings of the 12th International Conference on Intelligent Software Methodologies, Tools and Techniques*, 9–14.

Yu, S., & Ming, W. (2009). Research on individual motivation model of software engineering. *Journal of Communication and Computer, 6*(11), 12.

Zhou, M., & Mockus, A. (2012). What make long term contributors: Willingness and opportunity in OSS community. *Proceedings of the 34th International Conference on Software Engineering*, 518–528. 10.1109/ICSE.2012.6227164

Zhou, M., & Mockus, A. (2015). Who Will Stay in the FLOSS Community? Modelling Participant's Initial Behaviour. *IEEE Transactions on Software Engineering, 41*(1), 82–99. doi:10.1109/TSE.2014.2349496

Zhu, H., Kraut, R., & Kittur, A. (2012). Effectiveness of Shared Leadership in Online Communities. *Proceedings of the ACM 2012 Conference on Computer Supported Cooperative Work*, 407–416. 10.1145/2145204.2145269

Zhu, H., Zhang, A., He, J., Kraut, R. E., & Kittur, A. (2013). Effects of Peer Feedback on Contribution: A Field Experiment in Wikipedia. *Proceedings of the SIGCHI Conference on Human Factors in Computing Systems*, 2253–2262. 10.1145/2470654.2481311

ENDNOTE

[1] freeCodeCamp: https://www.freecodecamp.org/

Chapter 8
Building Teams and Developing a Career in the FOSS Industry

Renê de Souza Pinto
Zededa GmbH, Germany

ABSTRACT

The world has been recovering from the COVID-19 pandemic and is coming towards its post-pandemic era. Although many IT companies have experienced big growth during the pandemic caused by the increasing demand of several kinds of services, finding highly skilled IT professionals is essential to the expansion of the business and was never an easy task, even before the pandemic. The leveraging of remote work during the last years collaborated substantially with companies in order to expand their teams across the globe and find talented people that would never have been found within the pre-pandemic environment. However, apart from the new working models and environments in the IT sector, the FOSS model always posed as an outstanding framework not only to leverage projects but also to help in finding talented people throughout the world. This short chapter presents a brief overview about how FOSS can be used to help companies leverage their businesses and expand teams by reaching professionals with a good matching profile.

PROFESSIONAL CAREER

Although terms such as Open Source, Free Software, and Pervasive Computing might still sound like innovation for many people, they were coined decades ago. By the time the Open Source definition was coined in 1998 (Stone et al., 1999),

DOI: 10.4018/978-1-6684-4785-7.ch008

Free Software Foundation was more than 10 years old and GNU GPL licenses(GPL-Compatible Free Software Licenses, 2023) were well established even though the computing market was still dominated by proprietary software and business models. The hardware evolved fast and the development of microelectronics and manufacturing techniques of integrated circuits leveraged embedded systems and portable platforms, allowing miniaturization, reducing costs, and making them accessible to the general public. As a consequence, there was a boom of computer devices in our society: routers, smartphones, TVs, tablets, sensors, and several other devices became common in most environments and transformed the pervasive computing, already discussed and predicted years ago(Satyanarayanan, 2001), into a reality. In this context, FOSS also evolved through countless successful projects which have paved the way for newer (non-proprietary) business models, innovation, and acceleration of software development. Nowadays Open Source is everywhere, from robotic toys (Personal Robots, 2019) to Satellites(Labrèche et al., 2022), driving cloud and internet infrastructure, and running on billions of devices such as smartphones and TVs. Some of its main advantages are:

- The huge availability of high-quality FOSS: in 2023 there are more than 300 million of repositories hosted only by GitHub, where around 31 million are public(GitHub, 2023). Is easy to infer from this massive number that even considering only a small portion of all this software to be high quality, it still represents a big amount of artifacts, tools, and components that can be easily used by companies in their own business. However, this number can be much bigger considering the nature of Open Source, which usually counts on the collaboration of a community of developers working on several aspects of the software development process other than coding, such as reviewing, testing, and writing documentation, this joint force collaborates to improve the quality of the final product, bug fixes and evolution of the project throughout its lifetime. Also, it is worth mentioning that there are many other platforms hosting FOSS code apart from GitHub, which makes it harder to estimate the real numbers.
- Increase security: due to the FOSS working model, big projects draw a lot of attention of the community, which means that a lot of developers will not only code new features, but also review, test, find and fix bugs that could not be easily revealed by a smaller (corporative) team of developers. While the openness of the source code allows anyone to study it and find security flaws, it also allows a quick response from the community, providing fixes faster.
- Faster time-to-market: using available Open Source software can accelerate the development process by allowing companies to reuse FOSS artifacts

instead of writing their projects completely from scratch, which also saves development costs.

- Availability of tools, models, and use cases for project development: with so many FOSS projects carried on over the years throughout the community, a lot of valuable tools, models, and use cases were developed and designed for project management and software engineering, companies can define their own project development process based on successful FOSS projects and their open and transparent experience besides the use of open source tools for project management.

- Flexibility: by not charging customers for proprietary licenses (that give the rights to only run the software), but for the service (development, support, etc) instead, companies are actually giving much more flexibility to customers, which can be a big advantage when comparing with proprietary solutions from competitors. Customers can adapt the product for other needs and tend to be more open to reusing the software, leading to new contracts and service requests.

- Acceptance and propagation: the majority of protocols, APIs, and standards that build the internet infrastructure, cloud computing, operating systems, and several other areas are open standards with high acceptance from the community, industry, and manufacturers. A company trying to propagate a new standard (API, etc) has more chances to succeed following the FOSS model by making it transparent and open than trying to establish a new monopoly by making it closed-source and proprietary.

Developers play a central role in the FOSS model. All advantages brought by the FOSS approach can only be fully explored if the development team is composed of professionals who know how to work with the FOSS ecosystem. Breaking the numbers from the 10th Annual Open Source Jobs Report(The Linux Foundation, 2022) shows that 40% of hiring managers interviewed reported finding it very difficult to find professionals with open source skills; 53% said it was somewhat difficult; and only 7% said it was not difficult at all. The reasons why these professionals are very valuable for companies might be explained when the open-source career path is analyzed. In (Riehle, 2015), research on how open source is changing software development as a career was carried out by interviewing different professionals throughout a year and reviewing the literature. The authors explained different models for an open-source career ladder. In general, all of them establish three main phases:

- User: becoming a user is the very beginning step of any person that will eventually become a contributor to a FOSS project and a professional in this area. Because FOSS allows anyone to execute and use the software for their own needs as they wish, there are basically no barriers to a person becoming a user of Open Source software. Users can still be split into two categories: passive users, which are those who use the software but don't contribute with bug reports or participate in mail lists or other communication channels; and active users, which are those who use the software and contribute with bug reports, act as testers for new releases and usually are active members in the communication channels of the project. Active users tend to become contributors as they gain more experience with the project and its management model.

- Contributor: in the same way as the users, there are different types of contributors: they will usually start with little power over the project, by doing small bug fixes, improving documentation, or finding small issues throughout the code (typos, for instance). As contributors become more involved with the project, at some point they will become comfortable with the way how the project development is handled by the leaders and by the community of that project, so they know how to behave in the communication channels, how to push patches, write commit messages or follow the rules imposed by maintainers. At this stage, the contributor can be very involved with the project and become an active developer. Active developers are the core part of the team (community) that will actively push changes to the project, create new features, manage bug fixes, and documentation have more interaction with maintainers.

- Committer: this role has much more power over the project. Committers can be the maintainers of specific parts of the project, such as modules or subsystems (very common on big and complex software) or the project leaders. They have the power to decide which changes proposed by contributors should become upstreamed and the right to write in the main repository without prior permission. A regular development flow looks like the following: contributors push their patches proposing changes to the software®each patch is reviewed and discussed within the community®maintainers will give the final approval and merge those patches that were accepted to become upstreamed. Committees will help to lead the project and give its direction.

Foundations have evolved in order to guarantee the stability and the growth of relevant commercial Open Source projects. Well-known examples are the ASF(The Apache Software Foundation, 2023), Mozilla Foundation(Mozilla Foundation, 2023), OpenInfra Foundation(Open Infrastructure Foundation, 2023), and the Linux Foundation (Linux Foundation, 2023), which emerged from successful Open Source projects such as the Apache Web Server, Mozilla Firefox and the Linux kernel, all of them very explored also by commercial business. In this context, foundations have extended the open-source career path, extending the roles to management status as well(Riehle, 2015). In summary, there is a long (and very flexible) path through an open-source career, with many possibilities and knowledge levels of working. Additionally, the massive number of FOSS projects allows a professional to play different roles in more than one project at the same time.

A professional who went through the open source career path, or a large part of it, will have acquired a lot of experience going through different roles in different projects. As bigger and more successful the projects where it has participated are, the more comfortable this professional will be with the FOSS ecosystem and have experienced the software engineering development process and all its nuances. Both companies and professionals can take advantage of the FOSS model in order to find good employees and good places to work. From the recruiter's side, they have access to a large pool of professionals through the FOSS projects, where their information, work, and portfolio are publicly available. Not only the source code repositories, but also the communication channels (mail list, forums, etc) are easy ways to look for these professionals and quickly evaluate potential candidates for a role. Due to this openness and flexible model, companies have more tools and ways to evaluate the skills of an open-source developer who has a proven track record of delivering code and teamwork. These facilities can drastically reduce the costs of hiring.

From the developers' side, the ability to carry their source code throughout their career is really an advantage over those who work on proprietary solutions and do not own the copyright of their source code. By contributing to FOSS projects, developers can gain not only experience but high visibility in the community as well, drawing attention from companies and ending up receiving job offers. Professionals can also use their own FOSS projects to find companies that would be interested in leveraging them by funding through sponsorship or hiring the professional.

PROFESSIONAL DEVELOPMENT

In a number of ways, open source can have a big impact on someone's professional career advancement. Developing one's technical skills is possible through participating in open-source initiatives. They receive practical experience and learn the best practices in software development by working on real-world projects with seasoned engineers. Their technical skills may be improved, and potential employers may find them more appealing as a result of their practical experience.

Contributing to open-source projects allows individuals to showcase their expertise and knowledge in a tangible manner. By actively engaging in collaborative development, they can build a compelling portfolio that demonstrates their skills and dedication. This portfolio can prove invaluable when seeking freelance opportunities or applying for positions.

Open-source projects foster a vibrant community of developers who collaborate and share their expertise. By actively participating in these communities, individuals can expand their professional networks, connect with like-minded individuals, and learn from experienced developers. Building connections within the open source community opens doors to mentorships, job prospects, and other beneficial relationships throughout one's career. Making notable contributions to well-known open-source projects can also enhance an individual's reputation and establish them as an industry expert. This recognition can lead to job offers, speaking engagements, and leadership roles within the open-source ecosystem.

Employers highly value individuals who have made significant contributions to open source as it signifies their passion, knowledge, and commitment to their craft. Open-source projects provide a continuous learning environment where developers can stay up-to-date with the latest technologies, industry trends, and emerging techniques. Engaging in open source enables individuals to challenge themselves, solve complex problems, and acquire new knowledge and skills. Employers greatly appreciate this commitment to lifelong learning and growth, which ultimately contributes to long-term career success. In summary, involvement in open source brings numerous benefits, including technical skill development, portfolio enhancement, professional networking opportunities, recognition, and the fostering of a growth mindset. These qualities can significantly propel and advance a professional career in the technology sector.

In addition to the technical aspects, open-source software also raises a number of ethical issues when used professionally. The concept of cooperation and knowledge sharing comes first. Open source encourages experts to collaborate, add to the body of knowledge, and develop technology for the good of all. Professionals that actively participate in open-source projects have the chance to demonstrate their abilities, pick up knowledge from others, and advance the interests of the software industry. To preserve the honesty and fairness of open source projects, however, it is ethically required to uphold intellectual property rights, abide by licensing conditions, and provide adequate credit to contributions.

The promotion of inclusion and accessibility is another ethical aspect of open source in a professional setting. Open-source software has the potential to close the digital gap, strengthen the voices of marginalized groups, and open doors for people of all backgrounds. Professionals can help to a more diverse and fair IT sector by openly sharing code and offering free access to software. To make sure that open-source projects prioritize security, privacy, and code quality, ethical issues come into play. To provide dependable and dependable software solutions to the larger community, professionals must be cautious in fixing vulnerabilities, protecting users' data, and preserving high standards of workmanship.

Hard and soft skills developed through participation in FOSS communities yield personal and professional gains. Due to the distinctive abilities and experiences they acquire through their participation in open-source initiatives, open-source professionals frequently have the ability to find higher-paying jobs. Employers strongly value the knowledge, problem-solving skills, and collaborative approach that professionals actively contribute to open source to show. Open source experts can stand out from other applicants thanks to their practical experience gained from working on real-world projects and their ability to demonstrate concrete contributions in a portfolio. Their abilities may become more in demand as a result, opening up prospects for higher-paying jobs. Additionally, the open-source community offers a venue for networking and developing relationships with business titans, which may lead to lucrative career opportunities. Employers are frequently prepared to pay competitive remuneration packages in order to attract and keep the best personnel because they understand the commitment and enthusiasm displayed by open-source specialists. It's crucial to keep in mind, though, that individual circumstances, market conditions, and other variables also have a big impact on work chances and pay. While being active in the open source community might improve employment chances, it is only one of several elements that affect how competitive the job market is and how much money an individual can make.

A deliberate strategy, a mix of technical expertise, community engagement, and ongoing learning are needed to build a career in open source. First and foremost, it's essential to have a solid foundation in programming languages and pertinent technologies through formal schooling or independent study. It's crucial to get in-depth knowledge and proficiency in particular open-source software fields. One can demonstrate their abilities and dedication to collaborative development by actively engaging in open-source projects by submitting code, correcting bugs, and suggesting new features. To obtain experience and recognition, it's critical to start with modest initiatives before moving progressively toward bigger, more significant ones.

Networking possibilities, mentorships, and information exchange are made possible by participating in the open-source community through mailing lists, forums, and conferences. Creating a personal brand and online presence can assist enhance awareness and draw in potential employers. Examples include running a blog or contributing to technical publications. Maintaining current with the newest trends, techniques, and technology is essential if you want to stay competitive. Finally, looking for work with organizations that support and contribute to open-source projects might lead to additional career development and stability. A successful career in open-source can be achieved by combining technical proficiency, community involvement, ongoing learning, and strategic career decisions.

BUILDING OPEN-SOURCE TEAMS

It takes careful preparation, effective communication, and the creation of a collaborative environment to build an open-source team. You must first define your project by establishing specific objectives, identifying the areas in which you need assistance, and outlining the abilities needed for each team member. Then, actively seek out participants who have the required expertise and are passionate about your project. To assemble a diverse and competent team, use online platforms, developer forums, and social media to entice potential team members. Don't forget to promote inclusivity and diversity. Create lines of communication that will allow team members to work together productively next. Project management software, forums, chat rooms, and mailing lists are examples of this.

In order to encourage ideas to flow, problems to be solved, and choices to be taken jointly, open and honest communication is vital. In order to maintain responsibility and clarity within the team, roles and responsibilities must be clearly defined. Provide standards and documentation to help team members understand their roles, and assign work based on knowledge and interests.

Establish a culture where team members collaborate, evaluate one another's code, and offer helpful criticism in order to promote collaboration. A code of conduct that encourages courtesy, diversity, and professionalism must be established. Ensure that your team members have access to the materials, equipment, and documentation they require to properly contribute. Give newcomers opportunities for learning and skill development, as well as mentorship and support.

Create opportunities for personal and professional growth for your team members and publicly acknowledge their contributions by recognizing their work in project documentation or news updates. Use good project management techniques to keep your team on task and organized. Establish specific objectives, track your progress, and resolve any issues that may come up. Team members' regular updates and progress reports can be useful in this regard. Last but not least, concentrate on creating and sustaining an active community around your project. Encourage outside participation, plan gatherings or events, and actively hear and act on community feedback and suggestions.

These guidelines can help you build an effective open-source team that works cooperatively to accomplish the objectives of your project. Creating a personal brand and online presence can assist enhance awareness and draw in potential partners. Examples include running a blog or contributing to technical publications. Maintaining current with the newest trends, techniques, and technology is essential if you want to stay competitive. Finally, looking for work with organizations that support and contribute to open-source projects might lead to additional career development and stability. A successful career in open-source can be achieved by combining technical proficiency, community involvement, ongoing learning, and strategic career decisions.

Building an open-source team has its own set of difficulties and dangers that must be considered. The difficulty in attracting and retaining skilled contributors is one of the key threats. Finding people with the necessary competence who are also enthusiastic about the project's goals can be difficult because open-source projects frequently call for specific knowledge and experience. The team's success and the project's advancement may be hampered by this talent gap.

Maintaining team members' active engagement and dedication poses another threat. Since open-source contributions are often voluntary, people may not have as much time as they would like to devote to the project or may have other priorities. Long-term motivation and ensuring that team members consistently contribute can be difficult. If team members disengage, this threat could result in a lack of development, project stagnation, or even the team's breakup. To lessen these risks, it's critical to actively seek out possible collaborators and develop a compelling project vision that reflects their priorities and interests. Clear instructions, documentation, and assistance can aid in luring and keeping talented team members. Creating an environment where team members feel valued and appreciated can also increase their commitment and motivation. Within the team, regular feedback, coordination, and communication channels can assist solve problems and keep members engaged. Additionally, it's essential to offer chances for skill improvement and progress, acknowledge and appreciate contributions, and take proactive measures to resolve any disagreements or concerns that may develop. If team members disengage, this threat could result in a lack of development, project stagnation, or even the team's breakup. Open-source teams can increase their resilience and make sure that their projects are successful and sustainable by proactively addressing these concerns.

LONG-TERM SUSTAINABILITY

The viability and expansion of an open-source project depend on the team securing long-term funding, and here are some crucial actions.

First and foremost, you must create a compelling value proposition for your open-source project. Clearly state the special advantages it provides to the area, sector, or society at large. Emphasize the benefits it can provide, such as cost reductions, increased innovation, or meeting urgent demands. You can entice potential sponsors who share your aim and objectives by clearly outlining the value of your project.

Next, spread out your funding sources to lessen reliance on a single source of revenue. Investigate other options, such as private donations, corporate sponsorships, grants from foundations or governmental organizations, and income through business alliances. Increased financial stability and less danger of financing shortages are also benefits of diversifying funding sources.

It's critical to develop a vibrant community around your open-source project. Encourage a sense of ownership and support among your users, contributors, and stakeholders. To show the effect and advancement of your work, communicate project updates, accomplishments, and success stories on a regular basis. A devoted and encouraging community is more likely to support your initiative financially and vocally, which helps draw funds and maintain long-term financing.

Investigating sustainable revenue models may boost your financial security. Think about providing paid assistance, consulting services, or specialized solutions in connection with your open-source undertaking. This can create income while utilizing the knowledge from your project. Implementing a membership or subscription model is a further choice, in which individuals or organizations pay for deluxe features, assistance, or exclusive access to resources. These long-term revenue streams can support other financing sources and guarantee your open-source team's long-term financial stability.

Also, create strategic alliances with businesses that can both assist your initiative financially and share the same vision. Work with organizations that stand to gain from the success of your open-source project and who are eager to contribute to its advancement. Look for alliances that will not only provide financial support but also give you access to knowledge, tools, and networks that will help your team develop.

These actions will improve your prospects of finding long-term funding for your open-source team. Adapt your fundraising plan as the project develops and keep looking for additional funding sources. Maintain your commitment to the open-source principles and make sure that funding selections reflect the goals and principles of your project. Your open-source team can prosper and keep having a beneficial influence with a solid financial base.

PROFESSIONAL TEAMS AND THE COMMUNITY

Professional Free and Open Source Software (FOSS) development sets itself apart from community-based development in several fundamental ways. In the realm of professional FOSS development, there is typically a team of skilled developers who are employed and compensated by organizations or companies that hold a vested interest in the project's success. These developers adhere to predetermined timelines and project plans, working diligently towards achieving specific deliverables and milestones. Moreover, professional FOSS development often embraces a structured and hierarchical approach. Project managers or team leads play a pivotal role in overseeing the development process, assigning tasks, and ensuring seamless coordination among team members. Decision-making follows formal channels and often necessitates consensus or approval from higher-level stakeholders, adding a layer of structure and organization to the development workflow.

Conversely, community-based development thrives on the voluntary contributions of passionate individuals who possess a genuine interest in the project. These contributors stem from diverse backgrounds and frequently dedicate their personal time to the cause without any financial compensation. The development process itself adopts a more organic and decentralized nature, with contributions originating from various sources and individuals operating independently or in small groups. Within the community-based development landscape, decision-making tends to adopt a more democratic approach, with open discussions and dialogue taking place among community members. Consensus is usually reached through collaborative exchanges and debates, allowing the collective input of the community to shape the project's direction. Collaboration, knowledge sharing, and the cultivation of a sense of ownership among community members are often emphasized, fostering an inclusive and participatory development environment.

Both professional FOSS development and community-based development contribute to the advancement of open-source software, yet they function under distinct structures and dynamics. Professional FOSS development brings forth the advantages of dedicated resources, structured processes, and a heightened sense of accountability. Conversely, community-based development thrives on the voluntary contributions, diverse range of ideas, and collective wisdom of its participants. These contrasting approaches to FOSS development each possess their unique strengths and play vital roles in the broader open-source ecosystem.

Achieving a harmonious coexistence between professional and community open-source development entails striking a seamless balance between the structured nature of professional development and the inclusive ethos of community collaboration. One effective approach is to foster strong collaboration and communication channels that facilitate active engagement between the professional team and the broader open-source community. Encouraging the professional team to actively seek feedback, involve community members in decision-making processes, and establish regular forums and discussions can help facilitate the exchange of ideas and perspectives.

Transparency and inclusivity are key factors in successfully reconciling professional and community open-source development. Ensuring that the work of the professional team is transparent and accessible to the community by sharing regular updates, roadmaps, and openly discussing project plans is paramount. Inviting community members to contribute in various ways, such as through code contributions, documentation, or testing, further strengthens the sense of inclusiveness. Recognizing and valuing the contributions of community members and providing avenues for their growth and development within the project are essential.

Establishing clear guidelines and governance structures that delineate the roles and responsibilities of both the professional team and community contributors is vital. Defining decision-making processes that honor input from both sides and encourage collaborative decision-making based on the expertise of the professional team and the collective wisdom of the community can shape the project's direction effectively.

By cultivating a collaborative and inclusive environment that integrates the strengths of both professional and community development, it becomes possible to harness the advantages of each approach. This conciliation allows the project to leverage the resources and expertise of the professional team while embracing the passion, diversity, and collective intelligence of the open-source community. The result is a thriving open-source project that flourishes by combining the best elements of both realms.

Conflicts can arise between a commercial open-source developer and the community due to contrasting interests, expectations, and approaches. One area of contention revolves around striking a balance between commercial motives and the fundamental principles of open source. The community often places great importance on transparency, inclusivity, and collaboration, while commercial developers must consider profitability and safeguarding proprietary aspects of their work. This dichotomy can lead to disagreements concerning licensing, community involvement, and the level of control exerted by the commercial entity over the project.

Another source of conflict stems from the commercial developer's influence on the project's direction and decision-making. Community members may feel marginalized or undervalued when their ideas and input are overshadowed by the commercial entity's interests. Disputes may arise regarding release schedules, resource allocation, or a perceived prioritization of features catering primarily to commercial clients rather than the broader community's needs.

Conflicting expectations also arise in the realm of support and maintenance. The community often expects the commercial developer to be highly responsive and engaged, while the realities of limited resources and capacity can hinder the commercial entity's ability to address every community request. These disparities can result in frustrations and an imbalance in perceived support, straining the relationship between the commercial developer and the community.

To navigate and mitigate conflicts, establishing transparent and open lines of communication is vital. Actively listening to the community's concerns, involving community members in decision-making processes, and being transparent about commercial interests and limitations can foster understanding and bridge gaps. Embracing a collaborative approach that incorporates community feedback, promoting community-driven initiatives, and appropriately acknowledging community contributions can foster a sense of ownership and shared responsibility. Balancing the pursuit of commercial viability with the core values of the open-source community necessitates ongoing dialogue and a willingness to find mutually beneficial resolutions amidst conflicts.

Achieving a harmonious balance between a company's interests and the open-source community calls for a strategic and thoughtful approach. First and foremost, it is essential for the company to recognize and appreciate the significance of the open-source community. This community thrives on the contributions and feedback from a diverse group of developers, users, and enthusiasts. By acknowledging the value of the community and its collective knowledge, the company can lay a solid foundation for a mutually beneficial relationship.

Transparency and open communication are vital when it comes to balancing the interests of the company and the open-source community. The company should actively engage with the community, providing clear and accessible information about its goals, intentions, and decision-making processes. Regular updates, sharing roadmaps, and fostering public discussions can build trust and encourage collaboration. Seeking input from the community on important decisions demonstrates the company's commitment to inclusivity and openness.

In order to strike a balance, it is important for the company to align its interests with the broader objectives of the open-source community. This involves actively contributing back to the community by releasing relevant software as open source, sharing valuable insights, and supporting community events and initiatives. By giving back, the company not only enhances its reputation but also strengthens the interdependent relationship between its interests and those of the community.

Moreover, establishing clear guidelines and governance structures can help navigate potential conflicts of interest. Defining decision-making processes that take into account both the company's needs and the perspectives of the community is crucial. Striving for consensus and involving community members in decision-making fosters a sense of ownership and shared responsibility.

Ultimately, achieving a balance between a company's interests and those of the open-source community requires embracing collaboration, mutual respect, and a long-term perspective. By actively engaging with the community, maintaining transparency, and finding common ground, companies can create a mutually beneficial scenario where their interests align with the broader goals of the open-source ecosystem.

CONCLUSION

This chapter briefly discussed some of the main aspects of the FOSS model that can leverage software business: high availability of FOSS artifacts of high quality that can be reused by companies in order to reduce costs and time-to-market; increases security since a wider community of developers can audit the code, find bugs, security flaws and provide fixes quickly while proprietary solutions usually rely on a smaller number of developers, taking more time to delivery security fixes; use of tools, models and use cases for project management that were emerged from decades of history of open-source projects carried on throughout the years; flexibility for customers by using FOSS licensing model which allow them to adapt the product for their needs and/or reuse it in another projects; and a prepared environment for propagate innovation and newer open standards (such as APIs) which might help companies grow their open-source products that would be more difficult to achieve with a proprietary solution.

In order to explore and take advantage of FOSS, it's indispensable for companies to build their teams with professionals who have open-source skills. The open-source career comprises a long path that can be summarized into three main phases: users, when the professional it's just a regular user of the open-source software and can eventually contribute with bug reports and act as a tester for new releases; contributor, when the professional starts to push from bug fixes and small improvements up to new features and regular contributions; and comitter, when the professional became a core member of the project with powers of the decisions about contributions and project management. A professional can play different roles in different FOSS projects at the same time.

The FOSS model can help both companies and professionals to find good employees and good places to work. By considering FOSS projects, companies have access to a large pool of professionals and their portfolio, with a proven track record of their delivering code and teamwork. Communication channels can also be used to gather more insights about developers and their behavior. This information can help to find candidates with a good match for a given role. On the other hand, open-source professionals can carry their open-source code throughout their careers and use them to make a public portfolio that can draw attention from companies. The FOSS model has now countless successful projects and has become a key factor that must be considered by companies and professionals that want to succeed in their business and career.

REFERENCES

Błaszczyk, M., Popović, M., Zajdel, K., & Zajdel, R. (2022, October 17). The Impact of the COVID-19 Pandemic on the Organisation of Remote Work in IT Companies. *Sustainability (Basel)*, *14*(20), 13373. Advance online publication. doi:10.3390u142013373

GitHub. (2023). *GitHub Search*. Retrieved 2023, from https://github.com/search?q=is:public

GPL-Compatible Free Software Licenses. (n.d.). Free Software Foundation. Retrieved March 3, 2023, from https://www.gnu.org/licenses/license-list.html#GPLCompatibleLicenses

Labrèche, G., Evans, D., Marszk, D., Mladenov, T., Shiradhonkar, V., & Zelenevskiy, V. (2022). Agile Development and Rapid Prototyping in a Flying Mission with Open Source Software Reuse On-Board the OPS-SAT Spacecraft. *IAA SCITECH 2022 Forum*. 10.2514/6.2022-0648

Linux Foundation. (2023). Linux Foundation - Decentralized innovation, built with trust. Retrieved March 5, 2023, from https://www.linuxfoundation.org/

Mozilla Foundation. (2023). Mozilla Foundation - Homepage. Retrieved March 5, 2023, from https://foundation.mozilla.org/en/

Open Infrastructure Foundation. (2023). OpenInfra Foundation. Retrieved March 5, 2023, from https://openinfra.dev/about/

Personal Robots. (2019, March 30). *Vorpal Robot is a open source hexapod toy*. Personal Robots. Retrieved March 3, 2023, from https://www.personalrobots.biz/vorpal-robot-is-a-open-source-hexapod-toy/

Riehle, D. (2015). How Open Source Is Changing the Software Developer's Career. *Computer, 48*(5), 51–57. doi:10.1109/MC.2015.132

Satyanarayanan, M. (2001). Pervasive computing: Vision and challenges. *IEEE Personal Communications*, 10-17.

Stone, M., DiBona, C., & Ockman, S. (Eds.). (1999). *Open Sources: Voices from the Open Source Revolution*. O'Reilly.

The Apache Software Foundation! (2023). Welcome to The Apache Software Foundation! Retrieved March 5, 2023, from https://www.apache.org/

The Linux Foundation. (2022, June). *10th Annual Open Source Jobs Report*. The Linux Foundation. Retrieved February, 2023, from https://training.linuxfoundation.org/wp-content/uploads/2022/06/OpenSourceJobsReport2022_FINAL.pdf

KEY TERMS AND DEFINITIONS

FOSS: Stands for Free and Open Source Software.

Maintainer: Is the software developer responsible for an entire project or part of it, it takes the decisions about which code should be merged or purged from sources, analysis collaborations, mediate conflicts, can be the responsible for releases, it can be seen as a technical leader.

Software Development Process: Are the steps, procedures, the general approach followed to break the development of a software into several steps that can be smaller and executed sequentially or in parallel with the goal to improve the design and product management.

Time-to-Market: The total amount of time that takes a product to become available for sale since its conception.

Chapter 9
The Open Source Perspective in Education Technology:
A Digital Kon–Tiki Journey

Martin Dow
Open-Source Learning Academy Network, USA

David Preston
Open-Source Learning Academy Network, USA

ABSTRACT

Open source implies shared knowledge, one of the central virtues of the FOSS model. It is therefore natural that open-source technology constitutes a key resource for building accessible educational tools. Cost-effectiveness is not the only benefit brought about by the FOSS paradigm. Along with the flexibility permitted by unrestricted access to the source code, FOSS also implies public sovereignty, as community-driven development allows the society to regain control over the technology it uses and upon which it relies. Educational tools are especially critical in this context, as it directly impacts our autonomy to implement education programs free from technical, economic, or ideological biases dictated by corporate big tech. This chapter delves into this matter, exploring an illustrative case study based on the OSLAP experience. As in other application fields calling for new sustainable FOSS business models, open-source educational technology emerges as an area where fresh ideas are demanded, along with strategies for how to finance collaborative projects in the long term.

DOI: 10.4018/978-1-6684-4785-7.ch009

INTRODUCING TECHNOLOGY TO MEET UNMET NEEDS

The history and current landscape of education technology define both the need and the opportunity for OSLAP.

The history of technology has always been an adventurous journey. Popular accounts portray innovators and entrepreneurs as heroes in Joseph Campbell-esque monomyths, liminal figures who respond to calls that only they hear by venturing out to forge alliances and overcome obstacles so that they can share the benefits of vision and insight with the rest of us upon their return. However, our understandings and uses of technology have changed over time along with cultural norms and economic trends. Today's heavy emphasis on technology as a purchasable commodity — witness the line at the Apple Store — ignores the original concept of technology, which is rooted in the purposeful use of tools, not the tools themselves. The root of the word *technology* itself comes from the Ancient Greek word *techne*, which meant "cleverness."

Cleverness is a quality best illustrated through its strategic application. When Odysseus landed on the island of the Cyclops, he told the Cyclops that his name was Nobody. Later, when Odysseus blinded the Cyclops and the Cyclops ran around howling in pain, the other Cyclops asked who did it so they could punish the attacker. "It was Nobody! Nobody did this!" the Cyclops roared. The other Cyclops shrugged and went back to their business. There was Nobody to find, hiding in plain sight.

Odysseus' Strategy Exemplifies Cleverness In Practice: Techne

The spirit of techne infused the development of the internet and the World Wide Web. People took it upon themselves to learn how new tools could be used to make free long distance phone calls and communicate on screens over phone lines. They collaborated and coalesced around ideals. The members of the longest-running online community, The Well, are united by their motto, famously known as YOYOW: "You own your own words" (Well, n.d.).

The culture of Silicon Valley in the 1970s famously championed values of freedom, community, creativity, and collaboration. Stewart Brand expressed the sentiment in his seminal *Whole Earth Catalog* (1968) "A realm of intimate, personal power is developing — power of the individual to conduct his own education, find his own inspiration, shape his own environment, and share his adventure with whoever is interested."

Just five decades later, however, drastic changes in our relationship with technology have transformed our business practices, personal habits, and even our environment.

Today we have more tools than clever uses. Our inboxes are clogged with messages that hype the latest app, platform, game, or productivity software, promising revolution and disruption but in a way that is somehow different or better than the same features as 53 other options in the same space. We are constantly being encouraged and persuaded to buy someone else's cleverness, or the story of cleverness, rather than actually practice our own.

Many of these redundant products are designed to extract monetary value for small groups of entrepreneurs and investors. To paraphrase poet Jorge Luis Borges (n.d.) perhaps it is best not to develop new software unless we can improve upon the deafening cacophony of overpromising, underdelivering education technology that make it hard to hear the voices that want to learn.

And yet the alluring origin myth of techne persists. We are called by the internet's tantalizingly unrealized, unlimited promise for communication and collaborative learning — a space for real public education that has the capacity to facilitate interdisciplinary Medici effects (Johansson, 2004) of value on an unprecedented, even global scale.

On April 28, 1947, two years after Vannevar Bush wrote the seminal essay "As We May Think," (Bush, 1945). Thor Heyerdahl and the crew of the Kon-Tiki left Callao, Peru and set sail for Polynesia aboard the Kon-Tiki, a raft made of nine balsa tree trunks lashed together with hemp rope (*Kon-Tiki Expedition,* 2023).

Kon-Tiki was built in pursuit of understanding how people traveled the ancient world. Could people have made it from South America to Polynesia on rafts of balsa logs lashed together with hemp rope? There was only one way to find out.

As we considered building OSLAP, we didn't have to speculate or even look very far to understand the intentions, materials, or methodology of the internet's original architects. Vint Cerf, Bob Kahn, and others who built the modern internet are still here to tell their own stories. Kon-Tiki's builders could only verify its seaworthiness by setting sail. We already know that the internet's physical capacities can support a worldwide public learning architecture, and that members of existing communities will gravitate to that architecture when they become aware that it exists as a viable alternative to Big Tech.

However, just like the Kon-Tiki expedition, we are setting out to explore a hypothesis. We want to prove that the internet can in fact empower us to transcend the limitations of time, space, and the boundaries of existing social structures to accelerate and amplify the value of learning for individuals and communities. We believe that people will benefit greatly by making meaningful connections between the hardware, the command line software, the web interface, quantifiable evidence that documents participation, and emerging digital, cultural, and business trends. To test this hypothesis, we must build and introduce this software in alignment with the core values of Open-Source Learning itself. Our approach is consistent with the original communities that sprang up around techne decades ago when the internet first became accessible to the public.

Before embarking on this work we asked two fundamental questions about the present moment:

a)   Does existing education technology consistently help teachers and students build awareness about digital tools, strategies, and culture through the use of software that also provides opportunities to own their online identities, data, and any resulting value?

b)   Does the world really need another piece of education technology software?

From the TL;DR (too-long-didn't-read) perspective, the short answers are:

a)   No.

b)   Yes.

In his recent book *Failure to Disrupt*, MIT Professor Justin Reich observes how difficult it really is to change school: "Social inequality is a tenacious feature of educational systems" (Reich, 2022). As we saw during the pandemic-related campus closures, education technology exacerbated pre-existing inequalities. Algorithms discriminated against already disenfranchised students of color and students who logged on from noisy home environments (Young, 2020).

However, it is an oversimplistic disservice to evaluate education technology in broad terms of "good" and "bad." The commonly expressed post-pandemic desire to "return to normal" is a natural response to the trauma many experienced, but "normal" did a great deal of harm long before campuses closed, and many people thrived with the benefits of flexible schedules and personalized learning that online learning offered. Pitting education technology against in-person learning is a false dichotomy that ignores much of our lived experience. In addition, the "online learning" that people refer to during the pandemic was in most cases not developed, designed, or planned, but hastily implemented by well-meaning educators who did not have sufficient experience or training for the purpose (Adams, 2020).

Meanwhile, both politically imposed "normalcy" and technology adoption continue to grow in education without much critical analysis, which brings to mind the words of Paulo Freire: "It is not systematic education which somehow molds society, but, on the contrary, society which, according to its particular structure, shapes education in relation to the ends and interests of those who control the power in that society" (Freire, 1970).

Schools often promote core values of equity and inclusion in their vision statements, but how can a diverse campus truly be equitable and inclusive if it forces its constituents to upload their personal data and creative content onto LMS (learning management system) software that profits a small, off-campus group of shareholders whose identities are unknown and unlike those in the school community?

Many like to think of education technology as "disruptive." So far, however, the commodified technology alone has not led to promised change.

Christensen (1997) himself has clarified that few technologies are intrinsically "disruptive technologies." Disruptive innovations, in fact, can be the result of what are fairly crude technologies. The innovation, he argues, instead comes from the business model. That's why it doesn't matter to proponents of the "disruptive innovation" framework that Khan Academy or MOOCs suck, for example. It doesn't matter that they're low quality technologies featuring low quality instruction and sometimes low quality content. What matters is that they're free (or very, very cheap). What matters is that they change the market. It's all about markets after all. Students are consumers, not learners in this framework. What matters is that these innovations initially serve non-consumers (that is, students not enrolled in formal institutions) then "over time to march upmarket." That's why they're disruptive innovations, according to Christensen, who just this weekend published an op-ed in The Boston Globe insisting, "MOOCs' disruption is only beginning." Innovating markets. Not innovating teaching and learning (Watters, 2014).

These insights are consistent with our own observations as professional educators and parents. What exactly is being disrupted by education technology? The speed with which young people are moved through school board-approved, publisher-scripted content and shoved off to the assessment and data collection companies? That is not disruption. In fact, technology adoption raises serious questions about the purpose and function of education. In the words of Peter Drucker, "There is nothing quite so useless as doing with great efficiency something that should not be done at all" (Drucker, 1963).

As we considered developing software to support learning, we conducted informal research that began with a close examination of our own lived circumstances. Our students and our own children have not been given choices about which technology to use in their schooling. Their teachers and school administrators are not experts in the design or use of the mandated software. No one in the learning communities, schools, or school districts we approached could describe the basic value propositions, management structures, or core values of the software companies with whom they did business, much less the "under the hood" code or architecture of the software itself.

We asked these questions of dozens of schools. Stakeholders were unable to provide answers beyond basic explanations of the function of the software and instructions for use. We could not even determine what schools and school districts paid for the software. These were not closely guarded secrets; merely decisions that were made by one or two individuals in large organizations that were simply undocumented or buried so deeply in budgets and meeting minutes that they were difficult to find without extensive detective work and / or a legal demand for disclosure. We could not easily ascertain the terms of schools' agreements with software companies, nor could we determine if or how student data and original content is mined by the software companies to create value for their owners and shareholders.

Given that the education technology market is projected to grow to $404 billion over the next two years (HolonIQ, 2020) it stands to reason that corporate revenue streams include more than per-student license fees. In general, school personnel haven't a clue about how ed tech software is created, deployed, or managed for profit.

If the adults in the room are not knowledgeable of the technological architectures, applications, and business models of the online tools they use, they cannot reasonably be expected to teach young people how to navigate the digital environment.

The Appeal of 'Open' in a Closed Environment

The word "open" is attractive. It connotes expansiveness. Freedom. The easy transparency that comes with integrity. Even the warmth of human connection.

Describing products and services as open and evoking these qualities can make anything more appealing, including technology. But we should be mindful that marketing campaigns sometimes belie verifiable facts in the world. Modern education-related businesses and organizational cultures are not in fact generally open — they are closed and defended by privacy regulations, barriers to entry, and competition. The term "open source" came into being as a response to a context of increasing constraints (*Open Source,* 2023). The same is true for Open-Source Learning (Preston, n.d.) and the software we have developed to support it.

Over the last 50 years the internet has become an increasingly dominant influence on global culture and economy, and even our individual psychology and decision-making. However, to this day, there is no global awareness campaign or academic curriculum that exists to help us all understand and navigate the digital waters in which we now swim.

As a result, only those with the resources and motivation to learn become experts in the design and use of software. The rest of us are introduced to life online through the use of others' proprietary hardware and software platforms. With relatively few exceptions, social media, productivity software, learning management systems, and applications for every conceivable interest and purpose charge money and/or require "user agreements" that give them the rights to leverage the value of user-produced content and metadata in exchange for access.

Education has simultaneously accepted corporate terms and replicated traditional institutional hierarchies in a digital culture where data generates profit. When schools align themselves with investor interests, as opposed to the interests of their students and their communities, their use of technology reinforces and increases inequity. It wasn't long ago that no one profited from a student's homework assignments. Now, those homework assignments are the basis for analytics and data sets that become commodified assets in a market worth billions.

Freire's observation that "Washing one's hands of the conflict between the powerful and the powerless means to side with the powerful, not to be neutral" (Freire, 1970) is magnified exponentially in the digital world. School bears responsibility *in loco parentis* for the safety and security on campus; we believe that the same level of care should apply to school's online environments, in ways that honor individual identity and the value of the artifacts each person creates.

Forcing students onto software platforms that they don't choose, where they create data that generates value for platform owners, amounts to intellectual sharecropping. In today's platform environment students are not individuals with sovereign identities. They are assigned digital identifications that can be revoked without their knowledge or approval, along with access to the content they create. Students are directed on pain of failure and disciplinary action to create that content, which builds value for the owners of the digital real estate where it lives, without sharing in that value. Even if a student successfully completes an academic program, unless they learn how to back up their data onto their own drives or servers, they lose everything when they leave the program and their account is closed.

It seems disingenuous to promote learning communities as equitable and inclusive when those communities are built on digital infrastructure that so blatantly disregards the rights of so many for the benefits of so few.

Open-Source Learning: An Emerging Movement in Education

In the 20th century, educational philosophies and models such as Waldorf, Montessori, and Reggio Emilia enriched the field by providing meaningful alternatives and perspectives on school.

Today, we are in the midst of arguably the most dramatic transformation in human history. Where are the learning philosophies and models for the Information Age? Where, as Audrey Watters asked, is the innovation?

In 2004, the author of this essay, David Preston, took a sabbatical from a management consulting practice and teaching responsibilities at UCLA to teach English at a large urban high school in Los Angeles. He encouraged the use of technology and the public internet. His students developed websites, curated content, learned from and collaborated with experts all over the world, and achieved uncommon levels of success, from university admissions and scholarships to flying airplanes (Preston, 2020a) and leading expeditions and concerts in places like Yosemite National Park (Preston, 2021a).

The writer's philosophical foundation was the restoration of our connections: with others, with high-quality information, and even with our own curiosities and interests in ways that ignite passionate curiosity. To help remove the barriers that inhibit these connections, he abandoned the use of textbooks and actively encouraged mindful reflection and collaboration that transcended the temporal and spatial isolation of classrooms, the logistics of geography, and the inauthentic formality of hierarchical authority.

Collectively, those ideas and practices became known as Open-Source Learning (OSL). In schools OSL was defined as, "A guided learning process that combines timeless best practices with today's tools in ways that empower learners to ask big questions, create interdisciplinary paths of inquiry, develop communities of interest and critique, and curate their exploration in multiple media online so as to create a portfolio of knowledge capital that is directly transferable to the marketplace" (Preston, 2014a).

Over the years, OSL has been embraced by a variety of respected learning communities. OSL was presented by the author at the O'Reilly Open Source Conference (OSCON), the Royal Geographic Society, the Institute for the Future, the MacArthur Digital Media and Learning Conference, the Connected Learning Summit at MIT, TEDxUCLA, and elsewhere. The author's book *Academy of One* (Preston, 2021b) is used in teacher credential programs.

However, the organizational structure and culture of school are notoriously robust and resistant to change. To comply with institutional requirements, the framework's creator and other innovative practitioners integrated OSL as a complement to traditional, standardized curriculum that was defensible to administrators and boards of education. It would take a global pandemic to surface OSL as an independently viable curriculum.

On Friday, March 13, 2020, the author was teaching classes at a high school on California's central coast. The coronavirus loomed on the horizon and no one knew whether the campus would be open the following Monday (it would not — that campus would remain closed for more than a year). He reviewed the situation with learners. When asked what would change if they all met online the following week, the team answered back in unison: "Nothing!" The networked learning communities proved resilient. Every network member finished the school year in much the same way they chose to begin it (Preston, 2020b) — with Open-Source Learning.

The experience proved that: a) Open-Source Learning was ready to become a standalone model for interdisciplinary education, and b) OSL participants needed software that was informed and powered by the same philosophical DNA as the learning practice itself.

Software selection once represented an opportunity for critical thinking and collaborative decision-making in OSL. A generation of students was introduced to collaborative tools such as etherpads and mindmaps, and each exploration presented an opportunity for critical thinking in answer to the question: What are the best tools for the job?

However, software companies are driven by outcome-oriented business goals. Their core values are not in alignment with process-oriented learning models.

Over time, corporations have become extremely sophisticated in extracting value in ways that are not transparent to the casual user. Students need more awareness and protection when selecting online software, particularly with regard to platforms that are perceived as immediately accessible because they do not require payment or financial information to create an account and get started.

Open-Source Learning promotes active engagement and reframes learning community roles for the purpose of better understanding our lived experience. Classes and other organizational groupings are networks. Traditionally passive students are invited, encouraged, and challenged to become active learners. Teachers are lead learners who demonstrate what they advocate, and administrators are stewards who ensure smooth operation through an ethic of engaged care. The language that describes these roles carries specific meaning and day-to-day operational implications.

It is important to note that while Open-Source Learning is a viable programmatic option for schools, it can work for anyone, at any stage of life, in any context (Preston, 2021b). As a highly visible practitioner of Open-Source learning, the reporting author, acting as a Lead Learner, routinely seeks out experts to inform his own understanding and practice, in full view of his network and members who are learning with and from him (Preston, 2022a). This practice includes learning about technology. He asked his co-author, the technology architect Martin Dow about the online software environment facing today's students and teachers, specifically how the software "under the hood" may influence the experience or even provide a learning opportunity.

The question started a collaborative conversation. As one might expect from the aforementioned Medici Effect, the authors' diverse backgrounds, fields of expertise, and even cultures/continents of residence enriched their exchange of ideas. From their complementary perspectives, both identified glaring problems and promising opportunities that are not being addressed in the academic or popular media, much less in schools or the software market.

It was impossible to unring these bells or leave things the way we found them. We began to develop a solution.

THE OPEN-SOURCE LEARNING ACADEMY PROTOCOL

This section outlines the conception and implementation of the OSLAP (Open-Source Learning Academy Protocol), as an illustrative example of how FOSS technology can enable society's sovereignty in the education process.

Concept

We believe that the most effective education programs and software applications are built on a foundation of empathy — a genuine understanding of people's experiences and feelings. Providing an authentic sense of empathy begins with transparent integrity and a clear knowledge of ourselves.

Therefore, in the spirit of authenticity and transparent integrity, we set out to create software that relies and operates on the same values as the interpersonal practices that have made Open-Source Learning successful in practice.

Constructing software with this level of care is analogous to building the Kon-Tiki raft. There is nothing inherently special about balsa logs and hemp rope, and the materials and methods we used to build OSLAP have been available to many people for some time. What makes OSLAP unique is not the tools themselves, but the ways in which the tools are introduced and deployed.

For example, the practice of OSL "Begin(s) with the solution of the student-teacher contradiction, by reconciling the poles of the contradiction so that both are simultaneously teachers and students" (Freire, 1970). There are no (passive, game-playing) students in an OSL classroom, and there are no (dependent or addicted) users on an OSLAP instance. There are Learners. Participants. Network Members. Lead Learners. Stewards.

Semantic choices are important. Given all the attention currently being paid to Artificial Intelligence, we would do well to remember that each word, each search term, each command, and each line of code carries meaning that often stands alone in the absence of explanations or reference materials.

Consider the title "steward," which connotes a level of care and responsibility not found in the use of the terms "administrator" or "sysadmin."

Language sets a tone and creates expectations that flow through the strategies and tactics that form the decisions and daily operations in the OSL environment. Each instance of OSLAP requires stewardship. The development of stewardship practices bring the use of the software to life.

Just as we use precise language to define OSL roles, we make a clear distinction between protocols and platforms. The Open-Source Learning Protocol is so named because it is an environment that consists of protocols, i.e., "instructions and standards that anyone can use to build a compatible interface" (Masnick, 2019).

In contrast, the vast majority of education technology is platform-based, i.e., it exists on private digital real estate that can only be accessed via permission granted by the owner. Nearly every learning management system, student information system, curriculum content provider, and content creation and curation software is a walled garden with "a single set of policies and central control" (Electronic Frontier Foundation, 2020).

In the OSLAP environment FOSS integrations are designed to support stewardship practices and ultimately the learning community itself. For example, individual naming and group formation is designed to reflect each person's stated preferences about how they want to be known and the community's priorities related to openness and security. Each individual selects their identity and their password, which is known only to them and not stored anywhere else. The individual responsibility for password management is a first step in personal security that represents a learning opportunity. For those who want to dive deeper, local lead learners and stewards are available to support their explorations, along with external partners who are developing companion software and informational resources.

Web standards are used throughout OSLAP. Therefore, the entire system itself is open and unrestricted. FOSS software implements "social protocols" that enact OSL principles. For example, when a lead learner invokes online community principles to inform a problem-solving project, the conversation about selecting tools (such as a calendar, a mind map, cards, or spread sheets) represents an immediate opportunity to practice communication, critical thinking, and collaboration.

The OSLAP software is not a standalone product, but rather the vehicle through which OSL community members connect, communicate, collaborate, create, and curate. Whether or not a person participates in a formal offline learning community, their deployment of OSLAP defines them as an OSL community member online, and in the process makes available an abundance of software choices that feed thought processes such as critical thinking and decision-making in ways that demonstrably support workflows and valuable integrations. Packaging makes software accessible through a dashboard that is easy to navigate.

Building the Raft

Our development process followed OSLAP's defining philosophy and reason for existence.

In terms of installed software, OSLAP is a distribution that is based on a Linux server distribution plus software configuration management and maintenance software originally under OSS (some is now "Source-Available" license), with added packages and various configurations.

Here is a partial list:

Protocol support

- LDAP – Lighweight Directory Access Protocol
  - Directory of names known by the system
  - Central lookup for the OSLAP node which ties together and mediates access to all OSLAP-compatible software apps
  - Single-sign on (SSO) with optional 2FA (Two-factor Authentication) supported for apps
  - OpenLDAP is the main FOSS component
- Email - IMAP, SMTP, POP3 and security standard (DKIM)
  - Professional grade email services including list management
- W3C ActivityPub / ActivityStreams
  - Works within Learner Networks groups but can connect outside them according to the rules / policies / preferences of each specific OSL network's Stewards, Lead Learners, and Learners
  - Integrated with Learner's journal posts to provide combined live social feed for Learners, who can choose who to follow, post directly to feed,
  - Nextcloud supports a related standard to federate resources and documents
- Nextcloud Talk (Spreed)
  - video and audio communications, with strong support for groups
  - Instant messaging environments, supporting
    § Secure protocol between sender/receiver and server
    § 1:1 conversations
    § Groups / "rooms"
    § Comment threads on *any* resource that can be referred to in the OSLAP Dashboard, such as documents, spreadsheets, project schedules and appointments
- Matrix - Matrix is designed to interconnect / interoperate between all other messaging protocols
  - Bridges with NC:Talk
  - [To come: Bridges with ActivityPub]
  - Privacy-focused with end-to-end encryption (only sender and receiver can read)
  - Strong group support protects Learners
    § Privacy method is an improvement over WhatsApp and Signal messenger
    § Much stronger privacy support than Facebook Messenger, Telegram and other popular services
- WebRTC – the W3C standard for realtime audio-visual communications over the web

- ○ Big Blue Button – with Dashboard integration – a Zoom replacement, more functionality and security
- ○ Nextcloud Talk – with Dashboard integration – one-click / directly-integrated and very easy to use
- ○ Matrix, via Jitsi support – with Dashboard integration
  § privacy-oriented alternative to the above
  § helps support interconnects with those connected to Matrix infrastructure external to OSLAP
- ○ Jitsi Meet – WebRTC standard FOSS app
- ○ Optana Meet
- Git – the dominant distributed version control system
  - ○ GitLab – leading FOSS alternative to SaaS leaders Github and Bitbucket
  - ○ Gitea – emulates the Github interface and web experience
- WebDAV – distributed authoring and versioning
  - ○ Nextcloud fully supports via its "Files" app
- HTTP(S) – fileserving over the web
  - ○ Files – a simple web server with a simple web-based administration interface

Software BOM – in addition to the above:

- Identity and naming
  - ○ openLDAP
- Mail
  - ○ Server-side
  - ○ Choice of: Nextcloud ("Dashboard"), Rainloop and SoGo webmail clients
- Nextcloud "Dashboard" – central workspace with all apps integrated
  - ○ Groupware
    § Group functionality
    § Messaging (instant/group messaging and email)
    § Calendar
  - ○ "Deck" – functionality is analogous to Trello
  - ○ OpenOffice – each supports collaborative realtime editing
    § Word / Google docs replacement
    § Excel / Google sheets replacement
    § Powerpoint / Google slides replacement
  - ○ Cryptpad – quick and lightweight document collaboration
  - ○ Markdown-based notes editing
  - ○ Mindmapping software

- WordPress
  - Basis of Learner journals
  - Forms a portfolio for Learners – it's a "real" professional-grade web site
  - Ready to rehost with a Learner's provider of choice
  - Adapted for OSLpractices – themes, categories, menus and content structures make it ready to use for Learners yet fully customizable
  - Security-hardened – WordPress is notoriously difficult for non-experts to maintain securely
- PeerTube – video sharing and playout infrastructure and app
  - Federated with ActivityPub interoperability (Mastodon, e.g.)
  - YouTube-like interface
  - Each Learner Network can build a shareable video collection
  - Podcast potential
- Grav – full-featured web Content Management System
  - Used for static, non-journalled web content such instructions and walkthroughs, timetables, and general information
  - Can support "library" space or Lead Learner website for a Learner Network
- NodeBB – Modern forum software
  - Encourages community growth and peer support
- Bookstack – Modern documentation environment
  - Incorporates commenting abilities
  - Book-like finished quality
  - Web editing as well as markdown file support
- Wikis – modern wiki software
- Security Vault
  - Bitwarden – LastPass replacement
- Searx metasearch engine
  - From within the dashboard environment, Learners can search just like with Google but more efficiently; the software submits the search to not only Google but several other search engines (configurable), including Bing and Wikipedia, and neatly summarizes the results
  - Improved quality of Learners' research
  - Diversity of results encourages evaluation and critical thinking
  - Protects Learners from "bubbling" – i.e., whensearch engines build up databases and profile users for (their) cross-correlation sale
- Matomo analytics
  - The most sophiscticated open source analytics engine
- Kutt – URL shortener utility service (bit.ly, goo.gl etc replacement)
- Outlink, FilePizza, Nextcloud Files – link and filesharing utilities

WBS: Simple Whiteboard

We have integrated these and other elements of mature open source software based on our observations of the in-person and online learning processes of OSL individuals, groups, and classes. Our observations helped us evaluate — with learners — which FOSS software would most effectively meet their needs. Depending on the experience and skillsets of an OSL network, participants can modify and customize these elements to suit their unique needs.

What we did indicates that if we place the person (Learner) at the heart of the learning environment then it follows that we co-design / support their learning according to protocols – instructions and standards that anyone can use IRL – about which they have agency and foster healthy relationships.

So the practice of software architecture (which we have named OSLAP) necessitates mapping these protocols-for-learning to digital protocols that support information flows and allow the functioning of software. The software, the "things", are replaceable. We actually maintain a multiplicity of software systems, some of which have roughly the same features. We might want to prepare the dish with a variation or source the ingredients from somewhere else just because someone asks, or it's Wednesday. Being responsive and flexible matters around here. At every turn we remind ourselves and each other that the "thing" is not a static entity, but a way of meeting our needs and serving our priorities.

Improving technology from the learning perspective maps to improved technical protocols that support learning.

Which means supporting – truly supporting – diversity. To the granularity, in principle, of one individual in any given moment.

Customizing OSLAP requires awareness of individual and community needs, along with access to create forks and curating them, potentially in many varied recombinations [GNU/Linux distributions], and curating those too. It also means a culture of mutual respect, attribution, and helping others to help others to help.

Building community here must be differentiated from what we see from the VC-funded open source-as-disruptor, or the thinly veiled farm systems (such as Github) for identifying skilled devs and other future employees. Software may share OSS licensing terms, but the aims and objectives are not always clearly related.

OSLAP is NOT about features. OSLAP is NOT defined by product management around a software commodity. As a protocol, OSLAP adapts to people.

Most education technology – products and platforms – trains people to adapt to it. They become, to some degree or other, dependents. We cannot support our Declaration of Interdependence with integrity if we are working through various distorted prisms, funnels, blockades, and filters that are designed to surveil, refine and deplete dependents of their value.

Our approach is not compatible with "rentierware," "optimising dealflow," or any other construction that reduces learners to units or eyeballs in service to profit. OSLAP is FOSS because it makes our alignment of purpose through intentional software integrations possible.

A SECURE HUMAN SOFTWARE SUPPLY CHAIN

OSLAP is software that facilitates human learning. All education technology makes similar claims. However, OSLAP is unique in that it relies upon software that is constantly evolving and in many cases actually duplicates features or has them overlap across tools. These software dependencies represent a *supply chain* of open-source software.

OSLAP's relationship with software is flow-based and process-based. It's not exactly a distribution, although this is the closest commonly known likeness or manifestation. The software can be packaged and "stirred in" as needed. Other software can be pruned. Decisions to integrate or set aside software depend on the immediate needs of people. Stewards can evaluate the software's (lack of) usage, relevance, and complexity, as well as the requirements of developing the package configuration relative to the costs of time and attention required to maintain that package.

Closed source platforms are developed around a set of assumptions involving business and human psychology that point to building for people, as opposed to stewarding with people. While this makes sense when viewed through a lens of efficiency and investor/entrepreneur profit, it has also revealed some potentially dangerous vulnerabilities. According to Brian Fox, the Open Source Security Foundation Governing Board Member and CTO of Sonatype, "If you don't even know what's in your software to start with, you probably have no visibility into what's going on with the malware, which is almost a worse problem because it's not just the vulnerability that's latent, waiting for somebody to exploit" (*Supply Chain Attack*, 2023).

The devastation caused by the Solarwinds bug illustrates just how vulnerable closed-source software can be due to its supply chain. OSS allows code inspection and opens up the whole quality assurance process to a wider community, yet at the same time allows for the engineering of novel attacks. Closed-source software can suffer from quality limitations through a lack of transparency and community of interest. Organizations that are reliant on a closed-source approach to meeting their digital needs must rely on excellence from digital procurement through delivery, which in the case of education technology often involves children. Using an OSS supply chain opens up OSLAP adopters to a security model that benefits from the wider security industry, the best in the business with regards to experts from OSS suppliers from NextCloud through Canonical, for example.

As a FOSS ecosystem, OSLAP allows for a flexible and adaptable security posture in the face of a world of constant and varying security threats conducted against individuals and organizations alike. Further, OSLAP represents an important and unique approach to "learning by doing." All OSL network participants — Learners, Lead Learners, and Stewards, as well as families and community members — can in principle take an active part in securing their own software environment, with expertise close at hand. This meets a well-documented need: "According to analysis by Sonatype, the majority of the time that a company uses a vulnerable version of any component, a fixed version of the component is available — but they're not using it. That points to a need for more education, according to Fox, '96 percent of the problem is people keep taking the tainted food off the shelf instead of taking a cleaned-up one" (Burt, 2023).

The FOSS environment enables OSLAP to offer a context for curiosity and an invitation to engage.

INTELLECTUAL PROPERTY RIGHTS, COMMERCIAL EXPRESSIONS, AND SUSTAINABILITY

For many communities it is no longer sufficient to think in terms of code released under a "classic" open license. OSLAP values inclusivity and a reverence for the rights of creators. We hope that integrating software will raise awareness about the existence of that software and encourage success throughout the ecosystem.

The relationship between code and the data it produces and manipulates is also of interest. Groups are beginning to demand collective models beyond a simplistic commons whereby their data is first of all understood as "collective" and secondly used for known purposes (and sometimes with commercial valuation).

OSLAP supports commercial ecosystems without monopolistic practices. We believe that commercial support is entirely consistent with FOSS: "Open source software is also commercial software, not just in theory but in practice: there is commercial support available for most widely-used open source software packages, and often that support is available from more than one source (Fogel and Vasile, 2017).

The "fit" of appropriate commercial arrangements is a function of the purpose, desired impact, and perceived value as regards the amplification and acceleration of learning, as opposed to some intrinsic value of a piece of technology.

Here it is worth noting that commercial transactions are "one-offs." Purchases and rental agreements are not optimized for building relationships over time in ways that support emerging thought processes or collaboration; they don't even facilitate interest in or build an understanding of the parties' interests that underlie their positions at the moment. Commerce is typified by anonymity, commodification, and replaceability. Things, not people.

In contrast, as Boisot demonstrated in developing the Large Hadron Collider at CERN, human systems at chaotic boundaries self-organize at the edge. For the highest quality large-scale endeavors, rather than optimized design for commerce, OSLAP intends to promote awareness of "boundary object[s] around which the energy and focus of the [participants] involved can cohere to make meaning while engaged in a common purpose" (Boisot, 2010).

The need for a commercial code of conduct that can adapt to emerging software was highlighted recently by the controversy caused by Microsoft Github's Copilot offering, in which AI was trained on openly licensed material and then sold for profit by the AI operator (OSI Staff, 2022).

Stewarding members of the OSLAP development community, as opposed to building policies for them, can address many of these issues by inviting contributions and putting human beings in charge of the policies, instead of the other way around, which returns us to the foundational purpose of our endeavor.

BRINGING LEARNERS ON BOARD

We introduced OSLAP in real-time with an OSL network that was working completely online as a result of their physical school campus being closed due to the coronavirus pandemic. Moving online was of course, a departure from the norm — and it was an important opportunity to adapt and document the process of offering the software for acceptance.

In previous years, when he taught in the classroom, David introduced OSL on the first day of school as a possibility for students (who had not yet accepted the invitation to become Learners) to consider. After making a brief presentation to the class, he would step out of the room so that everyone could voice their perspectives and come to an agreement without feeling influenced or pressured by an authority figure. Then, to document the conversation and provide space for Learners to express their views, a blog post was published that summarized the process and invited comments (Preston, 2014).

During the pandemic, when schools required students to attend sessions and post work online, one degree of freedom (whether to communicate and collaborate online) in the OSL adoption process was removed. As a result, it became immediately important to consider the environment. The class talked about Big Tech and the ways in which we all interact online. The result was profound, in the view of the authors.

In the process of discussing online representation (we don't feel seen by online companies) and redress (we can't get an answer or help when we have a question or something goes wrong) we connected the concept of innovation with the concept of governance. Students admitted that they knew the term "Declaration of Independence" but didn't actually know or remember anything about it. This is consistent with a recent finding that only 13% of American students are proficient in their knowledge of history (Inside Daily Brief, 2023).

We revisited the institutionally required curriculum standard — the Declaration of Independence – by pasting it into an etherpad on OSLAP and editing it into our Declaration of Interdependence, which we then all signed electronically (Preston, 2021c).

Our signatures, the recording of our process, and ultimately our individual sign on to OSLAP provide three points of documented agreement in action. In the same way that classroom students were once asked to confirm their intentions in comments to a blog post, these data points signify a commitment to a learning community and protocol that is active and intentional.

OSLAP is a living ecosystem in the sense that it — through us as Stewards, Lead Learners, and Learners — responds to the needs of network members. In the same way that the brain develops through pruning, i.e., strengthening some neural pathways and losing others as we grow into patterns of more efficient, habituated thinking, each OSLAP instance evolves to integrate, prioritize, and decommission functionalities in ways that meet the needs of network members.

The next phase in OSLAP's development will be the journey from engagement with deployed and integrated software to community contribution. Stewards, Lead Learners, and Learners all stand to gain from learning more about the tools they use. Many people who interact with the internet every day are not aware of FOSS or the Fediverse, or the difference between platforms and protocols. Through "learning by engaging and doing," we want to raise awareness and support everyone's ability to make informed, reasoned choices about their online personhood and associated data. Rushkoff made waves when he wrote "Program or be programmed," (Rushkoff, 2011) but this is clearly no longer enough — we want to normalize a culture of being in "right relation" with technology.

As communities of practice emerge, we hope that some will fully integrate Open-Source Learning through the Open-Source Learning Academy model, which has been implemented for two full academic years in California. OSLAP can offer dedicated management for these organizational environments by integrating with Student Information Systems and providing additional support as needed.

Independently of who adopts OSLAP, we are planning better automation for monitoring and maintenance, and a dedicated package repository, and we will continue to consider and evaluate alternatives to upstream distribution technology and community.

PADDLING TO MARKET

According to the Harvard Business School, "Good go-to-market strategies are based on understanding who the customer is, what problem you are solving for them, and their journey and purchasing process." Many graduate schools and professional advisors advocate clear, data-based paths for education technology companies who believe they are ready to "go to market" (Shannon, 2022).

The qualitative data collection typically included in these processes presupposes that there is an existing market of prospective customers who are aware of specific needs or problems, and that they are capable of articulating those needs or problems in ways that invite reflection, proposals of potential solutions, and an assessment of fit.

We found it challenging to reconcile the apparent clarity of the typical late capitalist go-to-market strategy with the guiding principles of Open-Source Learning and the founding idealism that forms the nervous system and as-yet-unrealized promise of the internet, especially in the hype-saturated red ocean that constitutes the education technology marketplace.

And yet, the question remained: How can you convince cruise ship passengers to paddle a raft?

Professors W. Chan Kim and Renée Mauborgne have drawn attention to the fact that competing for current customers is less important and productive than raising awareness and meeting the needs of people who don't yet realize they are customers: "Blue ocean strategy is not about finding a better or lower-cost solution to the existing problem of industry. Instead, it is about redefining the problem itself" (Kim and Maubourgne, 2015). Educators are notoriously busy, stressed, and even traumatized by their current working conditions, and they generally do not have individual purchasing power or influence over institutional procurement, so why would we invite them to participate in this conversation? Because "noncustomers, not customers, hold the greatest insight into an industry's pain points and points of intimidation that limit the size and boundary of the industry."

Rather than attempt to compete for attention or customers in the existing red ocean marketplace, OSLAP seeks to create a new market by raising awareness. Most people who use the internet do not understand the nuts and bolts of code that make the internet work. Therefore, they are unaware of the damage being done and the existence of other available options.

OSLAP engages and prepares learners for OSL's practice of Civic Fitness (Preston, 2022b). Learners build a direct understanding through multiple lines of inquiry throughout the program around how our digital lives intersect and influence the physical world around us.

In contrast to many modern SaaS ("software as a service") offerings, OSLAP itself is deliberately agnostic to its installation requirements. For a good experience, a node installation requires at least one performant server and good connectivity, but this can be anywhere: public cloud, on-site, or somewhere in between. OSLAP is well-positioned to adopt machines from downstream markets.

OSLAP stands on the shoulders of giants. The software and the network/ community amplify, accelerate, and contribute to other people's work as it grows. This is true of each individual Learner, Lead Learner, and Steward, as well as the developers and distributors of component software, who stand to benefit from the increased collaboration and public presence. The rising tide of awareness carries the potential to lift all boats.

OSLAP is similar to an OSS operating system distribution, except that OSLAP is installed on at least one server and for participants works within their browser (with a companion bootable OS in the lab). The advantage of the FOSS approach is that OSLAP is maintainable using a tiny fragment of person-power required of a closed, competitive software product or SaaS. An example of a similar small-scale but big-impact distribution is the offline-capable educational software Endless OS (*Endless OS,* n.d.). On the bootable custom operating system side, a single developer is building a radically different and very promising version of Linux called "Chimera" (*Chimera Linux,* n.d.). Big impacts can come from such focus without requiring big tech-scale organizations.

This is blue ocean thinking. OSLAP is not designed to compete for existing customers based on crtieria such as features or price. OSLAP is designed to raise awareness in ways that create opportunities and solve problems that many people don't know they have. Big tech has convinced people that there is a finite world of software, and their choices are limited. OSLAP invites people to explore under the hood and learn about software for themselves as they become more able to leverage its functionalities.

PADDLING TO MARKET

If we were building a boat to sell, we could model our venture around fairly predictable costs, position our product in the marketplace, and make some reasonable projections about economic viability and sustainability.

Navigating this blue ocean requires a different mindset. Our digital Kon-Tiki is not only facing predictably unpredictable weather, but the very patterns of weather, seasons, and even the temperature and consistency of the ocean itself are displaying unprecedented characteristics that confound even the most experienced captains.

In this environment, the application of Open-Source Learning philosophy and strategy becomes an unfair competitive advantage. Traditional marketing feedback practices such as surveys and focus groups provide insight, but making substantial improvements based on those insights still depends on internal organizational approval and execution. OSL engages community members in real time who all have the power to actively engage with the software and immediately make changes that become use cases.

Apart from the initial software architecture and the invitation to participate, OSLAP is truly inclusive. That is to say, you, dear reader, are as much a part of OSLAP as you would like to be.

These community-based conversations and refinements also form the basis for connection. Communication opens channels for sharing ideas and resources. This has been demonstrated by companies that encourage their employees to connect with customers and prospects as individuals with shared interests (Levine et al., 2000).

Increasing entropy and removing structural and cultural barriers for exchanging information increases the complexity of information that can be shared throughout the OSLAP community (Wolpert, 2015).

Here is a seed for one such exchange of information: an idea for a commercial expression of OSLAP. Let's say, for example, that we propose a concrete business model to take capital investment to "stand up" an OSLAP node that we'll define as an administrative unit with 10-100 logins. We highlight the ways in which OSLAP nodes interconnect and federate. We support coordination and create scaffolds, such as training and collaborative spaces for Learners, Lead Learners, Stewards, as well as developers, entrepreneurs, and others.

This is a familiar opt-in subscription model that supports commercial involvment on a recurring donation basis. The software is capable of delivering features found in commercial, closed- source alternatives, and an organization could be built up to support sales and service to institutional and corporate clients whose procurement must take place on customer-provider terms. Revenue in this context could support delivery of further value via OSLAP for those in non-commercial settings.

Is that a good idea? Do you have a better one? Expressing answers to those questions in this moment is only a challenge because you're reading this in a textbook, and consequently you're the only one who knows what you're thinking. What if you were participating on OSLAP right now, exchanging ideas online in real time with people who cared about what you thought and provided feedback? That would be the ultimate learning by doing (by learning).

Take a moment to consider how the medium not only changes the message, but the structure of the exchange itself and the roles we play within that structure. OSLAP software not only does the things that software is intended to do; its existence also changes the structure of the organizational and commercial systems, cultures, and contexts in which it operates.

Eventually, the federation of OSLAP nodes may or may not serve numbers greater than those of commercial endeavors. Theoretically, it could unite everyone around the world in the very first global system of public education. It could also end up a novelty known only to us and a couple home-schooling families. Whatever the numbers, OSLAP is be a potentially impactful resource that operates across different groups while adapting in real time to each one.

This is a spread model of adoption. OSLAP's decentralized, inclusive nature makes it difficult to predict options – and it also makes OSLAP extremely resilient. The infrastructure and the data are distributed, and the investment model is incremental and localized. The characteristics that make OSLAP unappealing to venture capitalists and angel investors are the very same characteristics that will ensure its survival.

Making inductive arguments such as these are not the stuff of business plans. We understand that you're reading this in a business-oriented textbook, and we are grateful to the editors and publishers who are providing space for these ideas.

We also understand that the technological extensions of the natural world and human behavior are also irrational and predictably unpredictable, and although our perspective doesn't follow the logic of business planning, we are designing for technological future, not the industrial past. We believe this is a more timeless, less fragile pattern language. Here we appeal to nature: Primordial ooze didn't have a business plan either and that seems to have worked out ok.

NAVIGATING THE DEEP BLUE DIGITAL WATERS IN WHICH WE ALL SWIM

As we write this chapter, news outlets are reporting that the "godfather of AI" has stepped down from his position at Google (Taylor and Hearn, 2023) because our near-total lack of understanding and stewardship, combined with a profit-driven race to market, is creating and releasing AI sophisticated enough that it could kill humans and destroy truth, and society along with it, and we would be powerless to stop it. What if he's right? What if humanity is a passing phase in the evolution of intelligence?

It seems like a good time to learn more about technology while simultaneously putting human beings — not corporations, hardware, or software — in charge and creating value through learning.

Thor Heyerdahl and the crew of the Kon-Tiki embarked on their journey not because the Pacific Ocean was unknown at that time, but because he wanted to prove his theory that South American people could have reached Polynesia during pre-Columbian times using the tools, materials, and techne they had available. Ninety-seven days later, Kon-Tiki arrived at the Tuamotu Archipelago in French Polynesia. Today most scholars believe that Polynesia was originally populated in a westward expansion from Island Southeast Asia. In academic circles Kon-Tiki is regarded with skepticism as deeply flawed pseudoscience. And yet, proposing the idea, building the raft, and taking the trip made possibilities accessible and memorable to this day. The hero's journey continues to enlighten by keeping the conversation alive.

So it is with FOSS and OSLAP. We are assembling materials to embark on a journey that some say has already been completed, others say isn't possible, or makes no sense without a profit model, to a place where people think they have been, to settle a bet that has already been lost.

Nevertheless, we believe that people everywhere will be better off if they learn to navigate the digital waters in which we all swim. We intend to prove the blue ocean exists by sailing it.

REFERENCES

Adams, C. (2020, April 17). *Teachers need lots of training to do online learning well. Coronavirus closures gave many just days.* Hechinger Report. Retrieved from https://hechingerreport.org/teachers-need-lots-of-training-to-do-online-learning-well-coronavirus-closures-gave-many-just-days/

Boisot, M. (2010, November 18). *The City as a Complex Adaptive System: Lessons from the ATLAS Experiment at the LHC*. Retrieved from https://www.gcph.co.uk/assets/0000/0900/Max_Boisot__summary_paper_final.pdf

Borges' original quote: "Don't talk unless you can improve the silence." (n.d.). https://www.goodreads.com/quotes/670428-don-t-talk-unless-you-can-improve-the-silence https://en.wikipedia.org/wiki/Jorge_Luis_Borges

Burt, J. (2023, February 22). *Open source software has its perks, but supply chain risks can't be ignored*. The Register. Retrieved from https://www.theregister.com/2023/02/22/open_software_supply_chain_risks/

Bush, V. (1945, July). As We May Think. *The Atlantic Monthly*. Retrieved from https://web.mit.edu/STS.035/www/PDFs/think.pdf

Chimera Linux. (n.d.). Retrieved from https://chimera-linux.org/

Drucker, P. (1963, May). Managing for Business Effectiveness. *Harvard Business Review*.

Electronic Frontier Foundation. (2020, February 20). *The Future of the Internet: Protocols vs. Platforms*. Retrieved from https://www.eff.org/event/future-internet-protocols-vs-platforms

EndlessO. S. (n.d.). Retrieved from https://www.endlessos.org/os

Fogel, K., & Vasile, J. (2017, November 16). *Guidelines for Funding Open Source Software Development*. Retrieved from https://www.archesproject.org/wp-content/uploads/2018/01/guidelines_funding_OSS.pdf

Freire, P. (1993). Pedagogy of the Oppressed. The Continuum Publishing Company. (Original work published 1970)

Harvard Business School Professor Clayton Christensen introduced the popularized notion of disruption in his 1997 book *The Innovator's Dilemma*. (n.d.). https://en.wikipedia.org/wiki/Clayton_Christensen

Holon, I. Q. (2020, August 6). *Global EdTech market to reach $404B by 2025 - 16.3% CAGR. 'Post-COVID' update to HolonIQ's Global Market Sizing*. Retrieved from https://www.holoniq.com/notes/global-education-technology-market-to-reach-404b-by-2025

Inside Daily Brief. (2023, May 3). *American eighth-graders are performing worse on history & civics exams* [Blog post]. Retrieved from https://inside.com/daily/posts/american-eighth-graders-are-performing-worse-on-history-civics-exams-368163

Johansson, F. (2004). *The Medici Effect*. Harvard Business School Press.

Kim, W. C., & Maubourgne, R. (2015). *Blue Ocean Strategy: How to Create Uncontested Market Space and Make the Competition Irrelevant*. Harvard Business Review Press.

Kon-Tiki expedition. (n.d.). In *Wikipedia, The Free Encyclopedia*. Retrieved July 4, 2023, from https://en.wikipedia.org/wiki/Kon-Tiki_expedition

Levine, F., Locke, C., Searls, D., & Weinberger, D. (2000). *The Cluetrain Manifesto*. Basic Books.

Masnick, M. (2019, August 21). *Protocols, Not Platforms: A Technological Approach to Free Speech*. Knight First Amendment Institute at Columbia University. Retrieved from https://knightcolumbia.org/content/protocols-not-platforms-a-technological-approach-to-free-speech

Open source. (n.d.). In *Wikipedia, The Free Encyclopedia*. Retrieved July 4, 2023, from https://en.wikipedia.org/wiki/Open_source

Preston, D. (2014a, May 28). *Will this blog see tomorrow?* Retrieved from https://drprestonsrhsenglitcomp14.blogspot.com/2014/05/will-this-blog-see-tomorrow.html

Preston, D. (2014b, May 28). *Will this blog see tomorrow?* [Blog post]. Retrieved from https://drprestonsrhsenglitcomp14.blogspot.com/2014/05/will-this-blog-see-tomorrow.html

Preston, D. (2020a, August 4). *Achieve the impossible.* Retrieved from https://davidpreston.net/2020/08/04/achieve-the-impossible/

Preston, D. (2020b, June 3). *Last Post Of The School Year/ june 3 w online meeting #50.* Retrieved from https://drprestonsamlitsmhs1920.blogspot.com/

Preston, D. (2021a, August 27). *Learning without a ceiling.* Retrieved from https://davidpreston.net/2021/08/27/learning-without-a-ceiling/

Preston, D. (2021b). *Academy of One: The Power and Promise of Open Source Learning.* Rowman and Littlefield. https://rowman.com/ISBN/9781475859058/Academy-of-One-The-Power-and-Promise-of-Open-Source-Learning

Preston, D. (2021c, October 25). *Declare your digital interdependence (O...SLAP!)* [Blog post]. Retrieved from https://davidpreston.net/2021/10/25/our-declaration-of-digital-interdependence-o-slap/

Preston, D. (2022a, April 13). *Physical fitness is for lead learners too.* Retrieved from https://davidpreston.net/2022/04/13/physical-fitness-is-for-lead-learners-too/

Preston, D. (2022b, March 13). *The Five Fitnesses of Open-Source Learning* [Blog post]. Retrieved from https://davidpreston.net/2022/03/13/the-five-fitnesses-of-open-source-learning/

Preston, D. (n.d.). *This Is Open-Source Learning.* Retrieved from https://davidpreston.net/open-source-learning/

Reich, J. (2022). *Failure to Disrupt.* Harvard Business School Press.

Rushkoff, D. (2011). *Program or Be Programmed.* Soft Skull.

Shannon, A. (2022, November 17). *7 Best Go-to-Market Strategies for EdTech Companies.* Retrieved from https://salesintel.io/blog/7-best-go-to-market-strategies-for-edtech-companies/

Staff, O. S. I. (2022, November 17). *Open Source software started in academic circles, and AI is not different.* Open Source Initiative Blog. Retrieved from https://blog.opensource.org/open-source-software-started-in-academic-circles-and-ai-is-not-different/

Supply chain attack. (n.d.). In *Wikipedia, The Free Encyclopedia.* Retrieved July 4, 2023, from https://en.wikipedia.org/wiki/Supply_chain_attack

Taylor, J., & Hern, A. (2023, May 2). 'Godfather of AI' Geoffrey Hinton quits Google and warns over dangers of misinformation. *The Guardian.* Retrieved from https://www.theguardian.com/technology/2023/may/02/geoffrey-hinton-godfather-of-ai-quits-google-warns-dangers-of-machine-learning

Watters, A. (2014). *The Monsters of Education Technology.* CreateSpace Independent Publishing Platform via Creative Commons Attribution-ShareAlike 4.0 License.

Well, S. (n.d.). *Community Guidelines: Yoyow.* Retrieved from https://www.well.com/articles/community-guidelines/yoyow/

Whole Earth. (1968, Fall). *Whole Earth Catalog (complete).* Whole Earth. Retrieved from https://archive.org/details/1stWEC-complete/mode/2up9pa

Wolpert, D. (2015). *Information Width: A Way for the Second Law to Increase Complexity.* https://www.santafe.edu/research/results/working-papers/information-width-a-way-for-the-second-law-to-incr

Young, J. R. (2020, June 26). *Researchers Raise Concerns About Algorithmic Bias in Online Course Tools.* EdSurge. Retrieved from https://www.edsurge.com/news/2020-06-26-researchers-raise-concerns-about-algorithmic-bias-in-online-course-tools

Chapter 10
The Red Hat Enterprise Linux Business Model

Cesar Henrique De Souza
Universidade de Sao Paulo, Brazil

ABSTRACT

Red Hat, Inc. is a leading software company known worldwide for pioneering the FOSS industry. Its history offers a concrete example of a successful open-source business model. Red Hat Enterprise Linux (RHEL), taken as a study case, is one of the most successful commercial Linux distributions, thanks to its components' stability and company support. This chapter brings a brief historical perspective of the several Red Hat distributions and their communities, highlighting how decisions have impacted the enterprise product. The chapter also introduces the open-source model behind Red Hat's Linux development flow. For this purpose, the Linux kernel provides an excellent example of collaboration that goes through all distributions, maturing to their final destination. The discussion presents some aspects of quality, security, and testing that make RHEL one of the most reliable and secure distributions.

1. COMPANY HISTORY

In the literature, there are several books, documents, reports, and all kinds of material telling the story of Red Hat in the most varied ways. Even so, it is important to present the key aspects of this chronology that led and transformed the business model of the company that people know today. Red Hat was founded in the early 1990s by Marc Ewing and Bob Young. At that time, Linux was a newly created project by Linus Torvalds that had already crossed the ocean, reaching several universities including Carnegie Mellon. As the Unix source had been closed for

DOI: 10.4018/978-1-6684-4785-7.ch010

some years and with Tanenbaum's Minix being more of a teaching project than an expandable one, there were many enthusiasts of that new, promising, and totally open-source system. Many Unix user orphans started to use that project because they had similar compatibility.

Due to this fact, many students who tried to use the new operating system ended up facing various technical problems. However, as an accomplished computer expert, Marc Ewing always ended up collaborating with other enthusiastic students at Carnegie Mellon. More so, as he wore an old red lacrosse hat of his father, such adornment became his reference for students who didn't know him and looking for some help. That way, when someone had a problem, all they had to do was look for the student with the "red hat". That's how he and Bob Young met at university. Bob Young even tells an issue of Red Hat Magazine that Marc used to name his college projects with his trademark, just incrementing the number of each project: Red Hat 1, Red Hat 2, etc. Another interesting coincidence also mentioned by Bob in this interview is that during some revolutions, his revolutionaries wore red hats as a symbol of their libertarian ideals (Mears, 2006).

In the mid-90s and already getting to know each other, Marc and Bob opened two different companies, Bob's was called ACC Corporation, and Marc's, Red Hat obviously. Both provide versions of the new system called Linux. Later, in 1995, ACC purchased Red Hat and went under the name Red Hat, Inc. as default. From that moment, the company already had a very stable version of the operating system, offering support to its customers via email. The only problem with this model was that the computers were just inoperable due to failures. Therefore, it would not be possible to send emails requesting new support. Thus, the company later adopted telephone support and the subscription model used until today.

It has been noted so far how a symbol and supportive behavior have guided the company's culture and its project models for years. Also notice the emphasis on words such as reference, specialist, collaboration, freedom, and revolution. Today, Red Hat has some products in its internal portfolio, however, it is often said that the company does not sell software, but high-level support as well as innovations in the area. For this, it needs to have both experts who are references plus the freedom of discussion and collaboration. And yet, it is a company that has a massive and unparalleled presence in relevant projects of the free software community. The fact that the company itself sponsors two very important distributions for part of its success: Fedora and CentOS.

2. A BRIEF HISTORY OF FEDORA

In general, it is possible to call both Fedora and CentOS as Linux distributions. However, the correct way to refer to them is as variants of Red Hat Enterprise Linux.

To understand why it is necessary to remember that Red Hat's main product even before being purchased by ACC was precisely an open-source operating system initially called Red Hat Linux (RHL). In 1995, the first official release was released with the purpose of being focused on enterprise systems and mainly being stable. This resulted in a project shaped by the demand of the corporate market, with fewer innovative features.

Although RHL was a subscription product, its source was open. Soon, many developers began to generate and share the packages that formed the basis of the system, including new features. This project was called Fedora.us. The name was composed of Fedora (a type of hat) and the suffix "us" referring to the community, or a project aimed more at the people who developed it. This suffix, however, confused many users by associating it with the "United States" universal code. Later, the project was renamed to Fedora Project, the same name currently used.

In 2003, Fedora was released under the codename Yarrow. Also at the beginning, Fedora used many projects close to the development line, which caused several problems for users who used it. In the early days, it was common referring to Fedora as the "Linux for hackers" due to bugs that appeared. Ironically, this feature was also what attracted many users to chase them.

Over the years, Fedora has become a testing variant for RHEL and new features were incorporated into the system. Or even newer versions that were tested in that environment before being incorporated into RHEL. Not enough, Fedora itself has a version considered unstable called Rawhide. This entire flowchart of versions will be presented later.

3. A BRIEF HISTORY OF CENTOS

In the year 2003, Red Hat announced that it would discontinue the Red Hat Linux project to focus on corporate customers under the new name of Red Hat Enterprise Linux (in fact, it would be renamed Red Hat Advanced Server in 2003, assuming the current name later). With that, many users would be forced to migrate to some other distribution or use Fedora which, as is known, was an unstable version.

Thus, the Caos project announced a distribution called Community Enterprise OS which was basically the sources used in Red Hat Enterprise Linux recompiled and released to the community. Despite being indirectly helped by the company, the system did not have any logo or subscription system. It was completely free and maintained the stability paradigm proposed by RHEL (Smyth, 2019). Later in 2005, the announcement sent to the mailing list (Hughes, 2005) communicated that the Community Enterprise OS (already using the CentOS moniker) would become a single and independent project. In 2014, Red Hat has announced the inclusion of the project as part of its product portfolio (Vaughan-Nichols, 2014). So, today CentOS remains free and officially supported by Red Hat.

CentOS' proposal was precisely to maintain RHEL version parity. If RHEL releases version 6.2 for example, there would be an equally similar and free version of CentOS and so on. But, in 2020, under the control of Red Hat, the community announced a controversial paradigm shift in CentOS versioning, changing its name to CentOS Stream (Wright, 2020). Now, instead of parity, CentOS would always track the latest version of each major release.

4. DEVELOPMENT MODEL

4.1. Streams Concept

First, you need to understand some basic software development methodologies before understanding how the multi-variant model of the Red Hat ecosystem works. One of the concepts already mentioned was the stream concept. It's not exactly the same as that was adopted in CentOS from 2020 onwards, but it's similar. As also mentioned, Fedora is a version with newer features and newer projects. A version is more focused on innovations than stability. However, even Fedora has its development version called Rawhide as mentioned previously. This version contains almost the latest versions of the projects that compose the operating system, from the Kernel to window managers, among others. In the context of streams, Fedora Rawhide is called *upstream* and everything below it is called *downstream*. Fedora would be CentOS Stream 9's *upstream* and Fedora's *downstream* and so on until RHEL. Generally, projects in development are called *upstream* because they are exactly the origin of the functionality of what is below or *downstream*. In other words, it is a kind of fork model where the forked project is called *upstream* and the fork projects are called *downstream*. With this, the features, fixes, and/or codes can flow from *upstream* to *downstream*.

In Figure 1.1, it is possible to understand better how the development flow between each version works. Each block represents a variant and its respective Kernel project. Suppose a new functionality is proposed in the Linux Kernel maintained by Linus. It will arrive first in Fedora Rawhide, next in Fedora, then in CentOS Stream 9, and finally in RHEL. There is no possibility according to this model of something

Figure 1. The context of stream for all Red Hat variants

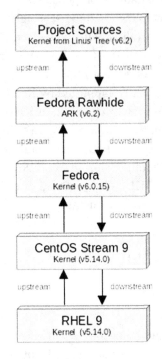

Figure 2. A dive deep into the variants generated by each respective stream based on a CentOS blog article
Source: Walter (2020)

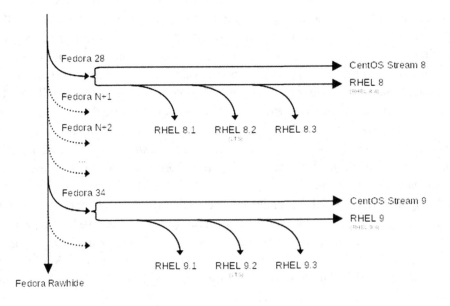

arriving earlier in RHEL than in CentOS Stream for example. Obviously, there are some corner cases that will be mentioned later.

In Figure 1, you can see an overview of how changes and versioning go through each variant in the context of *streams*. Otherwise, it does not show how each variant is defined. In Figure 2, it is possible to see how each branch is driven so that the variants are properly generated. Before the CentOS *streams* concept, its development line was basically a mirror of RHEL. Today, the project proposal is to become a development line similar to what happens with Fedora Rawhide for Fedora. However, the version is always ahead of the one being developed in RHEL. In the case of Figure 2, the two examples of development releases would be RHEL 8.4 and RHEL 9.4. The older versions (or the forked ones) like the latest 9.3 and 8.3 are stable releases.

It is possible to see that each fork generates two paths, one leading to the development version and another one to the stable version. Internally, the path that flows to the development branch is called Y branch or Y stream. For stable versions, the branches are called Z or Z streams and their lifecycle has some specific cadences (Freire, 2017). An important difference between them is that only Y streams accept new features coming from *upstream*. Stable releases or Z streams only accept bug and security fixes. It is quite rare when a Z stream receives a new feature.

In general, another interesting characteristic is that each even minor version (9.4, 9.2, 8.4, 8.2, and others) is practically considered a long support version (LTS). This support type depends on each version of RHEL, but usually, Red Hat supports it for an average of 10 years. It is not part of this chapter to explain the RHEL life cycle because each version has some peculiarities. You can find more details by visiting the company's product page (Red Hat Customer Portal, 2022a).

4.2. Always Ready Concept

Still referring to Figure 1, it is possible to notice that Fedora Rawhide uses a version called Always Ready Kernel (or ARK) (Red Hat Inc., 2020a) in the example. This version is very close to the development line of the tree maintained by Linus Torvalds. The idea is to experiment and propose everything new from the *upstream* project and thus anticipate trends, problems, design decisions, and so on and so forth. It's a good strategy to respond to customers' requests which could become the long-term standard in RHEL. A good example is a discussion of which would be the best standardization of hardware and power configuration: ACPI or Device Tree? (Corbet, 2013; Garrett, 2013). Discussions and decisions like these can affect the entire development and support of RHEL. That's why it is so important to the company. Therefore, they should be investigated and tested as soon as possible so the managers and engineers have enough time to plan the changes in the long term.

In parallel, there is another project called Fedora ELN. It stands for EL Niño originally, but it can be also referred to as the initials of Enterprise Linux Next. This project is not a distribution by the way. It is a development environment that uses the Fedora sources with RHEL configurations to early test RHEL. The Kernel is also a good example here where the configurations are taken from RHEL and applied to Fedora Kernel sources for development purposes.

4.3. Upstream First Motto

As mentioned earlier, features go through the flow from newest to most stable. Let's assume that, at some point, a problem is identified in RHEL 8.3 Kernel. Then, engineers identify which correction should be applied. From there, it is necessary to check if this defect occurs in newer versions. The purpose of this step is to identify whether this error is reproducible on newer versions of the Kernel. As the engineer goes through each *upstream* version and confirms the existence of the bug, he ends up getting closer to the development version (Linus' tree). If this happens, they should propose the fix to the general Kernel community, so that it can be applied in the *downstream* versions respectively. There is no possibility for a fix to be applied only to the RHEL Kernel without it being applied to the higher versions. Furthermore, every defect is always corrected in the source code regardless of the author.

If this error has already been fixed in some version *downstream*, the engineer needs to backport this correction, that is, apply the same set of changes that were made in that version to the lower versions. Of course, there are some precautions and points to consider before applying them. Red Hat has a list of some of these issues (Red Hat Customer Portal, 2022b).

The first question is whether changes are easily decoupled from new features. It is essentially important that commits or patches have a logical structure of minimal independence from other commits or patches. Some clear examples would be a patch set that introduces more than one change per patch or a patch granularity too high for a single change. The more cohesive the set of commits or patches is, the easier it becomes to backport a fix for example.

The second question to backport is whether that change does not generate any unexpected side effects for that version. A fix that consists in removing a driver functionality that is still supported for example.

4.4. An Embargoed Content

One of the most important fixes that engineers set as a high priority is security ones. They are usually associated with some vulnerability and when they are discovered, they get identifiers tracked by the Common Vulnerabilities and Exposures (CVE) system. The CVE is a public database that records the event of every vulnerability of sensitive projects like the Linux Kernel. Each vulnerability gains the prefix CVE plus an ID that is often tied to the year of discovery (Red Hat Inc., 2020b). A vulnerability can be tied to more than one CVE and is usually attached to public security reports from companies.

In the case of Kernel, a project maintained by multiple contributors, a vulnerability can be fixed by anyone. When this fix becomes public, it is quickly incorporated into *downstream* versions via backporting.

However, when a vulnerability is discovered or reported to Red Hat, it is reported to a vendor or the project that uses it. Once it is confirmed, engineers work with each other to define a plan of actions and a date for making it public. To make this possible, Red Hat keeps private copies of the original Kernel so that these patches can be set correctly and securely. This private security bug stage is called an embargoed flaw or an embargoed content (Rock, 2018).

Obviously, there is a discussion around the deprivation of access to discovery by other engineers. Many argue that leaving the patch restricted to a group can create patches poorly made to the point of generating other vulnerabilities in the future. As was the case with the Bash Shellshock vulnerability (CVE-2014-6271), generating more fixes after the first one, and SPECTRE (CVE-2017-5753) that generated 4 more versions of the fix (Red Hat Customer Portal, 2015).

For the argument that is still better to open the flaw publicly, there is the point that not all open-source projects have enough infrastructures that allow privacy for a vulnerability fix. When it does occur, it is often done using private messaging channels and local tests in order to correct them. It can cause another situation of poor fixes.

4.5. Review Process

As the basis of an operating system, the Linux Kernel source code is quite large. In addition, it has a huge number of drivers and subtrees to support as many platforms and hardware as possible. Therefore, each patch submitted to the Kernel must undergo a review before being applied. In the case of the main project, each driver or subtree usually creates a mirror project and accepts contributions from that clone. At a certain point, changes from that project are applied to the main project.

In the context of Fedora, CentOS and RHEL there is the same similarity. Once the Kernel version has been defined for each variant (see Figure 2), open-source projects such as Fedora and CentOS can also receive external contributions through Pull/Merge Requests. In order for a set of changes to be applied, each submission must be reviewed by the minimum criteria of reviewers. In the example of Figure 3, there is a Merge Request being proposed and being accepted by two reviewers

Figure 3. An example of a pull/merge request to Kernel ARK

as shown in the right column. Below the right column that indicates the reviewers, you can see some labels that indicate that certain requirements have been met. In the case of the review, you can see that there are two labels, one for Acks and one for Acks::net. Most likely, this change proposal refers to some network subtree, so it requires a review from a network expert.

As mentioned, the proposal of both Fedora and CentOS is for the community to collaborate, including revisions. However, it is sometimes difficult to recognize that a volunteer has enough experience to review content. Because both are sponsored by Red Hat, the company knows which engineers and groups have the ability to conduct the review process and automatically assigns them to each Pull/Merge Request. This is a guarantee of agility, accuracy, and higher quality in revisions.

A very interesting point to highlight is that the company has increasingly adopted the facilities of code management systems, even though many projects still use the system for submitting and reviewing patches via e-mail. Precisely, due to the large volume and the difficulty of obtaining adequate notifications, many patches for the main Kernel were not properly addressed or were even forgotten.

Still on Figure 3, note that there are also some other labels such as CodeChangeV4 indicating that this is the fourth version of the submission. There is also an indication of Configuration saying that there is a change even in the default configuration of the Kernel. Finally, there is an indication of the label Dependencies meaning that none or all dependencies have been fulfilled. Obviously, there are other labels available, but the important thing is to understand that they give an indication to the reviewer and even to the author himself what the status or summary of that Pull/ Merge Request is. The labels referring to CKI will be explained in the Continuous Integration section.

5. BUILD AND DEPLOY MODEL

5.1. RPM Package Manager

Any Linux operating system that is based on Red Hat will always use a file packaging system called RPM. Created in 1995 by Marc Ewing himself and engineer Erik Troan, the original acronym was just Red Hat Package Manager. Later in 2000, it took on the recursive acronym of RPM Package Manager. The main focus of RPM creation was to support pristine sources, be easy to create, and be easy to query metadata (Bailey, 1997; Ellis & Cotton, 2011).

All software and libraries on a Linux system are available as a package. Therefore, it is very important to understand the fundamental concepts of RPM because the Red Hat models that support package creation are oriented to the RPM structure. In Table 1, it is possible to see the structure of a package definition file. The template is called *spec* file due to its extension suffix. It contains a series of metadata that describes a package. However, with the exception of header metadata, each section is defined by the % character, that is %build, %description, %prep and others. The same is true for some standard RPM variables. For more information about each section, you can read the complete RPM guide (Miller, Svistunov, Doleželová, & et al., 2020).

For development purposes, the fields *Source* and *Patch* are important here. As RPM is based on offering pristine sources, you can see that it accepts as input a location containing a compressed file and a local file. As long as new fixes are introduced, even if they are not applied in the fixed version, they can be incorporated via backporting, through a patch file. In order for the file to be applied, it is sufficient to include the fields *Patch* plus a numeric identifier for each applied patch. The numeric identifier works as a sequence if they have dependencies on each other. It is important to finally understand how simple it is to backport corrections using the RPM structure.

5.2. *DistGit* Model

Unlike remote sources, you can also use local sources from existing files. Cases like this are more often when the project does not make compressed files available through download. Then, it is up to the engineer who will do the packaging to create

Table 1. An example of an ordinary SPEC file that describes a RPM package called eject

1	Name: eject
2	Version: 2.1.5
3	Release: 11%{dist}
4	License: GPL
5	Summary: A program that ejects removable media using software control
6	Source: http://metalab.unc.edu/pub/Linux/utils/disk-management/%{name}-%{version}.tar.gz
7	Source1: eject.pam
8	Patch1: eject-2.1.1-verbose.patch
9	Patch2: eject-timeout.patch
10	URL: https://www.pobox.com/~tranter
11	ExcludeArch: s390 s390x
12	BuildRequires: gettext
13	BuildRequires: automake
14	BuildRequires: autoconf
15	BuildRequires: libtool
16	
17	%description
18	The eject program allows the user to eject removable media (typically
19	CD-ROMs, floppy disks or Iomega Jaz or Zip disks) using software
20	control. Eject can also control some multi-disk CD changers and even
21	some devices' auto-eject features.
22	
23	Install eject if you'd like to eject removable media using software
24	control.
25	
26	%prep
27	%setup -q -n %{name}
28	%patch1 -p1 -b .verbose
29	%patch2 -p1 -b .timeout
30	
31	%build
32	%configure
33	make
34	
35	%install
36	rm -rf %{buildroot}
37	
38	make DESTDIR=%{buildroot} install
39	
40	# pam stuff
41	install -m 755 -d %{buildroot}/%{_sysconfdir}/pam.d
42	install -m 644%{SOURCE1} %{buildroot}/%{_sysconfdir}/pam.d/%{name}
43	install -m 755 -d %{buildroot}/%{_sysconfdir}/security/console.apps/
44	echo "FALLBACK=true" > %{buildroot}/%{_sysconfdir}/security/console.apps/%{name}
45	
46	install -m 755 -d %{buildroot}/%{_sbindir}
47	pushd %{buildroot}/%{_bindir}
48	mv eject ../sbin
49	ln -s consolehelper eject
50	popd
51	
52	%find_lang %{name}
53	
54	%files -f %{name}.lang
55	%doc README TODO COPYING ChangeLog
56	%attr(644,root,root) %{_sysconfdir}/security/console.apps/*
57	%attr(644,root,root) %{_sysconfdir}/pam.d/*
58	%{_bindir}/*
59	%{_sbindir}/*
60	%{_mandir}/man1/*
61	
62	%changelog
63	* Wed Apr 02 2008 Zdenek Prikryl <zprikryl at, redhat.com> 2.1.5-11
64	- Added check if device is hot pluggable
65	- Resolves #438610

Figure 4. The structure of a DistGit used to store huge RPM sources based on the same figure used in the project documentation
Source: Red Hat Release Engineering (2021)

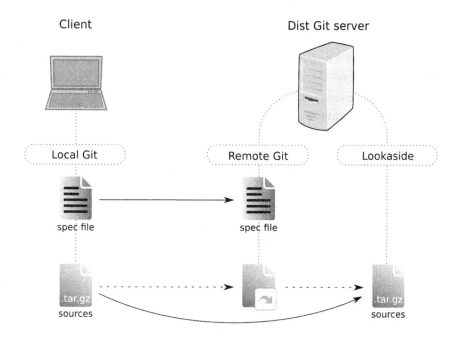

them somehow. For this, he needs to keep this code saved in some repository or make this process part of its automation, for example. The disadvantage of this process is that with each new release, a new compressed file has to be created. If the project is very large, there is an associated cost of generating a very large git diff from a binary compressed file and that diff is usually the same size as the file. Therefore, space consumption is excessive and useless.

To solve this problem, the Distribution Git (DistGit) (Red Hat Release Engineering, 2021) model was proposed. The design consists of keeping only a text file containing the data of the sources used. The fonts are in turn saved to remote storage services. So, when there is an update, only the metadata of the sources containing the names and the hashes of each file is updated by the git repository. Figure 4 shows that in a git repository the source is just a shortcut to the original source stored in some service. The lookaside repository is also responsible for a series of controls such as preventing the same source from being loaded twice or fixing a corrupted file with a new upload.

5.3. Koji Build System

To generate an RPM package, you need to use a tool called *rpmbuild*. The application requires as input the spec file and all its sources including patches. Then, to automate the process to build and generate packages, a system called Koji was created. It is composed of several components of front end and back end. This allows other instances to be cloned. The fact is that the same system exists for both Fedora (Fedora Community, 2016) and CentOS (CentOS Community, 2016) independently and other related forks. Even if they are used to generate RPMs, each one has its own peculiarity due to community needs.

Koji runs exactly the *rpmbuild* tool to generate the RPM, but the difference is in the centralization and isolation of the environment. Each build generates an encapsulated environment called Mock that is configured according to the target requirements.

If someone wants to generate a Kernel package for Fedora 34 for example, all the Fedora 34 libraries and applications needed are installed inside the *Mock*. Once generated, the package is published and pinned. If a build is completed with a successful result, Koji creates a unique identifier called the NVR (Name, Version and Release). After that, it is no longer possible to recreate that same version even if the source has changed. It is possible only if the release is incremented. This ensures compatibility with the published *Changelog* and ensures that no one has package mismatches on any given system.

6. CONTINUOUS INTEGRATION AND TESTING

One of Red Hat Enterprise Linux's guidelines is to always deliver a very stable system to its customers. Therefore, it is essential that the system is well-tested and well-evaluated. On the other hand, even fixing the versions and only receiving bug fixes and security fixes, some backports can be complex and introduce old bugs already solved for example. In software testing, the validation that no errors are introduced after a change is called regression testing. This is one of the types that are executed for Kernel quality assurance.

Imagine that a certain distribution has a bug in the Kernel and to fix it, it is necessary to apply a patch (following the workflow presented in the Development *Model* section). This patch A is a patch that unfortunately introduced another bug fixed by patch B. In this case, there is a dependency between them. Finally, if only patch A is applied, the regression tests will identify a problem precisely because patch B is missing. This scenario shows that tests for cases such as the Kernel are very important to guide the engineer on problems caused after patch applications.

So, even in the case of the Kernel, there are some specific solutions that help in this whole process and that will be presented below.

6.1. CKI Project

The CKI Project is the acronym for Continuous Kernel Integration (CKI Project Authors, 2022). Its proposal has the main goals of reducing the risks of applying a patch set and warning engineers and maintainers about possible problems found by regression tests. This process of testing is triggered for each patch set, for every Kernel package build or, as shown in subsection 1.4.5, for each Pull/Merge Request. With this, every contribution is tested before being effectively applied. In the case of Red Hat, it still has infrastructures that allow testing Kernel on every architecture supported by the product.

Once the Pull/Merge Request has been submitted, tests need to return feedback to stakeholders as quickly as possible. However, the compilation of a project like the Kernel can take hours to finish, which would make the agile process unfeasible. it's even worse if other submissions are coming and demanding new tests. For this, CKI uses some mechanisms that facilitate speed (Hayden, 2019a, 2019b) and avoid new requests being queued.

One such strategy is to use the *ccache project*. As you test small portions of changes, there is a high probability that each Merge Request of a fixed Kernel version will have similar objects to each other. Then there would be no need to recompile all the code from scratch. It would be enough to reuse the same objects generated in previous builds. This saves a lot of time in generating the test RPM.

Another engineering strategy present in the CKI infrastructure is Kernel Patch-Evaluated Testing (KPET). This project identifies which subtree the Merge Request changes or relates to and runs the tests specific to that change context. It also reduces the execution time of a pipeline because in many cases there is no need to test the entire kernel as it is done for a release build for example.

Finally, when the tests for that submission are completed, a label is added saying whether the tests via CKI are passed or not. If some test failed, the engineer needs to find out if there is a real problem or it was just a false positive.

6.2. KABI

Fundamentally, ABI stands for Application Binary Interface. It refers to how two compiled binary applications communicate with each other. A very simple example would be how a userspace application communicates with the Kernel. This can happen through several methods like system calls, ioctl() commands, etc. Ideally, a user space application code that was compiled for a certain version X of the

Kernel would have to be compatible with version X+1. Which may not happen. It is argued that maintaining compatibility across versions would create a big problem with maintaining legacy and old code, increasing the complexity more and more (Edge, 2017).

Considering the point of maintaining compatibility over major versions, the same does not occur for Kernel whose version is fixed as is the case with CentOS and RHEL. Suppose that at some point, there is a need to backport a bug fix for them. Patches that fix this bug change the Kernel ABI, this can create a problem for vendors that maintain drivers based on the Kernel version of both distributions (Masters & Blum, 2007).

In the case of CentOS, once the Merge Request of a fix or new feature is made, the test pipeline automatically checks for changes in the Kernel's ABI. Interestingly, even if something in the structure changes, tests run by pipelines like the CKI are not guaranteed to fail, but identifying when this occurs for deeper analysis is extremely important. In Figure 5, you can see a label added showing that the Merge Request changes the Kernel's ABI.

Figure 5. An example of a label notification of a merge request that changes some KABI symbol

The easiest way to check if the ABI of a version like CentOS is being changed is to compare the public symbol table of the current version with and without the included patch set. Once this is done, it is possible to compare whether any symbol is different from another.

6.3. Kernel Sanitizers

Another type of test that is quite important is the kernel memory management tests. Many of the security vulnerabilities and Kernel Panics arise from poorly constructed or poorly revised logic that generates memory pointers leaks. For that, there are some Kernel Sanitizers that propose to check for memory issues.

Both in the case of CentOS and RHEL they use the Kernel Address Sanitizer (KASAN) (Corbet, 2018; The Kernel Development Community, 2022b) as part of the CKI tests. KASAN is a dynamic memory error detector, that is, it is compiled and executed with the kernel to identify out-of-bounds and use-after-free problems. In this way, KASAN is usually added as part of the Kernel build that will be run by the CKI tests for that test suite. The fact that KASAN is only part of the CKI is precisely because it is a debug tool and mainly because of the latency it produces in terms of memory access. Thus, its use in the production Kernels is practically impossible.

Another test that is not part of the CKI debug scope but is quite relevant is the Kernel Electric-Fence (KFENCE) (Elver, 2020; The Kernel Development Community, 2022a). KFENCE is very similar to KASAN in terms of memory analysis. The major difference between them is the precision in which KFENCE has a lower one. The idea is that it has an almost minimal cost of performance and low latency compared to KASAN and therefore can be enabled in a production kernel. While KASAN is dedicated to being a unique test module, KFENCE, by analyzing Kernels in production, can cover structures that might not be possible in fixed tests.

6.4. *Rpminspect*

As mentioned earlier, Linux is made up of a series of packages that define the system.

These packages once generated must also undergo inspections to ensure that there are no regressions or errors being introduced. To make this possible, in the RPM-based variants it is possible to use the tool called *rpminspect* (Cantrell, 2021).

The *rpminspect* tool checks if the RPM complies with the policies defined in the analysis such as License, manual pages and others. It can also analyze the difference between two versions of the same package to report inconsistencies between them. These inconsistencies can be produced deliberately or by some problem in the build phase. Finally, he is also able to guide in a better RPM structuring focused on good packaging practices.

Regarding the target objects of the analysis, it is able to verify local RPMs files or Koji remote builds by analyzing the artifacts produced at the end of the process. In the case of the test model and Continuous Integration, *rpminspect* is only executed at the end of the generation of a Kernel release, for example. So the periodicity is much smaller compared to the CKI that is executed every Merge Request. On the other hand, as it is almost a test at the product level, its criticality is lower since at that moment it is expected that the Kernel has passed a long battery of tests.

6.5. Fedora Update System

Coming back to the point that both CentOS and Fedora are public projects and that, despite Red Hat's sponsorship and decision-making power, they are still maintained by the community. In this sense, there are also some initiatives of their own in relation to testing and quality.

One such initiative is the *Fedora Update System*. This system is a software quality and testing system in which any Fedora member can participate. Basically, it's a web system integrated with Koji that publishes the updates for each package before they actually go into production repositories. Each member can volunteer to run a set of tests, and once they are run, the user assigns a score called karma. The more positive *karma*, the greater the indication that this package is mature enough to be promoted to production. On the other hand, in cases of negative karma, the reason is investigated and if it is enough to embargo the package.

Figure 6 shows the example of a published kernel with some instructions of how to test and their respective current *karma*. It is possible to see that the minimum required *karma* to achieve maturity is 3 and to mark this package as embargoed the *karma* is -3.

In addition to the contribution of many people at an important stage of development, the community also ensures package testing on diverse hardware platforms. The greater the scope of the tests, the greater the guarantee of its quality, even more so if the package is strictly dependent on hardware such as the Kernel for example.

6.6. Fedora COPR

Another Fedora initiative is *"Cool Other Package Repo"* (COPR) which provides a free and open infrastructure for projects to be generated, compiled, and built for Fedora. This system also uses part of the Koji infrastructure like Mock to generate all the build process artifacts.

Figure 6. The example of a published kernel package with version 5.18.5-200 for Fedora 36 and its respective karma

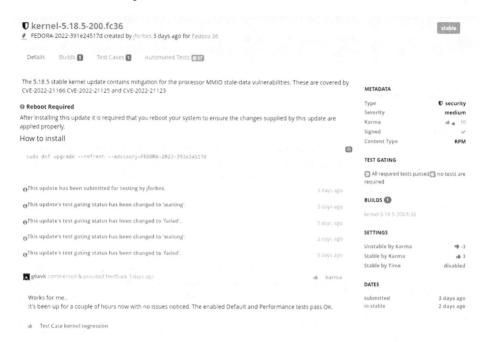

If someone develops a project and wants to generate an RPM to be made available to users, they can register, create their project and use COPR for that. Once generated, COPR creates a specific repository that can be added by users in a simple way. COPR is intended to serve as a testing instrument for new emerging projects. A project that is later relevant to users or the Linux community can be promoted and become an official project maintained by the community itself, rather than a user or a group maintaining the package on their own.

6.7. CentOS Special Group of Interests

On CentOS, besides the structures presented above as part of the testing and quality process, the community also maintains specific investigation and early testing groups called the *Special Group of Interests (SIG)* (CentOS Community, 2021).

The proposal allows that from fixed versions of CentOS, new features are added based on some specific customer demand. These features can get on RHEL's radar if they have any relevant arguments, criteria, and technical importance for it (Larabel, 2021). These groups may even use different versions of upstream and not Fedora itself.

Each SIG must be approved by the CentOS community council in view of the importance of investigating and debating that topic for future versions of CentOS and RHEL There are several SIGs nowadays such as the Virtualization group, Core, Kernel modules, and others that are still under analysis.

7. CONCLUSION

After presenting several components that are included in the development model of the two distributions, it is easy to see how the company has developed a model that is strongly oriented towards the open source model and, at the same time, is capable of providing stability, agility, and security for corporate customers. More than that, a model that has been present since its creation when it was proposed by its founders. This also proves that it is possible to have an extremely profitable company offering open source projects as business solutions.

There are obviously some dilemmas that are incorporated by the adoption of this model such as the resolution of vulnerabilities being always open to all or not, but the model satisfactorily addresses what is expected by customers using the private non-exposure model.

In addition to the use of open source projects for quality testing, there is also the adoption of many practices that are guided by community engagement. This extends Red Hat's testing and experimentation capabilities and serves as a thermometer for guiding new functionality or even new business.

Finally, the fact of the company is always close to the community and their discussions means that Red Hat is always seeing the transformations and innovations that constantly arise from the projects. Furthermore, if the company knows how to deal with them for its own benefit, it will always have a competitive advantage to offer.

DISCLAIMER

This article reflects the opinions of the author based on public information.

REFERENCES

Bailey, E. C. (1997). *Maximum rpm: Taking the red hat package manager to the limit*. Red Hat Software.

Cantrell, D. (2021). *Rpminspect*. Retrieved from https://rpminspect.readthedocs.io/en/latest/

Cent O. S. Community. (2016). *CentOS Kojihub*. Retrieved from https://kojihub.stream.centos.org/koji/

Cent O. S. Community. (2021). *Special interest groups*. Retrieved from https://wiki.centos.org/SpecialInterestGroup

CKI Project Authors. (2022). *Continuous Kernel Integration (CKI) Project*. Retrieved from https://cki-project.org/

Corbet, J. (2013). *ACPI for ARM?* Retrieved from https://lwn.net/Articles/574439/

Corbet, J. (2018). *Software-tag-based kasan*. Retrieved from https://lwn.net/Articles/766768/

Edge, J. (2017). *Specifying the kernel abi*. Retrieved from https://lwn.net/Articles/726021/

Ellis, S., & Cotton, B. (2011). *Rpm guide*. Fedora Documentation. Retrieved from https://docs.fedoraproject.org/en-US/Fedora_Draft_Documentation/0.1/html/RPM_Guide/index.html

Elver, M. (2020). *Kfence: A low-overhead sampling-based memory safety error detector*. Retrieved from https://lwn.net/Articles/835542/

Fedora Community. (2016). *Fedora Buildsystem*. Retrieved from https://koji.fedoraproject.org/koji/

Freire, R. (2017). *The code path - how does new code enter red hat products?* Retrieved from https://www.redhat.com/en/blog/code-path-how-does-new-code-enter-red-hat-products

Garrett, M. (2013). *ACPI vs Device Tree - moving forward*. Retrieved from https://lkml.org/lkml/2013/8/20/556

Hayden, M. (2019a). *Continuous integration testing for the Linux kernel*. Retrieved from https://opensource.com/article/19/6/continuous-kernel-integration-linux

Hayden, M. (2019b). *The Lifecycle of Linux Kernel Testing*. Retrieved from https://opensource.com/article/19/8/linux-kernel-testing

Hughes, J. (2005). *CentOS Mailing List - Official Announce List Notification*. Retrieved from https://lists.centos.org/pipermail/centos/2005-March/357451.html

Larabel, M. (2021). *Centos sig to help get community centos stream features into next rhel releases.* Retrieved from https://www.phoronix.com/scan.php?page=news_item&px=CentOS-Stream-Features-To-RHEL

Masters, J., & Blum, R. (2007). *Professional linux programming.* Wiley.

Mears, J. (2006). *Ever wonder how red hat got its name?* Computer World. Retrieved from https://www.computerworld.com/article/2548974/ever-wonder-how-red-hat-got-its-name-.html

Miller A. Svistunov M. Doleželová M. (2020). *RPM Packaging Guide.* Retrieved from https://rpm-packaging-guide.github.io/

Red Hat Customer Portal. (2015). *The hidden costs of embargoes.* Retrieved from https://access.redhat.com/blogs/766093/posts/1976653

Red Hat Customer Portal. (2022a). *Red Hat Enterprise Linux Life Cycle.* Retrieved from https://access.redhat.com/support/policy/updates/errata

Red Hat Customer Portal. (2022b). *What is backporting and how does it affect Red Hat Enterprise Linux (RHEL)?* Retrieved from https://access.redhat.com/solutions/57665

Red Hat Inc. (2020a). *Fedora/ARK Kernel.* Retrieved from https://cki-project.gitlab.io/kernel-ark/

Red Hat Inc. (2020b). *What is a CVE?* Retrieved from https://www.redhat.com/en/topics/security/what-is-cve

Red Hat Release Engineering. (2021). *DistGit provides home for linux distribution packages.* Retrieved from https://github.com/release-engineering/dist-git

Rock, L. (2018). *Security embargoes at Red Hat.* Retrieved from https://www.redhat.com/en/blog/security-embargoes-red-hat

Smyth, N. (2019). *Centos 8 essentials.* Payload Media.

The Kernel Development Community. (2022a). *Kernel electric-fence (kfence).* Retrieved from https://docs.kernel.org/dev-tools/kasan.html

The Kernel Development Community. (2022b). *The kernel address sanitizer (kasan).* Retrieved from https://docs.kernel.org/dev-tools/kasan.html

Vaughan-Nichols, S. (2014). *Red Hat incorporates 'free' Red Hat clone CentOS.* Retrieved from https://www.zdnet.com/article/red-hat-incorporates-free-red-hat-clone-centos/

Walter, S. (2020). *CentOS Stream is Continuous Delivery*. Retrieved from https://blog.centos.org/2020/12/centos-stream-is-continuous-delivery/

Wright, C. (2020). *CentOS Stream: Building an innovative future for enterprise Linux*. Retrieved from https://www.redhat.com/en/blog/centos-stream-building-innovative-future-enterprise-linux

Compilation of References

Acquier, A., Carbone, V., & Massé, D. (2016). L' Economie Collaborative: Fondements théoriques et agenda de recherche. In *2nd International Workshop on the Sharing Economy*. Paris: ESCP Europe.

Adams, C. (2020, April 17). *Teachers need lots of training to do online learning well. Coronavirus closures gave many just days*. Hechinger Report. Retrieved from https://hechingerreport.org/teachers-need-lots-of-training-to-do-online-learning-well-coronavirus-closures-gave-many-just-days/

Adler, A., Gujar, A., Harrison, B. L., O'Hara, K., & Sellen, A. (1998). A Diary Study of Work-related Reading: Design Implications for Digital Reading Devices. *Proceedings of the SIGCHI Conference on Human Factors in Computing Systems*, 241–248. 10.1145/274644.274679

Apache License. Version 2.0. (n.d.). *The Apache Software Foundation!* Retrieved August 20, 2022, from https://www.apache.org/licenses/LICENSE-2.0

Ascher, D. (2004). Is Open Source Right for You? *ACM Queue; Tomorrow's Computing Today*, *2*(3), 32–38. doi:10.1145/1005062.1005065

Bailey, E. C. (1997). *Maximum rpm: Taking the red hat package manager to the limit*. Red Hat Software.

Baldwin, C. Y. (2015). *Bottlenecks, modules and dynamic architectural capabilities*. Harvard Business School Finance Working Paper, (15-028).

Baldwin, C. Y. (2018). *Design Rules, Volume 2: How Technology Shapes Organizations: Chapter 14 Introducing Open Platforms and Business Ecosystems*. Harvard Business School, Harvard Business School Research Paper Series, 19-035.

Baldwin, C. Y., & Woodard, C. J. (2009). The architecture of platforms: A unified view. *Platforms, Markets and Innovation, 32*, 19-44.

Barbrook, R. (1998). The hi-tech gift economy. *First Monday*.

Bekkelund, K. J. (2011). *Succeeding with freemium*. Norwegian University of Science and Technology.

Benkler, Y. (2002). Coase's penguin, or, linux and" the nature of the firm. *The Yale Law Journal*, 369–446.

Benkler, Y. (2006). *The Wealth of Networks: How Social Production Transforms Markets and Freedom*. Yale University Press.

Benkler, Y. (2013). Commons and Growth: The Essential Role of Open Commons in Market Economies. *The University of Chicago Law Review. University of Chicago. Law School*.

Benkler, Y. (2017). Peer production, the commons, and the future of the firm. *Strategic Organization*, *15*(2), 264–274. doi:10.1177/1476127016652606

Benkler, Y. (2019). De la comunitat imaginada a la comunitat de pràctica, Sharing Cities. *Capítol*, *13*, 311–323.

Berlinguer, M. (2019). *Repensar la Smart City: Barcelona: ciudad abierta, colaborativa y democrática*. Icaria.

Berlinguer, M. (2020a). Commons, Markets and Public Policy. *Transform!*

Berlinguer, M. (2016). *Quantifying Value in Commons-based Peer production. Digital Method Winter School*. University of Amsterdam.

Berlinguer, M. (2018). The value of sharing. How commons have become part of informational capitalism and what we can learn from it. The case of FOSS. *Rassegna Italiana di Sociologia*, *59*(2), 263–288.

Berlinguer, M. (2020b). New commons: Towards a necessary reappraisal. *Popular Communication*, *18*(3), 201–215.

Berlinguer, M. (2021). Digital Commons as new Infrastructure: A new generation of public policy for digital transformation. *Umanistica Digitale*, (11), 5–25.

Bhartiya, S. (2016, August 27). *CIO. Linus Torvalds says GPL was defining factor in Linux's success*. Retrieved September 3, 2022, from https://www.cio.com/article/238985/linus-torvalds-says-gpl-was-defining-factor-in-linuxs-success.html

Blanke, T., & Pybus, J. (2020). The material conditions of platforms: Monopolization through decentralization. *Social Media + Society*, *6*(4).

Błaszczyk, M., Popović, M., Zajdel, K., & Zajdel, R. (2022, October 17). The Impact of the COVID-19 Pandemic on the Organisation of Remote Work in IT Companies. *Sustainability (Basel)*, *14*(20), 13373. Advance online publication. doi:10.3390u142013373

Blind, K., & Böhm, M. (2019). The Relationship Between Open Source Software and Standard Setting. EUR 29867 EN, Publications Office of the European Union. doi:10.2760/163594

Blind, K., Böhm, M., Grzegorzewska, P., Katz, A., Muto, S., Pätsch, S., & Schubert, T. (2021). The impact of Open Source Software and Hardware on technological independence, competitiveness and innovation in the EU economy. Final Study Report. European Commission.

Blind, K. (2004). *The Economics of Standards*. North Hampton.

Blind, K., & Jungmittag, A. (2008). The impact of patents and standards on macroeconomic growth: A panel approach covering four countries and 12 sectors. *Journal of Productivity Analysis, 29*(1), 51–60.

Boisot, M. (2010, November 18). *The City as a Complex Adaptive System: Lessons from the ATLAS Experiment at the LHC.* Retrieved from https://www.gcph.co.uk/assets/0000/0900/Max_Boisot__summary_paper_final.pdf

Bollier, D. (2014). *Think like a Commoner. A Short Introduction to the Life of the Commons. Gabriola Island.* New Society Publishers.

Boltanski, L., & Chiapello, E. (2005). The new spirit of capitalism. *International Journal of Politics Culture and Society, 18*(3), 161–188.

Bonaccorsi, A., & Rossi, C. (2004, January). Altruistic individuals, selfish firms? The structure of motivation in Open Source software. *First Monday, 9*(1), 1. doi:10.5210/fm.v9i1.1113

Bonvoisin, J., Thomas, L., Mies, R., Gros, C., Stark, R., Samuel, K., Jochem, R., & Boujut, J.-F. (2017). Current state of practices in open source product development. DS 87-2. In *21st International Conference on Engineering Design (Vol 2).* Design Processes, Design Organisation and Management.

Bonvoisin, J., Buchert, T., Preidel, M., & Stark, R. (2018). How participative is open source hardware? Insights from online repository mining. *Design Science, 4*(4), 1–31. doi:10.1017/dsj.2018.15

Bonvoisin, J., Mies, R., Boujut, J.-F., & Stark, R. (2017). What is the "Source" of Open Source Hardware? *Journal of Open Hardware, 1*(1), 1–18. doi:10.5334/joh.7

Borges' original quote: "Don't talk unless you can improve the silence." (n.d.). https://www.goodreads.com/quotes/670428-don-t-talk-unless-you-can-improve-the-silence https://en.wikipedia.org/wiki/Jorge_Luis_Borges

Bowman, C., & Ambrosini, V. (2000). Value Creation Versus Value Capture: Towards a Coherent Definition of Value in Strategy. *British Journal of Management, 11*(11), 1–15. doi:10.1111/1467-8551.00147

Bregman, R. (2021). *Human Kind a Hopeful History.* Bloomsbury Publishing PLC.

Breuer, H., & Lüdeke-Freund, F. (2018). Values-Based Business Model Innovation: A Toolkit. In Sustainable business models: Principles, Promise, and Practice. Springer. doi:10.1007/978-3-319-73503-0_18

Brooks, F. P. (1995). *The Mythical Man-Month: Essays on Software Engineering.* Addison-Wesley Professional.

Bryant, S. L., Forte, A., & Bruckman, A. (2005). Becoming Wikipedian: Transformation of Participation in a Collaborative Online Encyclopedia. *Proceedings of the 2005 International ACM SIGGROUP Conference on Supporting Group Work*, 1–10. 10.1145/1099203.1099205

Burke, M., Marlow, C., & Lento, T. (2009). Feed Me: Motivating Newcomer Contribution in Social Network Sites. *Proceedings of the SIGCHI Conference on Human Factors in Computing Systems*, 945–954. 10.1145/1518701.1518847

Burt, J. (2023, February 22). *Open source software has its perks, but supply chain risks can't be ignored.* The Register. Retrieved from https://www.theregister.com/2023/02/22/open_software_supply_chain_risks/

Bush, V. (1945, July). As We May Think. *The Atlantic Monthly.* Retrieved from https://web.mit.edu/STS.035/www/PDFs/think.pdf

Canfora, G., di Penta, M., Oliveto, R., & Panichella, S. (2012). Who is Going to Mentor Newcomers in Open Source Projects? *Proceedings of the ACM SIGSOFT 20th International Symposium on the Foundations of Software Engineering*, 44:1–44:11. 10.1145/2393596.2393647

Cantrell, D. (2021). *Rpminspect.* Retrieved from https://rpminspect.readthedocs.io/en/latest/

Capiluppi, A., & Michlmayr, M.F. (2007). From the Cathedral to the Bazaar: An Empirical Study of the Lifecycle of Volunteer Community Projects. In *Open Source Development, Adoption and Innovation.* Springer-Verlag Boston.

Castells, M. (2004). Informationalism, networks, and the network society: a theoretical blueprint. *The network society: A cross-cultural perspective*, 3-45.

Cennamo, C., Gawer, A., & Jacobides, M. G. (2018). Towards a theory of ecosystems. *Strategic Management Journal*, 39, 2255–2276.

Cent O. S. Community. (2016). *CentOS Kojihub.* Retrieved from https://kojihub.stream.centos.org/koji/

Cent O. S. Community. (2021). *Special interest groups.* Retrieved from https://wiki.centos.org/SpecialInterestGroup

Cha, S.-J., Jeon, S. H., Jeong, Y. J., Kim, J. M., & Jung, S. (2022). OS noise Analysis on Azalea-unikernel. *2022 24th International Conference on Advanced Communication Technology (ICACT)*, 81-84. 10.23919/ICACT53585.2022.9728776

Chandler, A. D. Jr. (1993). *The visible hand.* Harvard University Press.

Chengalur-Smith, I. N., Sidorova, A., & Daniel, S. L. (2010, November). Sustainability of Free/ Libre Open Source Projects: A Longitudinal Study. *Journal of the Association for Information Systems, 11*(11), 657–683. doi:10.17705/1jais.00244

Chen, K.-H., Günzel, M., Jablkowski, B., Buschhoff, M., & Chen, J.-J. (2022). Unikernel-Based Real-Time Virtualization Under Deferrable Servers: Analysis and Realization. *34th Euromicro Conference on Real-Time Systems (ECRTS 2022), 231.* 10.4230/LIPIcs.ECRTS.2022.6

Cherif, R., & Hasanov, F. (2019). *The return of the policy that shall not be named: Principles of industrial policy.* International Monetary Fund.

Chesbrough, H. (2006). *Open business models: How to thrive in the new innovation landscape.* Harvard Business Press.

Chimera Linux. (n.d.). Retrieved from https://chimera-linux.org/

Choi, B. R. (2012). *Essays on Socialization in Online Groups.* Tepper School of Business - Carneggie Mellon University.

Choi, B., Alexander, K., Kraut, R. E., & Levine, J. M. (2010). Socialization Tactics in Wikipedia and Their Effects. *Proceedings of the 2010 ACM Conference on Computer Supported Cooperative Work, 107–116.* 10.1145/1718918.1718940

CKI Project Authors. (2022). *Continuous Kernel Integration (CKI) Project.* Retrieved from https://cki-project.org/

Coase, R. H. (1937). The nature of the firm. *Economica, 4*(16), 386-405.

Colazo, J., & Fang, Y. (2009, May). Impact of License Choice on Open Source Software Development Activity. *Journal of the American Society for Information Science and Technology, 60*(5), 997–1011. doi:10.1002/asi.21039

Comission, E. U. (2021). *Study about the impact of open source software and hardware on technological independence, competitiveness and innovation in the EU economy.* https:// digital-strategy.ec.europa.eu/en/library/study-about-impact-open-source-software-and-hardware-technological-independence-competitiveness-and

Constantinides, P., Henfridsson, O., & Parker, G. G. (2018). Introduction—Platforms and infrastructures in the digital age. *Information Systems Research, 29*(2), 381–400.

Corbet, J. (2013). *ACPI for ARM?* Retrieved from https://lwn.net/Articles/574439/

Corbet, J. (2018). *Software-tag-based kasan.* Retrieved from https://lwn.net/Articles/766768/

Coriat, B. (2015). *Le retour des communs: & la crise de l'idéologie propriétaire.* Editions Les liens qui libèrent.

Council of the European Union. (2020). *Berlin Declaration on Digital Society and Value-based Digital Government.* Accessed December 15, 2021. https://digital-strategy.ec.europa.eu/en/news/berlin-declaration-digital-society-and-value-based-digital-government

Creative Commons website. (n.d.). *Creative Commons: When we share, everyone wins.* Retrieved August 28, 2022, from https://creativecommons.org/

Cubranic, D., Murphy, G. C., Singer, J., & Booth, K. S. (2005, June). Hipikat: A project memory for software development. *IEEE Transactions on Software Engineering, 31*(6), 446–465. doi:10.1109/TSE.2005.71

Cusumano, M. (2004). The business of software. Free Press.

Dagenais, B., Ossher, H., Bellamy, R. K. E., Robillard, M. P., & de Vries, J. P. 2010. Moving into a new software project landscape. *Proceedings of the 2010 ACM/IEEE 32nd International Conference on Software Engineering,* 275–284. 10.1145/1806799.1806842

Danish Design Center. (2018). *Remodel, A toolkit for Open Design Business Models.* https://remodel.dk

David, P. A. (2001). *Path dependence, its critics and the quest for historical economics.* Evolution and Path Dependence in Economic Ideas.

David, P. A., & Shapiro, J. S. (2008). Community-based production of open-source software: What do we know about the developers who participate? *Information Economics and Policy, 20*(4), 364–398.

De Filippi, P. (2018). Blockchain: A global infrastructure for distributed governance and local manufacturing. In Fab City the mass distribution of (almost) anything. Barcelona: IAAC Fab Lab Barcelona.

De Streel, A., & Ledger, M. (2021). *New ways of oversight for the digital economy.* CERRE Issue Paper.

Deshpande, A., & Riehle, D. (2006). The Total Growth of Open-source. *Open-source Development Communities and Quality, 275,* 197–209. doi:10.1007/978-0-387-09684-1_16

Dias, S. (2021). *Fabricademy 2021-22 Workshop HILO Machine Part 1.* https://vimeo.com/649695293/dddf9f225d

D-Link GPL source code support. (n.d.). *D-Link | Technical Support | Downloads.* Retrieved August 28, 2022, from https://tsd.dlink.com.tw/dlist?OS=GPL

Dopfer, K., Foster, J., & Potts, J. (2004). Micro-meso-macro. *Journal of Evolutionary Economics, 14*(3), 263–279.

Dosi, G. (1982). Technological paradigms and technological trajectories: A suggested interpretation of the determinants and directions of technical change. *Research Policy, 11*(3), 147–162.

Drucker, P. (1963, May). Managing for Business Effectiveness. *Harvard Business Review*.

Ducheneaut, N. (2005, August). Socialization in an Open Source Software Community: A Socio-Technical Analysis. *Computer Supported Cooperative Work, 14*(4), 323–368. doi:10.100710606-005-9000-1

Edge, J. (2017). *Specifying the kernel abi*. Retrieved from https://lwn.net/Articles/726021/

Eghbal, N. (2016). Roads and bridges. In *The Unseen labor behind our digital infrastructure*. Ford Foundation. Retrieved at: https://fordfoundcontent.blob.core.windows.net/media/2976/roads-and-bridges-the-unseen-labor-behind-our-digital-infrastructure.pdf

Eglash, R., Babbitt, W., Bennett, A., & Callahan, B. (2016). *Culturally Situated Design Tools: Generative justice as a foundation for stem diversity (Issue December)*. IGI Global.

Electronic Frontier Foundation. (2020, February 20). *The Future of the Internet: Protocols vs. Platforms*. Retrieved from https://www.eff.org/event/future-internet-protocols-vs-platforms

Ellis, S., & Cotton, B. (2011). *Rpm guide*. Fedora Documentation. Retrieved from https://docs.fedoraproject.org/en-US/Fedora_Draft_Documentation/0.1/html/RPM_Guide/index.html

Elver, M. (2020). *Kfence: A low-overhead sampling-based memory safety error detector*. Retrieved from https://lwn.net/Articles/835542/

Elworthy, S. (2020). *The Mighty Heart. How to transform conflict*. Pureprint Group. E-nable project. https://e-nable.fr/fr/

EndlessO. S. (n.d.). Retrieved from https://www.endlessos.org/os

Erhun, D. (2018). *An ICT4D initiative: FabLabs as a potential catalyst for constraint-based innovation in Rwanda* [Master Thesis]. University of Amsterdam.

Fab City Collective. (2018). Fabcity white paper. In *Fab City the mass distribution of (almost) anything*. Barcelona: IAAC Fablab Barcelona.

Fab Market. (n.d.). https://distributeddesign.eu/talent/

Fagerholm, F., Johnson, P., Guinea, A. S., Borenstein, J., & Münch, J. (2014, November). Onboarding in Open Source Projects. *IEEE Software, 31*(6), 54–61. doi:10.1109/MS.2014.107

Fang, Y., & Neufeld, D. (2009, April). Understanding Sustained Participation in Open Source Software Projects. *Journal of Management Information Systems, 25*(4), 9–50. doi:10.2753/MIS0742-1222250401

Farrell, J., & Klemperer, P. (2007). Coordination and lock-in: Competition with switching costs and network effects. Handbook of Industrial Organization, 3, 1967-2072.

Faulkner, R., Walling, S., & Pinchuk, M. (2012). Etiquette in Wikipedia: Weening New Editors into Productive Ones. *Proceedings of the Eighth Annual International Symposium on Wikis and Open Collaboration*. 10.1145/2462932.2462939

Fedora Community. (2016). *Fedora Buildsystem*. Retrieved from https://koji.fedoraproject.org/koji/

Fennell, L. A. (2011). Commons, anticommons, semicommons. In *Research handbook on the economics of property law*. Edward Elgar Publishing.

Fjeldsted, A. S., Adalsteinsdottir, G., Howard, T. J., & McAloone, T. (2012). Open Source Development of Tangible Products - from a business perspective. In NordDesign 2012. Creative Commons Netherlands, Premsela: the Netherlands Institute for Design and Fashion and Waag Society.

Fogel, K., & Vasile, J. (2017, November 16). *Guidelines for Funding Open Source Software Development*. Retrieved from https://www.archesproject.org/wp-content/uploads/2018/01/guidelines_funding_OSS.pdf

Fogel, K. (2005). *Producing open source software: How to run a successful free software project*. O'Reilly Media, Inc.

Fogel, K. (2013). *Producing Open Source Software: How to Run a Successful Free Software Project*. O'Reilly Media.

Foss, N. J., & Saebi, T. (2018). Business models and business model innovation: Between wicked and paradigmatic problems. *Long Range Planning*, *51*(1), 9–21. doi:10.1016/j.lrp.2017.07.006

França, A. C. C. (2009). An Empirical Study on Software Engineers Motivational Factors. *Proceedings of the 2009 3rd International Symposium on Empirical Software Engineering and Measurement*, 405–409. 10.1109/ESEM.2009.5316011

França, A. C. C., & da Silva, F. Q. B. (2010). Designing Motivation Strategies for Software Engineering Teams: An Empirical Study. *Proceedings of the 2010 ICSE Workshop on Cooperative and Human Aspects of Software Engineering*, 84–91. 10.1145/1833310.1833324

França, A. C. C., da Silva, F. Q. B., Felix, L. C., & Carneiro, D. E. S. (2014, January). A. de, Carneiro, D.E.S. 2014b. Motivation in software engineering industrial practice: A cross-case analysis of two software organisations. *Information and Software Technology*, *56*(1), 79–101. doi:10.1016/j.infsof.2013.06.006

França, A. C. C., Gouveia, T. B., Santos, P. C. F., Santana, C. A., & da Silva, F. Q. B. (2011). Motivation in software engineering: A systematic review update. *Proceedings of the 15th Annual Conference on Evaluation Assessment in Software Engineering*, 154–163. 10.1049/ic.2011.0019

Frankenberger, K., Weiblen, T., & Gassmann, O. (2014). The antecedents of open business models: An exploratory study of incumbent firms. *R & D Management*, *44*(2), 173–188. doi:10.1111/radm.12040

Fraser, N. (2017). A triple movement? Parsing the politics of crisis after Polanyi. In *Beyond neoliberalism* (pp. 29–42). Palgrave Macmillan.

Free Documentation License, G. N. U. v1.3. (n.d.). *GNU.org*. Retrieved August 28, 2022, from https://www.gnu.org/licenses/fdl-1.3.html

FreeRTOS website. (n.d.). *FreeRTOS - Market leading RTOS (Real Time Operating System) for embedded systems with Internet of Things extensions.* Retrieved August 31, 2022, from https://www.freertos.org/index.html

Freire, P. (1993). Pedagogy of the Oppressed. The Continuum Publishing Company. (Original work published 1970)

Freire, R. (2017). *The code path - how does new code enter red hat products?* Retrieved from https://www.redhat.com/en/blog/code-path-how-does-new-code-enter-red-hat-products

Frischmann, B. M. (2012). *Infrastructure: The social value of shared resources.* Oxford University Press.

Fugelstad, P., Dwyer, P., Moses, J. F., Kim, J., Mannino, C. A., Terveen, L., & Snyder, M. (2012). What Makes Users Rate (Share, Tag, Edit...)?: Predicting Patterns of Participation in Online Communities. *Proceedings of the ACM 2012 Conference on Computer Supported Cooperative Work*, 969–978. 10.1145/2145204.2145349

Fuster Morell, M. (2014). Governance of online creation communities for the building of digital commons: Viewed through the framework of the institutional analysis and development. In Governing Knowledge Commons. Oxford University Press.

Fuster Morell, M., Carballa Schichowski, B., Smorto, G., Espelt, R., Imperatore, P., Rebordosa, M., Rodriguez, N., Senabre, E., & Ciurcina, M. (2017). Decode. *Decentralised Citizens Owned Data Ecosystem.*, *1*(3), 1–144.

Fuster Morell, M., & Espelt, R. (2018). A Framework for Assessing Democratic Qualities in Collaborative Economy Platforms: Analysis of 10 Cases in Barcelona. *Urban Science (Basel, Switzerland)*, *2*(3), 1–13. doi:10.3390/urbansci2030061

Garrett, M. (2013). *ACPI vs Device Tree - moving forward.* Retrieved from https://lkml.org/lkml/2013/8/20/556

Gassmann, O., Frankenberger, K., & Csik, M. (2014). *The business model navigator.* Pearson Education.

Gavras, K. (2019). Open source beyond software: Re-invent open design on the Common's ground. *Journal of Peer Production*, *13*, 1–25.

Gawer, A. (2014). Bridging differing perspectives on technological platforms: Toward an integrative framework. *Research Policy*, *43*(7), 1239–1249.

Gawer, A., & Cusumano, M. A. (2014). Industry platforms and ecosystem innovation. *Journal of Product Innovation Management, 31*(3), 417–433.

Geels, F. W. (2002). Technological transitions as evolutionary reconfiguration processes: A multi-level perspective and a case-study. *Research Policy, 31*(8-9), 1257–1274.

Geels, F. W. (2010). Ontologies, socio-technical transitions (to sustainability), and the multi-level perspective. *Research Policy, 39*(4), 495–510.

Geels, F. W., & Schot, J. (2007). Typology of sociotechnical transition pathways. *Research Policy, 36*(3), 399–417.

Gérman, D., & Hassan, A. (2009). License integration patterns: Addressing license mismatches in component-based development. *2009 IEEE 31st international conference on software engineering*, 188-198.

Gérman, D., Penta, M. D., & Davies, J. (2010). Understanding and auditing the licensing of open source software distributions. *2010 IEEE 18th International Conference on Program Comprehension*, 84-93.

Gérman, D., Gonzalez-Barahona, J., & Robles, G. (2007). A Model to Understand the Building and Running Inter-Dependencies of Software. *14th Working Conference on Reverse Engineering (WCRE 2007),* 140-149. 10.1109/WCRE.2007.5

GitHub. (2023). *GitHub Search*. Retrieved 2023, from https://github.com/search?q=is:public

GNU Lesser General Public License v2.1. (n.d.). *GNU.org*. Retrieved August 20, 2022, from https://www.gnu.org/licenses/old-licenses/lgpl-2.1.html

GNU Library General Public License v2.0. (n.d.). *GNU.org*. Retrieved August 29, 2022, from https://www.gnu.org/licenses/old-licenses/lgpl-2.0.html

GNU. (2007a). *Gnu general public license.* https://www.gnu.org/licenses/gpl-3.0.html

GNU. (2007b). *Gnu general public license.* https://www.gnu.org/licenses/lgpl-3.0.html

Goffin, K., Åhlström, P., Bianchi, M., & Richtnér, A. (2019). Perspective: State-of-the-Art: The Quality of Case Study Research in Innovation Management. *Journal of Product Innovation Management, 36*(5), 586–615. doi:10.1111/jpim.12492

Gorwa, R. (2019). What is platform governance? *Information Communication and Society, 22*(6), 854–871.

GPL-Compatible Free Software Licenses. (n.d.). Free Software Foundation. Retrieved March 3, 2023, from https://www.gnu.org/licenses/license-list.html#GPLCompatibleLicenses

Halfaker, A., Geiger, R. S., Morgan, J., & Riedl, J. (2013a, May). The Rise and Decline of an Open Collaboration System: How Wikipedia's reaction to sudden popularity is causing its decline. *The American Behavioral Scientist, 57*(5), 664–688. doi:10.1177/0002764212469365

Halfaker, A., Keyes, O., & Taraborelli, D. (2013b). Making Peripheral Participation Legitimate: Reader Engagement Experiments in Wikipedia. *Proceedings of the 2013 Conference on Computer Supported Cooperative Work*, 849–860. 10.1145/2441776.2441872

Halfaker, A., Kittur, A., & Riedl, J. (2011). Don't Bite the Newbies: How Reverts Affect the Quantity and Quality of Wikipedia Work. *Proceedings of the 7th International Symposium on Wikis and Open Collaboration*, 163–172. 10.1145/2038558.2038585

Hannebauer, C., Book, M., & Gruhn, V. (2014). An Exploratory Study of Contribution Barriers Experienced by Newcomers to Open Source Software Projects. *Proceedings of the First International Workshop on CrowdSourcing in Software Engineering*, 11–14. 10.1145/2593728.2593732

Hardin, G. (1968). The tragedy of the commons: The population problem has no technical solution; it requires a fundamental extension in morality. *Science, 162*(3859), 1243–1248. PMID:5699198

Harvard Business School Professor Clayton Christensen introduced the popularized notion of disruption in his 1997 book *The Innovator's Dilemma*. (n.d.). https://en.wikipedia.org/wiki/Clayton_Christensen

Hasan, R. (2002). *History of linux*. https://www.cs.cmu.edu/~awb/linux.history.html

Hayden, M. (2019a). *Continuous integration testing for the Linux kernel*. Retrieved from https://opensource.com/article/19/6/continuous-kernel-integration-linux

Hayden, M. (2019b). *The Lifecycle of Linux Kernel Testing*. Retrieved from https://opensource.com/article/19/8/linux-kernel-testing

Henkel, J. (2004). Open-source software from commercial firms–tools, complements, and collective invention. *Journal of Business Economics, 4*(4), 1–23.

Herraiz, I., Izquierdo-Cortazar, D., Rivas-Hernández, F., Gonzalez-Barahona, J., Robles, G., Duenas-Dominguez, S., Garcia-Campos, C., Gato, J. F., & Tovar, L. (2009, March). Flossmetrics: Free/libre/open source software metrics. In *2009 13th European Conference on Software Maintenance and Reengineering* (pp. 281-284). IEEE.

Herraiz, I., Robles, G., Amor, J. J., Romera, T., Barahona, J. M. G., & Carlos, J. (2006). The processes of joining in global distributed software projects. *Proceedings of the 2006 International Workshop on Global Software Development for the Practitioners*, 27–33. 10.1145/1138506.1138513

Hertel, G., Niedner, S., & Herrmann, S. (2003, July). Motivation of software developers in Open Source projects: An Internet-based survey of contributors to the Linux kernel. *Research Policy, 32*(7), 1159–1177. doi:10.1016/S0048-7333(03)00047-7

Hess, C., & Ostrom, E. (2011). *Understanding Knowledge as Commons. From Theory to Practice.* MIT Press.

Hippel, E. V., & Krogh, G. V. (2003). Open source software and the "private-collective" innovation model: Issues for organization science. *Organization Science, 14*(2), 209–223.

Holon, I. Q. (2020, August 6). *Global EdTech market to reach $404B by 2025 - 16.3% CAGR. 'Post-COVID' update to HolonIQ's Global Market Sizing.* Retrieved from https://www.holoniq. com/notes/global-education-technology-market-to-reach-404b-by-2025

Hopkins, R. (2019). *From what is to what if: unleashing the power of imagination to create the future we want.* Somerset House.

Hsieh, G., Hou, Y., Chen, I., & Truong, K. N. (2013). Welcome! Social and Psychological Predictors of Volunteer Socializers in Online Communities. *Proceedings of the 2013 Conference on Computer Supported Cooperative Work*, 827–838. 10.1145/2441776.2441870

Huawei Open Source Release Center. (n.d.). *HUAWEI Consumer.* Retrieved August 28, 2022, from https://consumer.huawei.com/en/opensource/

Hughes, J. (2005). *CentOS Mailing List - Official Announce List Notification.* Retrieved from https://lists.centos.org/pipermail/centos/2005-March/357451.html

Hughes, T. P. (1987). The evolution of large technological systems: The social construction of technological systems. In W. E. Bijker, T. P. Hughes, & T. J. Pinch (Eds.), *New Directions in the Sociology and History of Technology* (pp. 51–82). MIT Press.

Huizingh, E. K. (2011). Open innovation: State of the art and future perspectives. *Technovation, 31*(1), 2–9. doi:10.1016/j.technovation.2010.10.002

Hunter, P., & Walli, S. (2013). The rise and evolution of the open source software foundation. *IFOSS L. Rev., 5*, 31.

iFross. (2006). *LG Frankfurt a.M., Urteil v. 06.09.2006, Az. 2-6 O 224/06.* Institut für Rechtsfragen der Freien und Open Source Software. https://www.ifross.org/Fremdartikel/urteil_lg_frankfurt_gpl. pdf

Inside Daily Brief. (2023, May 3). *American eighth-graders are performing worse on history & civics exams* [Blog post]. Retrieved from https://inside.com/daily/posts/american-eighth-graders-are-performing-worse-on-history-civics-exams-368163

Izquierdo, J. L. C., & Cabot, J. (2018, May). The role of foundations in open source projects. In *Proceedings of the 40th international conference on software engineering: software engineering in society* (pp. 3-12). Academic Press.

Izquierdo, J. L. C., & Cabot, J. (2020). *A Survey of Software Foundations in Open Source.* arXiv preprint arXiv:2005.10063.

Jaeger, T., Koglin, O., Kreutzer, T., Metzger, A., & Schulz, C. (2005). Die GPL kommentiert und erklärt. O'Reilly.

Jensen, C., King, S., & Kuechler, V. (2011). Joining Free/Open Source Software Communities: An Analysis of Newbies' First Interactions on Project Mailing Lists. *Proceedings of the 44th Hawaii International Conference on System Sciences*, 1–10. 10.1109/HICSS.2011.264

Jergensen, C., Sarma, A., & Wagstrom, P. (2011). The Onion Patch: Migration in Open Source Ecosystems. *Proceedings of the 19th ACM SIGSOFT Symposium and the 13th European Conf. on Foundations of Software Engineering*, 70–80.

Jergensen, N. (2007, May). Developer autonomy in the FreeBSD open source project. *The Journal of Management and Governance, 11*(2), 119–128. doi:10.100710997-007-9026-5

Jessop, B. (2001). Regulationist and autopoieticist reflections on Polanyi's account of market economies and the market society. *New Political Economy, 6*(2), 213–232.

Jessop, B. (2013). Revisiting the regulation approach: Critical reflections on the contradictions, dilemmas, fixes and crisis dynamics of growth regimes. *Capital and Class, 37*(1), 5–24.

Johansson, F. (2004). *The Medici Effect*. Harvard Business School Press.

Joyce, A., & Paquin, R. L. (2016). The triple layered business model canvas: A tool to design more sustainable business models. *Journal of Cleaner Production, 135*, 1474–1486. doi:10.1016/j.jclepro.2016.06.067

Kanfer, R. (1990). Motivation Theory and Industrial and Organizational Psychology. In Handbook of Psychology, Industrial and Organizational Psychology. Counsulting Psychologist Press.

Kattel, R., Drechsler, W., & Reinert, E. S. (2009). Introduction: Carlota Perez and evolutionary economics. Techno-Economic Paradigms: Essays in honour of Carlota Perez, 1-18.

Katz, M. L., & Shapiro, C. (1994). Systems competition and network effects. *The Journal of Economic Perspectives, 8*(2), 93–115.

Katz, M., & Sallet, J. (2018). Multisided platforms and antitrust enforcement. *The Yale Law Journal*, 2142–2175.

Kelly, K. (1999). *New rules for the new economy: 10 radical strategies for a connected world*. Penguin.

Ke, W., & Zhang, P. (2010, December). The Effects of Extrinsic Motivations and Satisfaction in Open Source Software Development. *Journal of the Association for Information Systems, 11*(12), 784–808. doi:10.17705/1jais.00251

Kim, W. C., & Maubourgne, R. (2015). *Blue Ocean Strategy: How to Create Uncontested Market Space and Make the Competition Irrelevant*. Harvard Business Review Press.

Knell, M. (2021). The digital revolution and digitalized network society. *Review of Evolutionary Political Economy, 2*(1), 9–25.

Köhler, J., Geels, F. W., Kern, F., Markard, J., Onsongo, E., Wieczorek, A., ... Wells, P. (2019). An agenda for sustainability transitions research: State of the art and future directions. *Environmental Innovation and Societal Transitions, 31*, 1–32.

Kollock, P. (1999). The economies of online cooperation: Gifts and public goods in cyberspace. *Communities in Cyberspace, 239.*

Kon-Tiki expedition. (n.d.). In *Wikipedia, The Free Encyclopedia.* Retrieved July 4, 2023, from https://en.wikipedia.org/wiki/Kon-Tiki_expedition

Kopnina, H., & Poldner, K. (2022). *Circular Economy. Challenges and opportunities for Ethical and Sustainable Business.* Routledge.

Kostakis, V. (2019). How to reap the benefits of the "digital revolution"? Modularity and the commons. *Halduskultuur, 20*(1), 4–19.

Kostakis, V., & Bauwens, M. (2014). *Network society and future scenarios for a collaborative economy.* Springer.

Kostakis, V., Niaros, V., Dafermos, G., & Bauwens, M. (2015). Design global, manufacture local: Exploring the contours of an emerging productive model. *Futures, 73*, 126–135. doi:10.1016/j.futures.2015.09.001

Kraut, R. E., Burke, M., Riedl, J., & Resnick, P. (2012). The Challenges of Dealing with Newcomers. In Building Successful Online Communities: Evidence-Based Social Design. MIT Press. doi:10.7551/mitpress/8472.003.0006

Krishnamurthy, S. (2005). An Analysis of Open-source Business Models. *Source, 54*, 267–278.

Kuenzer, S., Bădoiu, V.-A., Lefeuvre, H., Santhanam, S., Jung, A., Gain, G., Soldani, C., Lupu, C., Teodorescu, Ş., Răducanu, C., Banu, C., Mathy, L., Deaconescu, R., Raiciu, C., & Huici, F. (2021). Unikraft: Fast, Specialized Unikernels the Easy Way. *Proceedings of the Sixteenth European Conference on Computer Systems*, 376-394. 10.1145/3447786.3456248

Kuhn, T. S. (1974). Second thoughts on paradigms. *The Structure of Scientific Theories, 2*, 459-482.

Kumar, M., Tsolakis, N., Agarwal, A., & Srai, J. S. (2020). Developing distributed manufacturing strategies from the perspective of a product-process matrix. *International Journal of Production Economics, 219*, 1–17. doi:10.1016/j.ijpe.2019.05.005

Laadan, O., & Nieh, J. (2010, May). Operating system virtualization: practice and experience. *Proceedings of the 3rd Annual Haifa Experimental Systems Conference*, 1-12.

Labrèche, G., Evans, D., Marszk, D., Mladenov, T., Shiradhonkar, V., & Zelenevskiy, V. (2022). Agile Development and Rapid Prototyping in a Flying Mission with Open Source Software Reuse On-Board the OPS-SAT Spacecraft. *IAA SCITECH 2022 Forum.* 10.2514/6.2022-0648

Lakhani, K. R., & Wolf, R. G. (2003). Why hackers do what they do: Understanding motivation and effort in free/open source software projects. *Open Source Software Projects.*

Lakhani, K. R., & Wolf, R. G. (2005). *Perspectives on Free and Open Source Software.* The MIT Press.

Lampe, C., Obar, J., Ozkaya, E., Zube, P., & Velasquez, A. (2012). Classroom Wikipedia Participation Effects on Future Intentions to Contribute. *Proceedings of the ACM 2012 Conference on Computer Supported Cooperative Work*, 403–406. 10.1145/2145204.2145267

Larabel, M. (2021). *Centos sig to help get community centos stream features into next rhel releases.* Retrieved from https://www.phoronix.com/scan.php?page=news_item&px=CentOS-Stream-Features-To-RHEL

Lave, J., & Wenger, E. (1991). *Situated Learning : Legitimate Peripheral Participation.* Cambridge University Press. doi:10.1017/CBO9780511815355

Lazzarato, M. (1996). Immaterial labor. *Radical thought in Italy: A potential politics,* 133-47.

Lee, M. (2008, December 11). *Free Software Foundation Files Suit Against Cisco For GPL Violations — Free Software Foundation — Working together for free software.* Free Software Foundation. Retrieved August 13, 2022, from https://www.fsf.org/news/2008-12-cisco-suit

Lee, S., Park, D.-H., & Han, I. (2014, January). New members' online socialization in online communities: The effects of content quality and feedback on new members' content-sharing intentions. *Computers in Human Behavior*, *30*, 344–354. doi:10.1016/j.chb.2013.09.015

Lepak, D. P., Smith, K. G., & Taylor, M. S. (2007). Value creation and value capture: A multilevel perspective. *Academy of Management Review*, *32*(1), 180–194.

Lerner, J., & Tirole, J. (2005). Economic Perspectives on Open-source. *Perspectives on Free and Open-Source Software, 15*, 47-78.

Lerner, J., & Tirole, J. (2002). Some simple economics of open source. *The Journal of Industrial Economics*, *50*(2), 197–234.

Levine, F., Locke, C., Searls, D., & Weinberger, D. (2000). *The Cluetrain Manifesto.* Basic Books.

Lindman, J., & Rajala, R. (2012). How Open Source Has Changed the Software Industry: Perspectives from Open Source Entrepreneurs. *Technology Innovation Management Review*, *2*(1), 5–11. doi:10.22215/timreview/510

Linux Foundation. (2023). Linux Foundation - Decentralized innovation, built with trust. Retrieved March 5, 2023, from https://www.linuxfoundation.org/

Litman, J. (2014). The public domain. *Emory Law Journal, 39*(4), 965–1022.

Li, Z., & Seering, W. (2019). Does open source hardware have a sustainable business model? An analysis of value creation and capture mechanisms in open source hardware companies. *The International Conference on Engineering Design, ICED.* 10.1017/dsi.2019.230

Lüdeke-Freund, F., Breuer, H., & Massa, L. (2022). *Sustainable Business Model Design. 45 Patterns.* Academic Press.

Lundell, B., Butler, S., Fischer, T., Gamalielsson, J., Brax, C., Feist, J., ... Mattsson, A. (2021). Effective Strategies for Using Open Source Software and Open Standards in Organizational Contexts: Experiences From the Primary and Secondary Software Sectors. *IEEE Software, 39*(1), 84–92.

Madhavapeddy, A., Mortier, R., Rotsos, C., Scott, D., Singh, B., Gazagnaire, T., Smith, S., Hand, S., & Crowcroft, J. (2013). Unikernels: Library operating systems for the cloud. *Computer Architecture News, 41*(1), 461–472. doi:10.1145/2490301.2451167

Make Works. (n.d.). https://make.works/companies

Malone, T., Weill, P., Lai, R., D'Urso, V., Herman, G., Apel, T., & Woerner, S. (2006). Do Some Business Models Perform Better than Others? SSRN *Electronic Journal.* doi:10.2139/ssrn.920667

Martinez-Alier, J., Munda, G., & O'Neill, J. (1998). Weak comparability of values as a foundation for ecological economics. *Ecological Economics, 26*(3), 277–286.

Masnick, M. (2019, August 21). *Protocols, Not Platforms: A Technological Approach to Free Speech.* Knight First Amendment Institute at Columbia University. Retrieved from https://knightcolumbia.org/content/protocols-not-platforms-a-technological-approach-to-free-speech

Masters, J., & Blum, R. (2007). *Professional linux programming.* Wiley.

Mauss, M. (2002). *The gift: The form and reason for exchange in archaic societies.* Routledge.

Mazzucato, M., Entsminger, J., & Kattel, R. (2020). Public value and platform governance. *UCL Institute for Innovation and Public Purpose WP, 11.*

Mazzucato, M., Entsminger, J., & Kattel, R. (2021). Reshaping Platform-Driven Digital Markets. *Regulating Big Tech: Policy Responses to Digital Dominance, 17.*

Mazzucato, M., Kattel, R., & Ryan-Collins, J. (2021). Industrial Policy's Comeback. *Boston Review.* https://bostonreview.net/forum/industrial-policys-comeback/

Mears, J. (2006). *Ever wonder how red hat got its name?* Computer World. Retrieved from https://www.computerworld.com/article/2548974/ever-wonder-how-red-hat-got-its-name-.html

Meirelles, P., Santos, C., Miranda, J., Kon, F., Terceiro, A., & Chavez, C. (2010). A study of the relationships between source code metrics and attractiveness in free software projects. *Proceedings of the 2010 Brazilian Symposium on Software Engineering,* 11–20. 10.1109/SBES.2010.27

Menichinelli, M. (2015). Open Meta-Design. In D. Bihanic (Ed.), *Empowering Users through Design* (pp. 193–212). Springer. doi:10.1007/978-3-319-13018-7_11

Midha, V., Palvia, P., Singh, R., & Kshetri, N. (2010). Improving open source software maintenance. *Journal of Computer Information Systems*, *50*(3), 81–90.

Mies, R., Bonvoisin, J., & Jochem, R. (2019). Harnessing the Synergy Potential of Open Source Hardware Communities. In Co-Creation. Management for Professionals (pp. 129–145). Springer Nature Switzerland. doi:10.1007/978-3-319-97788-1_11

MillerA.SvistunovM.DoleželováM. (2020). *RPM Packaging Guide*. Retrieved from https://rpm-packaging-guide.github.io/

Moglen, E., & Choudhary, M. (2016, February 26). *The Linux Kernel, CDDL and Related Issues*. Software Freedom Law Center. Retrieved September 3, 2022, from https://softwarefreedom.org/resources/2016/linux-kernel-cddl.html

Moore, M. H. (2014). Public value accounting: Establishing the philosophical basis. *Public Administration Review*, *74*(4), 465–477.

Morell, M. F., Salcedo, J. L., & Berlinguer, M. (2016, September). Debate about the concept of value in Commons-Based Peer Production. In *International Conference on Internet Science* (pp. 27-41). Springer.

Morgan, J. T., Bouterse, S., Walls, H., & Stierch, S. (2013). Tea and Sympathy: Crafting Positive New User Experiences on Wikipedia. *Proceedings of the 2013 Conference on Computer Supported Cooperative Work*, 839–848. 10.1145/2441776.2441871

Moritz, M., Redlich, T., Grames, P. P., & Wulfsberg, J. P. (2016). Value creation in open-source hardware communities: Case study of Open Source Ecology. In *PICMET 2016 - Portland International Conference on Management of Engineering and Technology: Technology Management For Social Innovation*. Open Desk. https://www.opendesk.cc/

Mozilla Foundation. (2023). Mozilla Foundation - Homepage. Retrieved March 5, 2023, from https://foundation.mozilla.org/en/

Muegge, S. (2013). Platforms, communities, and business ecosystems: Lessons learned about technology entrepreneurship in an interconnected world. *Technology Innovation Management Review*, 5–15.

Nakakoji, K., Yamamoto, Y., Nishinaka, Y., Kishida, K., & Ye, Y. (2002). Evolution Patterns of Open- source Software Systems and Communities. *Proceedings of the International Workshop on Principles of Software Evolution*, 76–85. 10.1145/512035.512055

O'Mahony, S. (2007). The governance of open source initiatives: What does it mean to be community managed? *The Journal of Management and Governance*, *11*(2), 139–150.

O'Neall, G. (n.d.). *spdx/spdx-spec: The SPDX specification in MarkDown and HTML formats.* GitHub repository. Retrieved August 21, 2022, from https://github.com/spdx/spdx-spec

O'Neil, M. (2009). *Cyberchiefs: Autonomy and authority in online tribes.* Pluto Press.

O'Neil, M., Cai, X., Muselli, L., Pailler, F., & Zacchiroli, S. (2021). *The coproduction of open source software by volunteers and big tech firms.* News Media Research Centre, University of Canberra.

O'Reilly, T. (2019). *Antitrust regulators are using the wrong tools to break up Big Tech.* https://qz.com/1666863/why-big-tech-keeps-outsmarting-antitrust-regulators

Onetti, A., & Verma, S. (2009). Open-source Licensing and Business Models, ICFAI. *Journal of Knowledge Management, VII*(1), 68–95.

Open Infrastructure Foundation. (2023). OpenInfra Foundation. Retrieved March 5, 2023, from https://openinfra.dev/about/

Open source license usage on GitHub.com. (2015, March 9). *The GitHub Blog.* Retrieved August 27, 2022, from https://github.blog/2015-03-09-open-source-license-usage-on-github-com

Open source. (n.d.). In *Wikipedia, The Free Encyclopedia.* Retrieved July 4, 2023, from https://en.wikipedia.org/wiki/Open_source

Orcajada, A. (2021). *Material Driven. Fabricademy 2021 Recitation.* https://class.textile-academy.org/classes/2021-22/week06/

Oreg, S., & Nov, O. (2008, September). Exploring motivations for contributing to open source initiatives: The roles of contribution context and personal values. *Computers in Human Behavior, 24*(5), 2055–2073. doi:10.1016/j.chb.2007.09.007

Ostrom, E. (1990). *Governing the Commons. The Evolution of Institutions for Collective Action.* Cambridge University Press. doi:10.1017/CBO9780511807763

Ostrom, E. (1990). *Governing the commons: The evolution of institutions for collective action.* Cambridge university press.

Parker, G., Van Alstyne, M. W., & Jiang, X. (2016). *Platform ecosystems: How developers invert the firm.* Boston University Questrom School of Business Research Paper, (2861574).

Parker, G. G., & Van Alstyne, M. W. (2005). Two-sided network effects: A theory of information product design. *Management Science, 51*(10), 1494–1504.

Park, Y., & Jensen, C. (2009). Beyond pretty pictures: Examining the benefits of code visualization for open source newcomers. *Proceedings of the 5th IEEE International Workshop on Visualizing Software for Understanding and Analysis*, 3–10. 10.1109/VISSOF.2009.5336433

Pearce, J. M. (2012). Building research equipment with free, open-source hardware. *Science, 337*(6100), 1303–1304. doi:10.1126cience.1228183 PMID:22984059

Pearce, J. M. (2017). Emerging Business Models for Open Source Hardware. *Journal of Open Hardware, 1*(1), 1–14. doi:10.5334/joh.4

Perens, B. (1999). The open source definition. *Open Sources: Voices From the Open Source Revolution, 1*, 171-188.

Perens, B. (2005). The emerging economic paradigm of open source. *First Monday.*

Perez, C. (2003). *Technological revolutions and financial capital.* Edward Elgar Publishing.

Perez, C. (2010). Technological revolutions and techno-economic paradigms. *Cambridge Journal of Economics, 34*(1), 185–202.

Perez, C. (2012). Technological revolutions and the role of government in unleashing golden ages. *Journal of Globalization Studies, 3*(2), 19–25.

Perez, C. (2013). Unleashing a golden age after the financial collapse: Drawing lessons from history. *Environmental Innovation and Societal Transitions, 6*, 9–23.

Personal Robots. (2019, March 30). *Vorpal Robot is a open source hexapod toy.* Personal Robots. Retrieved March 3, 2023, from https://www.personalrobots.biz/vorpal-robot-is-a-open-source-hexapod-toy/

Pham, R., Singer, L., Liskin, O., Filho, F. F., & Schneider, K. (2013). Creating a Shared Understanding of Testing Culture on a Social Coding Site. *Proceedings of the 2013 International Conference on Software Engineering*, 112–121. 10.1109/ICSE.2013.6606557

Polanyi, K. (1957). Societies and Economic Systems. In *The Great Transformation.* Beacon Press.

Popp, K. (2019). *Best practices for commercial use of open source software.* Books on Demand.

Popp, K., & Meyer, R. (2010). *Profit from Software Ecosystems: Business Models, Ecosystems and Partnerships in the Software Industry.* Books on Demand.

Popp, K. (2011). Hybrid revenue models of software companies and their relationship to hybrid business models. In B. Regnell & I. Weerd (Eds.), *Software business* (pp. 77–88). Springer.

Popp, K. (2012). Leveraging open source licenses and open source communities in hybrid commercial open source business models. *CEUR Workshop Proceedings, 879*, 33–40.

Porter, D. E., Boyd-Wickizer, S., Howell, J., Olinsky, R., & Hunt, G. C. (2011, March). Rethinking the Library OS from the Top Down. *SIGPLAN Notices, 46*(3), 291–304. doi:10.1145/1961296.1950399

Powell, W. W. (1990). Neither market nor hierarchy. *Sociology of organizations: Structures and relationships*, 30-40.

Prattico, L. (2012). Governance of open source software foundations: Who holds the power? *Technology Innovation Management Review, 2*(12).

Preece, J. (2001). Sociability and usability in online communities: Determining and measuring success. *Behaviour & Information Technology, 20*(5), 347–356. doi:10.1080/01449290110084683

Preston, D. (2014a, May 28). *Will this blog see tomorrow?* Retrieved from https://drprestonsrhsenglitcomp14.blogspot.com/2014/05/will-this-blog-see-tomorrow.html

Preston, D. (2014b, May 28). *Will this blog see tomorrow?* [Blog post]. Retrieved from https://drprestonsrhsenglitcomp14.blogspot.com/2014/05/will-this-blog-see-tomorrow.html

Preston, D. (2020a, August 4). *Achieve the impossible.* Retrieved from https://davidpreston.net/2020/08/04/achieve-the-impossible/

Preston, D. (2020b, June 3). *Last Post Of The School Year/ june 3 w online meeting #50.* Retrieved from https://drprestonsamlitsmhs1920.blogspot.com/

Preston, D. (2021a, August 27). *Learning without a ceiling.* Retrieved from https://davidpreston.net/2021/08/27/learning-without-a-ceiling/

Preston, D. (2021b). *Academy of One: The Power and Promise of Open Source Learning.* Rowman and Littlefield. https://rowman.com/ISBN/9781475859058/Academy-of-One-The-Power-and-Promise-of-Open-Source-Learning

Preston, D. (2021c, October 25). *Declare your digital interdependence (O...SLAP!)* [Blog post]. Retrieved from https://davidpreston.net/2021/10/25/our-declaration-of-digital-interdependence-o-slap/

Preston, D. (2022a, April 13). *Physical fitness is for lead learners too.* Retrieved from https://davidpreston.net/2022/04/13/physical-fitness-is-for-lead-learners-too/

Preston, D. (2022b, March 13). *The Five Fitnesses of Open-Source Learning* [Blog post]. Retrieved from https://davidpreston.net/2022/03/13/the-five-fitnesses-of-open-source-learning/

Preston, D. (n.d.). *This Is Open-Source Learning.* Retrieved from https://davidpreston.net/open-source-learning/

Pujol, N. (2010). Freemium: Attributes of an Emerging Business Model. SSRN *Electronic Journal.* doi:10.2139/ssrn.1718663

Qureshi, I., & Fang, Y. (2011, January). Socialization in Open Source Software Projects: A Growth Mixture Modeling Approach. *Organizational Research Methods, 14*(1), 208–238. doi:10.1177/1094428110375002

Raasch, C., Herstatt, C., & Balka, K. (2009). On the open design of tangible goods. *R & D Management, 39*(4), 382–393. doi:10.1111/j.1467-9310.2009.00567.x

Rabis, F. (2019). *Open Source Ökonomie Diplomarbeit Ehrenwörtliche Erklärung* [PhD]. Technische Universität Dresden.

Rauch, E., Dallasega, P., & Matt, D. T. (2016). Sustainable production in emerging markets through Distributed Manufacturing Systems (DMS). *Journal of Cleaner Production, 135*, 127–138. doi:10.1016/j.jclepro.2016.06.106

Raworth, K. (2017). *Doughnut Economics: Seven ways to think like a 21st century economist.* Random House Business Books.

Raymond, E. (2001). *The Cathedral & the Bazaar* (Revised Edition). O'Reilly.

Raymond, E. S. (1998). Homesteading the noosphere. *First Monday.*

Raymond, E. S. (1999). *The Cathedral and the Bazaar.* O'Reilly & Associates, Inc. doi:10.100712130-999-1026-0

Red Hat Customer Portal. (2015). *The hidden costs of embargoes.* Retrieved from https://access.redhat.com/blogs/766093/posts/1976653

Red Hat Customer Portal. (2022a). *Red Hat Enterprise Linux Life Cycle.* Retrieved from https://access.redhat.com/support/policy/updates/errata

Red Hat Customer Portal. (2022b). *What is backporting and how does it affect Red Hat Enterprise Linux (RHEL)?* Retrieved from https://access.redhat.com/solutions/57665

Red Hat Inc. (2020a). *Fedora/ARK Kernel.* Retrieved from https://cki-project.gitlab.io/kernel-ark/

Red Hat Inc. (2020b). *What is a CVE?* Retrieved from https://www.redhat.com/en/topics/security/what-is-cve

Red Hat Release Engineering. (2021). *DistGit provides home for linux distribution packages.* Retrieved from https://github.com/release-engineering/dist-git

Reich, J. (2022). *Failure to Disrupt.* Harvard Business School Press.

Reichman, J. H., & Uhlir, P. F. (2003). A contractually reconstructed research commons for scientific data in a highly protectionist intellectual property environment. *Law and Contemporary Problems, 66*(1/2), 315–462.

Rideau. (2004). Patents are an Economic Absurdity. *A Journal for Western Man, 28.*

Riehle, D. (2010). The economic case for open source foundations. *Computer, 43*(01), 86–90.

Riehle, D. (2015). How Open Source Is Changing the Software Developer's Career. *Computer, 48*(5), 51–57. doi:10.1109/MC.2015.132

Riehle, D. (2021). The Open Source Distributor Business Model. *Computer, 54*(12), 99–103.

Rifkin, J. (2014). *Ushering In A Smart Green Digital Global Economy To Address Climate Change And Create A More Ecological And Humane Society.* https://www.troisiemerevolutionindustrielle. lu/wp-content/uploads/2016/01/6-9-2015_Digital-Europe_Ushering-In-A-Smart-Green-Digital-Global-Economy-To-Address-Climate-Change-And-Create-A-More-Ecological-And-Humane-Society-2.pdf

Roberts, J. A., Hann, I.-H., & Slaughter, S. A. (2006, July). Understanding the Motivations, Participation, and Performance of Open Source Software Developers: A Longitudinal Study of the Apache Projects. *Management Science, 52*(7), 984–999. doi:10.1287/mnsc.1060.0554

Rock, L. (2018). *Security embargoes at Red Hat.* Retrieved from https://www.redhat.com/en/blog/security-embargoes-red-hat

Rose, C. (1986). The comedy of the commons: Custom, commerce, and inherently public property. *The University of Chicago Law Review. University of Chicago. Law School, 53*(3), 711–781.

Rose, C. M. (2003). Romans, roads, and romantic creators: Traditions of public property in the information age. *Law and Contemporary Problems, 66*(1/2), 89–110.

Rosen, L. E. (2005). *Open source licensing: software freedom and intellectual property law.* Prentice Hall PTR.

Røvik, K. A. (2011). From Fashion to Virus: An Alternative Theory of Organizations' Handling of Management Ideas. *Organization Studies, 32*(5), 631–653. doi:10.1177/0170840611405426

Rullani, E. (2009). *I premi Nobel per l'economia anno domini 2009. Ovvero, l'economia dei commons e delle reti, che popolano la Terra di Mezzo tra mercato e piano.* Venice International University. Retrieved at: https://criticalmanagement.uniud.it/fileadmin/user_upload/Rullani_sui_Nobel_Economia_2009.pdf

Rullani, E. (2000). Le capitalisme cognitif: Du déjà vu? *Multitudes, 2*(2), 87–94.

Rushkoff, D. (2011). *Program or Be Programmed.* Soft Skull.

Sanguinetti, V. (2019). *Adoption de l'Open Source par les organisations: Articuler business model ouvert et implication dans les communautés.* Université Jean Moulin Lyon III.

Santos, C., Kuk, G., Kon, F., & Pearson, J. (2013, March). The Attraction of Contributors in Free and Open Source Software Projects. *The Journal of Strategic Information Systems, 22*(1), 26–45. doi:10.1016/j.jsis.2012.07.004

Satyanarayanan, M. (2001). Pervasive computing: Vision and challenges. *IEEE Personal Communications*, 10-17.

Scacchi, W. (2002, February). Understanding the requirements for developing open source software systems. *IEE Proceedings. Software, 149*(1), 24–39. doi:10.1049/ip-sen:20020202

Schilling, A., Laumer, S., & Weitzel, T. (2012). Who Will Remain? An Evaluation of Actual Person-Job and Person-Team Fit to Predict Developer Retention in FLOSS Projects. *Proceedings of the 2012 45th Hawaii International Conference on System Sciences*, 3446–3455. 10.1109/HICSS.2012.644

SFC. (2022). *The Glossary of terms by Software Freedom Conservancy.* https://sfconservancy.org/copyleft-compliance/glossary.html

Shah, S. K. (2006, July). Motivation, Governance, and the Viability of Hybrid Forms in Open Source Software Development. *Management Science*, *52*(7), 1000–1014. doi:10.1287/mnsc.1060.0553

Shannon, A. (2022, November 17). *7 Best Go-to-Market Strategies for EdTech Companies.* Retrieved from https://salesintel.io/blog/7-best-go-to-market-strategies-for-edtech-companies/

Sharp, H., Baddoo, N., Beecham, S., Hall, T., & Robinson, H. (2009, January). Models of motivation in software engineering. *Information and Software Technology*, *51*(1), 219–233. doi:10.1016/j.infsof.2008.05.009

Sidak, J. G. (2016). The value of a standard versus the value of standardization. *Baylor Law Review*, *68*, 59.

Smith, B. (2008). *A Quick Guide to GPLv3.* GNU.org. Retrieved August 27, 2022, from https://www.gnu.org/licenses/quick-guide-gplv3.html#neutralizing-laws-that-prohibit-free-software-but-not-forbidding-drm

Smith, B. (2009, May 20). *FSF Settles Suit Against Cisco — Free Software Foundation — Working together for free software.* Free Software Foundation. Retrieved August 13, 2022, from https://www.fsf.org/news/2009-05-cisco-settlement.html

Smith, H. E. (2000). Semicommon property rights and scattering in the open fields. *The Journal of Legal Studies*, *29*(1), 131–169.

Smyth, N. (2019). *Centos 8 essentials.* Payload Media.

Söderberg, J. (2015). *Hacking capitalism: The free and open source software movement.* Routledge.

Sony Linux Technical Information. (n.d.). *Sony Global - Source Code Distribution Service.* Retrieved August 28, 2022, from https://oss.sony.net/Products/Linux/common/search.html

SPDX. (2022). *SPDX License.* List Software Package Data Exchange, Linux Foundation.

Srnicek, N. (2017). *Platform capitalism.* John Wiley & Sons.

St. Laurent, A. M. (2004). *Understanding Open Source and Free Software Licensing.* O'Reilly Media.

Stacey, P., & Hinchliff Pearson, S. (2017). *Made with creative commons.* Ctrl-Alt-Delete Books. https://creativecommons.org/use-remix/made-with-cc/

Staff, O. S. I. (2022, November 17). *Open Source software started in academic circles, and AI is not different*. Open Source Initiative Blog. Retrieved from https://blog.opensource.org/open-source-software-started-in-academic-circles-and-ai-is-not-different/

Stallman, R. (1985). *The GNU Manifesto*. https://www.gnu.org/gnu/manifesto.en.html

Stallman, R. (2021). *Linux and GNU*. GNU.org. Retrieved August 18, 2022, from https://www.gnu.org/gnu/linux-and-gnu.html

Stallman, R. (2002). *Free software, free society: Selected essays of Richard M. Stallman*. Lulu. Com.

Steinmacher, I., Chaves, A.P., & Gerosa, M.A. (2013a). Awareness Support in Distributed Software Development: A Systematic Review and Mapping of the Literature. *Computer Supported Cooperative Work (CSCW), 22*(2-3), 113–158.

Steinmacher, I., Silva, M. A. G., & Gerosa, M. A. (2014c). Barriers Faced by Newcomers to Open Source Projects: A Systematic Review. In Open Source Software: Mobile Open Source Technologies. Springer.

Steinmacher, I., Chaves, A. P., Conte, T., & Gerosa, M. A. (2014a). Preliminary empirical identification of barriers faced by newcomers to Open Source Software projects. *Proceedings of the 28th Brazilian Symposium on Software Engineering*, 1–10.

Steinmacher, I., Chaves, A. P., & Gerosa, M. A. (2010). Awareness support in global software development: a systematic review based on the 3C collaboration model. *Proceedings of the 16th international conference on Collaboration and technology*, 185–201. 10.1007/978-3-642-15714-1_15

Steinmacher, I., Conte, T., & Gerosa, M. A. (2015a). Understanding and Supporting the Choice of an Appropriate Task to Start With In Open Source Software Communities. *Proceedings of the 48th Hawaiian International Conference in Software Systems*, 1–10.

Steinmacher, I., Conte, T., Gerosa, M. A., & Redmiles, D. F. (2015b). Social Barriers Faced by Newcomers Placing Their First Contribution in Open Source Software Projects. *Proceedings of the 18th ACM Conference on Computer Supported Cooperative Work & Social Computing*, 1–13. 10.1145/2675133.2675215

Steinmacher, I., Gerosa, M. A., & Redmiles, D. (2014b). Attracting, Onboarding, and Retaining Newcomer Developers in Open Source Software Projects. *Proceedings of the Workshop on Global Software Development in a CSCW Perspective*.

Steinmacher, I., Silva, M. A. G., Gerosa, M. A., & Redmiles, D. F. (2015, March). A systematic literature review on the barriers faced by newcomers to open source software projects. *Information and Software Technology, 59*, 67–85. doi:10.1016/j.infsof.2014.11.001

Steinmacher, I., Wiese, I. S., Chaves, A. P., & Gerosa, M. A. (2012a). Newcomers Withdrawal in Open Source Software Projects: Analysis of Hadoop Common Project. *Proceedings of the 2012 Brazilian Symposium on Collaborative Systems*, 65–74. 10.1109/SBSC.2012.16

Steinmacher, I., Wiese, I. S., Chaves, A. P., & Gerosa, M. A. (2013b). Why do newcomers abandon open source software projects? *Proceedings of the 2013 6th International Workshop on Cooperative and Human Aspects of Software Engineering*, 25–32.

Steinmacher, I., Wiese, I. S., Conte, T., Gerosa, M. A., & Redmiles, D. (2014d). The Hard Life of Open Source Software Project Newcomers. *Proceedings of the International Workshop on Cooperative and Human Aspects of Software Engineering*, 72–78. 10.1145/2593702.2593704

Steinmacher, I., Wiese, I. S., & Gerosa, M. A. (2012b). Recommending mentors to software project newcomers. *Proceedings of the Third International Workshop on Recommendation Systems for Software Engineering*, 63–67.

Stewart, K., Odence, P., & Rockett, E. (2010). Software package data exchange (SPDX) specification. *IFOSS L. Rev., 2.*

Stewart, K. J., Ammeter, A. P., & Maruping, L. M. (2006, June). Impacts of License Choice and Organizational Sponsorship on User Interest and Development Activity in Open Source Software Projects. *Information Systems Research*, 17(2), 126–144. doi:10.1287/isre.1060.0082

Stone, M., DiBona, C., & Ockman, S. (Eds.). (1999). *Open Sources: Voices from the Open Source Revolution*. O'Reilly.

Stürmer, M., & Myrach, T. (2006). Open-source community building. In Business Models and Community Relationships of Open-source Software Firms. Elsevier.

Stykka. (n.d.). https://www.stykka.com/

Sun-Times. Chicago. (2001). *Steve Ballmer's interview to Chicago Sun-Times on June 1 2001.* Author.

Supply chain attack. (n.d.). In *Wikipedia, The Free Encyclopedia*. Retrieved July 4, 2023, from https://en.wikipedia.org/wiki/Supply_chain_attack

Swann, G. P. (2010). *The economics of standardization: An update.* Report for the UK Department of Business, Innovation and Skills (BIS).

Tanenbaum, A. S., & Bos, H. (2015). *Modern Operating Systems*. Pearson.

Taylor, J., & Hern, A. (2023, May 2). 'Godfather of AI' Geoffrey Hinton quits Google and warns over dangers of misinformation. *The Guardian*. Retrieved from https://www.theguardian.com/technology/2023/may/02/geoffrey-hinton-godfather-of-ai-quits-google-warns-dangers-of-machine-learning

Teece, D. J. (2010). Business models, business strategy and innovation. *Long Range Planning*, *43*(2–3), 172–194. doi:10.1016/j.lrp.2009.07.003

The 3-Clause BSD License. (n.d.). *Open Source Initiative*. Retrieved August 20, 2022, from https://opensource.org/licenses/BSD-3-Clause

The academy of (almost) anything. (n.d.). https://academany.org/about/

The Apache Software Foundation ! (2023). Welcome to The Apache Software Foundation! Retrieved March 5, 2023, from https://www.apache.org/

The FreeBSD Project website. (n.d.). *The FreeBSD Project*. Retrieved September 2, 2022, from https://www.freebsd.org/

The GNU General Public License v2.0. (n.d.). *GNU.org*. Retrieved August 20, 2022, from https://www.gnu.org/licenses/old-licenses/gpl-2.0.html

The Kernel Development Community. (2022a). *Kernel electric-fence (kfence)*. Retrieved from https://docs.kernel.org/dev-tools/kasan.html

The Kernel Development Community. (2022b). *The kernel address sanitizer (kasan)*. Retrieved from https://docs.kernel.org/dev-tools/kasan.html

The Linux Foundation. (2022, June). *10th Annual Open Source Jobs Report*. The Linux Foundation. Retrieved February, 2023, from https://training.linuxfoundation.org/wp-content/uploads/2022/06/OpenSourceJobsReport2022_FINAL.pdf

The Linux Kernel website. (n.d.). *The Linux Kernel Archives*. Retrieved September 2, 2022, from https://kernel.org/

The MIT License. (n.d.). *Open Source Initiative*. Retrieved August 20, 2022, from https://opensource.org/licenses/MIT

The Open Group Base. (2017). *POSIX.1-2017*. The Open Group Base Specifications Issue 7, 2018 edition. Retrieved August 15, 2022, from https://pubs.opengroup.org/onlinepubs/9699919799.2018edition/

Thomas, L., & Samuel, K. (2017). Characteristics of Open Source Business Models. *XXVIII ISPIM Innovation Conference*.

Thomas, L. (2019). *Business models for Open Source Hardware*. Université Grenoble Alpes.

Thomson, C. C., & Jakubowski, M. (2012). Toward an open source civilization: innovations case narrative: open source ecology. *Innovations: Technology, Governance, Globalization*, *7*(3), 53–70. doi:10.1162/INOV_a_00139

Tiburski, R. T., Moratelli, C. R., Johann, S. F., Matos, E., & Hessel, F. (2021, March). A lightweight virtualization model to enable edge computing in deeply embedded systems. *Software, Practice & Experience, 51*(9), 1964–1981. doi:10.1002pe.2968

Tidwell, L. C., & Walther, J. B. (2002). Computer-Mediated Communication Effects on Disclosure, Impressions, and Interpersonal Evaluations: Getting to Know One Another a Bit at a Time. *Human Communication Research, 28*(3), 317–348. doi:10.1111/j.1468-2958.2002.tb00811.x

Tincq, B., & Bénichou, L. (2014). *Open Hardware Business Models*. Workshop at Open Hardware Summit. https://fr.slideshare.net/btincq/business-models-for-open-source-hardware?fbclid=IwAR1LzRMjs0fHn-0BjeP46G_tD9VyT9nKHZ1saDVJ4Le44h7R7GoTNxGdaEk

Torvalds, L., & Diamond, D. (2001). *Just for fun*. Harper Audio.

Troxler, P. (2010) Commons-based Peer-Production of Physical Goods. Is There Room for a Hybrid Innovation Ecology? *Third Free Culture Research Conference.*

Troxler, P. (2019). Building Open Design as a Commons. In The Critical Makers Reader: (Un)learning Technology. Academic Press.

Tsay, J., Dabbish, L., & Herbsleb, J. (2014). Influence of social and technical factors for evaluating contribution in GitHub. *Proceedings of the 36th International Conference on Software Engineering,* 356–366. 10.1145/2568225.2568315

Tucker, C. (2018). Network Effects and Market Power: What Have We Learned in the Last Decade? *Antitrust,* 72-79.

Unikraft website. (n.d.). *Unikraft*. Retrieved September 2, 2022, from https://unikraft.org/

Unterfrauner, E., Schrammel, M., Voigt, C., & Menichinelli, M. (2017). The Maker Movement and the Disruption of the Producer-Consumer Relation. *Internet Science, 342*(November), 1–51.

Valenduc, G. (2018). *Technological revolutions and societal transitions*. ETUI Research Paper-Foresight Brief.

Valimaki, M. (2002). Dual Licensing in Open Source Software Industry. SSRN *Electronic Journal*. doi:10.2139/ssrn.1261644

Van Abel, B., Evers, L., Klaassen, R., & Troxler, P. (2010). *Open Design Now. Why Design Cannot Remain Exclusive*. Bis publishers.

Vaughan-Nichols, S. (2014). *Red Hat incorporates 'free' Red Hat clone CentOS*. Retrieved from https://www.zdnet.com/article/red-hat-incorporates-free-red-hat-clone-centos/

Vercellone, C., Bria, F., Fumagalli, A., Gentilucci, E., Giuliani, A., Griziotti, G., & Vattimo, P. (2015). D3. 2 Managing the commons in the knowledge economy. *Decentralised Citizens Engagement Technologie*. http://www. nesta. org.uk/sites/default/files/d-cent_managing_the_commons_in_the_knowledge_economy. pdf

Ververs, E., van Bommel, R., & Jansen, S. (2011). Influences on Developer Participation in the Debian Software Ecosystem. *Proceedings of the International Conference on Management of Emergent Digital EcoSystems*, 89–93. 10.1145/2077489.2077505

Von Hippel, E. (2005). *Democratizing Innovation*. The MIT Press. doi:10.7551/mitpress/2333.001.0001

von Krogh, G., Haefliger, S., Spaeth, S., & Wallin, M. W. (2012, June). Carrots and Rainbows: Motivation and Social Practice in Open Source Software Development. *Management Information Systems Quarterly*, *36*(2), 649–676. doi:10.2307/41703471

von Krogh, G., Spaeth, S., & Lakhani, K. R. (2003). Community, joining, and specialization in open source software innovation: A case study. *Research Policy*, *32*(7), 1217–1241. doi:10.1016/S0048-7333(03)00050-7

von Krogh, G., & von Hippel, E. (2003, July). Editorial: Special issue on open source software development. *Research Policy*, *32*(7), 1149–1157. doi:10.1016/S0048-7333(03)00054-4

Vora, P., & Komura, N. (2010). The n00b Wikipedia Editing Experience. *Proceedings of the 6th International Symposium on Wikis and Open Collaboration*, Article 36. 10.1145/1832772.1841393

Walter, S. (2020). *CentOS Stream is Continuous Delivery*. Retrieved from https://blog.centos.org/2020/12/centos-stream-is-continuous-delivery/

Waltl, J. (2013). *IP modularity in software products and software platform ecosystems*. Books on Demand.

Wang, J., & Sarma, A. (2011). Which bug should I fix: helping new developers onboard a new project. *Proceedings of the 4th International Workshop on Cooperative and Human Aspects of Software Engineering*, 76–79. 10.1145/1984642.1984661

Wang, L. S., Chen, J., Ren, Y., & Riedl, J. (2012). Searching for the Goldilocks Zone: Trade-offs in Managing Online Volunteer Groups. *Proceedings of the ACM 2012 Conference on Computer Supported Cooperative Work*, 989–998. 10.1145/2145204.2145351

Wasserman, T. (2009). *Building a Business on Open Source Software*. Academic Press.

Watters, A. (2014). *The Monsters of Education Technology*. CreateSpace Independent Publishing Platform via Creative Commons Attribution-ShareAlike 4.0 License.

Weber, S. (2000). The Political Economy of Open Source Software. UCAIS Berkeley Roundtable on the International Economy, UC Berkeley.

Weber, S. (2004). *The success of open source*. Harvard University Press.

Well, S. (n.d.). *Community Guidelines: Yoyow*. Retrieved from https://www.well.com/articles/community-guidelines/yoyow/

Welte, H. (2013, June 26). *Regional court Hamburg judgement against FANTEC*. gpl-violations. org. Retrieved August 15, 2022, from https://gpl-violations.org/news/20130626-fantec_judgement/

What does seL4's license imply? (2019, December 9). *microkerneldude*. Retrieved August 28, 2022, from https://microkerneldude.org/2019/12/09/what-does-sel4s-license-imply/

Whole Earth. (1968, Fall). *Whole Earth Catalog (complete)*. Whole Earth. Retrieved from https://archive.org/details/1stWEC-complete/mode/2up9pa

Winter, S. G., & Nelson, R. R. (1982). *An evolutionary theory of economic change*. University of Illinois at Urbana-Champaign's Academy for Entrepreneurial Leadership Historical Research Reference in Entrepreneurship.

Wolff-Marting, V., Hannebauer, C., & Gruhn, V. (2013). Patterns for tearing down contribution barriers to FLOSS projects. *Proceedings of the 12th International Conference on Intelligent Software Methodologies, Tools and Techniques*, 9–14.

Wolf, P., & Troxler, P. (2016). Community-based business models Insights from an emerging maker economy. *Interaction Design and Architectures*, *30*(30), 75–94. doi:10.55612-5002-030-005

Wolpert, D. (2015). *Information Width: A Way for the Second Law to Increase Complexity*. https://www.santafe.edu/research/results/working-papers/information-width-a-way-for-the-second-law-to-incr

Wright, C. (2020). *CentOS Stream: Building an innovative future for enterprise Linux*. Retrieved from https://www.redhat.com/en/blog/centos-stream-building-innovative-future-enterprise-linux

Young, J. R. (2020, June 26). *Researchers Raise Concerns About Algorithmic Bias in Online Course Tools*. EdSurge. Retrieved from https://www.edsurge.com/news/2020-06-26-researchers-raise-concerns-about-algorithmic-bias-in-online-course-tools

Yu, S., & Ming, W. (2009). Research on individual motivation model of software engineering. *Journal of Communication and Computer, 6*(11), 12.

Zeitlyn, D. (2003). Gift economies in the development of open source software: Anthropological reflections. *Research Policy, 32*(7), 1287–1291.

Zhou, M., & Mockus, A. (2012). What make long term contributors: Willingness and opportunity in OSS community. *Proceedings of the 34th International Conference on Software Engineering*, 518–528. 10.1109/ICSE.2012.6227164

Zhou, M., & Mockus, A. (2015). Who Will Stay in the FLOSS Community? Modelling Participant's Initial Behaviour. *IEEE Transactions on Software Engineering, 41*(1), 82–99. doi:10.1109/TSE.2014.2349496

Zhu, H., Kraut, R., & Kittur, A. (2012). Effectiveness of Shared Leadership in Online Communities. *Proceedings of the ACM 2012 Conference on Computer Supported Cooperative Work*, 407–416. 10.1145/2145204.2145269

Zhu, H., Zhang, A., He, J., Kraut, R. E., & Kittur, A. (2013). Effects of Peer Feedback on Contribution: A Field Experiment in Wikipedia. *Proceedings of the SIGCHI Conference on Human Factors in Computing Systems*, 2253–2262. 10.1145/2470654.2481311

Zimmerman, L. (2014). *Open Design Platform.* https://larszimmermann.de/Open-platform-design-flowchart-vs-0-2-released

Zimmerman, L. (2019). *Mifactori, what is Open Circular Design.* https://mifactori.de

Zittrain, J. (2006). The Generative Internet. *Harvard Law Review*, *119*, 1974. https://ssrn.com/abstract=847124

Zott, C., & Amit, R. (2010). Business model design: An activity system perspective. *Long Range Planning*, *43*(2–3), 216–226. doi:10.1016/j.lrp.2009.07.004

About the Contributors

Francisco Jose Monaco, Ph.D. in Electrical Engineering, holds a professorship at the Department of Computer Systems, University of São Paulo, where he teaches courses on system software for both graduate and undergraduate students, and conducts scientific research in computational modeling and simulation. His main topics of investigation include evolutionary multiobjective optimization and unsupervised machine learning. He has authored several scientific articles, served in conferences' and journals' technical committees, and participated in national and international research projects. Dr. Monaco has been serving on the steering board of the USP Open Source Competence Center for over a decade, where he also coordinates the curricular course on Open-Source Systems for students of computer sciences, computer engineering, and information systems.

* * *

Marco Berlinguer has a Bachelor's Degree in Philosophy (La Sapienza University, Rome), a Master in Knowledge and Information Society (Universitat Obierta de Catalunya) and PhD in Public Policy and Social Transformation (Autonomous Universityt of Barcelona). He lives in Barcelona where he collaborates with the Institute of Government and Public Policies (IGOP), and teaches at the Superior School of Cinema and Audiovisual (ESCAC).

Martin Dow is Software Technical Architect & Project Lead for the Open-Source Learning Academy Protocol. Martin's background in professional software development spans three decades in both product and systems integration settings. Martin has innovated across a wide range of technologies, including: web-based interactive 3D systems; semantic and identifier systems for telcos, institutional repositories, digital asset management, and media value chain standards; and distributed computing techniques that foster new types of value propositions through collective agency. Martin's approach to OSLAP brings the benefits of open source software and practices to social learning and development. These situations – and our humanity – demand a different approach to building technical solutions that support informed stakeholders' owning their digital personhood. Martin lives with his family in rural Ireland and enjoys learning about and living within sustainable methods wherever possible.

Karine Evrard-Samuel is Professor of Management and Faculty Member at Université Grenoble Alpes, Grenoble Institute of Engineering and Management, member of the Center for Studies and Research Applied to Management. She has published numerous scientific articles and books or book chapters in the field of strategic business management and supply chain management. Her areas of expertise relate to supply risks and the resilience of organizations, in particular within innovation ecosystems. She co-drives several multidisciplinary research projects jointly with foreign universities. She is currently Vice-President for International Affairs of Université Grenoble Alpes, and President of the International Association for Research in Logistics and Supply Chain Management (AIRL-SCM).

Paulo Meirelles is currently an Assistant Professor at the University of São Paulo (USP), Institute of Mathematics and Statistics (IME). His primary research interests include Software Engineering, focusing on Free/Open Source Software, Agile Software Development, Static Code Analysis, and Mining Software Repositories.

Hillary Nyakundi is a passionate technical writer and visionary dedicated to inspiring and developing emerging talent. With a focus on open-source contribution and community development, Nyakundi strives to create high-quality content and learning opportunities for those seeking to empower themselves. His involvement in various tech communities has honed his writing and community development skills over the past years when he has contributed to numerous projects and led local tech communities. By embracing challenges and celebrating the unique skills of others, he aims at connecting and collaborating to inspire the next generation of talent.

Renê Pinto, graduated in Computer Engineering, holds master and doctorate degree in Computer Science. Over the last eight years he has been working on embedded systems development to the industry (automotive, medical, among others), specially with cutting edge Operating Systems and Virtualization technologies for Embedded Devices. He has a strong foundation on Operating Systems and Embedded Systems development with several hardware and software platforms. Currently working with Edge Computing (EVE OS).

Karl-Michael Popp, with a master in economics and a PhD in information systems, is a member of the Corporate Development and Strategy Team in the Office of the CEO at SAP SE in Germany. In his 30 year career at large and small software companies, he has worked on over 50 strategic partnerships and over thirty-five acquisitions and successful merger integrations as well as a few divestitures. He has lead open source licensing for SAP´s technology platform for several years. He is a speaker, author of many books and scholarly articles as well as advisor on software and platform business models, software ecosystems and merger automation and runs enticing workshops and trainings on software ecosystems and merger integration.

David Preston, Ph.D in Education, Management, and Communication studies, former lecturer at UCLA and Chapman University College, as well as k-12 courses, is the founder of the Preston Group, and of the Open-Source Learning Academy Network. Author of ACADEMY OF ONE, a book about the power and promise of Open-Source Learning, David speaks to organizational and conference audiences such as the MacArthur Foundation, the Royal Geographical Society, OSCON, and TEDxUCLA. He also mentors teachers and students through the Open-Source Learning Academy.

Marcelo Schmitt holds both a Bachelor's and Master's degree in Computer Sciences from the University of São Paulo. Marcelo's research interests focus on device driver testing methodologies. The author has long experience as a contributor to the FOSS community, including his participation as a founding member of the USP Free Hardware group, and the USP Free/Libre Open-Source student association.

Cesar Souza is a computer science graduate from the Federal Institute of Santa Catarina, Campus Lages. Currently pursuing a Master's degree at the University of São Paulo (USP) and collaborating with the FOSS Research and Education Center at USP, Brazil.

Laetitia Thomas, Ph.D., MBA, is a researcher on the circular economy. As a pedagogical engineer, she likes the game approach, to awaken emotions and get people into a state of flow to reflect on how to change our production and consumption patterns. A certified consultant with the Circulab method, she facilitates workshops on the value chain of microelectronics, and textiles. She is an adjunct professor at Grenoble INP and BSB Dijon where she teaches courses on impact entrepreneurship and organizational leadership. Her research topics include the open-source circular economy and business model innovation.

Peter Troxler is research director of the digital research institute at Rotterdam University of Applied Sciences, The Netherlands. His field of research is the impact of readily available direct digital manufacturing technologies and the design and manufacturing practice of "fabbers" and "makers" on the creative and manufacturing industries, and the emergence of networked co-operation paradigms and business models based open source principles – such as Open Design and Open Source Hardware. Moreover, Peter studies the emergence of third spaces and new manufacturing initiatives in Urban Open Innovation Environments, how they relocate production and research functions to the centres of neighbourhoods in the form of new spaces of production, and how the relationships between people and tools, people and capital, and people and authorities need to be remodeled to provide the conditions for radical innovations for the development novel socio-technical configurations. Peter is an industrial engineer by training (PhD 1999 from ETH Zurich). He worked in factory automation, attaching robots and automatic tool-changers to CNC milling machines before pursuing his career as a design consultant in Switzerland and later as a research manager in knowledge technologies and knowledge management at the University of Aberdeen, Scotland, UK. At new media think tank Waag in Amsterdam, the Netherlands, he worked on Fab Labs and the development and promotion of Creative Commons licences and the development of Open Design.

338

Index

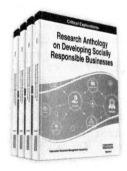

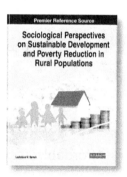